Kennedy, Johnson, and the Nonaligned World

In 1961, President John F. Kennedy initiated a bold new policy of engaging states that had chosen to remain nonaligned in the Cold War. In a narrative ranging from the White House to the western coast of Africa, to the shores of New Guinea, Robert B. Rakove examines the brief but eventful life of this policy during the presidencies of Kennedy and his successor, Lyndon Baines Johnson. Engagement initially met with real success, but it faltered in the face of serious obstacles, including colonial and regional conflicts, disputes over foreign aid, and the Vietnam War. Its failure paved the way for a lasting hostility between the United States and much of the nonaligned world, with consequences extending into the present. This book offers a sweeping account of a critical period in the relationship between the United States and the Third World.

Robert B. Rakove is a lecturer at Stanford University. He has held fellowships at the Miller Center for Public Affairs, the Mershon Center for International Security Studies at Ohio State University, and the University of Sydney's United States Studies Centre. This is his first book.

Kennedy, Johnson, and the Nonaligned World

ROBERT B. RAKOVE

Stanford University

To Kelly —
who helped me with this book,
even though she likes Ike.
Best wishes on all your future
endeavors,
Rob

CAMBRIDGE
UNIVERSITY PRESS

CAMBRIDGE
UNIVERSITY PRESS

32 Avenue of the Americas, New York NY 10013-2473, USA

Cambridge University Press is part of the University of Cambridge.

It furthers the University's mission by disseminating knowledge in the pursuit of education, learning and research at the highest international levels of excellence.

www.cambridge.org
Information on this title: www.cambridge.org/9781107449381

First published 2013
First paperback edition 2014

A catalogue record for this publication is available from the British Library

Library of Congress Cataloguing in Publication data
Rakove, Robert B., 1977–
  Kennedy, Johnson, and the nonaligned world / Robert B. Rakove.
  pages cm
  Includes bibliographical references and index.
  ISBN 978-1-107-00290-6 (hardback)
  1. United States – Foreign relations – 1961–1963. 2. United States – Foreign relations – 1963–1969. 3. United States – Foreign relations – Developing countries. 4. Developing countries – Foreign relations – United States. 5. Nonalignment – History. 6. Nonalignment –
Developing countries – History. 7. Kennedy, John F. (John Fitzgerald), 1917–1963.
8. Johnson, Lyndon B. (Lyndon Baines), 1908–1973. 9. World politics – 1945–1989.
I. Title.
  E840.R34   2012
  327.73009´046–dc23   2012021039

ISBN 978-1-107-00290-6 Hardback
ISBN 978-1-107-44938-1 Paperback

To my parents, Helen and Jack Rakove

Contents

Maps

Acknowledgments

Looking back across the past decade, the task of properly thanking the many people who played a vital role toward the completion of this book is a daunting one. This brief section cannot truly repay the individuals who helped me on the long road toward publication. Sober contemplation of the innumerable steps on that road only confirms the sometimes-obscured truth that scholarship in the humanities is a truly collaborative process. The following constitutes an attempt to at least recognize these debts.

In the spring of 2003, I, then still living in my native California, received the first of many messages from Melvyn Leffler, welcoming me to the University of Virginia. Over the succeeding years, Mel was a truly ideal graduate mentor. He is both demanding and generous: setting a high bar for his students, but also encouraging them to find their own way in terms of both topic and method. He expects both thorough research and strong writing from his graduate students, and he knows fundamentally when a draft chapter falls short of its potential. Above all, he has an inerrant knack for helping his students to sharpen their arguments, to consider weak points, and to revise relentlessly. This book's strengths are tributes to his dedication; its weaknesses most likely stem from instances when I did not listen to him as closely as I might have.

Although the inception of this project is difficult to pin down, wisps of it trace even further back in time, to my undergraduate years at Stanford University. Barton Bernstein, David Kennedy, James Sheehan, Norman Naimark, and Peter Stansky helped me develop my interest in the history of foreign relations and the Cold War. In an especially important class, Coit Blacker demonstrated the importance of close attention to the internal dynamics of presidential administrations. Scott Sagan did not hold my barely suppressed preference for writing history against me, offering me key counsel as both my undergraduate and thesis advisor.

Years later, I was happy to find myself at another institution that encouraged historians and political scientists to strive together. A predoctoral fellowship from the Miller Center for Public Affairs was instrumental in helping me finish on time. Brian Balogh has, alongside Mel, Jeffrey Legro, and Sidney Milkis, worked to put together a peerless institution for the study of policy and the presidency. At a time when fellowship programs sometimes fall under the budgetary axe, the Governing America in a Global Era program sets and maintains a much-envied standard.

Credit is due as well to my dissertation panelists. William Quandt helped me think about the broader conclusions of my work. Brian Balogh directed my attention toward institutional factors. Stephen Schuker provided vital assistance in preparation for my European archival visits and helped me think about the intellectual history of the 1960s. Olivier Zunz, although not on the panel, offered key comments on this project during its embryonic beginnings as a seminar paper in the spring of 2005. Tim Naftali, David Coleman, and Marc Selverstone, fellow New Frontier enthusiasts, offered helpful advice at various junctures. Thanks go as well to Ruhi Ramazani.

Some of the most helpful feedback I received during key junctures came from fellow students at the University of Virginia. Josh Botts and Barin Kayaoglu were invaluable sounding boards during my years in Charlottesville and afterward. Special thanks are due to Seth Center, James Wilson, Kelly Winck, and Kyle Lascurettes for gathering on an afternoon in August 2010 to discuss the manuscript in exhausting depth. They performed this vital service in exchange for a buffet lunch from Sticks Kebob Shop. Mr. Jefferson could not possibly be prouder.

Other Cavaliers were instrumental to the completion of this book. Bob Jackson, Phil Haberkern, and Jason Eldred offered tireless friendship and solidarity, often on long drives to and from a certain peculiar Ruckersville eatery. Melissa Estes Blair provided helpful counsel at various points. Kanisorn Wongsrichanalai was a tireless friend during my Charlottesville years, from the battlefields of the Civil War to the dining rooms of a staggering number of Virginia restaurants. Allison Robbins, fellow serial drama connoisseur, understood the important linkages between quality television series and the pursuit of scholarship.

My dissertation research was sponsored in substantial part by grants from presidential archives. I am grateful for the generosity of the John F. Kennedy Foundation for supporting a four-week visit to Boston in July 2006, and to the Lyndon Baines Johnson Foundation for underwriting a trip to Austin in the autumn of 2006. Thanks are due, as well, to the staffs of both libraries, as well as to the staff of the Dwight D. Eisenhower Library during two brief visits to Abilene. Thanks also go to the research room staff at the National Archives in College Park, and in particular to Stanford classmates Matthew and LaNitra Berger, who graciously offered me their guest room during my DC stays.

It was a rare privilege to be able to speak to individuals personally familiar with the Kennedy and Johnson administrations. I thank Ulric Haynes Jr., Jack Matlock, Thomas Cassilly, and Harold Saunders for speaking with me over the telephone. Thomas Hughes welcomed me into his home for an amazing period of time, providing invaluable insights on the inner workings of the two presidencies. At an early point in my research, Elspeth Rostow modestly offered helpful recollections. Phillips Talbot spoke candidly about his time in government and then treated me to lunch on the Upper East Side. Sadly, the last two individuals have since passed away.

Critical work revising my dissertation was undertaken during an invaluable postdoctoral year at the Mershon Center for International Security Studies at The Ohio State University. More than a dozen years after I took time away from a dreary summer job to read *The Cold War on the Periphery*, I had the privilege of working with Bob McMahon as I began the process of turning the dissertation into a book. Patient and discerning, Bob – whose books have shed unrivaled light on the key themes and problems confronting our study of U.S. policy in the Third World – helped ensure that I left Columbus with a viable book in hand. Thanks are also due to Rick Herrmann, Peter Hahn, and the staff of the Center. Andrew Rigney, then an OSU senior, offered helpful editorial assistance.

As an early champion of this book, Eric Crahan of Cambridge University Press provided indispensable editorial assistance on what could otherwise have been an arduous road to publication. I am indebted to him for his advice and support over the past several years. I received excellent feedback from two anonymous readers who were both supportive and constructive in their approach to the book. Thanks go as well to Abigail Zorbaugh for help on a wide range of issues. Newgen worked energetically at the typesetting, and Linda George of PETT Fox, Inc., contributed both grammatical and region-specific expertise to the copyediting process.

When I began this project, working in isolation, I wondered if I was the only person studying the interaction between the nonaligned world and the United States. Happily, this has proved not to be the case, and I have been honored to befriend a generation of scholars undertaking pathbreaking new work on related topics. Successive gatherings of the Society for Historians of American Foreign Relations (SHAFR) have afforded unique opportunities to present and refine my own work, while discovering the fascinating research of my peers. I owe deep gratitude in particular to Nick Cullather, Marc Selverstone, Ryan Irwin, and Jeffrey Byrne, who read the manuscript and provided thoughtful and challenging comments. Thanks are also offered to Jason Parker and Zach Levey for help with particular chapters. Paul Chamberlin, Alex Poster, Mark Lawrence, Andrew Preston, Mitch Lerner, Tanvi Madan, Douglas Little, Thomas Schwartz, Odd Arne Westad, Kristin Ahlberg, David Ekbladh, Mairi MacDonald, Dustin Walcher, Lien-Hang Nguyen, Phil Muehlenbeck, Brad Simpson, Laura Iandola, and others have been of considerable assistance along the way. The occasional false obituary read over our field cannot withstand the picture of intellectual vitality and methodological diversity offered by SHAFR today.

In between fellowships, I taught as a visitor at Old Dominion University, during the 2009–2010 academic year, and at Colgate University during the 2010–2011 year. While my peers at ODU and Colgate did not, for the most part, contribute directly to the completion of this book, their support over those two challenging years was, nonetheless, essential. Annette Finley-Croswhite, Kelly Duggins, Sharon Metro, and their peers did their utmost to help me settle into work on the eighth floor of Batten Arts & Letters. The following year, atop the giddy heights of Trainer Hill, my colleagues in the Colgate History Department helped make my visiting year there a delight. Special thanks are due to Andy Rotter for his trust and support over the year, to David Robinson for his assistance at numerous junctures, and to Alan Cooper for taking some time away from the Middle Ages to serve (briefly) as a research assistant. Thermometers aside, there are few warmer places than Hamilton, New York.

A project that began in Charlottesville concluded on the other side of the globe. Over the past year, I have been privileged to serve as a postdoctoral Fellow at the United States Studies Centre at the University of Sydney. Australia has truly proved to be the happy land, and I have been humbled by the hospitality of the staff of the USSC. Special thanks are due in particular to Margaret Levi, Rebecca Sheehan, Adam Lockyer, David Smith, and Brendon O'Connor.

I must conclude by thanking the people who helped me most toward the completion of this book: my family. My brother, Dan Rakove, has been a source of humor and good cheer in my life as long as I can remember. It is a delightful turn of fate that this book is emerging into print several years after he began a promising career as a diplomat. My parents, Jack and Helen Rakove, have been tireless supporters during my Bay Area childhood, my college years, graduate school, and afterward. My mother has offered key advice and encouragement along the way. My father has, needless to say, offered an ideal model, as a historian whose work is insightful, thoroughly researched, eloquent, and deeply relevant. Both in the office and in the home, his example has been inspiring; while he never pushed me toward this career, he and my mother made it possible in more ways than I can ever hope to describe. This book is lovingly dedicated to them.

A Note on Terminology

While writing this book, I have tried, whenever possible, to use contemporaneous names. Although now long known as Irian Jaya or West Papua, the final remnant of the Dutch East Indies is referred to here as West New Guinea, the name commonly used in the early 1960s. Portuguese Guinea refers to the country currently known as Guinea-Bissau.

I observe a similar principle with regard to the various names for nonalignment. As H. W. Brands has observed, the phenomenon was better known as neutralism in the 1950s, a term that lingered in American usage well into the following decade. Here the words are used somewhat interchangeably, although "neutralism" is used with reference to political sentiment and "nonaligned" with regard to foreign policy. Similarly the term "Non-Aligned Movement" (NAM) is reserved for the conclusion. Only with hindsight can we say that the 1961 Belgrade Conference marked the emergence of the NAM; debate about the movement's fundamental nature raged well into the 1960s. The NAM uses the hyphenated word "Non-Aligned." In common usage, however, the hyphen has long since become optional, so I have chosen to treat this as one word.

The names of capital cities are often used to refer to national governments. This choice is purely stylistic; it does not reflect a sense that any state in this era approached policy in a wholly unitary fashion.

Finally, my use of the term "Third World" simply reflects its political meaning in the 1950s and 1960s, as opposed to the uglier associations it has since acquired. The music group The Police put it best: one world is enough for all of us.

Abbreviations

BNSP	Basic National Security Policy
CIA	Central Intelligence Agency
FRELIMO	Liberation Front of Mozambique
NAM	Non-Aligned Movement
NATO	North Atlantic Treaty Organization
NSC	National Security Council
ONUC	United Nations Operation in the Congo
PAIGC	African Party for the Independence of Guinea and Cape Verde
PL-480	Food for Peace (Public Law 480)
PRC	People's Republic of China
UAR	United Arab Republic
UN	United Nations

IN CITATIONS

AA	Politisches Archiv des Auswärtigen Amtes, Berlin, Germany
CF	Country File
CFPF	Central Foreign Policy File
DDEL	Dwight D. Eisenhower Library, Abilene, Kansas
DDF	*Documents Diplomatiques Français*
DDRS	Declassified Document Reference Service
DOS	Department of State
DOSB	*Department of State Bulletin*
DSCF	Department of State Central Files
FO	Foreign Office
FRUS	*Foreign Relations of the United States*
GPO	Government Printing Office
GWBP	George W. Ball Papers
JFDP	John Foster Dulles Papers

JFKL	John F. Kennedy Library, Boston, Massachusetts
LBJL	Lyndon Baines Johnson Library, Austin, Texas
MAE	Ministère des Affaires Étrangères, Quai d'Orsay, Paris, France
MC	Miller Center, Charlottesville, Virginia
Memcon	Memorandum of Conversation
MfAA	Ministerium für Auswärtigen Angelegenheiten
(MS)	Microform Supplement to *Foreign Relations of the United States*
NA	National Archives and Records Administration, College Park, Maryland
NSAM	National Security Action Memorandum
NSF	National Security Files
NYT	*The New York Times*
OH	Oral Histories
POF	President's Office Files
PPP	*Public Papers of the Presidents of the United States*
PRP	Presidential Recordings Project
RG-59	Record Group 59, General Records of the Department of State
RWKP	Robert W. Komer Papers
TNA	National Archives, Kew, United Kingdom

Introduction: A Genuine Departure

On November 23, 1963, Egypt entered a state of mourning. The city of Cairo, in the words of an American diplomat, was "overcome by a sense of universal tragedy" over the death of United States President John F. Kennedy. As the embassy counselor, Donald Bergus, reported, a thousand Egyptians came to the American embassy to write messages of condolence. Many were prominent citizens, including Vice Prime Minister Ali Sabri and an influential member of the Presidency Council named Anwar al-Sadat. Others, though, were ordinary Egyptian citizens. Bergus observed: "The expressions on their faces left no doubt concerning the genuineness of their sorrow." Mourners remarked that "Kennedy was the first American President who really understood the Afro-Asian world." In the Egyptian media, journalists normally critical of the United States declared their heartfelt sense of shock and grief over the event. An editorial in the daily *Al-Ahram* stated that Kennedy had transformed the United States from the "repugnant rich brother" to the "cherished rich brother of the human family."[1]

Egypt's grief was not exceptional. The American embassy in Algiers reported "genuine shock and dismay" among average Algerians. U.S. Ambassador William J. Porter received a call of condolence from an "obviously shaken" Algerian President Ahmed Ben Bella, who quickly declared a week of official mourning.[2] In New Delhi, an American diplomat observed a "remarkable demonstration of admiration and sympathy by the people of India." Prime Minister Jawaharlal Nehru spoke before the Indian parliament, decrying "a crime against humanity" – the murder of "a man of ideals, vision and courage, who sought to serve his own people as well as the larger causes of the world."[3] The U.S. consulate in Bombay wrote: "Indians from all walks of life

---

[1] Airgram A-438, Cairo to Washington, December 9, 1963, NSF, box 430, "Reactions to Death, Miscellaneous" folder, JFKL.
[2] Airgram A-233, Algiers to Washington, November 30, 1963, ibid.
[3] Airgram A-442, New Delhi to Washington, November 27, 1963, ibid.

took occasion to mention their sorrow to Americans of their acquaintance."[4]
"Seldom have the Indian people been so shocked and dazed by the assassination of a leader of another country," observed the *Times of India*.[5] In
Indonesia, President Sukarno tearfully remarked in a lengthy eulogy, "The
good die young." Flags in Jakarta flew at half mast.[6] Ghana's President
Kwame Nkrumah eulogized "a great world statesman and a relentless fighter
for equality and human dignity."[7]

This striking outpouring by Indians, Indonesians, Egyptians, Algerians, and
other peoples across the newly independent states of Africa and Asia reflected
the profound power of the Kennedy image in the postcolonial world. As a
young, charismatic, dynamic American leader with an interest in fostering
development and, by the summer of 1963, combating segregation, Kennedy
was idolized in life and mourned in death. There was, however, another common feeling that brought ordinary people of Africa and Asia to grief: that
Kennedy seemed to have understood the issues that galvanized them. His policies had narrowed the gap between the United States and the postcolonial
world. At his death, millions of people in places like Egypt, India, and Algeria
viewed him as a friend. Kennedy's policies, as understood by the peoples of the
developing world, made them receptive to his image. Without this perception,
the murder in Dallas would have struck the average resident of Cairo or New
Delhi as a distant tragedy, not a universal calamity.

Contrast these scenes with those of successive years. In 1964, angry mobs
assaulted U.S.-owned libraries in Egypt and Indonesia. Leaders who had praised
and eulogized Kennedy denounced his successor, Lyndon Johnson, in increasingly fiery speeches. In 1967, Egypt broke relations with the United States
after the Six Day War, while other nonaligned states vehemently denounced
Johnson's war in Vietnam. With dismaying rapidity, the United States had come
to be seen not as an ally to Third World aspirations but as a malevolent foe.
Polarizing accusatory rhetoric unusual in the early 1960s became unremark-
able by the decade's end, emerging as a lasting feature of world politics, a recognizable precursor to contemporary denunciations of the United States.

Tumultuous by any accounting, the 1960s constituted a critically determi-
native era in the relationship between the United States and the postcolonial
world. Ties between the two moved between pendular extremes during the
eight years of Kennedy and Johnson – particularly in the cases of states that
declared themselves to be "nonaligned" in the Cold War. At stake was more
than a particular set of bilateral relations; the 1960s tested the ability of the
United States to comprehend and tolerate nonalignment itself. The concept of
nonalignment fused ideas of neutrality with ideals and agendas specific to the

[4] Airgram A-239, Bombay to Washington, December 13, 1963, ibid.
[5] "Delhi Grieved," *Times of India*, November 24, 1963, 1.
[6] Ganis Harsono, *Recollections of an Indonesian Diplomat in the Sukarno Era*, ed. C. L. M.
   Penders (Queensland: University of Queensland Press, 1977), 230.
[7] Kwame Nkrumah, *Selected Speeches*, Vol. 5, ed. Samuel Obeng (Accra: Afram, 1997), 158–160.

era of decolonization; it posed old and new challenges for its practitioners and the Cold War's major combatants.

Neutrality has been a controversial concept for as long as states have gone to war. Bystanders to conflict have, for millennia, protested their right to stay removed from the fighting, just as belligerents have received such claims warily and, on occasion, hostilely. The most famous instance of this debate is well known to classicists and innumerable students of international relations classes: during the Peloponnesian War, Athens invaded the neutral island-state of Melos, charging that Melian independence and neutrality constituted a standing rebuke to Athenian power. Having conquered Melos, the Athenians proceeded to massacre the male inhabitants and sell the others into slavery.[8]

The history of the United States provides ample proof of this tension. Memorably enshrined in George Washington's Farewell Address, neutrality emerged as the core principle of the young nation's foreign policy: to some Americans it offered an idealistic escape from Europe's cynical balance-of-power system; to others, it represented an acceptance of that balance and the most prudent choice available. Whatever the rationale, neutrality served as the lodestar of U.S. foreign policy for more than a century. At times commitment to the principles of neutrality superseded the desire to avoid war; broad definition of the commercial rights of neutral states lay behind U.S. involvement in the Quasi War and the War of 1812, and then, a century later, the First World War. An ironclad popular belief in the virtues of a neutral foreign policy delayed U.S. entry into the Second World War for more than two years, only to be punctured by the bombing of Pearl Harbor. After Pearl Harbor, however, came an eruption of enthusiasm for a crusade against the Axis powers – and over time, an altered view of neutrality during the war and in its immediate wake.

In the postwar years, the United States became embroiled in another global conflict largely understood along moral lines. The Cold War against the Soviet Union seemed, as the historian Melvyn Leffler has put it, a struggle "for the soul of mankind": an all-determining contest between democracy and tyranny.[9] Faced with this moral battle, Americans proved newly reluctant to accord respect to declarations of neutrality by the smaller and newer states of the international system.[10] These new states, many enjoying their first decade of independence, in turn sought to organize in defense of the rights to which the Melians had alluded. From their collaboration came a new and little-understood variant of

---

[8] Robert Strassler ed., *The Landmark Thucydides: A Comprehensive Guide to the Peloponnesian War* (New York: Touchstone, 1996), 350–357, 402–410, 482.

[9] Melvyn P. Leffler, *For the Soul of Mankind: The United States, the Soviet Union, and the Cold War* (New York: Hill and Wang, 2007), 1–10.

[10] Marc J. Selverstone, *Constructing the Monolith: The United States, Great Britain, and International Communism, 1945–1950* (Cambridge, MA: Harvard University Press, 2009), 139–142, 163–165.

neutrality: nonalignment. The stage was set for confrontation between the new faces of neutrality and its largest former practitioner.

Tracing nonalignment to its moments of inception is a complex project and not the one pursued in these pages. The term and concept first appeared in the immediate postwar years, if not before. Nonetheless, most agree that nonalignment emerged most prominently in April 1955 in the city of Bandung. There, Indonesian President Sukarno opened the first Asian-African Conference. Bandung drew a wide range of attendees, many representing countries that *had* taken sides in the Cold War. Nevertheless, it featured heartfelt declarations of the rights of the new states to remain uncommitted in the global struggle. However, Bandung was much more than a conference dedicated to the rights of neutrals. A meeting of decolonized states, still euphoric over their newfound independence, evoked feelings of solidarity, promises of cooperation, and professions of outrage over the perpetuation of colonialism elsewhere in the world and the growing risk of nuclear war between the superpowers. Nonalignment was more than a synonym for neutrality (it was regularly and mistakenly termed "neutralism"): it also expressed a strong sense of solidarity among postcolonial peoples and an activist agenda directed against remnants of empire. These two facets of nonalignment coexisted uneasily at best; both could be heard in Sukarno's passionate opening address to the gathering.[11] Although no cohesive organization emerged from the conference, Bandung signaled a growing activism and cohesion among postcolonial states.

Neither superpower was initially prepared to deal with this vocal group of states. The Soviet Union was still undergoing a political transition following the 1953 death of Joseph Stalin, who had taken little interest in the postcolonial world. Over the 1950s, however, Moscow developed a sophisticated strategy for appealing to the nonaligned states, founded in large part on a shared vision of development and a common antipathy to European colonialism. The United States was slower to respond. Under President Dwight D. Eisenhower, Washington balanced uneasily between expressions of sympathy for newly decolonized states and annoyance at their refusal to choose sides in the Cold War. The 1950s were years of ambivalence for the United States in its dealings with the nonaligned world. During the following decade, however, President Kennedy pursued an ambitious program of outreach toward the nonaligned states, one that constituted, in the words of one key policy maker, a genuine, if temporary, departure from established Cold War foreign policy.[12]

---

[11] George McT. Kahin, *The Asian-African Conference, Bandung, Indonesia, April 1955* (Ithaca: Cornell University Press, 1956), 39–51; Jason C. Parker, "Small Victory, Missed Chance: The Eisenhower Administration, the Bandung Conference, and the Turning of the Cold War," in Kathryn C. Statler and Andrew L. Johns eds., *The Eisenhower Administration, the Third World, and the Globalization of the Cold War* (New York: Rowman & Littlefield, 2006), 153–174; Odd Arne Westad, *The Global Cold War: Third World Interventions and the Making of Our Times* (New York: Cambridge University Press, 2006), 97–104.

[12] See Westad, *The Global Cold War*, 57–67.

THE POLICY OF ENGAGEMENT

This book examines a foreign policy without an official name that, even so, profoundly shaped the modern history of United States foreign relations. Kennedy came to office convinced that the Cold War would be decided on the battlefields of the Third World: in Latin America, and in the postcolonial states of Africa and Asia. Believing that his predecessors in the Eisenhower administration had waged the Cold War with insufficient vigor or subtlety in this new arena, Kennedy and his advisors adopted a diverse array of programs. JFK authorized the development of counterinsurgency programs to defend against communist rebellions in friendly, impoverished countries. He established the Peace Corps, dispatching eager young volunteers across the globe to burnish the image of the United States as a supporter of Third World development. With a particular concern about the political ramifications of poverty in Latin America and the dangers posed by the recent Cuban revolution, Kennedy inaugurated the Alliance for Progress, a deeply ambitious but ultimately unsuccessful program to advance prosperity and social stability in the lands south of the Rio Grande.

Alongside these named policies, he pursued one that never received a public christening, a policy that will be referred to in these pages as "engagement." Alarmed by the spread of Soviet influence in the nonaligned states of Africa and Asia, Kennedy sought to appeal to these states. By and large, he did this not expecting to win their formal support against communism but to forestall their enlistment as allies of Moscow or Peking. Broadly comprehending the distinction between nationalism in the Third World and the communism of the First World, Kennedy believed that the former could be separated readily from the latter. The new states did not need to be formal allies; simply by remaining independent of the communist bloc, they stood to limit the expansion of Moscow's control and influence. Economic development and the ebbing of colonial-era animosity would, over time, narrow the divide between the West and the postcolonial world. Kennedy and his advisors believed the democratic West held an intrinsic advantage when it came to dealing with an international system made diverse by decolonization.

Engagement was also a product of the high age of modernization theory; indeed, nonaligned states held special significance to theorists of economic development. Unlike mainland Latin America, where Soviet aid was essentially nonexistent, nonaligned states represented active battlefields between the two blocs and their legions of economists, experts, and technicians. Troublingly to Americans, the Soviet and Chinese models of centrally planned industrialization held real appeal to Third World leaders, seeming to offer a quick and proven road to economic modernization. Both communist powers approached the postcolonial world with avid interest, seeing it as a decisive ideological proving ground. So, too, did the Americans. At stake was not only the position of the United States amid a world of rising postcolonial powers, or its continued access to vital resources, but also the validity and relevance of the

American ideology of democracy and free markets. By the end of the decade, modernization theory faced sharp challenges, but it was reaching its intellectual zenith when Kennedy took office.

Engagement employed three distinct tactics. In the first place, Kennedy made prominent use of presidential diplomacy. He met frequently with nonaligned leaders, forged personal bonds with them, and thereby better conveyed the views of the United States on key global issues. Economic assistance programs constituted the second leg of the triangle. Aid was intended both to foster economic development in the nonaligned states and also to serve as a political statement of U.S. friendship. Finally, and most critically, the task of engaging these states necessitated policy adjustments on the part of the United States, requiring American decision makers and diplomats to heed their views on the issues that most concerned them – particularly colonial questions. In this third area, Kennedy's departure from Cold War precedent is most clearly discernible.

Kennedy's pursuit of this policy is one of the less-well-understood aspects of his presidency. Scholarship on Kennedy's foreign policy has traveled between far-flung extremes. The first wave of accounts – immediately following his assassination and including key memoirs by administration insiders – seemed to idealize Kennedy. He was depicted as an astute practitioner of diplomacy, able to see past the stale doctrines of 1950s-era Cold War strategy. To these authors, JFK stood apart from his Cold War peers as a president likely to have drawn down Cold War tensions and avoided entanglement in Vietnam.[13] A second wave, emerging in the wake of the Vietnam War, found Kennedy far less remarkable amid his Cold War peers, terming him aggressive, even reckless, in his pursuit of Cold War victory. Kennedy has been taken to task for his support of coups in Latin America, as well as for his culpability in the overthrow and murder of South Vietnamese President Ngo Dinh Diem.[14] The end of the Cold War and the release of recordings made during the Cuban Missile Crisis have begun to move scholarship back toward the middle ground. Although third-wave Kennedy scholars acknowledge his avid pursuit of Cold War victory, they also note his prudence amid crises. To varying degrees, they have renewed speculation that Kennedy had called into question cardinal Cold War precepts, that he might have further eased tensions with the Soviet Union, and that he was at least less likely than Johnson to go to war in Vietnam.[15]

[13] See Theodore Sorensen, *Kennedy* (New York: Harper & Row, 1965); and Arthur M. Schlesinger Jr., *A Thousand Days: John F. Kennedy in the White House* (Boston: Houghton Mifflin, 1965).
[14] See John Gaddis, *Strategies of Containment: A Critical Appraisal of Postwar National Security Policy* (New York: Oxford University Press, 1982), 198–273; Thomas Paterson ed., *Kennedy's Quest for Victory: American Foreign Policy, 1961–1963* (New York: Oxford University Press, 1989); Stephen G. Rabe, *The Most Dangerous Area in the World: John F. Kennedy Confronts Revolution in Latin America* (Chapel Hill: University of North Carolina Press, 1999); and Stephen G. Rabe, *John F. Kennedy: World Leader* (Washington: Potomac Books, 2010).
[15] Howard Jones, *Death of a Generation: How the Assassinations of Diem and JFK Prolonged the Vietnam War* (New York: Oxford University Press, 2002); Robert Dallek, *An Unfinished Life: John F. Kennedy, 1917–1963* (New York: Little, Brown, & Co., 2003); Aleksandr Fursenko and Timothy Naftali, *One Hell of a Gamble: Khrushchev, Castro, and Kennedy, 1958–1964*

Kennedy's ability to mix lofty rhetoric with pragmatic, sometimes ruthless, strategy presents a perennial challenge to historians, as do innumerable questions of how he might have proceeded in office after November 1963. Much about him must remain unknowable.[16]

To date, scholars have yet to examine comprehensively Kennedy's and Johnson's policies toward the nonaligned states. Broad overviews of Kennedy-era foreign policy have tended to define the Third World geographically, encompassing both aligned and uncommitted states. Accordingly, they have fundamentally blurred a distinction that was cardinal to the Kennedy administration. This dividing line between aligned and nonaligned is of little consequence when making an argument about the morality of Kennedy's foreign policy, but it has broad import when we examine his outlook toward what his contemporaries considered the "Third World." His approaches to India, Egypt, and Indonesia, among others, reveal a more cautious, tolerant Kennedy, and the disparity is worth pondering. Where individual Third World states or regions are concerned, we have outstanding books by scholars such as Robert J. McMahon, Andrew J. Rotter, Douglas Little, H. W. Brands, Thomas J. Noer, Thomas Borstelmann, and Bradley R. Simpson. Such accounts not only illuminate policies toward particular countries or areas, they also cast light on its broader outlook toward the Third World. Even so, the task of surveying in a comprehensive fashion the Kennedy-Johnson approach to the nonaligned world has yet to be undertaken.

Much has been written recently on the topic of modernization theory and its policy impact in the 1960s. To borrow a phrase from Walt W. Rostow, modernization theory's most prominent advocate, this decade represented a period of political "takeoff," when means and ends seemed to move into harmonious alignment and successive Democratic administrations enjoyed the opportunity to tackle directly the interlinked problems of underdevelopment and social instability in the Third World. Scholars have examined aid programs toward both aligned and nonaligned states; here I have stuck strictly to the latter.[17] I focus more on the politics of aid than the concepts behind it but am struck by the range of visions on the part of both aid recipients and their American donors. For some, aid programs were an expression of American mission in the poorer parts of the world; for others they served largely political ends,

---

(New York: W. W. Norton, 1997); and Fredrik Logevall, *Choosing War: The Lost Chance for Peace and the Escalation of War in Vietnam* (Berkeley: University of California Press, 1999).

[16] See, for example, Leffler, *For the Soul of Mankind*, 174–192; and James N. Giglio, *The Presidency of John F. Kennedy* (Lawrence: University Press of Kansas, 1991), 221–254.

[17] On this, see David Ekbladh, *The Great American Mission: Modernization and the Construction of an American World Order* (Princeton: Princeton University Press, 2010); Bradley R. Simpson, *Economists with Guns: Authoritarian Development and U.S.-Indonesian Relations, 1960–1968* (Stanford: Stanford University Press, 2008); Nick Cullather, *The Hungry Word: America's Cold War Battle Against Poverty in Asia* (Cambridge, MA: Harvard University Press, 2010); and Michael Latham, *Modernization as Ideology: American Social Sciences and "Nation Building" in the Kennedy Era* (Chapel Hill: University of North Carolina Press, 2000).

regardless of what the proffered funds accomplished. My examination of the politics of aid to nonaligned states reveals an uneasy coexistence between the goal of modernization and expectations of gratitude on the part of recipients. Above all, the uncommitted status of nonaligned states tended to enhance their leverage in obtaining aid from the United States and in advancing their own ideas about development, while posing substantial political difficulties for the two administrations.

Scholarly work on nonalignment is largely recent, but promising. Historians have begun to discern, in the rise of revolutionary nationalism in the post-colonial states of Africa and Asia in the middle of the twentieth century, fundamental shifts in the nature of the international system, characterized by the tentative emergence of new fault lines and new international norms that challenged prior notions of global politics. In *The Specter of Neutralism* H. W. Brands postulates that Bandung initiated a new era in which states could not be compelled to choose sides in the Cold War. Subsequent research has examined the interplay between Cold War combatants and noncombatants. Odd Arne Westad's *The Global Cold War* and Matthew Connelly's *A Diplomatic Revolution* look broadly at the calamitous interrelationship between the Cold War and decolonization as the rival superpowers applied their ideologies and conceptions of progress in the underdeveloped global south. Both Connelly and Westad confront the complex multidirectional interaction between decolonization and the Cold War. The emergence of nonalignment served to delineate the limits of superpower influence, allowing its adherents to coordinate action on common issues. It represented the most significant reaction by the uncommitted states of Africa and Asia to the expanding superpower struggle.

Kennedy's policy of engagement offers a vital window on his conceptions of foreign policy and the tectonic shifts in world politics during his era. In his reflections on the new forces of nationalism and nonalignment, Kennedy emerges as a perceptive observer of international politics, convinced that the Cold War could not be treated as a Manichean affair, and highly cognizant of the strength of nationalism in the postcolonial states. Kennedy approached the nonaligned countries as states to be persuaded, not coerced. Differentiating between his policies toward these states and those he believed to be in the Western sphere of influence illuminates much about his outlook. While he adopted intervention-ist policies elsewhere in the world, notably in Latin America and mainland Southeast Asia, Kennedy grasped the counterproductive consequences of treat-ing nonaligned states forcefully. Although he famously swore in his inaugural address to bear every burden in the global struggle for freedom, engagement testifies to his grasp of the limits of U.S. power.

This policy came with real costs. Nervous allies in Europe, Africa, and Asia demanded and often obtained statements of continued American solidarity. At home Kennedy's approach to the nonaligned world came at considerable expense to his political standing, particularly in the summer of 1963 when his foreign aid bill faced a devastating Congressional gauntlet. Kennedy did not live to see the end of this struggle, but his statements and actions during his final months leave no doubt that he planned to continue the policy. Even though politically cautious and preparing for the 1964 election, Kennedy clearly thought engagement was worth the attendant risks.

His successor, Lyndon Baines Johnson, departed substantially from Kennedy's approach at a critical time in U.S.-nonaligned relations. Johnson, too, is the subject of much debate among historians. Scholarship has understandably focused on Johnson's escalation of the Vietnam War, but recent accounts have insightfully examined his policies elsewhere in the world.[18] Although often portrayed as a novice in the realm of foreign policy, Johnson was his own man, with a distinct outlook and a uniquely forceful way of crafting policy. He held substantially greater experience in the political arena than his predecessor. He also brought his own particular interests and passions to the table, and these differed deeply from Kennedy's.[19]

Whereas Johnson was capable of dealing subtly and prudently with other foreign policy issues, this was much less often the case in his relations with nonaligned states. His policies toward them reveal a reliance on coercion – a tactic that Kennedy had largely forsworn. At heart, Johnson lacked Kennedy's interest in the Third World and his comprehension of nonalignment. Consequently, LBJ's goals in this realm were far less lofty. The product of an impoverished upbringing in the Texas Hill Country, he empathized with peoples struggling against deprivation; but, as a legislative maestro who expected that no favor would go unrewarded, he was reluctant to aid or otherwise abet states that refused to side with the United States. Johnson's own utterances reveal a general exasperation with the proclamations and demands of nonaligned states, an attitude shared by much of the American public.

Johnson's ambivalence about engagement attests to his own core concerns about U.S. credibility and his understanding of the Cold War. He famously remarked that he could not yield South Vietnam without being subsequently chased halfway across the Pacific by the communists. Like Kennedy, he considered the global power balance to be fragile, but he accorded far more concern to the signals his policy sent to allies. Facing his own war, Johnson instinctively sought solidarity from allies, the same solidarity he felt obligated to offer them in their own regional conflicts. He had comparatively little patience for states that refused to choose sides or, even worse, that accepted U.S. aid while continuing to criticize or oppose his policies. He held, at heart, a more traditional

---

[18] Thomas Schwartz, *Lyndon Johnson and Europe: In the Shadow of Vietnam* (Cambridge, MA: Harvard University Press, 2003); Warren I. Cohen and Nancy B. Tucker eds., *Lyndon Johnson Confronts the World: American Foreign Policy, 1963–1968* (New York: Cambridge University Press, 1994); and H. W. Brands, *The Wages of Globalism: Lyndon Johnson and the Limits of American Power* (New York: Oxford University Press, 1994).

[19] The leading biographies of Johnson are Robert Dallek, *Flawed Giant: Lyndon Johnson and His Times, 1961–1973* (New York: Oxford University Press, 1998); and Randall Woods, *LBJ: Architect of American Ambition* (New York: Free Press, 2006). Fredrik Logevall painstakingly examines the impact of the Kennedy-Johnson transition in *Choosing War*; as does Melvyn Leffler in *For the Soul of Mankind*, 201–224.

view of the Cold War, as a struggle in which states ultimately should choose sides, and it meshed seamlessly with the vote-counting outlook of a senate majority leader. Thus, with Johnson's ascendance, the departure that Kennedy initiated came to its end – not immediately, but inexorably.

The next seven chapters chronicle the ebbs and flows of relations between the United States and the nonaligned world in the Kennedy and Johnson years. Chapter One provides a prologue to the New Frontier, offering a brief sketch of U.S.-nonaligned relations during the Eisenhower presidency. Chapter Two profiles the most senior policy makers in the Kennedy and Johnson administrations, focusing on the outlooks that they carried into office. Chapter Three chronicles early policy toward the nonaligned movement as a whole, particularly responses toward the 1961 Belgrade Conference, while also examining nonaligned reactions to the major Cold War crises of the period. It concludes at the end of 1962, when Kennedy and his advisors believed their efforts in the nonaligned world had begun to yield real dividends.

Chapters Four through Seven examine fundamental problems that frustrated and ultimately undermined the policy of engagement. Chapter Four offers an integrated history of four key colonial disputes that pitted nonaligned states against European allies of the United States. Regional conflicts – rivalries between African or Asian states – are the subject of Chapter Five, which also chronicles four cases. Both of these chapters focus on the period between 1961 and the end of 1964, by which point U.S.-nonaligned relations stood in a state of crisis. Going past the close of 1964, Chapter Six depicts the problems that plagued U.S. aid: both the domestic difficulties that the aid program faced and the futile efforts of both administrations to resolve the question of what the United States could expect in return for American aid. Finally, Chapter Seven looks at the decline of engagement in the era of Vietnam, linking the political damage done by the war with the evolving character of nonalignment in the middle of the 1960s.

Two interrelated phenomena fundamentally altered the Cold War in the 1960s: the Sino-Soviet split and the formal establishment of the Non-Aligned Movement. Both emerge throughout these chapters. The former redefined the global struggle as a fundamentally multipolar affair, particularly as China and the Soviet Union engaged in a costly battle for influence across the Third World. The latter, however, weakened the pull that any one pole could exert upon states caught in the middle. Nonalignment, consequently, ushered in an era of weak polarity, in which major, midsized states such as Egypt, India, and Indonesia could exert substantial leverage on the superpowers. Determined headstrong national leaders charted their own courses, playing great power patrons against one another, sometimes to beneficial outcomes, sometimes as preludes to disaster. In the political map of the 1960s, we can recognize some of the contours of our contemporary world.

This book focuses its attention on the American side of the story: on the outlooks held by policy makers and other actors, the ways these were expressed in acts of policy, and the outcomes that followed. It is my belief that sustained attention to the personalities, views, and debates of these two administrations is needed to understand the profound shifts in U.S.-nonaligned relations over the course of the 1960s. In key ways, the challenges presented by nonaligned states in 1965 were not substantially different in character from what they had been in the 1950s. What had changed over the preceding years were the ways in which they were perceived within the White House. As an informal policy, engagement rose and fell based on the internal politics of the Kennedy and Johnson presidencies. It is best understood – and thereafter situated in a broader international history of the 1960s – through intensive examination of American sources.

Nevertheless, any consideration of outcomes must necessarily make this, at least in part, an international story. I utilize British, French, and German archival documents to complement the perspective offered by American sources, providing for a fuller understanding of events. Transcripts, memoirs, and news reports from key nonaligned countries have yielded further insights. Studying the U.S.-nonaligned relationship led me to observe that changes in American politics and policy were accompanied by concurrent shifts in the leadership and direction of the movement. Chronicling the evolution of this vast diverse grouping is the task for another book; yet I think this story of U.S. policy gains further insight from a (tentative) examination of nonaligned politics – a fascinating story in its own right.

Readers may note the relative brevity of discussion of the more familiar events of the 1960s: the Berlin and Cuba crises and the descent into the Vietnam War. I came to this project with the belief that there were other revealing stories to tell about the Kennedy-Johnson years and that the foreign policies of these two administrations could not be reduced to Cold War crises and war in Southeast Asia. Discussion of the Vietnam War has, understandably, dominated interpretations of American foreign policy in this period; yet we stand to benefit from setting the familiar narrative of the war alongside developments that it has long overshadowed. Where Kennedy and Johnson are concerned, the crushing weight of Vietnam tilts the scales of historical judgment sharply to one side but does not remove our obligation to examine carefully the contents of both baskets. Although this book accords more direct attention to less familiar events such as the West New Guinea crisis and the Belgrade Conference, it also speaks to the broader impact of the long war in Vietnam and the myriad ways that a single war can affect seemingly far-off relationships. In the end, I found that I was writing this book not to dismiss Vietnam but to add something to our understanding of this tragedy.

It is my belief that engagement offers its practitioners a measure of credit. For good and for ill, nonalignment and the Cold War's emerging multipolarity transformed the world. Kennedy and Johnson were among the first to attempt to come to grips with the ensuing diffusion of political power. Their response – engagement – was at once a success and a failure. The New Frontiersmen were myopic planners yet skilled tacticians. They overestimated engagement's benefits and underestimated its costs. Early triumphs obscured the ways in which engagement was irreconcilable with preexisting commitments. The Cold War concerns that had initially spurred engagement increasingly circumscribed it; indeed, engagement came undone because it was fundamentally incompatible with long-standing popular views of the global struggle. As the costs came due, Lyndon Johnson shifted away from his predecessor's endeavor. Yet it remained a worthwhile policy. Engagement, for all the misconceptions embedded in it, was a prudent reaction to the emerging phenomenon of nonalignment. Its failure yielded grave and lasting consequences for the United States and the world.

"Walking a Tightrope": Eisenhower and Nonalignment

Every policy is a product of its era, of the ideas, events, and perceptions that shape the time before it is enacted. The Kennedy-era policy of engagement emerged from the debates of the 1950s, not only within the government but also outside of it. It came as both a reaction to and a continuation of the policies of President Dwight D. Eisenhower in the Third World, policies that were themselves responses to the fall of China to Mao Zedong's communists in 1949 and the eruption of the Korean War the following year.

As was the case with so many other presidencies, the Kennedy administration held a pronounced sense of the shortcomings of its immediate predecessor, particularly with regard to the Third World. In the eyes of Kennedy and his advisors, Eisenhower had failed to meet a growing Soviet political offensive in Africa and Asia. His secretary of state, John Foster Dulles, compounded the problem with his own stern and highly moralistic pronouncements on the nature of the Cold War. When forced to choose between European allies and postcolonial states, Dulles seemed to favor Europe consistently, at the expense of American credibility in the postcolonial world. The New Frontiersmen thought Dulles disastrously myopic, driven to divide the world between friend and foe. They believed that he had harshly overreacted to Third World nationalism, failing to grasp that it could in fact act to restrict the spread of communism.

The new administration came to office determined not to prolong or repeat what Kennedy's first undersecretary of state, Chester Bowles, later dubbed the "everyone stand up and be counted" approach of Dulles.[1] Kennedy, wrote his friend Arthur Schlesinger, was bored by "the John Foster Dulles contrast between the God-anointed apostles of free enterprise and the regimented hordes of atheistic communism."[2] Undersecretary of State George Ball scathingly

---

[1] Chester Bowles, *Promises to Keep: My Years in Public Life, 1941–1969* (New York: Harper & Row, 1971), 250, 478–479.
[2] Arthur M. Schlesinger Jr., *A Thousand Days: John F. Kennedy in the White House* (Boston: Houghton Mifflin, 1965), 298.

recalled Dulles's "Manichean crusade."[3] Robert Komer of the National Security Council acidly opined: "Stalin had the same black and white approach to the less developed world that John Foster Dulles did."[4]

There was truth to these complaints, but the New Frontiersmen entered office without giving the Eisenhower administration its full due. Whereas the Manichean image of their predecessors held some validity, it also reflected the acrimonious atmosphere of the 1950s. Eisenhower enjoyed both triumphs and failures in his policies toward the uncommitted states. The former aided the efforts of his successor, whereas the latter left obstacles strewn across Kennedy's path. Eisenhower, moreover, set important precedents for JFK, committing the United States to combat communism in key areas of the Third World, assuming the burdens that Kennedy subsequently promised to bear.

THE EISENHOWER OUTLOOK

As much as any other aspect of his presidency, Eisenhower's policies toward the Third World have generated considerable debate. His interventions in Guatemala, Iran, Indochina, and Indonesia reinforce the image of a hawkish administration, that often mistook Third World nationalism for communism.[5] Recent scholarship, however, has argued that Eisenhower's approach to the postcolonial world was ultimately more prudent and less ideological than previously believed. Most saliently, H. W. Brands makes the case that pragmatism ultimately trumped ideology in Eisenhower's approach to the key nonaligned states of India, Egypt, and Yugoslavia.[6] Both theses are tenable and illuminate the distinction between public image and policy. Eisenhower was acutely aware of the dilemmas facing the nonaligned states and was often sympathetic toward them. However, the pattern sketched by Brands does not apply universally, particularly where Southeast Asia and sub-Saharan Africa are concerned. In addition, the rhetoric and the public image of the administration created a cloud that Eisenhower's quiet diplomacy never quite dispelled. Brands acknowledges but understates the damage done by administration rhetoric.

John Foster Dulles played a critical role in shaping nonaligned opinion of the administration. Dulles earned an unenviable reputation among the elites of the nonaligned world, seeming to personify what they saw as Washington's

[3] George W. Ball, *The Past Has Another Pattern* (New York: W. W. Norton, 1982), 174–177.

[4] First Interview, Robert W. Komer, June 18, 1964, 4, OH, JFKL.

[5] See Chester J. Pach and Elmo Richardson, *The Presidency of Dwight D. Eisenhower* (Lawrence: University Press of Kansas, 1991); Robert J. McMahon, "Eisenhower and Third World Nationalism: A Critique of the Revisionists," *Political Science Quarterly* 101 (Fall 1986), 453–473; Odd Arne Westad, *The Global Cold War: Third World Interventions and the Making of Our Times* (New York: Cambridge University Press, 2006), 119–157; Melvyn Leffler, *For the Soul of Mankind: The United States, the Soviet Union, and the Cold War* (New York: Hill and Wang, 2007), 129–135, 149–150.

[6] H. W. Brands, *The Specter of Neutralism: The United States and the Emergence of the Third World, 1947–1960* (New York: Oxford University Press, 1989).

stark, inflexible, Cold War outlook, a worldview providing little sympathy for or understanding of the problems of postcolonial states. They believed that a pro-European bias shaped his policy toward colonial questions. Years after his death in 1959, nonaligned leaders continued to invoke Dulles as the personification of a Manichean Cold Warrior.[7]

Despite this image, Dulles was no admirer of European colonialism. He worried that colonial conflicts might distract states from the looming threat of communism. He described the anticolonial resolutions adopted at the 1955 Asian-African Conference at Bandung as being "in accord with what we feel in our hearts (though we are unable to say them publicly)."[8] He comprehended that U.S. prestige throughout Africa and Asia rested on "the confidence of the peoples in those areas in our basic and unshakeable devotion" to their right of national self-determination.[9] Dulles saw himself as an adherent to the American tradition of anti-imperialism, and he perceived the American experience as offering valuable lessons for the postcolonial world.[10]

Eisenhower shared these views. He approved of decolonization in principle (although not always in practice) and emphatically believed the United States could and should serve as a natural guide to the postcolonial states.[11] He could be surprisingly indifferent to the internal economic policies of nonaligned states, one commonly used measure of Cold War allegiances. In 1956, he responded to warnings about the statist direction of the Indonesian economy by asking how Indonesia could possibly avoid creating a centralized system when it lacked any historical basis for a free-market system. Socialist economics were to be expected from "such immature countries."[12]

As a question of general principle, Eisenhower and Dulles believed that the United States should respond tolerantly to states professing neutrality in the Cold War, and they incorporated this tenet into their overarching strategy statements. In January 1955, the National Security Council (NSC) released a statement entitled NSC 5501, which elucidated the general outlines of foreign policy for the coming year. This statement, known as the Basic National Security Policy (BNSP), outlined two central principles pertaining to relations with the nonaligned world. NSC 5501 called for broadly aiding "constructive nationalist and reform movements." Aid was to be allotted "on the basis of the willingness and ability of countries to strengthen and develop their independence

[7] See, for example Telegram 4793, Cairo to Washington, February 24, 1967, in DOS, *FRUS, 1964–1968, Vol. 18: Arab-Israeli Dispute, 1964–1967* (Washington: GPO, 2000): 767.

[8] Minutes of Cabinet Meeting, April 29, 1955, in DOS, *FRUS, 1955–1957, Vol. 21: East Asian Security; Laos; Cambodia* (Washington: GPO, 1990): 91–92.

[9] Letter, Dulles to Julius Holmes, July 13, 1955, JFDP, Subject Series, box 6, "North African Survey," DDEL.

[10] See, for example, Memorandum, Dulles to Eisenhower, May 14, 1956, in DOS, *FRUS, 1955–1957, Vol. 22: Southeast Asia* (Washington: GPO, 1989): 267–268.

[11] William R. Louis, "American Anti-Colonialism, Suez, and the Special Relationship," in Louis ed., *Ends of British Imperialism: The Scramble for Empire, Suez, and Decolonization* (New York: Palgrave Macmillan, 2006), 603; Westad, *The Global Cold War*, 131.

[12] Editorial Note in *FRUS, 1955–1957*, 22: 254.

against Communist expansion rather than on their formal alignment with the U.S." The document forswore the exertion of "pressure" to convert recipients into outright allies. Furthermore, it was incumbent on the United States to alleviate "disputes and tensions" that might undermine "free world strength and cohesion." Particular attention was needed to "develop long-term policies to deal with deep-seated problems (such as those involved in the evolution of colonial peoples)."[13]

Eisenhower emphasized the positive value of neutrality the following year when discussing NSC 5602, the successor document to NSC 5501. Speaking before the NSC on February 27, 1956, Eisenhower "very forcefully" cited the nation's own historical neutrality, while noting that it was "erroneous" to charge "that there could be no genuine neutrality in the world between the Communist and the Western nations." Indeed, in some cases states allying with the United States "often made themselves highly vulnerable to Communist attack." Ike thought it imperative to define neutrality more precisely: "It should mean a moral, spiritual and, possibly, a political commitment to our side, but not necessarily a military commitment."[14] Similarly, in a letter to his brother Edgar written the same day, Eisenhower argued emphatically that, whereas "we want every nation we can reach to stand with us," it would be "a very grave error to ask some of these nations" to announce that they stood with the United States.[15]

These statements embodied the president's confusion on neutrality. Eisenhower was at once both somewhat tolerant and somewhat uncomprehending of the phenomenon. Neutrality in the classical sense requires no commitments – moral, spiritual, political, or otherwise – from its adherents toward belligerents – quite the opposite, in fact. Although he spoke against forcing states to choose sides in the Cold War and argued vehemently that the United States could benefit from accepting neutrality, Eisenhower's definition of the term was exceedingly narrow, leaving little room for deviations from expected "commitments." At heart, this statement advanced a stark view of the Cold War. The expectation of "moral" support left scant leeway for uncommitted states to be neutral in thought and deed.[16] Nonalignment, which incorporated an activist agenda, fell further outside the allowed range of behavior.

In its final form, NSC 5602 bolstered the language in the preceding year's BNSP. Again, the drafters eschewed using pressure to make allies of neutral states, but rather recognized that the independence of such governments served U.S. interests. The document further clarified the language regarding colonial conflicts. When faced with disputes between its allies and their colonies, it

---

[13] NSC Report, "Basic National Security Policy," January 7, 1955, in DOS, *FRUS, 1955–1957, Vol. 19: National Security Policy* (Washington: GPO, 1990): 24–38.

[14] Memorandum of Discussion, 277th Meeting of NSC, February 27, 1956, ibid.: 201–202.

[15] Letter, Dwight D. Eisenhower to Edgar Eisenhower, February 27, 1956, JFDP, White House Memoranda Series, box 4, "White House Correspondence – General 1956 (6)," DDEL.

[16] One case illustrative of Eisenhower's ambivalence toward conventional neutrality is that of Finland. See Jussi M. Hahnimäki, *Containing Coexistence: America, Russia, and the "Finnish Solution," 1945–1956* (Kent, OH: Kent State University Press, 1997), 139–193.

declared, the United States should "use its influence in behalf of an orderly evolution of political arrangements toward self-determination." The national interest of the United States in engaging "constructive nationalist and reform movements" in colonial Africa and Asia was also reaffirmed.[17]

By themselves, the sentiments of Eisenhower and Dulles, along with the pragmatic outlook embodied in NSC 5501 and NSC 5602, might have steered the United States toward relative concord with the nonaligned states. Other priorities, however, trumped these inclinations and propelled the United States and the nonaligned states into far more antagonistic relationships. Foremost among these were the White House's strategic goals of ringing the Soviet Union with alliances and excluding communism from key regions. These twin imperatives brought deep entanglement in three critical areas: the Middle East, Southeast Asia, and sub-Saharan Africa. Ensuing regional commitments shaped the geopolitical priorities of the Eisenhower administration and its successors, and brought confrontation with nonaligned states.

"ONE OF THE MOST DANGEROUS POLITICAL TRENDS"

Between 1953 and 1955, the Middle East emerged as the first arena of conflict between Eisenhower and the nonaligned states, particularly India and Egypt. In 1953, Eisenhower and Dulles grew deeply concerned about Britain's diminishing influence in the oil-rich Persian Gulf region and sought to shield the area from Moscow's advance. This drove them to mount a successful CIA-sponsored coup against Iranian Prime Minister Mohammed Mossadeq, who lacked their anticommunist fervor and had nationalized his country's oil reserves.[18] It also led them to look for local allies to share the burden of regional defense.

Of the states in the region, Pakistan most impressed Dulles. After a visit there in May 1953, he deemed it the one country in the Gulf region "that has the moral courage to do its part in resisting communism." He contrasted it favorably with India, which had criticized the United States on occasion and eschewed any alliance with Washington. Dulles and Eisenhower approved the shipment of arms to Karachi and a subsequent treaty of mutual assistance. U.S. military aid to Pakistan incensed New Delhi, bringing bilateral relations to their lowest point since Indian independence.[19] Prime Minister Jawaharlal Nehru spoke anxiously about the administration's expansion of military pacts into the Middle East and Southeast Asia, terming it "a wrong approach, a dangerous approach, and a harmful approach," jeopardizing both India and the general peace of the world.[20]

[17] Memcon, 277th Meeting of NSC, February 27, 1956, in *FRUS, 1955–1957*, 21: 201–202.
[18] On this, see Zachary Karabell, *Architects of Intervention: The United States, the Third World, and the Cold War, 1946–1962* (Baton Rouge: Louisiana State University Press, 1999), 63–91.
[19] Robert J. McMahon, *The Cold War on the Periphery: The United States, India, and Pakistan* (New York: Columbia University Press, 1994), 123–153.
[20] Jawaharlal Nehru, *India's Foreign Policy: Selected Speeches, September 1946-April 1961* (New Delhi: Ministry of Information and Broadcasting, 1961), 94–96.

Egypt, too, objected to Anglo-American efforts to bolster the "northern tier" of the Middle East, particularly after the signing of the Baghdad Pact in 1955, which established a regional security organization that included Turkey, Iran, Pakistan, Iraq, and the United Kingdom. British participation made the Pact suspect to Arab nationalists such as Egyptian President Gamal Abdel Nasser, who feared the expansion of the Cold War into the Middle East and Western efforts to build up Iraq as an Arab counterweight to Egypt. Nasser's opposition displeased the White House, which concluded that he was – to Moscow's benefit – undermining regional security.[21]

Nonaligned states had, in these instances, obstructed the consolidation of regional pacts. Their actions, consequently, bolstered U.S. suspicions that nonalignment was something exploitable by Moscow, particularly when its adherents opposed U.S.-sponsored alliances. Evidence of a new dynamism in Soviet foreign policy after the death of Joseph Stalin aroused fears that Moscow might gull wavering Western allies into outright neutrality. An October 1955 assessment of NSC 5501 by the State Department's Policy Planning Staff predicted that Moscow would promote neutralism so as to drive a wedge between the United States and its allies. A National Intelligence Estimate the next month forecast Soviet efforts to advance neutralist policies in "vulnerable areas," such as Southeast Asia. To senior analysts in the CIA, the Pentagon, and the State Department, the "blurring of the lines which have divided the Communist and non-Communist worlds" and the consequent "trend toward a greater number of uncommitted states" represented "one of the most dangerous political trends" of the 1950s.[22]

At heart, the Eisenhower administration held two conflicting ideas about neutrality in the Cold War. In certain regions and situations, neutrality stood to benefit the United States. As a broader philosophy – as nonalignment (or "neutralism") – however, it menaced the integrity of the new American system of regional alliances. Neutralist sentiment seemed to be something that could be exploited by the Soviet Union. The containment of Soviet power and the maintenance of existing alliances remained Eisenhower and Dulles's paramount goal in the Third World. Their alliance system depended predominantly on two types of states: European powers and conservative Asian nations – neither of which tended to enjoy favorable relations with nonaligned states. With this imperative, Dulles and Eisenhower saw little advantage in placating neutrals at the cost of unnerving allies. Consequently, disputes related to decolonization and the U.S. alliance system served to divide Washington from the nonaligned world.

---

[21] Salim Yaqub, *Containing Arab Nationalism: The Eisenhower Doctrine and the Middle East* (Chapel Hill: University of North Carolina Press, 2004), 38–40; Peter L. Hahn, *The United States, Great Britain, and Egypt, 1945–1956: Strategy and Diplomacy in the Early Cold War* (Chapel Hill: University of North Carolina Press, 1991), 197–200.

[22] State Department Paper, "General Comments on NSC 5501," October 3, 1955, in *FRUS, 1955–1957*, 19: 123–125; National Intelligence Estimate, November 1, 1955, ibid.: 131–145.

Neither man, moreover, stood prepared to set aside the conviction that the Cold War was a moral struggle. Eisenhower remained amenable to neutrality in a purely geopolitical sense, but still expected truly neutral states to signal their disapproval of communism and Soviet policy. Dulles opined to the president at the end of 1956 that there could not be true neutrality between American and Soviet world orders.[23] He chafed at the silence of nonaligned powers in the face of Soviet domination of Eastern Europe and expansionist agendas within their own ranks, which he viewed as Soviet-sponsored.[24] Critically, believing that the Cold War was the defining struggle in world affairs, he tended to perceive malicious Soviet influence behind colonial and regional conflicts in the Third World, while understating the salience of local factors.[25] The willingness of nonaligned states to engage in these conflicts thus represented an acquiescence on their part to Moscow's grand design. All this and their open courting of Soviet aid nurtured a belief in Dulles and other Americans that the nonaligned states were guilty of gross hypocrisy. This perception fostered a profound sense of unease on the administration's part when it confronted the phenomenon of organized nonalignment in early 1955.

EISENHOWER AND BANDUNG

If neutrality in individual cases appeared tolerable to Eisenhower, an organized, activist group of nonaligned states was something else altogether. When the planned Bandung Conference was announced at the end of 1954, the meeting elicited real concern in Washington, but the Eisenhower administration reacted with restraint. Dulles shared the common fear that the conference could easily be manipulated by pro-communist delegations to produce unfriendly resolutions, especially on the ongoing Taiwan Straits crisis, which pitted the United States against the PRC. He worried that China's foreign minister, Zhou Enlai, would dominate the proceedings, perhaps working to forge a broader anti-Western alliance founded on pan-Asianism and a shared anticolonialism. Dulles also, however, perceived that Washington stood to lose prestige among the attendees if it tried to undermine the conference. Dulles's reaction to Bandung revealed his own ambivalence about the emerging phenomenon of nonalignment: whereas he felt profound misgivings toward it, he also feared the consequences of actively opposing it. Overruling the recommendations of several advisors, Dulles tellingly chose a middle path.[26]

---

[23] Memcon, Eisenhower and Dulles, December 3, 1956, JFDP, White House Memoranda Series, box 4, "Meetings with the President, August–December 1956 (2)" folder, DDEL.

[24] Memorandum, Philip Young to Walter Robertson, January 3, 1956, in *FRUS, 1955–1957*, 22: 222–225.

[25] Letter, Dulles to Konrad Adenauer, December 27, 1955, in DOS, *FRUS, 1955–1957, Vol. 26: Central and Southeastern Europe* (Washington: GPO, 1992): 63–64.

[26] Jason Parker, "Small Victory, Missed Chance: The Eisenhower Administration, the Bandung Conference and the Turning of the Cold War," in Kathryn Statler and Andrew Johns eds., *The Eisenhower Administration, the Third World, and the Globalization of the Cold War*

In a meeting on January 7, 1955, several of Dulles's colleagues – most notably his brother, CIA Director Allen W. Dulles – advised him that Bandung was likely to be a "rigged conference" intended to generate anticolonial resolutions directed against the United States and its European allies. Allen Dulles and others advised working with pro-Western invitees to delay the gathering. The secretary shared their trepidation. He feared that the meeting could create a "very solid block of anti-Western votes in the United Nations." He did not, however, recommend attempting to stall the event, instead advising that the United States ask friendly governments to neither accept nor decline invitations, pending a study of Bandung's objectives. Dulles essentially adopted a wait-and-see attitude.[27] With apparent frustration he wrote:

We wish that the conference were not held; but if it is to be held, we must try to get the best representatives of friendly countries to Bandung, and they must be armed with the best available information.... We cannot afford to be simply negative, but if we are unduly constructive we might help the sponsors.[28]

Broader Cold War concerns soon intruded. Escalating tensions in the Taiwan Straits heightened the significance of Bandung. Dulles feared that the conference could sanction a more aggressive Chinese policy; he also hoped that coordinated action by friendly attendees might serve to constrain Peking with a resolution calling for a negotiated solution.[29] The unwanted conference now posed both dangers and opportunities. As it became clear that the conference would occur as planned, Dulles consulted extensively with friendly invitees.[30]

As it happened, Bandung witnessed neither a harmonious meeting of the new states of Africa and Asia nor any great forward step for international communism. Invitations had been based on geography, not Cold War nonalignment. The attendees represented a wide spectrum of opinion and included dedicated U.S. allies such as Japan, Turkey, and the Philippines on the one hand and the PRC on the other. Other nations, notably Iran, Iraq, and Ceylon, brought strong anticommunist leanings to the table. Sub-Saharan Africa was barely represented. India backed the conference in hopes of attracting international support for what Nehru termed the principles of Panchsheel: noninterference and peaceful coexistence. To Nehru's consternation, this agenda faced strong resistance from outwardly aligned and anticommunist states. Ceylon's prime minister delivered an impassioned condemnation of Soviet repression in

(New York: Rowman and Littlefield, 2006), 153–174; Brands, *The Specter of Neutralism*, 110–118; Matthew Jones, "A 'Segregated' Asia?: Race, the Bandung Conference, and Pan-Asianist Fears in American Thought and Policy, 1954–1955," *Diplomatic History* 29, No. 5 (November 2005), 854–862.

[27] Minutes of Meeting, January 7, 1955, in *FRUS, 1955–1957,* 21: 1–5; DOS, *FRUS, 1952–1954, Vol. 12: East Asia and Pacific, Part 1* (Washington: GPO, 1984): 1085n.

[28] Minutes of Meeting, January 18, 1955, in *FRUS, 1955–1957,* 21: 11–16.

[29] Memcon, Dulles and Sir Roger Makins, April 7, 1955, in DOS, *FRUS, 1955–1957, Vol. 2: China* (Washington: GPO, 1986): 453–455.

[30] Circular Telegram 401, Washington to Various Missions, January 25, 1955, in *FRUS, 1955–1957,* 21: 23; Parker, "Eisenhower and Bandung," 156–162.

Eastern Europe. Turkey, Iran, and Iraq – all recent signatories to the Baghdad Pact – offered staunch defenses of their choice to align. The conference declaration emphasized the brotherhood and common struggles of the Afro-Asian peoples, but the ideological disunity of the attendees was clear to diplomatic observers.[31]

Dulles declared victory, as the PRC had failed to marshal the attendees in support of its policy against Taiwan. He told Eisenhower on April 29 that he had originally thought the conference "was going to be dominated by Zhou. Actually, it turned out that the conference was dominated by a group of friendly Asian nations who believed in association with the West." The final document had been largely agreeable – even its statements about colonialism resonated with what Dulles and Eisenhower privately believed.[32] Dulles attributed U.S. success at the conference to the cooperation of existing friends and allies, who had checked Nehru's advocacy of nonalignment. The staunch anticommunism of the Ceylonese and Turkish delegations reassured him that he could count on African and Asian opposition to Soviet influence or to the emergence of a neutralist bloc. In a concurring report, the Operations Control Board observed that "the free world scored a considerable substantive success" at Bandung.[33]

The "success" at Bandung had not altered the administration's ambivalence toward nonalignment; it continued to fret that neutralist sentiment, now legitimated by the conference, could penetrate the U.S. alliance system. If Zhou had not dominated the conference, he had still struck many observers as its most charismatic and impressive participant.[34] Nonalignment continued to evoke a sense of unease, and Dulles was not content to leave the leadership of the postcolonial states to the likes of Nehru or Sukarno. In November, he discussed with British Foreign Secretary Harold Macmillan the possibility of staging a "Bandung Conference in reverse." Bringing together postcolonial and European attendees, this counter-conference would have aspired to develop a comprehensive plan for decolonization. Notably, Dulles asked Rockefeller Foundation President Dean Rusk to study the proposal further, although no conference was ever held.[35]

The administration's post-Bandung confidence, moreover, contributed to the administration's belief that it could count on states to be both notionally neutral and broadly sympathetic to the West. This contributed to serious missteps in the following year. Events in 1956 played a disproportionate role in shaping the image of the Eisenhower administration among the nonaligned

[31] G. H. Jansen, *Nonalignment and the Afro-Asian States* (New York: Praeger, 1966), 182–225.
[32] Minutes of Cabinet Meeting, April 29, 1955, in *FRUS, 1955–1957*, 21: 91–92; Memcon, Dulles and Turkish Counselor Savut, May 4, 1955, ibid.: 94–95.
[33] Memorandum, "Bandung Conference," OCB Staff, May 12, 1955, White House Office, NSC Staff Papers, 1948–1961, OCB Central File Series, box 86, OCB 092.3 (File #2), DDEL.
[34] Memorandum, Roy P. McNair to H. S. Craig, May 13, 1955, ibid.
[35] Letter, Dulles to Winthrop Aldrich, January 9, 1956, in John Foster Dulles Papers, Subject Series, box 7, "Policy of Independence for Colonial Peoples," DDEL; Memcon, Dulles and Harold Macmillan, November 16, 1955, ibid.

leaders, overshadowing the more careful diplomacy practiced in the decade's final years.

NEUTRALITY AND MORALITY

No act brought Dulles greater notoriety in the nonaligned world than a statement he made at the commencement exercises of Iowa State College in Ames, on June 9, 1956. In an address entitled "The Cost of Peace," which broadly surveyed the goals and methods of U.S. foreign policy, he commented on the value of Washington's forty-two active treaties of alliance:

These treaties abolish, as between the parties, the principle of neutrality, which pretends that a nation can best gain safety for itself by being indifferent to the fate of others. This has increasingly become an obsolete conception and, except under very exceptional circumstances, it is an immoral and shortsighted conception. The free world today is stronger, and peace is more secure, because so many free nations courageously recognize the now demonstrated fact that their own peace and safety would be endangered by assault on freedom elsewhere.[36]

This was just a short passage in a commencement address, but Dulles's brief shot at the nonaligned states was heard around the world. It cemented into place an image of American contempt for the attendees of Bandung.

Dulles had not set out to offend the nonaligned states, but rather to reassure allies. The Eisenhower administration faced a delicate predicament: in trying to remind allies that their support was valued, it had inadvertently insulted nonaligned states. Dulles also directed his statement toward a domestic audience. As Brands has observed, Dulles and Eisenhower often made complementary statements on foreign policy: Dulles, acting as the lightning rod, played to the conservative base, whereas Eisenhower was the more amiable, moderate spokesman for administration foreign policy.[37] Indeed, Ike had previously expressed his understanding of why states would plausibly choose neutrality in the Cold War:

Now today there are certain nations that say they are neutral. This doesn't necessarily mean what it is so often interpreted to mean, neutral as between right and wrong or decency and indecency.

They are using the term "neutral" with respect to attachment to military alliances. And may I point out that I cannot see that this is always to the disadvantage of such a country as ours.[38]

Notably, Eisenhower promised that a fuller statement on the question of neutrality was to be delivered by Dulles in Ames a few days later. In all likelihood,

---

[36] *DOSB*, Vol. 34, June 18, 1956, 999–1000; "Dulles Shifts on Neutrality," *The Washington Post*, July 12, 1956, 8.
[37] Brands, *The Specter of Neutralism*, 306–310.
[38] *Public Papers of the President: Dwight D. Eisenhower, 1956* (Washington: GPO, 1957), 555.

the two men were coordinating their messages, pitching Ike's remarks for a global audience and Dulles's for domestic ears.

Missed in the ensuing clamor was Dulles's defense of foreign aid in general and aid to Yugoslavia in particular. Conceding that Yugoslavia "does not have the form of society that we like," he proceeded to praise Tito for his defiance of Stalin and termed his state "a notable case of national independence in Eastern Europe." More generally, he defended foreign aid against the charge that it represented a "give away" and asserted that the success of aid programs was to be measured not in terms of the subservience of recipients but rather by the extent to which such assistance strengthened freedoms around the world (an argument later echoed by the Kennedy administration). Dulles intended, in sum, to define foreign aid – even aid to countries not fully supportive of the United States – as part of his "cost of peace."[39] He certainly intended no volte face on U.S. policy toward nonalignment, and implemented no such change in basic policy statements. The next draft of the BNSP, NSC 5707, retained the exact language of its predecessor on the question of neutrality.[40]

If Eisenhower and Dulles had hoped to perform in counterpoint, the arrangement nevertheless failed. The president's remarks in Washington were overshadowed by the secretary's speech in Ames. The administration had taken a calculated risk in trying to advance its aid budget, and it incurred a serious cost to its image. Dulles's statement on the immorality of nonalignment came to symbolize the outlook of the Eisenhower administration. Across the world, Dulles was perceived as embodying American inflexibility and insensitivity toward the postcolonial states. A decade later, he was remembered, first and foremost, as the man who deemed their foreign policies immoral.

ASWAN AND ITS AFTERMATH

The following month, Eisenhower and Dulles's decision to withdraw a $400 million Anglo-American loan to Egypt further widened the breach between the United States and the nonaligned world and set the Suez crisis into motion. The loan had been intended to fund the construction of Nasser's pet project, the Aswan High Dam. Driven into a panic by the loan cancellation, Nasser chose to raise the ante by nationalizing the Suez Canal, and thereby setting Egypt onto a fateful collision course with Britain, France, and Israel.

Ironically, the Aswan debacle had its origins in a risky effort by Eisenhower and Dulles to stem Egypt's leftward drift. Alarmed at reports of Egyptian arms purchases from the Soviet Union, the administration, acting with the United Kingdom, had committed to lend $400 million toward the High Dam project.

---

[39] *DOSB*, Vol. 34, June 18, 1956, 1001–1002; Lorraine Lees, *Keeping Tito Afloat: The United States, Yugoslavia, and the Cold War* (University Park, PA: Pennsylvania State University Press, 1997), 183–185.

[40] NSC Report, "Basic National Security Policy," June 3, 1957, in *FRUS, 1955–1957*, 19: 507–524.

In so doing, it faced opposition from members of Congress incensed by either Nasser's denunciations of the Baghdad Pact or his enmity toward Israel. In early 1956, the government of British Prime Minister Anthony Eden, which still owned and operated the Suez Canal, concluded that it had to oppose Nasser at all costs, seeing him as a dangerous expansionist: a Hitler on the Nile.[41] All these factors made an Aswan loan more difficult, but they did not pose insurmountable obstacles for the Eisenhower administration.[42]

Nasser's own choices, however, added new obstacles. As the Anglo-Egyptian relationship worsened, Nasser extended recognition to the PRC and informed Washington that Moscow would be happy to supply him with funds for the dam. In March, presidential emissary Robert B. Anderson traveled to Israel and Egypt, seeking support for Arab-Israeli peace negotiations. Nasser responded unfavorably, and Eisenhower and Dulles blamed the Egyptian leader when Anderson returned empty-handed.[43] In July, they withdrew their offer to fund the dam.

Months later, retrospectively explaining his decision, Dulles asked rhetorically: "Do nations which play both sides get better treatment than nations which are stalwart and work with us?"[44] He had already answered that question in his Ames speech. As Dulles wrote in March 1956 after Anderson had returned, his goal was to "let Colonel Nasser realize that he cannot cooperate as he is doing with the Soviet Union and at the same time enjoy most-favored-nation treatment from the United States."[45] To Ike, the core problem seemed to be "the growing ambition of Nasser, the sense of power that he has gained out of his associations with the Soviets, his belief that he can emerge as a true leader of the entire Arab world."[46]

The Aswan debacle came as prologue to the Suez crisis. Nasser responded to the cancellation of the loan by nationalizing the Suez Canal. Britain, France, and Israel then famously plotted to destroy Nasser. An Israeli invasion of the Sinai Peninsula was planned as the pretext for a subsequent Anglo-French operation to recapture the canal. The Israeli invasion began on October 29, 1956; the next day, Britain and France issued an ultimatum to Israel and Egypt, calling for both belligerents to withdraw their forces to a distance of ten miles from the canal. The three powers had assumed that they would enjoy U.S.

---

[41] Hahn, *The United States, Great Britain, and Egypt*, 202–206.

[42] Townsend Hoopes, *The Devil and John Foster Dulles* (Boston: Little, Brown and Company, 1973), 337.

[43] Douglas Little, *American Orientalism: The United States and the Middle East Since 1945* (Chapel Hill: University of North Carolina Press, 2004), 168–171; Yaqub, *Containing Arab Nationalism*, 41–47.

[44] Hoopes, *The Devil and John Foster Dulles*, 337.

[45] Memorandum, Dulles to Eisenhower, March 28, 1956, in DOS, *FRUS, 1955–1957, Vol. 15: The Arab-Israeli Dispute, January 1–July 26, 1956* (Washington: GPO, 1989): 419–421.

[46] Memcon, Eisenhower, Dulles, and others, March 28, 1956, in *FRUS, 1955–1957*, 15: 421–425; Robert Ferrell ed., *The Eisenhower Diaries* (New York: Norton, 1981), 318–324; Richard Immerman, *John Foster Dulles: Piety, Pragmatism, and Power in U.S. Foreign Policy* (Wilmington: Scholarly Resources, 1999), 147–153; Pach, *Eisenhower*, 127–128.

support or acquiescence.[47] Dulles's own rhetoric may have reinforced this belief. Had he not, during his Ames speech, declared that Washington ultimately stood by its allies?

In fact, Dulles was appalled by the actions of the three powers, which had, without informing him, acted to enflame yet another localized conflict to Moscow's potential benefit. In an NSC meeting, Dulles bemoaned the fundamental dilemma posed by Suez:

For many years now the United States has been walking a tightrope between the effort to maintain our old and valued relationships with our French and British allies on the one hand, and on the other trying to assure ourselves of the friendship and understanding of the newly independent countries who have escaped from colonialism.... Unless we now assert and maintain this leadership, all of those newly independent countries will turn from us to the USSR.[48]

The shock of Suez spurred Eisenhower to take an unusually strong stance against two European allies, employing political and economic pressure to force a withdrawal. In part, this reflected shock at the deceit of the allies. At the core of Washington's opposition, however, lay concern that the invasion would gravely damage U.S. influence among the uncommitted states of the Arab world, opening the region to Soviet influence and jeopardizing Western access to valued bases and oil resources.[49]

The administration's strong reaction to the Suez crisis could not undo the damage done by the Aswan decision. Although Nasser welcomed Eisenhower's rhetorical support, the accord between Washington and Cairo proved temporary. Eisenhower and Dulles were alarmed by the expansion of Soviet influence in Egypt and by Nasser's own regional policies, which threatened conservative, pro-Western regimes in the region. Seeking to contain the Egyptian leader, Eisenhower and Dulles adopted the "Eisenhower Doctrine," supplying military and economic aid to friendly regimes in the area. For two years, the United States and Egypt waged a bitter, inconclusive battle on the Middle Eastern chessboard.[50]

STALLING FOR TIME: GOA AND WEST NEW GUINEA

The Ames speech and the fallout from Aswan dealt sharp blows to U.S. prestige in the nonaligned world. Staunch support for European powers in colonial disputes, in contravention to the principles outlined in the BNSP, further alienated nonaligned states from the administration. Faced with disputes between new states and their former colonizers, the White House pleaded neutrality

---

[47] Harold Macmillan, *Riding the Storm, 1956–1959* (London: Macmillan, 1971), 148–151.
[48] William Roger Louis, "Dulles, Suez, and the British," in Richard H. Immerman ed., *John Foster Dulles and the Diplomacy of the Cold War* (Princeton: Princeton University Press, 1990), 654–656.
[49] Yaqub, *Containing Arab Nationalism*, 51–55; Immerman, *John Foster Dulles*, 147–156.
[50] Yaqub, *Containing Arab Nationalism*, 57–85; Little, *American Orientalism*, 128–137.

but largely deferred to the preferences of the metropole. If Eisenhower and Dulles wanted an end to the problems of decolonization, they did not seek a means to expedite the process. Suez proved a unique exception to the rule of pro-European neutrality.

The case of Portuguese India was more representative of the administration's policy toward lingering colonial questions. Lisbon retained several small territorial enclaves on the Indian subcontinent, with Goa the most prominent among them, to the expressed outrage of Nehru's government. The dispute placed Washington in a bind. Portugal was a key NATO ally, providing the alliance with vital aerial refueling bases in the Azores. India, on the other hand, was the largest and most influential nonaligned state.

An early public statement on the Goa question came in August 1955, in the form of a noncommittal call for the two parties to resolve the dispute without violence.[51] This did not satisfy India, which was irked subsequently by a joint U.S.-Portuguese statement issued on December 2, 1955. This declaration, made by Dulles and visiting Portuguese Foreign Minister Paulo Cunha, contained a reference to "the Portuguese provinces in the Far East," implying full American recognition of Portugal's claim to its South Asian enclaves.[52] Nehru remarked that no American action "could have been more calculated to irritate Indian opinion" than Dulles's statement.[53]

Nehru raised the issue when Dulles visited India in March 1956 and when he in turn came to the United States the following December. Both times, Dulles responded evasively.[54] Privately the secretary felt that he had already done his utmost to avoid taking any stance on Goa – much more than Nehru had done when issuing a communique with Khrushchev on the Taiwan question.[55] Eisenhower offered Nehru more in the way of sympathy, confiding that he thought the Portuguese claim was "spurious." Still, citing Portugal's membership within NATO and the value of the Azores bases, he asked if Nehru could defer the issue.[56] A subsequent Indian effort in 1960 to solicit U.S. mediation drew a similar response. Secretary of State Christian Herter replied that although the United States wished to see the Goa dispute resolved, it did not intend to "insert itself" into the matter.[57] Goa was left to fester until Kennedy took office.

Similarly, Washington maintained strict neutrality on the question of West New Guinea. Indonesia claimed the western half of the island of New Guinea,

---

[51] Department of State, Review of U.S.-Indian Relations, January 20, 1956, in DOS, *FRUS, 1955–1957, Vol. 8: South Asia* (Washington: GPO, 1987): 301–306.

[52] *DOSB*, December 12, 1955, 966–967.

[53] Operations Control Board, "Progress Report on U.S. Policy Towards South Asia," March 30, 1956, in *FRUS, 1955–1957*, 8: 1–8; McMahon, *Cold War on the Periphery*, 223–225.

[54] Memcon, Dulles and Nehru, March 9, 1956, in *FRUS, 1955–1957*, 8: 307–308.

[55] Letter, Dulles to John Sherman Cooper, December 19, 1955, JFDP, Chronological Series, box 13, "December 1955 (4)" folder, DDEL.

[56] Memcon, Eisenhower and Nehru, December 19, 1956, in *FRUS, 1955–1957*, 8: 331–41.

[57] Telegram 435, Washington to Lisbon, March 11, 1960, ibid., 753D.00/3-1060, NA.

which had remained under Dutch governance after Indonesia gained independence in 1949. Dulles avoided taking a public stance on the issue and tried to keep it out of the UN. He worried that Indonesia might move closer toward communism if the United States took an unambiguous position on the question. At heart, Dulles felt "strongly opposed" to the prospect of Indonesian control of West New Guinea, not out of sympathy for the Dutch but because he saw the government in Jakarta as dangerously unstable.[58]

This policy of neutrality mandated avoidance of any efforts at mediation between the two parties. In December 1955, when India sponsored a UN resolution calling for peaceful dialogue on the territory's future – a position that both The Hague and Jakarta had supported – Dulles declined to cosponsor the measure. In January 1956, the Dutch and Indonesian governments asked the United States to play a mediating role in the dispute. Dulles again demurred, and urged them to resolve their dispute bilaterally. Each party had placed different requests, but active efforts by the United States might have yielded a broader, more comprehensive set of negotiations.[59] Dulles did not want to commit the U.S. government to resolving the dispute, despite – or perhaps because of – warnings from the embassy in Jakarta about how Sukarno was fanning popular anger on the issue.[60] At the same time, he was unwilling to be seen backing Dutch colonialism.[61] Once again, Washington had taken a stance that – although strictly neutral – served to reinforce the status quo. As U.S. policy turned increasingly against Sukarno, the fleeting prospects of U.S. mediation between the Dutch and the Indonesians dimmed.

By tabling the questions of Goa and West New Guinea, the Eisenhower administration bequeathed these nettlesome disputes to its successors. In so doing, it both reassured allies and risked the deepening of anticolonial sentiment in India and Indonesia and the alienation of both countries from the United States.

UNDERMINING SUKARNO: INTERVENTION IN SOUTHEAST ASIA

The choice of the Eisenhower administration to avoid the question of West New Guinea in 1955 and 1956 proved fateful. During those years following the end of the First Indochina War, Washington moved to supplant the spent power of France in its former colonial possessions, becoming the predominant Western power in mainland Southeast Asia. Despite the French defeat, the economically vital region remained a critical Cold War arena, where

---

[58] Memcon, Dulles and Robert Menzies, March 15, 1955, in *FRUS, 1955–1957*, 22: 143–144; Memcon, Dulles and others, August 24, 1955, ibid.: 182–185.

[59] Telegram 1213, Washington to Jakarta, January 23, 1956, ibid.: 226–227.

[60] George McT. Kahin and Audrey Kahin, *Subversion as Foreign Policy: The Secret Eisenhower and Dulles Debacle in Indonesia* (New York: Norton, 1995), 77–83.

[61] Transcript, Dulles and Livingston Merchant, March 23, 1956, Papers of John Foster Dulles/ Telephone, box 4, "Memoranda of Telcon, General, 1/3/56–4/30/56" folder, DDEL.

Eisenhower sought to contain the PRC and establish stable non-communist regimes, notably in South Vietnam.

The mid-1950s marked a relative lull in tensions between the United States and Indonesia and the zenith of a policy of outreach to Sukarno, climaxing in the Indonesian's June 1956 visit to the United States. When the Indonesian leader visited Moscow later in the year, his stock plummeted in Washington. Indonesia faced economic crisis and the splintering of government authority across the far-flung archipelago. In response, Sukarno sought to consolidate central authority under what he termed "guided democracy," and he accepted Soviet economic aid and allied himself with the powerful Indonesian communist party, the PKI. Dulles, mindful of earlier "successes" in the cases of Guatemala and Iran, began to consider covert action as the best means to combat communism in Indonesia. Washington provided generous assistance to rebels on the islands of Sumatra and Sulawesi, including Second World War–vintage combat aircraft that briefly gave the rebels air superiority over the government in Jakarta.[62]

By any accounting, the policy turned out disastrously. Although the rebels capitalized upon lavish American support, a determined reaction from Jakarta stamped out the rebellions on both islands. Washington's role in supplying pilots and aircraft to the rebels proved impossible to conceal. As the insurrections foundered, Indonesia obtained definitive evidence of CIA involvement when it shot down a B-26 bomber and captured its American pilot. Faced with this Indonesian trump card and the dwindling of the rebellions and impressed by the strength of anticommunist sentiment in the Indonesian armed forces, Dulles and Eisenhower reversed course and abandoned the rebels.[63]

Eisenhower's anti-Sukarno policy was not exceptional in Southeast Asia. Partly as echoes of policies conceived during the Chinese civil war, the Korean War, and the First Indochina War, the Eisenhower administration pursued stratagems that had either the intended or the incidental effect of weakening nonaligned governments in mainland Southeast Asia. In Burma, Eisenhower supported a recalcitrant fragment of the defeated Chinese Nationalist army that had fled south across the Sino-Burmese border after the fall of Chiang Kai-shek's government. In Cambodia and Laos, the administration aided militant factions opposed to the neutral governments of Prince Norodom Sihanouk and Souvanna Phouma.[64]

---

[62] Kahin and Kahin, Subversion as Foreign Policy, 81–84; Robert J. McMahon, "'The Point of No Return': The Eisenhower Administration and Indonesia, 1953–1960," in *Statler and Johns, Globalization of the Cold War*, 80–89; Andrew Roadnight, *United States Policy towards Indonesia in the Truman and Eisenhower Years* (Palgrave: Hampshire, 2002), 139–143.

[63] Kahin and Kahin, *Subversion as Foreign Policy*, 180–216; McMahon, "The Point of No Return," 88–96.

[64] Kahin and Kahin, *Subversion as Foreign Policy*, 10–16; Robert J. McMahon, *Colonialism and Cold War: The United States and the Struggle for Indonesian Independence, 1945–1949* (Ithaca: Cornell University Press, 1981), 78–83, 98–101; Robert J. McMahon, *The Limits of Empire: The United States and Southeast Asia Since World War II* (New York: Columbia University Press,

These cases stand in sharp contrast to those of other nonaligned states, notably Egypt, India, and Yugoslavia. Although Dulles had no love for Nasser, he and Eisenhower had ruled out toppling the Egyptian leader through subversion.[65] Nor did Washington's relations with India, however difficult, descend to the level of outright hostility. In the case of Yugoslavia, the White House opted to support Tito and publicly defended the often-controversial aid that it sent to Belgrade. Why, then, did it pursue a far more aggressive set of policies in Southeast Asia?

A confluence of factors following the end of the Second World War had drawn the United States into the region. In the first place Southeast Asia was, after the Middle East, the second region of the postcolonial world identified by Eisenhower as an area of critical concern. Here, Eisenhower followed in Truman's footsteps, continuing his predecessor's policy of aiding the French in their struggle against Vietnamese nationalism. At stake, by Ike's reckoning, was the containment of Chinese communism. Fears of a domino effect were heightened by the area's pronounced economic importance to European and Japanese reconstruction, its proximity to major maritime arteries, and the relative weakness of its constituent states.[66]

State stability represented a critical distinction between the cases of India, Egypt, and Yugoslavia, on the one hand, and the Southeast Asian states on the other. Whereas each of the former was, by the mid-1950s, an established state with a strong national government, the latter were significantly more fragile. Cambodia and Laos had barely come into being; Indonesia and Burma battled strong centrifugal pressures from separatist regions. In this region, Dulles applied "lessons" learned from the fall of China in 1949. He felt his predecessors had erred in allowing Chiang Kai-shek to begin his ill-fated Manchurian campaign and thereby risk his southern power base. Far better would have been creating two Chinese states: a small communist-dominated north and a larger pro-Western south. What held true for China – a state with long-established historical boundaries – could only apply even more strongly to multi-ethnic, seemingly artificial states like Indonesia and Burma, with their sizable ethnic Chinese populations. In this region, concerns about spreading Chinese communist influence further drew the White House away from its own stated policy toward the uncommitted world.[67]

INTO AFRICA

By 1958 the White House had identified the Middle East and Southeast Asia as Third World areas of concern. Now, Africa began to merit this designation

---

1999), 79–84, 98–101; Kenton Clymer, *Troubled Relations: The United States and Cambodia Since 1870* (DeKalb: Northern Illinois University Press, 2007), 26–48.

[65] Louis, "Dulles, Suez, and the British," 147.

[66] McMahon, *The Limits of Empire*, 63–70.

[67] Kahin and Kahin, *Subversion as Foreign Policy*, 74–91; McMahon, "The Point of No Return," 87.

as well. That year, the State Department finally created a bureau charged with African affairs. (African policy had previously been implemented by the European bureau.) Although the continent never received as much attention as other areas of the uncommitted world, toward the end of the decade leading policymakers began to discern a national interest in excluding communism from Africa. In 1957 Dulles told the visiting British Foreign Secretary Lord Selwyn Lloyd that the West "would be in serious trouble" if Africa was lost to the Free World.[68] At stake were a range of strategic facilities, largely in North Africa, but also vast mineral resources that the United States considered essential to the economic health of Europe. Although the status quo of white minority rule seemed acceptable or even desirable, administration officials recognized the likelihood of widespread African independence, particularly after Ghana gained its freedom in 1957, and fretted that this was occurring "prematurely."[69] State Department officials wrote of pursuing a "triangular" policy, taking U.S., European, and African needs into account.[70] In practice, however, the administration considered the imperative of preserving European influence and economic access to Africa far more pressing than meeting the demands of Africans for political and economic independence. This is apparent in two cases: the crises of Guinean and Congolese independence.

In 1958, in the inaugural year of the Fifth Republic, French President Charles de Gaulle proposed a new constitutional arrangement for his African colonies. This new partnership would offer the colonies substantial financial aid and internal autonomy if they ceded jurisdiction over foreign affairs to Paris. Each colony needed to ratify this new arrangement by a referendum; any colony that voted against it would be excluded from the new union. De Gaulle's new constitution faced one especially determined foe in Africa, Sekou Touré, the premier of the Guinean colonial government. Touré called for his countrymen to reject an arrangement that chained twelve small African dependencies to a powerful metropole. In a shocking rebuke, some 95 percent of Guineans voted "non." This was an anomaly; Guinea was the only colony to reject the constitution.[71]

De Gaulle was not inclined to let Guinea's defiance pass unnoticed. France withdrew its personnel from Guinea, and de Gaulle sought to make Touré's victory a Pyrrhic one. As they departed, the French destroyed records and property; they smashed light bulbs, cut telephone wires, and diverted shipments of

---

[68] Memcon, Dulles and Selwyn Lloyd, March 23, 1957, in DOS, *FRUS, 1955–1957, Vol. 18: Africa* (Washington: GPO, 1989): 53–56.

[69] James H. Meriwether, "'A Torrent Overrunning Everything': Africa and the Eisenhower Administration," in Statler and Johns, *Globalization of the Cold War*, 175–186; George H. White Jr., *Holding the Line: Race, Racism and American Foreign Policy toward Africa, 1953–1961* (New York: Rowman & Littlefield, 2005), 28–33.

[70] Memorandum, Office of African Affairs, August 4, 1955, in *FRUS, 1955–1957*, 18: 13–18.

[71] See Elizabeth Schmidt, *Cold War and Decolonization in Guinea, 1946–1958* (Athens: Ohio University Press, 2007); Ebere Nwaubani, *The United States and Decolonization in West Africa, 1950–1960* (Rochester: University of Rochester Press, 2001), 206–211.

food and medicine. This was not merely a matter of pique for de Gaulle. As he saw it, no other African government could be tempted to follow in Guinea's footsteps, nor could France be seen offering favors to the one colony that had spurned it. He employed his foreign ministry to ensure that the desperate Guineans received no diplomatic recognition or economic succor from any of France's allies.[72]

Although U.S. diplomats fretted that nonrecognition of Guinea could well drive it into the arms of the communist powers, Dulles withheld recognition. Touré pleaded for both recognition and immediate economic assistance, adding that he would prefer U.S. aid to communist aid but would have to accept the latter should the former prove unavailable.[73] All he received in reply in the critical month following the referendum were vague promises of recognition at some future date.[74]

Touré did not spend the time sitting on his hands. While France held its allies back, the communist and nonaligned powers acted. In the week following Guinea's de facto independence, it received notices of recognition from Ghana, Egypt, the Soviet Union and its Warsaw Pact allies, and the PRC. Khrushchev cabled Touré on October 6, offering substantial economic and technical assistance. Touré's secretary of finance declared that Europe would only be able to blame itself, should Guinea become "the door to Africa for the Soviets."[75]

Although Paris held fast to its policy of nonrecognition, Guinea's broadening ties with the communist bloc brought Washington's patience to an end. At the end of October, Dulles signaled his intent to recognize Guinea, which France grudgingly accepted. Paris still urged its allies to delay the establishment of relations with Conakry, and sought to keep the new state out of the UN. Dulles assented to these two requests.[76] Another three and a half months passed before full relations were established and Washington opened an embassy in Conakry.[77] Without formal diplomatic relations, Eisenhower was unable to answer Guinean pleas for economic assistance. To the Guineans, it seemed that the United States was incapable of taking any action with regard to them without consulting their enemy.[78]

Touré could hold a grudge as well as de Gaulle; he remembered who had shown him support during October 1958. For the next few years, the communist bloc profited from Touré's sense of gratitude, while Washington chafed at the expansion of Soviet influence in West Africa. Delegations from the Warsaw Pact countries streamed into Conakry, and Czechoslovakia began supplying

[72] Schmidt, *Cold War and Decolonization*, 171–176.
[73] Telegram 150, Dakar to Washington, October 23, 1958, in DOS, *FRUS, 1958–1960, Vol. 14: Africa* (Washington: GPO, 1992): 675–8.
[74] Telegram 92, Washington to Dakar, October 17, 1958, ibid.: 674.
[75] Thomas F. Brady, "Guinea Awaiting Move By France," *NYT*, October 6, 1958, 13.
[76] Memorandum, Dulles to Eisenhower, October 31, 1958, in *FRUS, 1958–1960*, 14: 679–680.
[77] Memcon, Herter and Telli Diallo, December 1, 1958, in *FRUS, 1958–1960*, 18: 680–683.
[78] John H. Morrow, *First American Ambassador to Guinea* (New Brunswick: Rutgers University Press), 69.

Guinea with light arms in the spring of 1959.[79] To the consternation of West Germany, Touré edged toward recognition of East Germany; only an intense diplomatic campaign by Bonn prevented the East Germans from gaining a full diplomatic foothold in West Africa.[80]

Guinea had demonstrated Eisenhower's continued deference to Europe in African affairs. The same can be said of his handling of the Congo crisis in 1960. When Belgium granted independence to the Congo, on June 30, 1960, it created a power vacuum in the heart of Africa. Executed as badly it was, the transfer of power was a recipe for anarchy. Brussels clearly expected to retain control over its notionally independent former colony, which possessed vast reserves of precious minerals, including uranium. At the time of independence, the officer corps of the Congolese army remained entirely white and Belgians dominated the civil service. Many Congolese found this an entirely unacceptable state of affairs; within a week, units of the army mutinied against their white officers. Brussels responded by dispatching troops to protect its citizens and restore control of key cities.[81]

The Belgian deployment to the Congo brought widespread African condemnation, and the Congolese government, led by Premier Patrice Lumumba, declared itself to be at war with Belgium. Adding to the chaos, Belgium openly abetted a separatist rebellion in the mineral-rich southern Congolese province of Katanga, headed by a businessman named Moise Tshombe. Faced with Katanga's secession, Lumumba sought military assistance to restore order and evict the Belgians; Khrushchev proved eager to offer food aid and technical assistance, which Lumumba gladly accepted. The UN dispatched troops to restore order and facilitate the withdrawal of the Belgians. Washington supported the UN mission, however many of the soldiers sent to the Congo came from nonaligned states supportive of Lumumba.[82]

Lumumba visited Washington in July 1960 and attempted to explain to Eisenhower that evicting the Belgians was his top concern; he had no desire to join the communist bloc. The Eisenhower administration regarded him with the deepest skepticism, deeming him incoherent, volatile, and socialist-leaning. Inflammatory reports from the Congo of the rape of white women further inflamed opinion in the United States government and public. The Eisenhower administration concluded that Lumumba was a dangerous radical and began contemplating how he might be removed from the political scene.[83] In

---

[79] Morrow, *First American Ambassador to Guinea*, 37–38; Sergey Mazov, *A Distant Front in the Cold War: The USSR in West Africa and the Congo* (Stanford: Stanford University Press, 2010), 63–75.

[80] See William Glenn Gray, *Germany's Cold War: The Global Campaign to Isolate East Germany, 1949–1969* (Chapel Hill: University of North Carolina Press, 2003), 107–115.

[81] Madeleine G. Kalb, *The Congo Cables: The Cold War in Africa – From Eisenhower to Kennedy* (New York: Macmillan, 1982), 3–16.

[82] Ibid, 17–71.

[83] Richard Mahoney, *JFK: Ordeal in Africa* (New York: Oxford University Press, 1983), 36–41; White, *Holding the Line*, 115–122.

September the Congolese government cleft itself in two when President Joseph Kasavubu, the pro-Belgian head of the government, dismissed Lumumba, with the active backing of the United States.[84] This dismissal ultimately fragmented political power in the Congo. A week later, faced with unrest by pro-Lumumba elements, Colonel Joseph Mobutu, an army officer, led a coup in the capital, Leopoldville. Lumumba was placed under protective UN custody in a residence within the city. By November, two rival governments claimed to rule the Congo: Kasavubu's from Leopoldville and Lumumba's from the eastern city of Stanleyville.

That autumn brought Kennedy's election, fueling hopes among African leaders that a change of Congo policy was imminent. The eleven weeks separating Kennedy's November victory and his January inauguration, however, proved fatal for Lumumba, as the Eisenhower administration sought to neutralize him. Lumumba lived precariously in Leopoldville under UN protection. Fearing for his life, he attempted to flee for friendly Stanleyville at the end of November. Working together, the CIA and Mobutu located and captured him.[85] Three days before Kennedy assumed office, Mobutu, in connivance with the Katangans, had his rival murdered.

Lumumba died because the Eisenhower administration had deemed him an enemy. He was not, at the time of his death, a member of the nonaligned caucus, but his politics much resembled those of Nkrumah, Touré, and other African nationalists. These men saw him as their ideological kin; when his safety was threatened, they reacted sharply. Nkrumah and Touré had written to Eisenhower in August, demanding the immediate removal of Belgian troops. Both reiterated their pleas when they visited the United States in the autumn.[86] It made no difference. Faced with the prospect of left-leaning nationalism in the Congo, the Eisenhower administration saw red, sided with its Belgian allies, and involved itself in an act of murder. The ensuing catastrophe was left to Eisenhower's successor, along with a visible U.S. commitment to keep communist influence from the heart of sub-Saharan Africa.

When viewed in a broader perspective, Eisenhower's Congo policy reveals a fundamental continuity in his approach to Third World nationalism and nonalignment. Abstract statements about the desirability of assisting local nationalists or the possible utility of neutrality invariably clashed with active support of European allies and panicked responses to the behavior of Third World leaders. Over the same period Eisenhower adopted policies of covert intervention readily, in cases such as Iran and Indonesia, despite all the manifest uncertainty these acts entailed. The tension between intervention and situational tolerance of nonalignment remained unresolved to the end of his presidency.

[84] Suspected for years, this was documented, albeit sparsely, in Larry Devlin, *Chief of Station, Congo: A Memoir of 1960–1967* (New York: PublicAffairs, 2007), 66–68.
[85] Mahoney, *JFK: Ordeal in Africa*, 55–61; Kalb, *The Congo Cables*, 128–174.
[86] Telegram 176, Accra to Washington, August 6, 1960, in *FRUS, 1958–1960*, 14: 390–392; Message, Touré to Eisenhower, August 7, 1960, ibid.: 395; Memcon, J. C. Satterthwaite and Touré, October 6, 1960, ibid.: 515–516.

TOWARD THE NEW FRONTIER

Eisenhower never abandoned intervention as a tactic in the Third World, but he showed a greater prudence toward the nonaligned states in his final years in the White House. If his concerns about nonalignment did not change, he did display a capacity to refine and improve policies and occasionally to reverse course and cut his losses. Consequently, the end of the 1950s witnessed a general improvement in relations with several key uncommitted states.

This shift in policy came as a reaction to increased Soviet efforts to woo the nonaligned states. Unlike his predecessor, Joseph Stalin, General Secretary Nikita Khrushchev actively and eagerly sought to spread revolution in the Third World, and proved quite willing to court noncommunist nonaligned governments, offering aid to India, Egypt, Guinea, and Indonesia. Khrushchev courted Nehru, Nasser, and Sukarno, staging two visits to India and one to Indonesia during the Eisenhower years. In 1959 he enthusiastically embraced Cuban revolutionary leader Fidel Castro and the following year he sought to aid Lumumba.[87] With each passing year, the Soviets appeared to be gathering momentum in the Third World, and the American public took uneasy notice.

Key to Moscow's appeal was the shared interest of the Soviets and their nonaligned peers in the virtues of planned economies. As he called for peaceful coexistence and competition between the superpowers, Khrushchev sought to expand Soviet economic assistance programs in the Third World.[88] Nasser, Nehru, Touré, Nkrumah, and Sukarno all sought to develop industrial economies rapidly. The Soviet Union offered a statist blueprint, based on mass mobilization, with the promise of economic equality. Socialism, as such, was an intrinsically appealing economic model to nonaligned leaders and Moscow proved eager to fund public-sector industrial projects such as the Aswan High Dam and India's Bhilai steel mill; this put the United States, already tarred by its association with European colonialism, at a greater disadvantage.[89] From New Delhi, U.S. Ambassador Ellsworth Bunker warned of an "all-out" Soviet offensive designed to tie India to Moscow through trade, aid, and propaganda.[90]

Soviet diplomatic progress in the Third World compounded broadly felt American anxieties in the late 1950s. The trauma of the loss of China and the frustrations of the Korean War remained recent memories. The U.S. electorate

[87] Westad, *The Global Cold War*, 66–72; William Taubman, *Khrushchev: The Man and His Era* (New York: W. W. Norton, 2003), 392–395; Vladislav Zubok and Constantine Pleshakov, *Inside the Kremlin's Cold War: From Stalin to Khrushchev* (Cambridge, MA: Harvard University Press, 1996), 205–210.

[88] See Michael R. Adamson, "'The Most Important Single Aspect of Our Foreign Policy': The Eisenhower Administration, Foreign Aid, and the Third World," in Statler and Johns, *Globalization of the Cold War*, 55–61.

[89] Westad, *The Global Cold War*, 90–97; Leffler, *For the Soul of Mankind*, 169–171; McMahon, *Cold War on the Periphery*, 259.

[90] Telegram 2791, New Delhi to Washington, May 13, 1959, White House Office of the Special Assistant for National Security Affairs Records, NSC Series, Briefing Notes, box 16, "South Asia, 1957–1959" folder, DDEL.

was further unsettled by the 1957 launch of the Soviet satellite Sputnik, which seemed to augur an age of communist technological superiority. Such fears were only compounded by the release of the Gaither Report, a Ford Foundation study that deemed the United States to be in grave danger of a preemptive Soviet nuclear strike. Moscow's new sway in the uncommitted states added to public unease about the Cold War in the late 1950s. Amid this sense of a nation adrift, the clear appeal of socialism in the postcolonial world represented, in the words of noted British political scientist D. W. Brogan, "an affront to the American belief in an intelligible and manageable world."[91]

Some Americans sought to restore intelligibility, to explain why the self-apparent qualities of their system were not appreciated in the Third World. No explanation was received more broadly than that offered by the bestselling 1958 novel *The Ugly American*, advertised by its publisher, W.W. Norton, as "the inside story of how we are losing the Cold War."[92] Written by William J. Lederer and Eugene Burdick, *The Ugly American* depicted an incompetent U.S. diplomatic corps falling behind in the battle for hearts and minds in the fictional Southeast Asian state of Sarkhan. The novel's portrait of whiskey-swilling, culturally insensitive diplomats, unable to speak the language of their host countries, largely defined the public debate over U.S. diplomatic efforts in the Third World during the late 1950s. Accompanying its assault on the State Department, however, was an argument that the United States needed to be subtler and less Manichean in its pursuit of the Third World, coupled with both a moral and a geopolitical case for saving Sarkhan – and countries like it – from communist tyranny. With Moscow and Washington at near nuclear parity, the Cold War was likely to be decided by "a multitude of tiny battles." If the United States could not win these battles, the authors wrote,

We had better retreat to our shores, build Fortress America, learn to live without international trade and communications, and accept the mediocrity, the low standard of living, and the loom of world Communism.[93]

These popular concerns were mirrored by less hyperbolic analyses within the U.S. government. Moscow's diplomatic offensive in the postcolonial world exploited the weakness of U.S. policy toward the Bandung attendees, evident in the broad gap between the sentiments of the annual BNSP and the administration's regional strategy. Doubts permeated the administration as to whether alliances with unstable Asian governments were preferable to their neutralization under more stable regimes. Within the State Department, some analysts felt dismayed at the absence of a comprehensive policy toward neutral states and unnerved by spreading Soviet influence.

[91] D. W. Brogan, *America in the Modern World* (New Brunswick: Rutgers University Press, 1960), 21–22.
[92] Display Ad, *Chicago Tribune*, September 30, 1958, 10.
[93] William J. Lederer and Eugene Burdick, *The Ugly American* (New York: Norton, 1958), 266–269, 271–285.

Among these men was Robert M. McClintock, a former ambassador to Cambodia, who served on the State Department's Policy Planning Staff (PPS). McClintock complained in 1957: "One at times has the impression that we are following antithetical positions on neutrality." Echoing suggestions made by one of his PPS predecessors, Charles Burton Marshall, McClintock questioned whether the United States was benefiting from a surfeit of alliances, observing that it would cost substantially less to tacitly support neutral states than it would to bankroll weak, dependent allies. In particular, he thought a neutral India might safeguard Southeast Asia from communist expansion.[94]

McClintock's memoranda both signified internal discord within the Eisenhower administration over its policy toward uncommitted nations and coincided with an emerging determination on the part of the White House to improve relations with prominent states such as India, Egypt, and Yugoslavia. Indeed, real progress was achieved in the administration's later years; with the task of alliance building seemingly complete and in the relative absence of serious regional conflict, Eisenhower and Dulles worked to improve relations with major nonaligned states.

The White House showed political courage and persistence in its efforts to engage Yugoslavia. Eisenhower and Dulles waged a bruising but ultimately successful battle to obtain Congressional approval for economic and military assistance to Belgrade. A successful visit by Tito near the end of Eisenhower's second term signaled the fundamental health of the relationship. The case of Yugoslavia demonstrates a fundamental pragmatism on the part of the administration, a willingness to abide the difficulties posed by Tito's communism.[95]

Similarly, Eisenhower presided over a gradual improvement in relations with Egypt. In the years immediately following the Suez crisis, the Eisenhower Doctrine had led the United States to intervene against a potential coup in Jordan in 1957 and to land 15,000 Marines in Lebanon in 1958 to preempt another possible change of government in the region. The much-trumpeted union of Egypt and Syria in the name of the United Arab Republic that year, coupled with a radical coup in Iraq, further alarmed Eisenhower. Nonetheless, in 1959, the rising popularity of Nasser and the increasingly pro-Moscow tilt of the new government in Baghdad caused Washington to reevaluate its stance. Dulles and Eisenhower agreed on the need to reengage Nasser, and in the summer of 1959 the administration offered economic aid to Cairo – the first offer made since the withdrawal of Aswan funding. Most pivotally, Eisenhower offered Nasser generous sales of surplus grain at concession prices through the Food for Peace program, ultimately providing two thirds of Egypt's grain imports. Although serious disagreements with Nasser remained, Eisenhower

94 Memorandum, Robert McClintock to Robert Bowie, January 25, 1957, RG-59, Records of the Policy Planning Staff, 1957–1961, PPC-123, "Neutralism" folder, NA.; Memorandum, McClintock, March 12, 1957, ibid.; Charles Burton Marshall "Alliances with Fledgling States," in Arnold Wolfers ed. *Alliance Policy in the Cold War* (Baltimore: The Johns Hopkins Press, 1959), 213–223.
95 Lees, *Keeping Tito Afloat*, 227–236; Brands, *The Specter of Neutralism*, 215–219.

left office with the justifiable conviction that real improvements had been achieved in Egyptian-American relations.[96]

India, too, moved closer to the United States in the waning years of the Eisenhower administration. Having tilted toward Pakistan in the mid-1950s, the White House ultimately took a greater interest in bolstering India. New Delhi faced a severe economic crisis, particularly a growing foreign exchange gap. The failure of India's industrialization program stood to strengthen the country's communist opposition. The urgency of aiding India drew Eisenhower into conflict with his own party. After Styles Bridges, a Republican senator from New Hampshire, questioned the rationale for aid to New Delhi, he endured a sharp tongue-lashing at the hands of his president the following day. "If that country goes Communist, where are we going?" Eisenhower worried aloud.[97] India's perceived rivalry with China extended into the realm of developmental economics; the White House did not wish to see Peking's model validated by the implosion of New Delhi's. Accordingly, in March 1958, Eisenhower and Dulles approved a $225 million loan to India. Eisenhower also approved, in 1956 and 1960, two large sales of U.S. grain to India at concession prices.[98] Meetings between Eisenhower and Nehru in 1956 and 1959 further dispelled the suspicion and acrimony that had clouded the relationship. The tie grew closer as India became increasingly concerned by Chinese claims on its northern border. In 1960, the Eisenhower administration sold C-119 transport aircraft to New Delhi, initiating a new military aid relationship.[99]

Apparent in both instances was a greater use of economic aid as a tool of policy toward the uncommitted states. Well before Kennedy came to office, the White House began to approach nonaligned states as proving grounds for Western models of modernization, using foreign aid as a tool to gain leverage and influence development. Anxiety about Moscow's burgeoning aid programs in the Third World drove this shift, as did concern that poverty was creating breeding grounds for communist unrest. These worries were vividly illustrated when Vice President Richard Nixon was violently accosted by irate Venezuelans on a 1958 trip to Caracas, and confirmed when Fidel Castro took power in Cuba at the beginning of the following year. Eisenhower's travels abroad convinced him of the imminence of decolonization and the importance of aiding Third World development. Against

[96] Little, *American Orientalism*, 132–137; Brands, *The Specter of Neutralism*, 282–302; Yaqub, *Containing Arab Nationalism*, 237–267; William J. Burns, *Economic Aid and American Policy toward Egypt, 1955–1981* (Albany: SUNY Press, 1985), 114–120.

[97] Memcon, Eisenhower and Styles Bridges, May 21, 1957, Eisenhower Papers as President, Ann Whitman Series, box 24, "May '57 Miscellaneous (2)" folder, DDEL.

[98] Dennis Merrill, *Bread and the Ballot: The United States and India's Economic Development, 1947–1963* (Chapel Hill: University of North Carolina Press, 1990), 122–168; McMahon, *Cold War on the Periphery*, 233–239; Nick Cullather, *The Hungry World: America's Cold War Battle Against Poverty in Asia* (Cambridge, MA: Harvard University Press, 2010), 137–146.

[99] McMahon, *Cold War on the Periphery*, 259–271; Dennis Kux, *India and the United States: Estranged Democracies, 1941–1991* (Washington: National Defense University Press, 1992), 139–173.

this backdrop, India took on a unique symbolic value as a potential proving ground for non-communist – albeit somewhat statist – development.
Similarly, Eisenhower approved funding for Ghana's grandiose Volta River
Dam project in 1960, hoping to improve the U.S. position in West Africa.[100]
With his evolving aid policy, Eisenhower anticipated the Kennedy outlook
toward the nonaligned world, although Ike proved less radical in his thinking
than the New Frontiersmen.[101]

Eisenhower also proved a successful practitioner of presidential diplomacy.
He was a less polarizing figure to nonaligned leaders than Dulles. Indeed there
was something about the former general to which these revolutionary leaders could relate. Sukarno greatly enjoyed his 1956 trip to the United States,
and Eisenhower was, improbably, the president whom Nehru most enjoyed
meeting.[102] The triumphant head of state visit – a frequent occurrence in the
Kennedy years – was in fact patented during the previous administration. In
Sukarno's case, his second visit, in 1960, contributed to a quiet shift in U.S.
policy toward the West New Guinea dispute, as Dulles's successor, Christian
Herter, began to ponder ways by which the conflict could be mediated.[103]
Although the issue continued to fester, U.S.-Indonesian relations had improved
substantially from their nadir in 1957 and 1958.

The roots of the Kennedy administration's policy thus lay partially in the
sometimes prudent diplomacy of the late Eisenhower years. Even though the
new administration was loath to say it publicly, the Eisenhower administration
had begun the vital work of reaching out to some of the nonaligned states.
Eisenhower's problems were largely in terms of timing, perception, and tone:
of presiding over the era of alliance building, and of often yielding to the temptation to see and describe the rivalry between the free and communist worlds
in zero-sum terminology. Domestic politics and regional strategy had put a
premium on anticommunism, and the administration's efforts to cover its right
flank produced episodes like the Ames speech. The perception that the Cold
War was being lost in the Third World, particularly in areas such as the Middle
East, Southeast Asia, and Africa, prompted public alarm and interventions on
one hand, and the use of aid and presidential diplomacy on the other. In each
case, Eisenhower and Dulles acted to deepen U.S. involvement in the Third
World.

[100] Nwaubani, *Decolonization in West Africa*, 180–204.
[101] McMahon, *Cold War on the Periphery*, 260–262; Adamson, "'The Most Important Single
    Aspect of Our Foreign Policy'," 61–66; Burton I. Kaufman, *Trade and Aid: Eisenhower's
    Foreign Economic Policy, 1953–1961* (Baltimore: The Johns Hopkins University Press, 1982),
    58–68, 197–199.
[102] Andrew J. Rotter, *Comrades at Odds: The United States and India, 1947–1964* (Ithaca, Cornell
    University Press, 2000), 277–278.
[103] Editorial Note, in DOS, *FRUS, 1958–1960: Vol. 17: Indonesia* (Washington: GPO, 1994):
    564–565; Memorandum, Livingston Merchant to Herter, October 27, 1960, RG-59, DSCF,
    656.9813/10–2760; Memorandum, James Bell to Parsons, November 22, 1960, RG-59, DSCF,
    656.9813/11–2260.

The Eisenhower administration can be credited with devising farseeing, well-calibrated policies in a number of areas. Its response to the emerging phenomenon of nonalignment, however, deserves less credit. Eisenhower and Dulles recognized the power of nationalism in Africa and Asia, and thought that it could, in fact, be beneficial to the United States. Yet if neutrality in principle remained acceptable, nonalignment in practice evoked concern. The administration expected sympathy from uncommitted states and held limited tolerance for deviations from its own narrow definition of neutrality. The goals of preserving alliances and combating communism warred with the objective – stated in NSC 5501 and subsequent documents – of engaging the new governments of the postcolonial world.

Consequently, the administration erred significantly: by reneging on the Aswan loan, in its efforts against Sukarno, in its slow reaction to Guinean independence, and in its panicked response in the Congo. Furthermore, Dulles and Eisenhower avoided opportunities to act in the cases of Goa and West New Guinea, thereby passing these simmering conflicts along to their successors. In the case of the Congo, the New Frontiersmen were bequeathed a raging inferno. A fundamental ambivalence toward nonalignment brought repeated conflict in U.S.-nonaligned relations in the 1950s, doing damage that was painful but not permanent. As this tone ebbed in the waning years of the 1950s, the more prudent policies of the Eisenhower administration partially paved the way for broader strides forward as Kennedy took office. Komer admitted as much in 1963, when he termed engagement "a genuine departure from previous policy," but added, "(though the last Administration was gradually shifting in this direction.)"[104]

---

[104] Memorandum, Komer to Kennedy, January 18, 1963, in DOS, *FRUS, 1961–1963, Vol. 8: National Security Policy* (Washington: GPO, 1996): 456–457.

Rationales for Engagement: The New Frontiersmen Approach Nonalignment

Romanticized views of the Kennedy administration summon to mind images of unleashed dynamism and vision, heralding the arrival of a new American government with bold ideas and the determination to bear any burden to see them fulfilled. Such is the familiar portrait of the New Frontier offered by Kennedy's rhetoric and by the later reflections of his advisors. Kennedy thrived on this perception of vitality and vigor, but it was not simply a mere persona projected for political benefit. On many fronts, the New Frontiersmen perceived a dire need to clear away thickets that had grown during the Eisenhower years, conceiving of the period as an era of wasted opportunities and stale doctrines.

The New Frontier began with the pervasive sense of work yet undone, of having, as Kennedy's favorite poet had once written, "promises to keep / And miles to go before I sleep." The Cold War seemed to be entering a volatile new phase, with the emergence of a pro-Soviet regime in Cuba, the escalation of tensions over the divided city of Berlin, civil war in Laos, and the disintegration of the Congo. These events added a sense of urgency to the presidential transition. The veteran journalist Marquis Childs likened the change of power to a high-wire balancing act.[1]

The new administration took office determined to seize the opportunities and face the dangers presented by recent events. Kennedy's inaugural address projected an image of implacable resolve: the United States stood poised to defend its interests and the cause of freedom anywhere in the world, to – in the famous words – "pay any price, bear any burden, meet any hardship, support any friend, oppose any foe, in order to assure the survival and the success of liberty." Kennedy, moreover, pledged "the loyalty of faithful friends" to America's "old allies" in Europe.[2]

However eloquent, these were the kind of promises Kennedy's predecessors had also made in their inaugurals. It remained for Kennedy to distinguish his

---

[1] Marquis Childs, "Shifting Burden to the New Man," *The Washington Post*, January 17, 1961, A12.
[2] *PPP: John F. Kennedy, 1961* (Washington: GPO, 1962), 1–12.

rhetoric from that of Eisenhower. Kennedy was speaking to a domestic and an international audience, the latter not limited to allies. Having pledged his support to existing allies, Kennedy reached out to the new states of Africa and Asia:

To those new States whom we welcome to the ranks of the free, we pledge our word that one form of colonial control shall not have passed away merely to be replaced by a far more iron tyranny. We shall not always expect to find them supporting our view. But we shall always hope to find them strongly supporting their own freedom – and to remember that, in the past, those who foolishly sought power by riding the back of the tiger ended up inside.[3]

This passage signaled to the Third World that the Kennedy administration would chart a new course. It stood as a rebuke to the rhetoric of Dulles and a signal that Kennedy would broadly engage the nonaligned world. Different individuals within the administration, from a wide range of professional and intellectual backgrounds, invested great hopes in the project of engagement.

Two intellectual frameworks motivated the policy of engagement in the 1960s: the pragmatic and the liberal. These two outlooks provided distinct rationales for courting the nonaligned states but sometimes seemed to recommend different approaches and different geographic emphases. Pragmatists like NSC staffers McGeorge Bundy and Robert Komer expressed support for engagement by referring to the changing balance of power in the world. As they saw it, the emergence of new states and power centers obliged the United States to redraw the balance between existing allies and the postcolonial states of Africa and Asia. In particular, large nonaligned states such as Egypt, Indonesia, and India stood to influence their immediate regions, arguably more effectively than present U.S. allies were capable of doing. The reality of a global Cold War, the importance of retaining economic access to key regions, and the weakness or unreliability of existing allies, the pragmatists argued, required basic and immediate efforts to reconcile U.S. goals with the agendas of nonaligned powers. The three most powerful nonaligned states were, thus, of greatest interest to the pragmatists.

Liberals did not disagree that a geopolitical shift was underway; they were, however, more likely to approach the nonaligned states with a broadly felt sense of American mission. For State Department appointees like Chester Bowles, G. Mennen Williams, and, to a lesser extent, Adlai Stevenson, the task of engaging the nonaligned states held a distinct moral imperative and drew upon the same core principles as the New Deal and the civil rights struggle. Liberals agreed with pragmatists that decolonization required a more robust approach to the nonaligned states. If anything, liberals believed so even more fervently, inspired by the possibilities decolonization offered to the peoples of Africa and Asia and conceiving of a distinct, historic American responsibility toward the newly independent states. Whereas pragmatists focused on

[3] Ibid.

the larger states, liberals pursued engagement more broadly; even though they shared the NSC's concern with regional powers, liberals took a deeper interest in policies directed at smaller – often African – states, and had a greater pre-occupation with questions of development. This fusion of ideals and strategy made the prescriptions of the liberals truly elastic, applicable everywhere in the Third World.

These two outlooks were not mutually exclusive. Liberals like Williams and Bowles knew they needed to embrace arguments about power in order to advance their preferences. Walt Rostow incorporated aspects of both out-looks, along with his well-known academic interest in development economics. Kennedy, at heart, was a pragmatist but at the outset he proved receptive to liberal advice and certainly believed in the importance of nonaligned states as proving grounds for an American vision of development. Nonetheless, some characterizations can be made about these different outlooks, with reference to position, style, philosophy, and efficacy.

The pragmatic outlook dominated the NSC, and adherents such as Bundy and Komer held general expertise. Pragmatists operated as crisis managers, applying lessons from one problem to another, seeking immediate outcomes. They were more concerned with the balance of power than they were with humanitarian ends. Their embrace of ideas about development was tenta-tive and connected intimately to their belief that aid served political ends. Pragmatists liked to regard themselves as dispassionate, unmoved by moral-istic arguments.

Liberals held several key positions at the Department of State, where they had geographically specific concerns and experience. Bowles served as under-secretary of state, informal representative to the Third World, and ambassador to India. Williams directed the Department's African Bureau. Stevenson's posi-tion as ambassador to the United Nations put him in direct contact with many representatives of the nonaligned world. Liberals were intellectually inclined to take the longer view, feeling compelled (often to the frustration of their NSC counterparts) to fit present policy issues into a broader historical context, making arguments that fused conceptions of the national interests with moral imperatives.

Liberals and pragmatists shared one essential tenet: the spread of commu-nism in the Third World posed a fundamental threat to the United States. They held this view for complementary reasons: a conviction that uncommitted states stood to be key balancers in the evolving global system; the belief that nonalignment could be a particularly effective form of containment; a con-ception of the Cold War as a test of rival models of development; and a sense of a particular American mission in the postcolonial world. These views were far from uncontroversial, however. Liberals and pragmatists alike ran against streams of Cold War thought that dated back to the beginning of the struggle.

More skeptical policymakers contested the liberal and pragmatic cases, especially their contention that the Third World was becoming the cockpit of the Cold War. This viewpoint was well represented by Secretary of State Dean

Rusk, his deputy, Undersecretary of State George Ball, and a Europe-oriented faction of the State Department. Even though the skeptics did not oppose engagement outright, they doubted that it would yield the promised rewards and balked at the costs it seemed to require. They rejected the contention that the Cold War would be decided in the Third World, some doubted the promises of modernization theory, and they looked warily upon the emotional appeals of liberals. At first outpaced by events, this group steadily accrued influence, particularly in the Johnson years.

The changing fortunes of these groups in the Kennedy and Johnson White Houses determined the course of U.S. policy toward the nonaligned states. To understand why engagement emerged when it did, and why it came to be eclipsed by other policy priorities, one must examine the outlooks and personalities of those policymakers who influenced it most profoundly. Naturally, one must begin with the thirty-fifth president of the United States, John Fitzgerald Kennedy.

JOHN F. KENNEDY

When he entered the White House in 1961, John F. Kennedy was well suited to begin a new phase of engagement with the nonaligned world. Kennedy brought real interest in the dilemmas of postcolonial societies, an attentive and engaging style of interpersonal diplomacy, and a preference for new thinking. His Irish-American heritage offered something of a counterweight to this pragmatic outlook, shaping his own feelings about colonialism and giving him a degree of empathy for the challenges faced by the postcolonial nations. This was a legacy that he explicitly referenced on occasion.[4]

Well before he took office, Kennedy made clear his personal sentiments about colonialism. Speaking on July 2, 1957, before the Senate, Kennedy made what *The New York Times* deemed "perhaps the most comprehensive and outspoken arraignment of Western policy toward Algeria yet presented by an American in public office."[5] Breaking with the Eisenhower administration, which supported Paris in its bloody war to retain Algeria, Kennedy declared that the war was damaging the American image throughout the Third World. Whatever the "original truth" of French claims about Algeria's constitutional status, Kennedy argued, "the blunt facts of the matter today are that the changing face of African nationalism and the ever-widening byproducts of the growing crisis have made Algeria a matter of international and consequently American concern." He proposed that the Eisenhower administration back independence for Algeria and facilitate talks between France and the nationalist rebels.[6]

---

[4] See Letter, Kennedy to Nehru, January 18, 1962, in DOS, *FRUS, 1961–1963, Vol. 19: South Asia* (Washington: GPO, 1996): 197–199.
[5] Russell Baker, "Kennedy Urges U.S. Back Independence for Algeria," *NYT*, July 3, 1957, 1.
[6] Ibid.

Kennedy's speech about Algeria was the most controversial one he gave as a senator and his remarks attracted more criticism than praise. A *New York Times* editorial observed that he had "probably added fuel to a raging fire," noting that the speech was likely both to anger France and reinforce the hopes of the rebels. The French government attacked him bitterly. Dulles suggested that Kennedy would be well advised to direct his scorn at Soviet colonialism instead. Adlai Stevenson, twice a Democratic candidate for president, told his good friend George Ball that Kennedy's speech had been "a great mistake," that early Algerian independence would lead only to mass bloodshed.[7] Despite such criticism, the speech marked Kennedy around the globe as a Democrat willing to rethink policies toward colonial questions.

Kennedy's willingness to question administration policy also extended to his thoughts on nonalignment, particularly those revealed in his 1957 article in *Foreign Affairs*. Although drafted by his speechwriter and close friend Ted Sorensen, the article offers a revealing window into Kennedy's thinking about foreign policy in the postcolonial world. Examining current U.S. policy, Kennedy identified two principal shortcomings: the general timidity and indecisiveness of the Eisenhower administration, and a failure to "appreciate how the forces of nationalism are rewriting the geopolitical map of the world." Kennedy perceived an ongoing "diffusion of power." The two superpowers were not only magnets, attracting allies and clients, they also exerted "repellent forces" on other states in the international system. Consequently, the world was witnessing the "reemergence of small and middle states as important international factors" leading to a "more complicated and fluid balance of power." There was no evading this fact, and Kennedy wrote scornfully of the popular American "ill-conceived and ill-concealed disdain for the 'neutralists' and 'socialists'" who, in fact, represented the "free world's strongest bulwarks to the seductive appeal of Peking and Moscow." Advancing the argument of his Algeria speech, Kennedy called for recognizing the power of anticolonial sentiment in the Third World, particularly in Africa, observing that communists had benefited from declaring their opposition to empire. He warned against the "illusion" that neutrality toward colonial struggles insulated the United States from their fallout, advising that the United States should avoid the "prolongation of Western colonialism where it is stagnant."[8]

Kennedy's use of the phrase "diffusion of power" reflected the influence of Walt W. Rostow, who was then a professor of economics at the Massachusetts Institute of Technology. Kennedy fundamentally accepted Rostow's view that the position of the United States in the Third World hinged on its ability to offer a viable pathway to economic growth. Both men, furthermore, shared

---

[7] Robert Doty, "Paris Is Bitter," *NYT*, July 4, 1957, 13; Roger Baldwin et al., "Support for Kennedy," *The Washington Post*, August 7, 1957, A12; George W. Ball, *The Past Has Another Pattern: Memoirs* (New York: Norton, 1982), 149.

[8] John F. Kennedy, "A Democrat Looks at Foreign Policy," *Foreign Affairs* 36, No. 1 (October 1957), 44–59.

a particular interest in India, which Kennedy characterized as "a centerpiece of the 'middle zone' of uncommitted nations extending from Casablanca to Djakarta," and as "the leading claimant for the role of a 'broker' middle state" in the Cold War. His article recommended the adoption of Rostow's proposals for aid to India, recognizing the importance of affirming the Indian approach to development as an alternative to the communist model.[9] In 1958 and 1959, along with Republican Senator John Sherman Cooper of Kentucky, a former ambassador to India, he submitted the Kennedy-Cooper resolution, calling for expanded aid to India.

Kennedy made repeated mention of the nonaligned states during his presidential campaign in 1960. Repeatedly in his debates with Vice President Richard Nixon, he drew attention to growing Soviet influence in the Third World and the waning of American prestige in the world. He cited the Eisenhower administration's slow response to Guinean independence as evidence of its lack of interest in Africa. In part, his discussion of Africa was designed to improve his appeal among African-American voters, but it also reflected his belief that the Third World would play a deciding role in the Cold War. He questioned Nixon's ability to appeal to nonaligned states, noting that his foe had challenged India's right to be neutral.[10] This went beyond a targeted appeal to one segment of the electorate; Kennedy's emphasis on nonaligned states reflected his views of both the Eisenhower administration's failings and the shifting nature of the Cold War.

In his presidency, Kennedy maintained a consistent interest in improving relations with the nonaligned states. Although his attention to the issue was sporadic, eclipsed by pressing crises in the Caribbean, Central Europe, and mainland Southeast Asia, Kennedy remained convinced of the importance of the nonaligned states within the global balance of power. Even though this view mandated a primary focus on Egypt, India, and Indonesia, he took occasional interest in the affairs of smaller, less prominent states, such as Mali and Guinea. Moreover, as both Mary Dudziak and Thomas Borstelmann have persuasively shown, his interest in improving relations with African states provided substantial motivation over time for his growing support of civil rights for African-Americans.[11]

Kennedy felt his share of frustration with the nonaligned leaders, sometimes finding them mercurial and unpredictable. Regarding nonalignment as being largely akin to neutrality, Kennedy wanted the nonaligned states to be fully neutral. Unlike Eisenhower, he did not seek private communications of

---

[9] Ibid.

[10] "Kennedy Attacks Nixon 'Weakness,'" *NYT*, October 21, 1960, 1; James H. Meriwether, "'Worth a Lot of Negro Votes': Black Voters, Africa, and the 1960 Presidential Campaign," *Journal of American History*, December 2008, 737–763.

[11] Mary Dudziak, *Cold War Civil Rights: Race and the Image of American Democracy* (Princeton: Princeton University Press, 2000), 152–202; Thomas Borstelmann, *The Cold War and the Color Line: American Race Relations in the Global Arena* (Cambridge, MA: Harvard University Press, 2001), 135–171.

support, but he did expect balance. Moments of apparent hypocrisy incensed him. The silence of the nonaligned states on Soviet misdeeds angered him (although he would have had no complaint if they endorsed American stances and condemned those of Moscow).[12] He nursed, but never acted on, the occasional notion that nonaligned countries held double standards.

A broader character trait also impeded Kennedy's approach to the uncommitted states: his profound sense of caution, abetted by his penchant for avoiding hard choices whenever possible. Even as he sought to answer the Soviet offensive in the Third World, Kennedy was – understandably – loath to face the costs that came with engagement. In large part he showed little sign of having anticipated these tradeoffs. Growing complaints and threats from allies, ranging from Portugal to Pakistan, drew Kennedy away from stances he had previously supported. He was susceptible to arguments that the United States could somehow have it both ways and balance between allies and nonaligned states. His concern with the domestic fallout from appealing to the nonaligned states further constrained him. By 1963, he clearly had become more cautious, cognizant of the complications posed by engagement. Yet Kennedy continued to defend key components of the policy in the weeks immediately preceding his death, risking a significant political cost.

Kennedy's ultimate tolerance of nonalignment and his belief that those states could not be coerced has not been fully recognized by scholars. Indeed some astute overviews of the Kennedy years thematically group together his policies toward aligned Asian or Latin American states with those toward India, Egypt, or Indonesia.[13] Reflective of prevailing opinion is the assessment that Kennedy ultimately "wanted to defeat neutralism and bring its adherents into the American Cold War network," and the charge that he invariably favored anticommunist governments, be they imperial or authoritarian, over nonaligned nationalists.[14] Kennedy's own remarks about the phenomenon shed a different light on his conception of nonalignment and his strategy toward its adherents. Far from thinking nonalignment could be erased, Kennedy believed it was a lasting phenomenon, requiring patience and caution on his part. Faced with the more familiar stories of his policies toward South Vietnam and Latin America, one must constantly distinguish between Kennedy's policy toward truly uncommitted states and his approach to aligned states. The evolution of the term "Third World" over five decades has obscured political distinctions starkly apparent in the early 1960s.

---

[12] Walt W. Rostow, *The Diffusion of Power: An Essay in Recent History* (New York: Macmillan, 1972), 192; Dean Rusk, *As I Saw It* (New York: Norton, 1990), 295.

[13] See, for example, James N. Giglio, *The Presidency of John F. Kennedy* (Lawrence: University Press of Kansas, 1991), 237–270; Stephen G. Rabe, *John F. Kennedy: World Leader* (Washington: Potomac Books, 2010), 18.

[14] Thomas Paterson, "John Kennedy's Quest for Victory and the Global Crisis," in Thomas Paterson ed., *Kennedy's Quest for Victory: American Foreign Policy 1961–1963* (New York: Oxford University Press, 1989), 22.

Kennedy twice spoke to the members of the NSC on the topic of policy toward nonaligned states – once in January 1962 and again a year later. His remarks reveal not an expansive agenda to redefine or eliminate nonalignment, but a policy with far more modest, calibrated expectations. His first statement came not long after the nonaligned conference at Belgrade, when both Yugoslavia and Ghana seemed to support the Soviet position on Berlin and other major Cold War issues. Kennedy observed that U.S. policy required promoting a "world of free and independent countries." This could create problems, he observed, as was the case with Yugoslavia and Ghana. Even so, the relationship between those states and the United States could never be like the relationship between the Soviet Union and its Warsaw Pact allies. The United States would simply have to "live with the difficulties" posed by a world of independently minded states.[15]

The following January, at Komer's request, Kennedy again defended engagement. His advisor had warned of a growing sense of frustration within the government toward the nonaligned states. Kennedy noted Pakistani objections to U.S. aid to India, but remarked that these should be weighed against India's sheer size. His primary concern was not enlisting Nehru as an ally in the global Cold War but rather helping to keep India itself noncommunist. Engagement's overriding goal was to keep nonaligned states out of the communist bloc, thus "we must keep our ties to Nasser and other neutralists even if we do not like many things they do because, if we lose them, the balance of power could swing against us."[16]

Such remarks outlined conservative, geopolitically centered goals for engagement, revealing a striking gap between the public and private rationales for the policy. Kennedy publicly spoke of his long-term goal of a community of free nations, encompassing Western democracies and postcolonial states. In the immediate term, however, he operated from the conviction that there was a real danger that nonaligned states would drift into the arms of the communist bloc if the West proved unreceptive and unresponsive to them. He spoke in terms of immediate results – necessarily so, because he felt obliged to defend this policy from its critics both within his administration and among the public. He perceived progress over time in his approach to the nonaligned world, but understood that it could be quickly overturned by abrupt shifts in policy.

With his concern for the balance of power, it is unsurprising that Kennedy took a different stance toward the prospect of neutralism among existing allies than he did toward nonaligned states. Engagement was formulated to arrest the drift of postcolonial states toward the communist bloc. Where these states were concerned, alliance – though unlikely – was preferable to nonalignment, which was, in turn, clearly preferable to alignment with the communist bloc.

[15] President Kennedy's Remarks to the 496th NSC Meeting, January 18, 1963, in DOS, *FRUS, 1961–1963, Vol. 8: National Security Policy* (Washington: GPO, 1996): 238–239.

[16] Record of 508th Meeting of NSC, January 22, 1963, in *FRUS, 1961–1963*, 8: 460.

Kennedy, therefore, opposed neutralism within the American alliance system and saw no inconsistency in this.

Kennedy advanced engagement and made the appointments he did because he was convinced that this policy was essential to the national security of the United States in a rapidly changing world. At the same time, his caution and his lack of executive experience led him to avoid making engagement an explicit policy goal. Fatefully, he never undertook steps to institutionalize it. No presidential memoranda or explicit policy statements created durable machinery to pursue engagement. No presidential speeches offered the public a comprehensive explanation of the policy. So long as JFK and his favored advisors remained in positions of power, this informality was not a serious obstacle, and, indeed, engagement seemed unlikely to receive a sympathetic public hearing. The notion of the Cold War as an all-encompassing moral struggle did not reconcile easily with generous recognition of a right to neutrality in its midst. Kennedy, however, was sadly denied the chance to serve out his elected term; in his absence, his policy faced an uncertain future. The Africans and Asians who mourned him did so for good reason.

PRAGMATISTS AND CRISIS MANAGERS: BUNDY AND KOMER

Kennedy broadly envisioned engagement; the responsibilities of the presidency obligated him to entrust its daily execution to trusted subordinates. The two men most critical to the implementation of engagement both served on the staff of the NSC: National Security Advisor McGeorge Bundy and NSC staff member Robert Komer. Like Kennedy, Bundy was obligated to focus on major crises, yet a pattern was apparent during his tenure: Bundy consistently offered strong support for the policy of engaging nonaligned states and backed the suggestions of Komer, its most aggressive advocate.

Bundy served as Komer's gateway to the NSC; as such his own intellectual development is worthy of examination. Bundy was, by the 1950s, a seasoned observer of foreign affairs and a dedicated internationalist, having been profoundly influenced by veteran policymaker Henry Stimson.[17] During that decade, he became increasingly disaffected with the foreign policy of Eisenhower and Dulles. He thought Dulles's approach to the Cold War was overly focused on power and heedless of the need to marry ideals and strategy. Bundy instinctively sought a middle path that would meld pragmatism to idealism, avoiding the excesses of either nuclear confrontation or isolationism. At the same time, he made his own partial embrace of modernization theory. These inclinations led him, as a matter of intellectual habit, to seek a middle path on policy toward the uncommitted states.[18]

[17] Andrew Preston, *The War Council: McGeorge Bundy, the NSC, and Vietnam* (Cambridge, MA: Harvard University Press, 2006), 12–35; Kai Bird, *The Color of Truth: McGeorge Bundy and William Bundy: Brothers in Arms* (New York: Simon and Schuster, 1998), 23–41, 54–99.
[18] Bird, *The Color of Truth*, 147–153; Preston, *The War Council*, 32–35.

Upon his selection to head Kennedy's NSC, Bundy sought intellectual kin. He was particularly interested in fresh thinking and creative responses to emerging crises in the developing world. Komer, who had made the acquaintance of Bundy's brother William, presented the future national security advisor with recommendations on improving relations with Nasser's Egypt and resolving the West New Guinea dispute. Komer's case for improving relations with the nonaligned states won him a position on Bundy's NSC.[19]

Henceforth, Bundy's influence on policy toward the nonaligned states was most discernible from his relative silence on these questions. Having largely entrusted these issues to Komer, Bundy allowed his subordinate a direct line of communication with both Kennedy and Johnson – which the ambitious Komer seized and utilized eagerly. Assistant Secretary of State Phillips Talbot recalled that Bundy "worked basically from Komer's analyses and recommendations" and consequently "it was basically Komer in the White House counsels who would stake out the foreign policy position."[20] Bundy sometimes added his own opinions, in cover memoranda. These added mild caveats to Komer's suggestions but mostly criticized Komer's prose, which Bundy regarded as unbefitting a fellow Harvard man.[21] When he did write to the president on such issues, Bundy tended to support engagement and did so consistently during the Kennedy years and well into the Johnson presidency.

Like his colleagues, Bundy believed that the United States needed to be more flexible and tolerant toward neutral states. Here, too, he instinctively sought a middle stance. A 1967 *Foreign Affairs* article he penned decried "either/or" views of the world, praising the Kennedy administration for its rejection of Manichean categories.[22] In a 1962 article in the same journal, he pointedly declared, "We have chosen neutrality for enough of our history to recognize and respect the similar choice of others." As he saw it, the United States held "a deep interest in the effort toward stable and progressive freedom" in both "small states and in great sub-continents" – a clear reference to India.[23] Also implied was a correspondingly moderate stance on questions that divided European allies from postcolonial states. He wrote:

As we are the most powerful, we have the largest number of associations – and so we face the largest number of conflicts of interest. Both interest and sympathy can pull us two ways, and our policy will often put us in positions which both sides would like to disapprove. It is becoming that we should accept that responsibility coolly – as we have tried to do … in the Congo, in West New Guinea, in the Dominican Republic, and in the Middle East.[24]

Three of these four were areas or disputes that involved nonaligned powers.

[19] Fifth Interview, Robert W. Komer, December 22, 1969, 4, OH, JFKL.
[20] Second Interview, Phillips Talbot, August 13, 1970, 10–11, OH, JFKL.
[21] See Second Interview, Robert Komer, July 16, 1964, 22, OH, JFKL.
[22] McGeorge Bundy, "The End of Either/Or," *Foreign Affairs*, Vol. 45, No. 2 (January 1967), 189–201.
[23] Bundy, "Friends and Allies," *Foreign Affairs*, Vol. 41, No. 1 (October 1962), 14–23.
[24] Bundy, "Friends and Allies," 22.

Bundy supported engagement for geopolitical reasons. Like Kennedy, he believed that the national security of the United States depended on improving its relationships with the leading states of the nonaligned world, even if this occasionally came at some cost to existing alliances. A cool pragmatism guided Bundy, distancing him from the legalism of Dean Rusk and the idealism of Chester Bowles. In this he resembled his hard-driving, ambitious subordinate, Komer.

Beyond hiring Komer, Bundy created an environment in which his aide would thrive. With Kennedy's authorization, he reinvented the NSC, transforming it from a large body dedicated in considerable part to long-term planning, to one that acted to coordinate policy. Bundy's NSC was small, collegial, and agile. He exploited the council's proximity to the president and created what peers saw as a State Department in miniature. He enjoyed a good rapport with Kennedy, but he also provided his staff with direct access to the president. Bundy's system, therefore, empowered men like Komer during the Kennedy years – with critical results for the policy of engagement.[25]

Robert William Komer is best known to history for his ill-starred role in the Vietnam War, a job that left him the dubious sobriquet of "Blowtorch Bob." From 1966 to 1968, he directed the White House's counterinsurgency efforts in South Vietnam, with his efforts coming disastrously undone during the Tet Offensive of 1968. Other parts of Komer's career have earned him comparatively less attention, particularly his service on the staff of the NSC between 1961 and 1966.

He rose to this position after more than a decade of work for the CIA, culminating in a role as the agency's liaison to the NSC in the later Eisenhower years. Eisenhower treated the NSC as an analytical tool; Komer was "rather unimpressed" with its workings, disparaging the council as a "giant paper mill."[26] As he saw it, Eisenhower's NSC had languished in obscurity without a strong special assistant, and ignored by Dulles's State Department.[27] Komer leaped at the opportunity to serve on Bundy's newly invigorated NSC, under a president who shared his distrust for entrenched bureaucracy. A distaste for what he saw as useless bureaucratic process became a hallmark of Komer's approach to policy. Kennedy's aspiration to act as his own secretary of state meshed with Komer's desire to sidestep the bureaucracy at Foggy Bottom and directly shape policy.

Komer was an intense, argumentative man. His memoranda testify both to his hard-working, assertive personality and to his inimitable sense of humor. Bundy valued him for his "unusual combination of energy and experience and his abrasiveness."[28] Elspeth Rostow, the wife of National Security Advisor Walt

---

[25] Preston, *The War Council*, 39–47.
[26] Ibid.
[27] Fourth Interview, Robert W. Komer, October 31, 1964, 18, OH, JFKL.
[28] Memorandum, Bundy to Johnson, February 27, 1966, NSF, Memos to the President, box 6, "February 5–28, 1966" folder, LBJL.

Rostow, recalled Komer as someone who enjoyed making his opinion heard through "forceful verbiage."[29] He valued candor over tact, and this did not endear him to his peers. This trait has left a visible paradox for scholars. Komer is omnipresent amid records of the era but a ghostly presence at best in the memoirs of his colleagues. Allusions to him are invariably brief and fleeting.[30]

Komer had little difficulty communicating his views. He formed close working relationships with both Kennedy and Johnson. This was made possible by the unusually close collegial bond he enjoyed with Bundy. Their office correspondence has the tenor of a dialogue between close friends. Komer saw no need to write formally to his boss; Bundy was treated to the gripes, wisecracks, and offhand suggestions of his subordinate. For his part, Bundy clearly thought highly of Komer; "I love you," he wrote jokingly in response to a mock-indignant note from his subordinate.[31]

Working in Bundy's informal NSC, Komer assumed responsibility for a vast swath of the globe, stretching from Morocco, through the Middle East and South Asia, to Indonesia. Atop his expansive domain, Komer tirelessly advocated for expanding relations with the largest states of the nonaligned world, paying particular attention to Egypt, Indonesia, and India. His absence was felt, however, with regard to policy in sub-Saharan Africa. Komer's focus on other regions of the world and the priority he assigned to the larger nonaligned states made his contributions to African questions sporadic and comparatively less effective, although he came to assign an increasing importance to African questions by 1965. In that year, Bundy formally named him as his deputy; following Bundy's resignation in February 1966, Komer served as Interim National Security Advisor, before Walt Rostow assumed the position permanently.

Komer was motivated not by an idealistic sense of mission, but by the belief that the critical battlefields of the Cold War had shifted away from Europe and toward the developing world. He perceived states such as Egypt, India, and Indonesia as presenting both great opportunities and great dangers for American strategy. If they forged stronger political and economic ties with the West, they would offer a powerful counterbalance to the Soviet Union and China. If, however, they continued an erratic, anti-Western course, edging closer to the established positions of the Communist bloc, or perhaps engaging in regional adventures, they would tip the global balance of power away from the capitalist powers, perhaps impairing Western access to critical economic resources and military facilities. Correspondingly, Komer shared Kennedy's

[29] Elspeth Rostow, Interview with the author, October 8, 2006.
[30] Komer appears – barely – in memoirs such as Chester Bowles, *Promises to Keep: My Years in Public Life, 1941–1969* (New York: Harper & Row, 1971); Rostow, *The Diffusion of Power*; Ball, *The Past Has Another Pattern*; and Rusk, *As I Saw It*. Neil Sheehan paints a vivid portrait of Komer during his Vietnam years as the friend and eulogist of John Paul Vann, in *A Bright Shining Lie: John Paul Vann and America in Vietnam* (New York: Random House, 1988).
[31] Memorandum, Komer to Bundy, February 27, 1963, NSF, box 322, "Robert Komer, 1/63–2/63" folder, JFKL. See also: Memorandum, "On Bob Komer's Future," Bundy to Johnson, NSF, Memoranda to the President, box 3, "Vol. 9: 3/65–4/14/65" folder, LBJL.

concern about neutralism making inroads within allied countries.[32] While liberals like Bowles and Williams were animated by a sense of the raw human potential present in the new states of Africa and Asia, Komer was concerned with their potential impact on the balance of power and therefore tended to focus on the largest of the nonaligned states. He saw himself as a hardheaded, realistic counterpart to Williams and Bowles, making use of them as needed, but eschewing their idealism and occasionally belittling their enthusiasm.[33] He was not a theorist, but saw himself instead as a man of action, a manager of crises. An eager generalist, he disdained Rostow's lengthy memoranda. To a point, Komer accepted Rostovian notions of development, but he largely concerned himself with near-term outcomes.

Komer advocated an active foreign policy that would thrust the United States into regions hitherto dominated by Europe. This brought him into some conflict with individuals in the government who preferred to defer to European preferences where postcolonial issues were concerned. By virtue of his regional specialization, his focus on the Middle East, South Asia, and Southeast Asia, and his belief that these regions constituted the key battlegrounds of the Cold War, he tended to favor advancing U.S. interests there over assuaging the concerns of European allies. He believed unsentimentally that colonialism was doomed and that it benefited the United States to advise its European allies to accept the inevitable.

Invariably, as a matter of tactical principle, he believed in engaging nonaligned governments, even when faced with the most trying of reactions. Engagement, even if it did not achieve positive goals, stood to stanch the leftward drift of nonaligned states or at least play for time. Komer's experiences in the Eisenhower years left him little confidence that covert action or political pressure could improve America's position with the nonaligned states. He wrote in 1963:

All these guys who advocate "tough" policies toward neutralists like Nasser and Sukarno blink at the fact that it was precisely such policies which helped influence these countries to accept Moscow offers in the first place. The best way to keep Nasser or Sukarno from becoming prisoners of the USSR is to compete for them, not thrust them into Soviet hands.[34]

This outlook made Komer the staunchest advocate for engagement within the White House. After he left the NSC staff, no one embraced the policy with the same passion and trenchancy he had employed.

Komer won the respect of his superiors for his forceful manner, but this attribute was also, in considerable part, his deepest flaw. He had great

[32] See Komer, Memorandum to Bundy and Rostow, May 22, 1961, JFKL, NSF, box 321, "Robert Komer, 5/16/61–6/14/61" folder.
[33] See, for example Letter, Bowles to Komer, December 17, 1965, NSF, RWKP, box 13, Chester Bowles Vol. 1 folder, LBJL; Memorandum, Komer to Bundy, Undated (Doc. 61), ibid.; Memorandum, Komer to Johnson, July 27, 1965, ibid.
[34] Memorandum, Komer to Bundy, January 16, 1963, in DOS, *FRUS, 1961–1963, Vol. 23: Southeast Asia* (Washington: GPO, 1995): 656–658.

self-confidence; although he prided himself on his unsentimental pragmatism, Komer tended toward dangerous optimism when assessing the benefits of proactive diplomacy. When faced with regional conflicts, he believed the United States could play a constructive role by engaging both sides – a stance that, though it offered the greatest possible dividends, entailed risking relations with both combatants. This preference for conflict management complemented Kennedy's sense of caution, seeming to promise the best of both worlds. Komer's optimism – he playfully characterized himself as a pollyanna – had a defensive quality: he had a vested interest in defending policies that he had helped to put into place. This was a dangerous tendency on his part, and Komer's overly sanguine outlook proved to be his personal undoing after he was dispatched to Vietnam.

LIBERAL AND MODERNIZER: WALT WHITMAN ROSTOW

Immediate geopolitical considerations alone did not drive engagement. Working in tandem with concerns about regional power balances were fundamental ideas about the historic role of the United States as an anticolonial nation and its unique capacity and obligation to lead the new states toward prosperity by promoting its own model of development. Notions of moral obligation and geopolitical necessity intertwined themselves in the outlook of liberals, leading to broad advocacy of developmental assistance and anticolonial policies.

A cardinal distinction must be noted here. Liberals agreed on the need to be more responsive to the developmental agendas of the postcolonial states, to provide noncommunist counterparts to the narratives emerging from Moscow and Peking. Prominent appointees such as Bowles, Williams, and Stevenson also advocated a more openly anticolonial policy, perceiving that the United States stood to lose ground so long as it remained associated with the European powers on colonial questions. Walt Rostow, on the other hand, focused on economic questions, seeing underdevelopment as the core problem in the Third World. These different emphases proved significant over time, as Rostow's star rose and those of the other liberals descended.

Walt Whitman Rostow played a central role in the development of U.S. policy toward the nonaligned world, comparable and complementary to that of Komer. Whereas Komer thrived as a crisis manager, intervening in particular conflicts and disputes, Rostow developed the broader assumptions and goals behind U.S. policy. Rostow made two unique contributions to the policy of engagement, both through his prolific writings during the 1950s. First, he helped to articulate an intellectual framework for understanding the changes in world affairs over the decade preceding Kennedy's inauguration. He argued that Washington faced a volatile global environment characterized by the intersecting phenomena of Third World industrialization, decolonization, and nationalism. Communism, by its aggressive nature, would seek to prey on the underdeveloped states of Africa, Asia, and Latin America. Secondly, as a scholar dedicated to studying economic growth, Rostow posited that the

United States could assist impoverished societies toward what he termed "economic take-off": regular growth and innovation. Rostow, in essence, helped to define both the problem – the radical transformation of the political map and the gradual weakening of the main powers – and the solution – collaborative efforts toward shared prosperity.[35]

While he taught developmental economics at MIT, Rostow was among the foremost advocates of engagement with the new states, and he linked this goal emphatically with both the historic ideals and the national security of the United States. He observed the growing Soviet focus on the Third World, which affirmed his belief that the battleground of the Cold War was shifting, and not to the advantage of the West. Thinking Eisenhower's focus on existing alliances inadequate, Rostow sought to articulate a distinctly American vision of development that could be pursued in the developing world. Only growth and stability in the postcolonial states could produce a world safe for democracy.[36]

Rostow's outlook combined economic theory and his own concept of American mission. As he and his colleague Max Millikan wrote in 1957:

Down to the present day the peoples of the United States and of the world have not wholly lost the sense that this nation represents a continuing, unique experiment in the development of free societies. If over the coming decades the United States should turn its back on the great revolutionary transformations going forward in the underdeveloped countries ... American society will progressively lose some of those basic spiritual qualities which have been historically linked to the nation's sense of world mission.[37]

Rostow was not merely concerned with the preservation of the American spirit; his writings also reflect a belief – shared by many of his academic peers – in a universal human right to material prosperity and democratic governance and the conviction that the United States could play a central role in achieving this end.[38] By the same coin, communists – the "scavengers of the modernization process," as he termed them – threatened to divert developing societies away from advancement and into the abyss of totalitarianism and stagnation.[39]

Once in office, Rostow articulated the central assumptions of White House strategy toward the nonaligned states, mixing geopolitical and developmental arguments, leaving his more ideological assumptions implicit. His most critical argument for engagement was made several weeks after the nonaligned

---

[35] Michael E. Latham, *The Right Kind of Revolution: Modernization, Development, and U.S. Foreign Policy from the Cold War to the Present* (Ithaca: Cornell University Press, 2011), 53–58.

[36] David Milne, *America's Rasputin: Walt Rostow and the Vietnam War* (New York: Hill and Wang, 2008), 40–55.

[37] Walt W. Rostow and Max Millikan, *A Proposal: Key to an Effective Foreign Policy* (New York: Harper & Bros., 1957), 150–151.

[38] Walt W. Rostow, *The Stages of Economic Growth: A Non-Communist Manifesto* (New York: Cambridge University Press, 1960), 166–167; Nils Gilman, *Mandarins of the Future: Modernization Theory in Cold War America* (Baltimore: The Johns Hopkins University Press, 2003), 192–202.

[39] Walt W. Rostow, *View from the Seventh Floor* (New York: Harper & Row, 1964), 114.

states met in Belgrade, in September 1961. Rostow sent Kennedy a detailed memorandum arguing for a continuation of the policy of engagement. The nonaligned states were critical, he argued, because the United States retained a crucial interest in seeing them develop along non-communist lines and also in guiding them toward foreign policies that would not indirectly aid the communist bloc. Their stances on international issues in the UN represented a third concern. Above all, Rostow stressed, these states took positions based on their own calculation of national interest – and this could be altered over time. States receiving U.S. aid, he argued, had generally taken more moderate positions at Belgrade.[40]

Rostow's background in economics predisposed him toward a universalist conception of what motivated nonaligned leaders. He believed that the key distinctions between postcolonial states and their European counterparts could be made in terms of power and prosperity: the relative poverty and weakness of the underdeveloped areas dictated an overriding concern with local issues. With prosperity the key determinant of foreign policy, Rostow reasoned, there was "fundamentally very little difference" between the motivations of Pakistan's leader, Mohammed Ayub Khan, and India's Nehru.[41] Such an analysis discounted deep differences in ideology and culture. Komer thought Rostow insufficiently cognizant of the strength of anticolonial sentiment in nonaligned states.[42]

Rostow's solution to the problems posed by this turbulent process of diffusion was, paradoxically, to seek a "community of free nations." The Basic National Security Policy (BNSP) that he and the State Department's Policy Planning Council drafted in the late autumn of 1961 proposed a kind of association between the industrialized democracies and the developing world. Rostow envisioned Europe, Japan, and the United States contributing capital and expertise to assist developing societies in their progress toward economic takeoff, thereby inoculating them against communist subversion. Citing the preamble of the Constitution in its opening paragraphs, the BNSP declared America's national purpose to be: "The creation of a world environment in which a nation with values and purposes such as ours can flourish." Instrumental toward the creation of such a community would be an immediate, comprehensive program to promote economic modernization in developing economies – putting economic priorities *ahead* of "the promotion of special ties with these countries."[43]

His outlook owed much to an idealism and triumphalism based upon a sense of American mission and a belief that his country had solved the fundamental

---

[40] Memorandum, "Neutralism and Foreign Aid; or Belgrade Reconsidered," Rostow to Kennedy, September 27, 1961, DDRS.

[41] Ibid.

[42] Memorandum, Komer to Rostow, October 2, 1961, NSF, box 439, "Nonaligned Conferences [White House Memoranda]" folder, JFKL.

[43] Memorandum, "Basic National Security Policy," George McGhee, December 5, 1961, in DOS, *FRUS, 1961–1963, 8: National Security Policy (MS)* (Washington: GPO, 1997): doc. 285.

problems of economic development. The United States and its allies were well suited to promote a community of free nations because they were, as democracies, more tolerant of variety and of pluralism. Rostow abjured seeking overseas replicas of the American system. He wrote in the June 1962 draft of the BNSP, "We do not need societies abroad in our own image; and in any case, the democratic process must be viewed as a matter of underlying purpose ... not as an absolute condition." Compared to the flexibility that democratic culture afforded the West, communism seemed hampered by its totalitarianism and its emphasis on the centralization of power.[44] His anticommunism and veneration of the American model checked his analytical abilities; here Rostow dangerously understated the capacity of the communist powers to deal subtly and patiently with non-Marxist states, while treating his own country as non-ideological and entirely pragmatic.

Rostow and Komer were not close. Komer's assertive style did not couple well with Rostow's more soft-spoken demeanor. On another level, though, the two men complemented one another. Whereas Komer specialized in drafting pointed, sometimes scathing memoranda specific to individual issues, Rostow was more comfortable describing in broad terms the ongoing evolution of the international system. Consequently, his memoranda helped to articulate the overarching assumptions of American policymakers – tenets less likely to emerge in the terse, issue-oriented dispatches of his peers. Rostow, moreover, lacked Komer's enthusiasm for geopolitical gamesmanship and aggressive diplomacy geared toward short-term goals. Far more than Rostow, Komer believed that aid could be used as leverage, "to influence nations to stand up more often on our side."[45] Rostow was skeptical about this use of aid. "It is crucial that we do not permit our short-term tactics to disrupt the long-term strategy," he warned in September 1961, arguing that long-term aid stood to have far greater effect on the foreign policies of recipients.[46]

Rostow's caution toward using aid for short-term goals was well founded, but his own outlook erred on the side of universalism. Significant differences existed between a Nehru and an Ayub, and these transcended the distinctions between the geopolitical vantage points of India and Pakistan. Rostow's emphasis on commonalities, on measurements largely defined by scales and quantities, led him to neglect the very qualities that distinguished the nonaligned leaders from one another: ideology, culture, and memory, in particular. His writings about nonalignment were half-conscious of these differences, making broad statements about the neutralists, followed by caveats about not painting over local distinctions with a broad brush. As his biographer David Milne notes, Rostow proved blind to the power of nationalism in the Third World,

[44] Rostow, "Basic National Security Policy," June 22, 1962, ibid.
[45] Memorandum, Komer to Rostow, October 2, 1961, NSF, box 439, "Nonaligned Conferences [White House Memoranda]" folder, JFKL.
[46] Memorandum, "Neutralism and Foreign Aid," Rostow to Kennedy, September 27, 1961, DDRS.

perceiving left-leaning movements there as pawns of communist states – most fatefully in the case of Vietnam.[47]

By the time Rostow succeeded Bundy as national security advisor in 1966, he faced severe geopolitical and economic constraints posed by the Vietnam War and was unable to advance the broad agenda he had previously advocated. Preferring development over engagement, he sought to reinforce key states in particular regions as models for modernization. These states tended to be those more openly friendly to the United States as LBJ's commitment to Vietnam neared its zenith. This policy departed substantially from engagement as pursued by Kennedy.

THE LIBERAL APPOINTEES: BOWLES, WILLIAMS, AND STEVENSON

Some Kennedy appointees at the highest level of the Department of State sought friendship with the nonaligned states as an outgrowth of their liberal ideology. Chester Bowles, G. Mennen Williams, and, to a lesser extent, Adlai Stevenson approached the nonaligned world with a sense of mission. These men were supporters of the American civil rights struggle at home and former elected officials. Just as Americans were striving to break the pernicious chains of poverty and racial discrimination, so, too, would they struggle in concert with the peoples of Africa and Asia to undo the historic legacy of colonial exploitation and underdevelopment.

These liberal advocates played an important role in advancing the policy of engagement, but their passion for it also limited their effectiveness. All three men were political appointees with little, if any, diplomatic experience, former politicians placed in the midst of the State Department. Each of them was marginalized over time, beginning with the quick replacement of Bowles by George Ball in the autumn of 1961, depriving the other two of their main ally in the Department.

Chester Bowles was the only one of the three to remain in government through the Johnson years. He stood among the earliest and most vocal advocates of engaging the postcolonial world. A onetime isolationist who later embraced the foreign policies of Franklin Roosevelt and a successful advertising executive who traced his American ancestry back three centuries, Bowles believed in a distinct American mission to aid the newly decolonized states, seeing his country as a shining city on the hill and Europe as a decadent, debased continent. Involvement with colonialism, he believed, fundamentally betrayed American ideals.[48]

Bowles's concern with the United States' standing in the postcolonial world dated back to the onset of the Cold War. Between 1946 and 1948, while working

---

[47] Milne, *America's Rasputin*, 97–100.
[48] Howard B. Schaffer, *Chester Bowles: New Dealer in the Cold War* (Cambridge, MA: Harvard University Press, 1993), 14–32; Richard P. Dauer, *A North-South Mind in an East-West World: Chester Bowles and the Making of United States Cold War Foreign Policy, 1951–1969* (Westport: Praeger, 2005), 13–25; Ball, *The Past Has Another Pattern*, 170.

for a range of different UN-affiliated bodies, Bowles formulated a broader set of principles that ultimately dictated his approach to the Afro-Asian world. Writing to Secretary of State George Marshall in 1948, Bowles expressed his concern that the United States would face real danger if it allowed itself to be positioned "as the great reactionary power in a revolutionary world." This would cost Washington the support of the Third World and deprive it of access to the region's economic resources. He called for broad, New Deal-style programs of social assistance targeted not only at Europe but also at the Middle East and Latin America. Even at the outset of the Cold War, he seemed most concerned by the economic gap between the industrial north and the underdeveloped south.[49]

In October 1951, Bowles was confirmed as the U.S. ambassador to India. Though he served in New Delhi for slightly less than a year and a half, Bowles made a profound impression on his Indian hosts. The historian Andrew Rotter observes that Bowles was the most successful American ambassador in India during the Nehru years, endearing himself to the Indian prime minister and people. Bowles failed, however, in his efforts to convince the Truman administration and his fellow countrymen of India's strategic importance as a counterweight to communist China. The Republican victory in 1952 brought an early end to Bowles's service in India.[50]

After his return to the United States, Bowles became one of the leading advocates of American engagement in the Third World. In 1954, he published *Ambassador's Report*, a chronicle of his short tenure in New Delhi. A visit to Africa in 1955 inspired him to write *Africa's Challenge to America*, in which he argued for an active American role in advancing self-determination and economic progress on the continent. In 1959, in *The Coming Political Breakthrough*, Bowles likened revolutions in Africa and Asia to the American Revolution. Analyzing the declaration issued at Bandung – which featured resolutions that pledged the attendees to combat poverty and colonialism and advance human dignity, peace, and economic progress – Bowles wrote: "These concepts are no more and no less than an assertion from these decisive, restless new continents of the continuing American Revolution for which Jefferson, Lincoln, Wilson, and Franklin Roosevelt spoke so eloquently."[51] He perceived nonalignment as a positive development, representing the emergence of a "world conscience" capable of mediating Cold War crises.[52] Bowles did not oppose the Cold War – indeed, he profoundly feared the spread of communism, particularly the Chinese type. He did object to the prevailing emphasis on military forms of containment and the stark division of the world into friendly and

---

[49] Schaffer, *Chester Bowles*, 32–33; Dauer, *A North-South Mind*, 13–25.

[50] Andrew J. Rotter, *Comrades at Odds: The United States and India, 1947–1964* (Ithaca: Cornell University Press, 2000), 278–280; Robert J. McMahon, *The Cold War on the Periphery: The United States, India, and Pakistan* (New York: Columbia University Press, 1994), 110–122; Schaffer, *Chester Bowles*, 44–112.

[51] Chester Bowles, *The Coming Political Breakthrough* (New York: Harper, 1959), 18.

[52] Memcons, Bowles and Nehru, August 8 and 9, 1961, in *FRUS, 1961–1963, 19:* 80–86.

unfriendly zones, believing such a partitioning would harm both the United States and the postcolonial world.

In 1959 Bowles accepted an offer to advise Senator Kennedy on the campaign trail. Kennedy's choice of Bowles rested on his need to reassure the liberal wing of the Democratic Party, which held Bowles in high regard. This marked the start of a troubled partnership. Differences of personality kept the two men apart: although Kennedy valued succinctness, Bowles had a tendency to speak elliptically and to repeat himself. While listening to Bowles, Kennedy could sometimes be observed tapping his teeth with a pen – a sign that his patience had run out.[53] He still felt indebted to Bowles for his support in 1960, and offered him the position of undersecretary of state, making him deputy to Rusk. The two men were one of the administration's odder couples.

Bowles lasted only ten months as undersecretary. He and Rusk operated at a distance: the secretary was concerned with the daily functioning of the department; the undersecretary seemed more preoccupied with the general than the specific. Rusk's reticence hampered coordination, and Bowles's tendency to float in abstractions led some to believe that he was still drawing on his background in advertising.[54] Bowles damaged his standing within the administration when he made it known that he had opposed the Bay of Pigs invasion. Frustrated, he complained that the bureaucracy was still "full of Eisenhower left-overs."[55] By the summer of 1961, rumors of Bowles's impending demotion circulated in Washington. Stevenson and Williams petitioned Kennedy to keep Bowles where he was but won him only a temporary reprieve. Finally, around Thanksgiving, Rusk asked Bowles if he would take the position of roving ambassador to the Third World. Bowles accepted, but felt humiliated by the apparent demotion.[56] He served in this makeshift position until resigning at the end of 1962. Kennedy kept him in mind for the position of ambassador to India, and, in July 1963, after John Kenneth Galbraith resigned from the post, Bowles returned happily to New Delhi.

Bowles was unable to manage the State Department, but even so, U.S. diplomacy suffered in his absence. Among engagement's advocates, he was the one most aware of the psychological and cultural influences behind the outlook of nonaligned leaders. His moral outrage over the abuses of colonialism gave Bowles a natural feeling for the anger and fear lingering in its wake. As he noted about Indian perceptions of the United States:

The Indians were hurt that we didn't understand them better. They said, 'We admit that we have a chip on our shoulders and certainly we moralize too much. We're not being

[53] Elspeth Rostow, Interview with the author, October 8, 2006.
[54] Ball, *The Past Has Another Pattern*, 170.
[55] Unsent Letter, Bowles to Kennedy, April 22, 1961, Chester Bowles Papers, Series 1, Part 6, Box 297, Yale University Library, New Haven.
[56] Arthur M. Schlesinger Jr., *A Thousand Days: John F. Kennedy in the White House* (Boston: Houghton Mifflin, 1969), 437–444; Schaffer, *Chester Bowles*, 192–231.

logical in all of our reactions, but neither were you.' They felt very deeply about this. For two hundred years there were signs that hung on the benches saying 'For Europeans Only,' and signs outside of restaurants, 'No Dogs or Indians Allowed.' ... these things hurt them and affected them.[57]

Bowles's pronounced sense of what colonialism had wrought made him unique among senior policymakers. Like Rostow, he took particular note of the vast disparity of incomes separating the West from its former colonies; unlike Rostow, however, Bowles believed that this gulf further hampered Western efforts to understand the motivations of the nonaligned world. As he remarked in 1970, "We are very well off, very affluent, and as a result it's impossible for us to understand developing nations and how they feel and how sensitive they are." Poverty did not merely bestow a desire for material development; it also made poorer nations resentful of being steered or managed by would-be benefactors.

His most lasting contribution to policy came through his ambassadorial appointments. Bowles helped to appoint like-minded liberals to ambassadorships throughout the Third World. Long after his departure from formal power, men like Galbraith, William Attwood in Guinea, and John Badeau in Egypt pursued Bowlesian programs of outreach on the ground while advocating engagement in their cables to Washington.

Bowles was farsighted – in all senses of the term. He was uncommonly perceptive of the long-term challenges and burdens faced by states like India. More than almost all of his colleagues, he grasped why and how the traumas of colonial occupation were not easily overcome. Unfortunately, Bowles was prone to long-term prognostication, yet he served in administrations that valued concise, dispassionate, immediate analysis. As Ball observed, not unsympathetically, "He tried to see every question in the long view, whereas the Kennedy *modus operandi* required quick answers and prompt action."[58] These limitations diminished the impact of his often insightful observations.

Gerhard Mennen "Soapy" Williams gained particular acclaim and notoriety when Kennedy appointed the Michigan governor to head the African Bureau of the State Department. Known for his bow ties, his role in the construction of the Mackinac Bridge, and his sterling civil rights record, Williams seemed a peculiar choice for the job. Nonetheless, he embraced his new job with optimism and energy. His passion for civil rights gave Williams an instinctive empathy for the new nations of Africa. To Africans, he presented a far more sympathetic profile than his predecessors had in the 1950s.[59]

Williams gained acclaim and some notoriety when he was erroneously reported as having proclaimed "Africa for the Africans!" during a visit to Kenya. Williams had, in fact, stated: "What we want for Africa is what the

---

[57] Interview, Chester Bowles, November 11, 1969, 17, OH, LBJL.
[58] Ball, *The Past Has Another Pattern*, 172; Schlesinger, *A Thousand Days*, 438.
[59] Thomas Noer, *"Soapy": A Biography of G. Mennen Williams* (Ann Arbor: University of Michigan Press, 2005), 11–221.

Africans want for themselves." The incident endeared Williams to countless Africans and made him anathema to the Portuguese, the Rhodesians, and white South Africans. It also alarmed both Rusk and Kennedy, and, despite the president's public avowal of support – he dryly mused, "I do not know who else Africa should be for" – Williams was discouraged from further impromptu oratory.[60]

In other respects, Williams was clearly effective at his job. Kennedy valued his advice and took care to consult the notes that Williams gave him in advance of the visits of African leaders. The African bureau of the State Department, which had only been created in 1958, benefited from Soapy's energetic style. He fought, with some success, to redress acts of discrimination perpetrated by segregationist establishments against African diplomats.[61] On the road, Williams was a spirited, engaged traveler and presented himself as a friendly, sympathetic ally to the newly decolonized states of Africa. Although he was far from fluent in French, his efforts to speak it were appreciated by the continent's many Francophone leaders.[62]

Williams was a staunch partisan of aid to Africa and a stalwart anticommunist. His visits to the continent in 1961 reinforced his sense that the U.S. position there depended on Washington's willingness to finance African development as broadly as possible.[63] He viewed his job as having both international and domestic responsibilities: representing the United States to Africa and advocating for the continent within the domestic arena. Inevitably, his support for African nationalism led Williams to take strong stances against Portuguese colonialism and against the continuation of white rule in Rhodesia and South Africa. Williams viewed apartheid and other forms of racial discrimination as morally troubling and politically dangerous. Like Bowles, he tended to produce long reports that were likely to be, at most, skimmed by his superiors.

Despite his energetic style, Williams was unprepared for the administrative challenges of the State Department. He faced an uphill struggle during the administration's long internal debate over policy toward the Congo and considered resigning at least once. Veterans like Rusk, Ball, and Averell Harriman, who eventually superseded him during the Johnson years, possessed greater experience and a far sharper grasp of bureaucratic strategy. Williams, like his friend Bowles, had more success representing the United States in Africa than advocating for Africa at home.[64]

---

[60] Noer, "*Soapy*," 239–241.

[61] Renee Romano, "No Diplomatic Immunity: African Diplomats, the State Department, and Civil Rights, 1961–1964," *The Journal of American History* 87, no. 2 (2000): 546–579.

[62] William Attwood, *The Reds and the Blacks: A Personal Adventure* (New York: Harper & Row, 1967), 94.

[63] Memorandum, Williams to Bowles, September 29, 1961, in DOS, *FRUS, 1961–1963, Vol. 21: Africa* (Washington: GPO, 1995): 303–305.

[64] Carl Watts, "G. Mennen Williams and Rhodesian Independence: A Case Study in Bureaucratic Politics," *Michigan Academician* 36 (2004), 225–246.

Adlai Stevenson held the greatest prominence of the three liberals. A former governor of Illinois and twice the Democratic nominee for the presidency, he brought considerable personal prestige to his position as American representative to the United Nations, but uneasy personal relations with JFK hampered his effectiveness. Stevenson had nursed hopes of reclaiming the Democratic nomination in 1960; these were quashed by Kennedy's candidacy. Like Bowles, he helped Kennedy to shore up his left flank in 1960, but to JFK he seemed too outspoken and too famous for the position of secretary of state. Stevenson's appointment confirmed the importance the administration vested in the UN but ensured that he would not outshine Kennedy from his office in New York City.[65]

Stevenson shared the liberal beliefs of Bowles and Williams, although his tendency to espouse gradualist solutions made him less respected by civil rights advocates. During his campaigns against Eisenhower, he had spoken out against the Manichean view of the Cold War. He took an interest in the opportunities offered by decolonization, visiting Ghana several times after it gained independence in 1957 and corresponding with its president, Kwame Nkrumah. In 1957, he spoke of the inexorable disintegration of the European empires and the need for the Western nations to jointly assist the new states of Africa and Asia.[66] Yet Stevenson tempered his anticolonial sentiment. He supported the French in Indochina, fearing that their defeat would open the region to communist influence, and he had real misgivings about Kennedy's speech on Algeria.[67]

As the head of the U.S. mission to the UN, Stevenson confronted the daunting task of preserving the American position in that body as its membership continued to expand. The addition of seventeen new African members in 1960 underscored the potential difficulties that Washington faced. An ardent Cold Warrior, Stevenson sought to appeal to new delegations – and to apprise Washington of their concerns. As such, he became a strong advocate for policies more in accordance with the growing tide of anticolonial sentiment. Though seen as a capable representative, he remained peripheral in both the Kennedy and Johnson administrations, serving until his death, on July 14, 1965.

Williams, Bowles, and Stevenson mixed a sense of American mission toward the postcolonial world with a firm anticommunism. They shared an intense, idealistic commitment to a broad American role across the Third World, with a greater emphasis on combating racism and poverty. But their political influence within the administration was always precarious. Bowles was undermined by

---

[65] On the life of Stevenson, see John Bartlow Martin, *Adlai Stevenson of Illinois: The Life of Adlai E. Stevenson* (New York: Doubleday, 1976); Porter McKeever, *Adlai Stevenson: His Life and Legacy* (New York: Morrow, 1989); Jeff Broadwater, *Adlai Stevenson and American Politics: The Odyssey of a Cold War Liberal* (New York: Twayne, 1994).

[66] Walter Johnson ed., *The Papers of Adlai Stevenson, Vol. VII: Continuing Education and the Unfinished Business of American Society, 1957–1961* (Boston: Little, Brown, 1977), 7–23, 94–95.

[67] Ball, *The Past Has Another Pattern*, 170.

his bureaucratic inefficiency and his unabashed advocacy. Williams came to be seen as a starry-eyed idealist lost in the State Department. Stevenson battled in vain to establish his position and bridge the distance between the UN mission and Washington. The three of them did much to redefine the U.S. image in the nonaligned states, but their impact on policy peaked in 1961 and fell off thereafter.

THE SKEPTICS: RUSK AND BALL

Skepticism toward engagement existed within the government, but its adherents did not oppose the policy on principle. Opposition to engagement waxed and waned in response to particular policy questions. As with so many issues, where one stood on policy toward the nonaligned states depended upon where one sat. Officials dealing with the internal cohesion of NATO, with preserving access to vital bases such as the Portuguese Azores, or with reassuring nervous allies outside Europe tended to have less patience with nonaligned leaders. The European division of the Department of State, concerned about the impact of the policy on Euro-American relations, sought to check what it saw as the giddy enthusiasm of Bowles and Williams. When Ball replaced Bowles, the tide seemed to be turning in favor of the Europeanists, who reportedly exulted, "One down and Williams to go!"[68]

None of the administration's senior appointees, however, opposed the policy outright – given Kennedy's well-known preferences, this was hardly surprising. Although it would be inaccurate to term either Dean Rusk or George Ball consistent foes of engagement, both men espoused a greater skepticism toward the endeavor than did their peers on the NSC staff. To them, the costs of this policy tended to exceed the benefits.

Among the New Frontiersmen, Rusk was the advisor who was most consistently critical of the nonaligned leaders. This was not because he was unfamiliar with or unsympathetic toward the postcolonial states. Rusk had considerable experience in the non-European world, including wartime service in the China-Burma-India theater and subsequent work on the question of Indonesian independence in Dean Acheson's State Department. During that time, he was hardly an unflinching advocate of supporting colonial powers against African and Asian subjects.[69] Unrecognized at the time of his appointment, however, was the fact that Rusk was substantially more conservative than many of his peers within the administration. Although a liberal on domestic matters, his foreign policy views hewed more closely to those of Dulles than

[68] Thomas J. Noer, *Cold War and Black Liberation: The United States and White Rule in Africa, 1948–1968* (Columbia: University of Missouri Press, 1985), 82.

[69] Warren I. Cohen, *Dean Rusk* (Totowa: Cooper Square, 1980), 15; Philip C. Jessup, *The Birth of Nations* (New York: Columbia University Press, 1974), 73–77, 87–88; Robert J. McMahon, *Colonialism and Cold War: The United States and the Struggle for Indonesian Independence, 1945–1949* (Ithaca: Cornell University Press, 1981), 161–162, 291–295.

either his liberal or pragmatist counterparts. Dulles, in fact, had been a close friend; even though the men held different political allegiances, they viewed the Cold War similarly. Dulles had shielded Rusk from the onslaught of Joe McCarthy and, as president of the Rockefeller Foundation, Rusk often assisted the administration, including when the secretary of state inquired about staging a counter-Bandung conference. Like his friend, Rusk proved particularly sensitive to the rhetoric of nonaligned leaders. "Some of these fellows were just plain rascals," he later wrote.[70] Facing choices between existing allies and unpredictable nonaligned powers, Rusk preferred the birds already in hand. Bowles thought Rusk unimaginative, easily irritated by the rhetoric of nonaligned leaders, and biased toward Europe.[71]

Rusk's prior experience with the UN left one singular imprint on his outlook: he wholeheartedly believed in the UN Charter. Unilateral Indian and Indonesian action against colonial vestiges struck Rusk as blatant attacks on the international system he had worked to create. The new states seemed happy to utilize the institutions of the postwar order when it suited them and to flout them when it did not. Rusk chafed at this perceived hypocrisy.[72] As he saw it, the United States was deeply invested in its treaty commitments and in the United Nations; neither of these obligations could be neglected without terrible cost. Bundy observed critically, "The Secretary occasionally has the disadvantage of being a very conscientious man with strong moral feelings."[73]

During the Kennedy administration, Rusk maintained a cordial distance from the president. As he later recounted, he and Kennedy spoke on a formal basis, without the use of first names. He was the only cabinet member whom the president called "Mr. Secretary." Although Kennedy respected Rusk's administrative abilities, he likely would have chosen another secretary of state, had he lived to win a second term.[74] Rusk and Johnson, however, instinctively liked and respected each other; in the words of one contemporary, they were "almost two peas in a pod."[75] The increased trust that Rusk enjoyed during the Johnson years contributed to the declining effort accorded to engagement after 1963. Rusk was more doubtful about the returns this policy offered and less receptive to the advice of its advocates.

Unlike Rusk, George Ball had little direct experience with Africa or Asia before 1961. Although his long career in public service and his private law practice brought him into contact with a truly global range of issues, Europe

[70] Rusk, *As I Saw It*, 160–161, 398.
[71] Schaffer, *Chester Bowles*, 229–230; Thomas L. Hughes, Interview with the author, July 16, 2009.
[72] Cohen, *Dean Rusk*, 207–209.
[73] Bundy, Memorandum for the Record, April 1, 1963, Personal Papers of McGeorge Bundy, box 35, "Daily Memoranda for the Record, 7/63–12/62; 1963: April-Feb" folder, JFKL.
[74] Schlesinger, *A Thousand Days*, 927; Thomas L. Hughes, Interview with the author, July, 16, 2009.
[75] First Interview, Dean Rusk, July 28, 1969, 10, OH, LBJL; Thomas L. Hughes, Interview with the author, July, 16, 2009.

was Ball's area of primary expertise – in this he was a kind of diametric opposite to Chester Bowles. This did not, however, entail any dogmatism on the issues that divided Europe from the emerging nonaligned group. From his frequent trips to France in the 1950s, Ball observed firsthand the trauma of the Algerian war. He concluded that France was engaged in a futile struggle against the "tides of history" and felt similarly skeptical about Belgian colonialism in the Congo. Ball still did not wholly approve of Kennedy's Algeria speech, believing that the senator risked involving the United States in a conflict only France could solve.[76]

Like his peers, Ball held critical opinions of Eisenhower-era foreign policy. During the 1952 and 1956 elections, he worked on the presidential campaigns of his old friend and colleague Adlai Stevenson. He believed that Eisenhower and Dulles were pursuing a Manichean foreign policy and resented the underhanded attacks made against Stevenson by Nixon. Although the two men parted paths in their respective foreign policy outlooks – especially toward the Third World – Ball retained a lifelong affection for Stevenson, which softened their frequent disagreements on matters of policy.

Ball was no supporter of colonialism, but he evinced a far greater skepticism that the United States could play a positive role in the resolution of colonial disputes. Ever anxious to avoid disagreements with major allies, he consistently advocated close coordination with NATO members on issues outside the European theater. This limited, in turn, Washington's ability to placate the demands of the nonaligned states. Privately, advocates of engagement such as Komer fumed at Ball's Eurocentric approach, but Ball – an experienced lawyer – came to the table with forceful, compelling arguments and a canny appreciation of the art of bureaucratic warfare.

Ball was especially doubtful of Rostow's grand design for foreign aid and its idealistic underpinnings. He later wrote despairingly of the "theological ... overblown nomenclature" advocated by the more fervent proponents of development. He felt particular ire at the "presumptuous undertaking" of nation-building, with its hubristic underlying assumption that the same "bricks" could be made with "infinitely various kinds of clay." As Ball saw it, this mania for development came at a real cost to established American alliances. He chafed at the tendency of development advocates to regard NATO allies as a "bank" for "grandiose Third World programs," noting the strains this placed on trans-Atlantic cooperation.[77]

Ball prided himself on his realism, on not espousing what he termed "moralistic mush." This applied especially in his attitude toward the newly decolonized states of Africa and Asia. He felt profoundly skeptical, not only of the claims of Western economists that vigorously executed aid programs could better the standard of living in newly decolonized states, but also of the underlying assumption that these new states would be the deciding ground of the

---

[76] Ball, *The Past Has Another Pattern*, 154–157, 166–167, 224–225.
[77] Ibid., 183–184.

Cold War. Ball believed their profound poverty, halting economic progress, and the crippling weight of expanding populations made the new states burdens on any patron. He wrote in 1968, "For the life of me, I cannot see how we would be endangered by a Communist regime in Mali or Brazzaville or Burundi; its most likely effect would be to cost Moscow or Peking some money." Ball once responded to a telegram from Zanzibar warning of the ascendance of a pro-Chinese leader by observing, "God watches every sparrow that may fall, but I do not see why we need to compete in that league."[78]

Ball believed that America's critical geopolitical relationships were "most heavily concentrated in the world's north temperate zone," meaning the states of Western Europe, the Soviet Union, Canada, and Japan. He regarded China and India as too impoverished and too far away from mature industrial development to be more than "light heavyweights." Only among the industrial democracies of the northern hemisphere could the "fragile *bipolar* balance of power" truly be shifted. Here lies a critical distinction between Ball and the major advocates of engagement. Unlike Rostow, Ball did not perceive the diffusion of power to be continuing. Certainly decolonization had forced the states of Western Europe to accept that they were now "medium-sized powers," but for Ball the absence of meaningful economic development outside the northern hemisphere meant that the Cold War remained a bipolar fray centered in Europe.[79] This is not to say that Ball embraced the Manichean outlook he associated with Dulles: he explicitly rejected Dulles's moralistic style and never equated neutrality with immorality. For Ball, the most salient fact about the nonaligned states was not that they were declaring a kind of neutrality but that they were underdeveloped and peripheral to the Cold War, as he understood it. Their views would have little bearing on its outcome.

Ball decried the evils of colonialism and the white supremacist governments of Rhodesia and South Africa, but doubted whether economic sanctions could move either Portugal or the governments of Rhodesia and South Africa away from racist policies. In his 1968 discussion of the Portuguese colonies, Ball wrote with particular sympathy for the Portuguese dilemma, noting the dire economic consequences Lisbon would face from a sudden loss of its colonies. Only through a course of engagement could Ball see Portugal prepared – politically, economically, and psychologically – to concede the independence of its colonies. He took a similar position on the question of South Africa. Ball considered apartheid abhorrent, but – as he put it – "abhorrence is a state of mind, not a principle of political action." Here again he inveighed against the "self-righteous" tendency of Westerners to isolate South Africa, which he saw as fostering a "siege mentality" on the part of South Africa's white population.[80]

---

[78] George W. Ball, *The Discipline of Power: Essentials of a Modern World Structure* (Boston: Little, Brown, 1968), 7, 221–234; Edwin Guthman and Jeffrey Shulman eds., *Robert Kennedy, in His Own Words: The Unpublished Recollections of the Kennedy Years* (New York: Bantam, 1988), 324.

[79] Ball, *The Discipline of Power*, 12–13, 169–183, 344–345. Emphasis added.

[80] Ibid., 245–259.

Ball's professed disapproval of Portuguese colonialism and apartheid was likely genuine, but these systems did not outrage him in the way they did liberals like Bowles or Williams.

Ball related exceedingly well to Rusk. The two men came from the same generation, shared many of the same views on foreign affairs (although not on Vietnam), and balanced each other personally, with the self-effacing Rusk often ceding the stage to the outspoken Ball. They played a significant role in the shaping of policy during the Kennedy years but especially came to the fore during the Johnson years.

LYNDON JOHNSON AND ENGAGEMENT

Lyndon Johnson bears the unhappy distinction of being the only vice president in history to witness the murder of his running mate. On November 22, 1963, at the moment of the fatal shots, he rode four cars behind the presidential vehicle. Pinned to the seat of his car by a quick-acting Secret Service agent, LBJ was driven to Parkland Hospital, where grief-stricken presidential aide Kenneth O'Donnell told him simply, "He's gone."[81] Himself overwhelmed, the thirty-sixth president of the United States now shouldered an unfathomable burden of responsibilities and legacies, public and private, known and unknown. Kennedy's policy of engagement lay among them, now subject to the uncertain inclinations of a man who had been largely excluded from the counsels of foreign policy. Although LBJ more than shared the anguish felt throughout the nonaligned world, his own outlook led the United States into an inexorable collision course with the nations and governments his predecessor had done so much to court.

Why the divergence? Like Rusk, LBJ had had a relationship with the Eisenhower administration during the 1950s that was fundamentally different from that of other New Frontiersmen. As Democratic leader in the Senate, he clashed on occasion with the Eisenhower White House. It was often, though, a cooperative relationship. Johnson perceived a need, on occasion, to assist Eisenhower against the right wing of his party, including on matters of foreign policy. Differences of opinion remained, but LBJ formed a durable working relationship with Eisenhower and Dulles, sometimes at the expense of his standing among liberal Democrats. More than any of his peers, Johnson cultivated personal ties to the administration. In March 1959, in the final months of his battle against cancer, a grateful Dulles thanked Johnson for "your many kindnesses and your friendly concern on my behalf." LBJ had just sent him a basket of yellow chrysanthemums and red dahlias.[82]

---

[81] Lyndon B. Johnson, *The Vantage Point: Perspectives of the Presidency, 1963–1969* (New York: Holt, Rinehart and Winston, 1971), 7–17; Robert Dallek, *Flawed Giant: Lyndon Johnson and His Times, 1961–1973* (New York: Oxford University Press, 1998), 46–48.

[82] Letter, Dulles to Johnson, March 16, 1959, JFDP, Chronological Series, box 17, "March 1959," DDEL.

Johnson is often portrayed as a president who perceived the world in starker terms than Kennedy did, who seemed less comfortable with diplomacy, and who was more inclined to divide the globe between friend and foe.[83] That case has at times been overstated. The image of LBJ as a Texas bumpkin, uncomprehending of the world, has long since been proven false. Whereas the Vietnam tragedy looms foremost in our understanding of his foreign policy, recent years have witnessed new pathbreaking accounts of his approach to other areas of the world. As Thomas Schwartz has argued, Johnson's policies toward Europe and the NATO alliance were generally both prudent and successful, hinging substantially on his ability to grasp the nature of power within the Western alliance system – much as he had while Senate majority leader.[84]

Johnson clearly had the capability to be as successful in his dealings with nonaligned leaders as his predecessor. The Texan's intense charm and exhaustive appetite for information fully matched Kennedy's. Johnson, as much as any other president, believed in government's capacity to address and remedy social ills. The product of an impoverished upbringing in the Texas Hill Country, he could identify with the developmental aspirations of leaders in the postcolonial world – but to do that he first had to meet them. Johnson proved to be a far less avid practitioner of presidential diplomacy toward the nonaligned leaders than JFK had been.

In part, Johnson's shift on nonalignment came as an unintended consequence of his marginalization within the Kennedy White House. Kennedy intentionally excluded Johnson from both critical and routine policy discussions. When asked why he did not offer his vice president more of a role, Kennedy explained, "It's awfully hard because once you get into these crunches you don't really think of calling Lyndon because he hasn't read the cables." This was, as Robert Dallek notes, circular, self-reinforcing logic: Johnson was not reading cables because JFK had decided that he need not be kept up to date on outstanding issues.[85] On some occasions, Johnson played a role in foreign policy. Largely, however, he sat fretfully on the bench. When he took office, he felt obligated to fulfill Kennedy's agenda, but this never applied to engagement – a policy that Kennedy had never formalized as he had his commitment to the defense of South Vietnam.

Johnson's most visible contribution to foreign policy during his vice presidency occurred through his work as a roving ambassador for the administration. His trips overseas brought him into contact with a wide range of international leaders, some of them nonaligned. He had a triumphal visit to Senegal in April 1961 as the head of an American delegation attending celebrations of that

[83] See Fredrik Logevall, *Choosing War: The Lost Chance for Peace and the Escalation of War in Vietnam* (Berkeley: University of California Press, 1999), 79–80, 389–395; David Kaiser, *American Tragedy: Kennedy, Johnson, and the Origins of the Vietnam War* (Cambridge, MA: Harvard University Press, 2000), 285–287.

[84] Thomas A. Schwartz, *Lyndon Johnson and Europe: In the Shadow of Vietnam* (Cambridge, MA: Harvard University Press, 2003), 223–237.

[85] Dallek, *Flawed Giant*, 16–17.

country's independence. Impressed by the welcome he received at the hands of Prime Minister Leopold Senghor, LBJ expressed understanding for Senegalese (and African) nonalignment in the Cold War. "The most harmful Western course would be to interpret each African move as a West-East choice," he wrote to Kennedy. "This is clearly repugnant to the Africans and we must leave them 'room to assert their independence' of both West and East." He identified with Senegalese aspirations for material prosperity and advised his colleagues to regard Senghor's conception of socialism as a far cry from the Cuban model.[86] His report from Senegal showed Johnson's views on nonalignment to be a far cry from those of Dulles: states could be uncommitted without hazarding charges of immorality.

On other trips, however, LBJ was called upon to reassure allies and show solidarity; these missions largely characterized his vice presidential travels. He is best known for his visit to West Berlin during the summer of 1961, at the height of the Berlin crisis. Earlier in the year, however, he visited South and Southeast Asia in the wake of the Geneva Agreement to neutralize Laos. He had an amicable exchange with Nehru, but found the prime minister noncommittal when asked for his support in Southeast Asia. Pakistan's Ayub offered a strong endorsement for the Western position in Indochina and deeply impressed Johnson. His subsequent report to Kennedy noted a serious decline of confidence in U.S. leadership after the Laos settlement, conveying Johnson's belief that "there is no alternative to United States leadership in Southeast Asia" or elsewhere.[87] Once in office, notions of American global leadership and the need to reinforce allies no longer coexisted easily with Johnson's reluctance to seek Cold War solidarity from states such as Senegal.

Johnson's passion for advancing civil rights and alleviating poverty did not have an entirely, or perhaps even primarily, positive impact on his views of engagement. These were goals he sought, above all, to pursue domestically. Johnson was sworn into the presidency with less than a year remaining before the 1964 election. Few men, if any, better understood what that contest would demand. An emphasis on domestic issues both advanced his prospects for reelection and catered to his own aspirations. Politically risky enterprises, such as aid to nonaligned states and furthering détente with the Soviet Union, offered fewer rewards – these could rationally be tabled until after the election. Engagement, as such, did not merit the tireless effort that Johnson accorded to civil rights and antipoverty legislation.

By the time he won election in his own right, Johnson had substantially altered the internal dynamic of the policymaking process. He came to office with his

---

[86] Memorandum, Johnson to Kennedy, undated, Vice President's Security File, box 1, "Vice President's Trip to Europe, Africa" folder, LBJL.

[87] Memorandum, Johnson to Kennedy, undated, Vice President's Security File, box 1, "Vice President's Visit to Southeast Asia I (1)" folder, LBJL; Memcon, Ayub and Johnson, May 20, 1961, in *FRUS, 1961–1963, 19:* 45–50. See also Mitchell Lerner, "A Big Tree of Peace and Justice": The Vice Presidential Travels of Lyndon Johnson, *Diplomatic History,* Vol. 34, No. 2 (April 2010), 357–393.

own managerial style and preferences. Kennedy had favored debate among his advisors, with himself acting as arbiter, paying less attention to formal hierarchy. Johnson did not enjoy playing referee; he asked his advisors and cabinet secretaries to come to conclusions *before* raising issues with him. This stylistic change significantly altered the dynamic within the executive branch. The freewheeling Kennedy style, oriented around debate, had favored outspoken men like Bundy and Komer. The Johnson method bolstered Rusk's position in the chain of command, while reducing the influence of the national security advisor. Interpersonal dynamics further reinforced Rusk's centrality in the administration. Both Rusk and the president were Southern liberals, born into poverty a few months apart. These similarities allowed the formation of a far stronger, more instinctive bond between the two men than Rusk had ever enjoyed with Kennedy.

Though the pragmatists of the NSC weathered the Johnson transition, their influence gradually ebbed. Johnson's relationship with Bundy was ambivalent. He had ample respect for his special assistant's dazzling intellect, but a wide cultural chasm loomed between the two men, one a former Texas schoolteacher, the other a former Harvard dean of faculty. Johnson valued the advice Bundy provided – often professorially – but he took inordinate pleasure in tweaking the fastidious New Englander as well.[88] Komer, on the other hand, was someone Johnson liked personally. Like Kennedy, LBJ appreciated the man's energy and candor, although in 1964 and 1965 he increasingly drew away from Komer's recommendations. Johnson also appreciated Rostow's advice and interest in economic development. The two men worked harmoniously together after Rostow became national security advisor in 1966 – too harmoniously, some critics of the administration thought.[89]

A greater gulf existed between Johnson and the liberals, Bowles, Williams, and Stevenson. The president grew weary of the emphatic requests sent by his ambassador in India and openly doubted Bowles's capacity to separate the interests of the United States from those of India. Williams received more attention than he predicted – he worried that he had earned Johnson's wrath by opposing his vice presidential nomination in 1960 – but still felt himself further marginalized before he resigned to run for the governorship of Michigan in 1966. Stevenson hoped that Johnson would prove more receptive to him, but he also felt largely ignored.[90]

His inauguration to the presidency, moreover, changed Johnson's approach to the nonaligned world. If his post-Senegal memorandum indicates that he was intellectually inclined to accept differences of opinion with nonaligned states, once in office he was not *temperamentally* prepared to do so. As Fredrik Logevall observes, LBJ had a strong tendency to personalize questions of policy.[91] Johnson approached international disputes with a pronounced sense

---

[88] See, for example, Bird, *The Color of Truth*, 297–300.
[89] Ibid., 348–349.
[90] McKeever, *Adlai Stevenson*, 540–541; Noer, "*Soapy*," 271–299.
[91] Logevall, *Choosing War*, 390–394.

that he was being tested and increasingly resented international criticism of his policies – particularly from countries receiving U.S. aid.

By the same coin, he believed allies should be consistently supported. Johnson retained the habits of a Senate majority leader, regarding international disputes as akin to contests between the leaderships of rival parties, ultimately to be resolved by the side with the more effective whip. As Bundy later observed:

Johnson treated Third World leaders like Senators. He presumed that they were all reasonable men who could be persuaded to compromise on almost any issue if the right combination of threats and incentives was employed.[92]

The quote is telling, particularly when one recalls the earlier argument by Thomas Schwartz that LBJ's successful European policy derived in part from his experience as majority leader. In the case of the NATO alliance, he could employ the same kind of logrolling that he used to pass bills in Congress. This instinctive approach failed him when dealing with willful, mercurial nonaligned states, which had no real analogue within the United States Congress. To his intense vexation, these states felt free to accept U.S. aid and simultaneously criticize LBJ's foreign policies.

Such criticism tended to annoy Johnson. In November 1964, he met with Bundy, Rusk, and Stevenson to discuss impending votes in the UN to seat a delegation from the People's Republic of China, which had hitherto been excluded from the body. Stevenson noted a troubling erosion of support among African states for blocking PRC membership and argued that a compromise solution – the seating of two China delegations – would show flexibility and avoid a humiliating defeat. Rusk challenged Stevenson's position, observing that it would seem to reward the hard line taken by both the PRC and the USSR and would serve only to spur the Chinese communists toward increasingly confrontational acts. Tellingly, Johnson remarked that he was most persuaded by Rusk's argument that changing policy would represent "a pay-off for the Soviet and Chinese hard line." When Stevenson insisted doggedly that the PRC, which spoke for more than 700 million people, needed to be reincorporated into the world community, Johnson observed sharply that "he did not pay the foreigners at the UN to advise him on foreign policy but he did pay Rusk" and he preferred the latter's counsel.[93]

The exchange fundamentally reflected LBJ's instinctive reaction to the unsolicited policy views of the nonaligned states. He understood U.S. prestige to be defined primarily by maintaining the credibility of prior commitments to allies. He also noted the domestic fallout that would result from any modification of policy on the representation question. Moreover, he favored the counsel of

---

[92] William J. Burns, *Economic Aid and American Policy toward Egypt, 1955–1981* (Albany: Suny Press, 1985), 152.

[93] Memorandum for the Record, "Meeting with the President on United Nations Matter," November 18, 1964, in DOS, *FRUS, 1964–1968, Vol. 30: China* (Washington: GPO, 1998): 125–128.

his trusted advisor, Rusk, over the pleadings of Stevenson. So long as he felt tested across the globe and so long as he feared eroding American credibility though unreciprocated concessions, he was ill disposed toward unsolicited advice. These tendencies only deepened as he committed the United States to the military defense of South Vietnam.

Johnson also held a different attitude toward aid, one informed by his grasp of the linkages between foreign policy and domestic politics. Modernization and the war against poverty engaged him, but, dealing with a Congress skeptical of assistance to nonaligned states, he felt a consistent need to see real political results for his aid dollars. His patience and generosity were tried by ingratitude on the part of nonaligned aid recipients, leading to increased efforts on his part to use aid for political leverage. All of this was in keeping with his experiential belief in the need for reciprocity in world politics, and yet this thinking diverged substantially from Kennedy-era policies.

Intellectually, Johnson had no fundamental objections to engagement, but a combination of circumstance and personality made him less receptive to nonaligned opinion than Kennedy had been. His view of the world, based in substantial part on his long experience as a legislator, accorded less value to those states unwilling to choose sides. The Vietnam War only sharpened this shift in Johnson's thinking. His approach to the uncommitted world thus diverged greatly from Kennedy's. In many respects an astonishingly effective president, Johnson never thought engagement worthy of the heroic levels of determination he brought to bear on other issues.

THE ERODING CONSENSUS

Several key fault lines separated advocates of engagement from those more skeptical of the policy, and liberal supporters from pragmatists. The most fundamental point of contention was the relative importance of the Third World. A vast gulf separated the rival assessments of Komer and Ball: one man saw the postcolonial world as a fulcrum of power in the Cold War world, the other vehemently doubted that the Cold War would be decided outside the industrial centers of the northern hemisphere. Another key argument concerned how to receive nonaligned criticism of the United States. Liberals and some pragmatists preferred to treat such barbs as a minor irritant, while pointing to other indicators of progress. These explanations could not always carry the argument, and even advocates of engagement tired of what they perceived to be hypocritical, shortsighted criticism of the United States.

The consensus in favor of engagement was never ironclad. It depended on an uncertain coalition between unsentimental pragmatism and heady, optimistic liberalism – on two very different types of inclinations, worldviews, and temperaments. A shaky partnership existed between those who wanted to steer a more prudent course in the world and those who fundamentally wanted to change the world. Pragmatists shared, to a degree, the liberal concern with development, but were cognizant of the domestic political costs of foreign aid. They also tended to view aid as a tool for gaining influence or leverage. Pragmatists always held the upper hand and liberals were always in a position of dependence. The pragmatic rationale for engagement, moreover, depended on evidence that was not always visible. Komer liked to argue that engagement had halted the leftward drift of the leading nonaligned states and that progress needed to be measured not only in terms of gains realized but also in terms of losses averted. This was often true, but proving it required counterfactual, speculative reasoning.

Eventually Komer lost the argument. The logic of the skeptics proved stronger over time as the United States became increasingly embroiled in Southeast Asia. The Vietnam War increasingly limited the time and resources available for the uncommitted world. The strains of warfare made Johnson less willing to accept criticism from the nonaligned states with patience or equanimity, even as it increased in both volume and severity.

None of these men entered office wanting to validate the stark, polarized view of the Cold War that they associated with Dulles. All, to some degree, believed that the United States could deal more prudently with the nonaligned states, whether to avert calamities or to seize opportunities. None opposed outright the tenet that neutrality and Third World nationalism could ultimately act to contain communism. Competing conceptions of the Cold War, however, and conflicting assessments of the ultimate importance of the uncommitted world fostered serious internal divisions within both administrations. The U.S. commitment to engagement depended on the fortunes of the bureaucratic factions that supported it. So long as liberals and pragmatists enjoyed a position of relative strength, the path lay open for an unprecedented program of outreach to the nonaligned world.

3

Conferences Amid Crises: The United States and Nonalignment, 1961–1962

On January 6, 1961, before an international meeting of communist leaders in Moscow, Soviet Chairman Nikita Khrushchev delivered one of the most noted speeches of his career. In what became known as his "wars of national liberation speech," the Soviet leader enthusiastically affirmed his country's support for nationalist movements in Africa, Asia, and Latin America, declaring the three continents "the most important centers of the revolution against imperialism." He also emphatically defended his policy of appealing to non-communist, non-aligned states, such as India, Indonesia, and Egypt.[1] To the incoming Kennedy administration the speech signaled the importance that the Kremlin invested in the uncommitted states. Amid the air of general crisis at the beginning of 1961, the perception of growing Soviet influence in the nonaligned world galvanized the White House to devise and execute a policy response: engagement.

For much of that year, Khrushchev appeared to be a man on the move, confronting the West in Berlin, while continuing to shift the emphasis of his country's foreign policy toward the postcolonial world. When he met Kennedy in June, in Vienna, Khrushchev took pleasure in goading the president about U.S. policy toward colonial questions, stating that the United States was effectively a colonial power in its own right. Kennedy expressed his unease with Khrushchev's January speech, remarking that wars of national liberation were likely to be destabilizing. Khrushchev, in turn, chided the president on U.S. policy toward uncommitted states, remarking that Washington, unlike Moscow, recognized neutrality only among countries that effectively supported its policies. Rhetorically he asked, with regard to the nonaligned states:

What is socialism in the view of all those people? Nasser, Nehru, Nkrumah, Sukarno – all of them have said that they want their countries to develop along socialist lines; but what kind of a socialist is Nasser when he keeps communists in jail? Nehru certainly does not

[1] CIA, Current Intelligence Weekly Review, January 26, 1961, in DOS, *FRUS, 1961–1963, Vol. 5: Soviet Union* (Washington: GPO, 1998): 39–46; Jussi Hanhimäki and Odd Arne Westad eds., *The Cold War: A History in Documents and Eyewitness Accounts* (New York: Oxford University Press, 2003), 358–360.

favor the Communist Party of India either. However, the Soviet Union helps these people and this is a manifestation of its policy of non-interference.[2]

Khrushchev's barbs spoke to one of the Kennedy administration's deepest worries: that the United States was losing the struggle for influence in the nonaligned world. In leaders such as Egyptian President Gamal Abdel Nasser, Indian Prime Minister Jawaharlal Nehru, Ghanaian President Kwame Nkrumah, and Indonesian President Sukarno, Khrushchev had found friends who shared his belief in rapid economic growth through central planning and who welcomed Soviet support for the anticolonial struggle. The specter of rising Soviet influence galvanized Kennedy and his advisors toward dramatic efforts to improve their position in the uncommitted world.

The United States was not merely concerned with particular nonaligned states; in 1961, it had cause to worry about the direction of nonalignment itself. By the time of the Vienna summit, the nonaligned states had laid plans for the Belgrade Conference, their first major meeting since Bandung. With the Berlin crisis continuing to escalate, civil wars raging in Laos and the Congo, and anticolonial revolts breaking out in Portuguese Africa, Kennedy and his advisors feared that a conference would forge a bond between the Soviets and the nonaligned leadership. The Kennedy administration sought, at the peak of the Berlin crisis, to sway the opinions of attendees to the Belgrade Conference. Faced with disappointing results, Kennedy nonetheless continued to engage the nonaligned states, using bilateral presidential diplomacy to considerable effect. These forays were generally successful, but the shift to bilateral approaches accompanied a gradual cessation of efforts to comprehend nonalignment as an international phenomenon. Events the following year, particularly the Cairo Economic Conference, the Cuban Missile Crisis, and the Sino-Indian War, spurred hopes within the White House that the policy of engagement was bearing real fruit, with Khrushchev's boasts refuted and communist influence in the postcolonial world on the wane.

THE BASES OF ENGAGEMENT

Engagement is best understood as an overarching strategy that, in turn, spurred Kennedy and his advisors to fashion particular stances on individual issues, most often involving questions of economic aid and local conflicts. Although some conflicts were understood to broadly affect a wide range of relationships, and whereas some aid initiatives assumed an Aswan-like symbolism, most of these questions were either bilateral or regional. Engagement – aimed at a broad swath of the globe, from West Africa to the Indonesian archipelago – required a continual effort to reconcile wider goals with particular circumstances and, in the face of limited resources, to focus on some relationships rather than others.

---

[2] Memcon, Kennedy and Khrushchev, June 3, 1961, in *FRUS, 1961–1963*, 5: 182–197.

The nonaligned states represented a diverse group, ranging from the second-most populous state in the world to some of the smallest. Their leadership included revolutionaries, generals, elective leaders, priests, and monarchs. Several of these nonaligned states were recognizable as regional powers, particularly Egypt, Indonesia, and India. Others, although militarily weak, possessed a symbolic importance: Ghana held a special significance as the first sub-Saharan state to gain independence. Revolutionary leaders such as Algeria's Ahmed Ben Bella and Guinea's Sekou Touré enjoyed broad acclaim for their defiance of the colonial powers. Yugoslavia could legitimately claim a founding role where nonalignment itself was concerned. Size was not the sole determinant of influence within the group.

The nonaligned states that commanded the most attention from the Kennedy and Johnson administrations were still, unsurprisingly, the most powerful and populous: India, Egypt, and Indonesia. The New Frontiersmen considered India to be a proving ground for Western models of development and a major power with broad influence among the nonaligned states, potentially able to check the advance of China and thereby safeguard Southeast Asia.[3] Concern for the same region militated engagement with Indonesia, the area's largest state, itself rich in economic resources and positioned along critical sea lanes.[4] Egypt occupied a similarly important position at the juncture of Africa and Asia; its size, its proximity to the oil-rich Persian Gulf, and the unparalleled influence of its leader within the Arab world made engagement with Cairo a priority.[5] Traditional liberal capitalist concern with the preservation of global trade and access to strategic resources loomed in each case.

The diversity of the nonaligned caucus ensured a wide variance in the value assigned by U.S. policymakers to particular states and the bilateral goals associated with each relationship. Even during the Kennedy years, engagement was rarely discussed in a trans-regional manner. Policymakers, notably Robert Komer and Walt Rostow, sometimes wrote of policy toward nonaligned states in a global or comparative fashion, but the case-specific challenges of engagement most often required bilateral arguments. It is unsurprising, consequently, that the most general discussions and studies of nonalignment occurred during the first year of the Kennedy administration, in the months preceding the conference at Belgrade.

---

[3] Paper, Bureau of Near East and South Asian Affairs, "United States Relations with South Asia," undated, in DOS *FRUS, 1961–1963, Vol. 19: South Asia* (Washington: GPO, 1996): 181–189; Nick Cullather, *The Hungry World: America's Cold War Battle Against Poverty in Asia* (Cambridge, MA: Harvard University Press, 2010), 152–158.

[4] Robert J. McMahon, *The Limits of Empire: The United States and Southeast Asia Since World War II* (New York: Columbia University Press, 1999), 105–106; Matthew Jones, *Conflict and Confrontation in South East Asia, 1965: Britain, the United States, Indonesia, and the Creation of Malaysia* (New York: Cambridge University Press, 2002), 31.

[5] Memorandum, Robert Komer to Walt Rostow, June 30, 1961, in *FRUS, 1961–1963, Vol. 17: Near East, 1961–1962*: 173; Warren Bass, *Support Any Friend: Kennedy's Middle East and the Making of the U.S.-Israel Alliance* (New York: Oxford University Press, 2003), 76–78.

The most cohesive study of nonalignment made during the Kennedy-Johnson years came in a May 1961 paper by the State Department's Policy Planning Council (PPC). This was, in turn, based in large part on a British study drafted earlier in 1961.[6] The PPC paper spelled out fundamental assumptions about nonalignment and the purposes of engagement. Neutralism, as the PPC termed nonalignment, "is rather a political attitude than a moral conviction." Countries adhering to this outlook "cherish a spirit of militant anti-colonialism" with "anti-Western and anti-capitalist" inclinations. Neutralists were "susceptible to Communist lures" and their "craving for status and material advancement." At times they were "myopic, seeing issues through the haze of their own preoccupations and antipathies." This made them "difficult to deal with" as their policies reflected "irrational attitudes and extremist tendencies."[7]

Having offered these assessments, the PPC paper still recommended engaging the neutralists, with the aim of encouraging their development and independence. It reasoned that the West held a fundamental long-term advantage over the communist bloc in its dealings with uncommitted states. Whereas Washington and its allies could accept diversity, the bloc was irredeemably totalitarian and obsessed with "monolithic conformity." Consequently, the nationalism of nonaligned states could act as a "barrier to Communist penetration" so long as it was "exploited tactfully." These key beliefs undergirded engagement during its active lifetime. The PPC recommended a number of policies and provisos. Chief among these was a Rostovian emphasis on setting the development of nonaligned states ahead of seeking their support on major Cold War issues. In fact, the paper cautioned against regarding nonalignment as "a way station on the road to alignment" and against pressing uncommitted states "into a Cold War mold." Restraint and "dignified partnership" were the order of the day.[8]

Much of this was sensible, but the PPC study held two telling omissions. Although it referred frequently to the phenomenon of anticolonial sentiment within the nonaligned group, it treated this as an emotion, a psychological byproduct of decolonization. This not only infantilized the nonaligned states; it also ignored the real fears felt by the new states of neocolonial assaults on their freedom. It also ignored the heartfelt conviction of Nehru and his peers that there was a moral case to be made for Cold War neutrality. Most critically, the document failed to recommend policies toward colonial conflicts. In a year already marked by strife in Algeria, Angola, and the Congo, and a growing crisis over West New Guinea, this absence was significant and consequential.

In other ways, the PPC document made apt statements. It cautioned against treating the nonaligned states as a unified bloc or making broad assumptions

---

[6] Planning Paper, Planning Section, "Neutralism: The Role of the Uncommitted Nations in the Cold War," January 30, 1961, FO 371/161211, TNA.

[7] Paper, Policy Planning Council, "Neutralism: Suggested United States Policy Toward the Uncommitted Nations," May 29, 1961, NSF, box 303, "Neutralism, General" folder, JFKL.

[8] Ibid.

about them. It reinforced the notion that successful nonalignment could serve to contain communism. It was, however, more platitudinous than specific. The study reflected a new tolerance of nonalignment but did not lay out tactics for engagement or a hierarchy of states to be targeted. No successor studies on nonalignment were to follow. As a result, engagement, from its very outset, was a bilateral or regional affair, with only occasional efforts to understand nonalignment comparatively, to grasp the problems that transcended individual relationships. This lack of subsequent study did not hamper the initial execution of engagement, but it denied policymakers a broader framework for grasping the challenges this endeavor was bound to face across cases.

THE PROBLEM OF CONFERENCES

After May 1961, U.S. analyses of the nonaligned movement as a whole were almost entirely tied to the group's regular conferences. The rapid decolonization of Africa in the late 1950s and early 1960s augured an expansion of the ranks of the nonaligned movement. With its greater size came enlarged influence – especially in votes on the floor of the United Nations – and profound debates about its future.

One consideration was whether the movement might ultimately evolve into a bloc in its own right. The Soviet Union seemed to hope for this outcome, which would assist it in remaking the structure of the United Nations and the broader international system. Angry at the role of the UN in advancing what he saw as Western aims in the Congo, Khrushchev proposed dramatically revising the body by designating three blocs: a Western bloc, a Communist bloc, and a nonaligned bloc. Each bloc would have equal representation within the UN bureaucracy and a veto. This proposal, tendered in the fall of 1960, worried the Eisenhower and Kennedy administrations – enough so that Kennedy mentioned it in two of his annual addresses to Congress. A nonaligned bloc promised to assist the Soviet Union on a number of issues, creating incentives for each partner to trade votes: Communist support on anticolonial issues, for African and Asian support on East-West disputes. Persistent collaboration between the two risked forging a tight bond and opening the nonaligned states to Soviet influence, paving the way for the communization of the postcolonial world. In the eyes of Western policymakers, the "troika" proposal, as it was known, was a kind of worst-case scenario for the nonaligned movement.

For this and other reasons, Washington and its allies regarded each major meeting of the nonaligned states with apprehension. Greater openness to the nonaligned powers on an individual basis did not reduce fears of how these states would act in concert. Holding little hope that the conferences would endorse Western stances on Cold War issues, the White House hoped at least to keep them from producing group statements endorsing Soviet positions.

Liberals and pragmatists argued for greater American involvement in the conferences. By encouraging attendance and publicly welcoming the contributions that the conferences offered toward world peace, the United States might reduce or minimize the damage done by the events. The State Department favored a far more restrained approach; Secretary of State Dean Rusk and his subordinates suspected that the United States would be perceived as meddling, should it take an active role in influencing the conferences. As they saw it, these conferences were likely to exacerbate feeling against the West, their agendas were stacked with grievances against European colonial powers, and their leaders were loath to admit wrongdoing by either communist power. Any attempt to influence their proceedings would merely disturb the bees' nest further.

Both factions, however, supported engaging particular nonaligned states bilaterally through presidential diplomacy. Kennedy's direct dealings with nonaligned leaders offered what seemed to be the best antidote to the problems posed by ideologically charged conferences. Working actively, through direct communication between heads of state, the administration sought to address the issues that most concerned the nonaligned world, while forging interpersonal bonds with the new elites of Africa and Asia.

The ultimate goal of this approach was the creation of what Rostow termed a community of free nations: a deep, collaborative bond between the Americas, Europe, and the former colonies of Africa and Asia, that would secure its constituents from communist subversion, while easing the former colonies' path toward development and prosperity.[9] This was, in effect, the polar opposite of the nightmare scenario offered by the troika proposal. A vital first step toward this new, transformative ordering of the international system would be the evolution of the nonaligned conferences into more moderate events – meetings more concerned with promoting collaboration than offering condemnation. That in turn would enable the White House to surmount Congressional opposition to aiding the nonaligned states. By 1961, the nonaligned leaders already suffered from poor reputations in the United States; editorialists and Congressional foes of foreign aid depicted them as sanctimonious, demagogic, often pro-communist windbags. United States policymakers and diplomats were, themselves, dismayed at the failure of the nonaligned leaders to condemn Moscow and Peking, even as they engaged in what seemed to be ritualistic condemnations of the Western powers and colonialism.

Much of this frustration stemmed from semantic confusion. Americans in and out of government largely understood the term nonalignment as a synonym for neutrality. The term "neutralist" was commonly used to describe nonaligned states; yet that word found little currency among the peoples and elites to whom it referred. "Neutralist" added a false familiarity to nonalignment. It seemed to link it to fundamentally Western ideas of neutrality, which did not accommodate the more expansive agendas of nonaligned states. Thus, when Kennedy and Eisenhower sought to reach out to nonaligned states, they often reflected upon America's own period of neutrality, particularly in the first decades of the Republic. Valid comparisons could be made, but

[9] See Memorandum, George McGhee, December 5, 1961, in DOS, *FRUS, 1961–1963, Vol. 8: National Security Policy (MS)* (Washington: GPO, 1997): doc. 248.

this Americanization of the word obscured the striking differences between classical or American neutrality and the new phenomenon of nonalignment. Accordingly, the votes of nonaligned states at the United Nations were carefully tallied from year to year, as gauges of how each government leaned: had they voted with the United States or the Soviet Union? These scorecards came bereft of analyses of the particular issues at hand. The same logic was applied to the conduct of nonaligned conferences, with only occasional reference to their overall character and direction.

U.S. policymakers should have noted how often nonaligned leaders defined nonalignment at their gatherings; this would have conferred a sense of just how amorphous, disputed, and flexible this term remained. Some conceptions of nonalignment – notably that of Nehru – roughly approximated the Western idea. Nehru saw the group as a barrier against the expansion of the Cold War, a movement committed to national self-determination, concerned about broad issues of war and peace, but especially committed to noninterference. Nehru wanted as broad a group as possible. He was eager to see its ranks extend outside the postcolonial world to include states in Europe and Latin America. He implicitly rejected developing a politically unified movement, standing against ideological or geopolitical litmus tests. The Indian prime minister was a devoted supporter of the UN, believing that it offered mankind its best hope of avoiding another world war. Though he was capable of resorting to force when necessary, Nehru showed a consistent concern that disputes might escalate into war; accordingly he fretted at excesses of anticolonial ideology or the notion of forming a nonaligned "Third Force."[10]

Other nonaligned leaders, notably Indonesia's Sukarno and Ghana's Kwame Nkrumah, contended that nonalignment required positive commitments to combat colonialism and expedite the freeing of peoples still under the colonial heel. Their more militant or "positive" approach made them less interested in the abstract principle of noninterference. In their view, the freedom struggle was paramount. International institutions such as the UN were gauged and supported according to their effectiveness in advancing this goal. Nkrumah and Sukarno repeatedly emphasized their commitment to advancing the welfare of African and Asian peoples above all else. They proclaimed colonialism, neo-colonialism, and imperialism to be the greatest threats to peace and held that solidarity among nonaligned states was essential to the common defense.[11]

To Nkrumah and Sukarno, Nehru's principles were perhaps noble in their own right but beside the point while many millions of Africans and Asians still languished under colonial rule. Furthermore, the sense of balance that

[10] Sarvepalli Gopal, *Jawaharlal Nehru: A Biography, Vol. 3: 1956–1964* (London: Jonathan Cape, 1984), 185; Jawaharlal Nehru, *India's Foreign Policy: Selected Speeches, September 1946–April 1961* (Bombay: Government of India, 1961), 77–79, 86, 184–187, 216–225.
[11] See, for example, Kwame Nkrumah, *I Speak of Freedom* (New York: Praeger, 1961), 175–177, 245–281; George McT. Kahin, *The Asian-African Conference, Bandung, Indonesia, April 1955* (Ithaca: Cornell University Press, 1956), 39–51.

Washington might have expected of a truly neutral power was also a useless quality. Insofar as the Soviet Union and the People's Republic of China were willing to support the anticolonial struggle, they were to be regarded as valuable friends; their misdeeds in Eastern Europe or Tibet did not merit the same kind of disapproval as those of the colonial powers. Much confusion might have been averted had the organization been christened the Anticolonial Movement, but the name endured – long after the Nehruvian conception of nonalignment was superseded by this more activist outlook. The increasing prevalence of the anticolonial stance, rising in tandem with decolonization and colonial conflicts, served only to complicate Washington's efforts to comprehend the phenomenon of nonalignment.

THE ROAD TO BELGRADE

The U.S. goal of averting the emergence of a cohesive nonaligned bloc benefited greatly from these internal divisions among the nonaligned states themselves. As at Bandung, differences in geopolitical interests, ideology, and personality divided the leaders of the nonaligned states. Even as it sought to maintain its position in the movement, India played a pivotal role in shaping U.S. expectations of the upcoming summit. India's consequent role as a tacit ally of the United States among the nonaligned states is one of the lesser-known aspects of the Indo-American relationship.

As chronicled by the Indian journalist G. H. Jansen, Nehru waged a long, uphill struggle to define nonalignment, both at Belgrade and afterward. Over time Nehru had become increasingly wary of his nonaligned peers, whom he viewed as headstrong and incautious. Dependent on Western aid, and hoping to avoid the fallout of another Bandung-like meeting, Nehru tried in vain to forestall another conference. Nasser and Tito, however, served him with a fait accompli, publicly declaring that they would hold a conference later in 1961.[12] Nehru was displeased, although Nasser and Tito made no effort to exclude him from critical discussions about the impending conference. Having been "dragged" into Belgrade, Nehru wanted to prevent the conference from becoming dominated by militant sentiment. Failing that, he wanted to clearly distinguish India's position from that of its peers. He stipulated to Nasser and Tito that the conference should not offer a platform for attacking adversaries or pursuing national agendas. In addition, Nehru called for inviting European neutrals, such as Austria – thereby stifling the possibility that the conference might catalyze the emergence of a third bloc.[13] He told U.S. Ambassador John

[12] Telegram 1893, Cairo to Washington, May 22, 1961, NSF, box 252A, "Belgrade, Conference of Non-Aligned Nations [1 of 2]" folder, JFKL; G. H. Jansen, *Nonalignment and the Afro-Asian States* (New York: Praeger, 1966), 280–282. More than four decades after publication, this remains the best account of the early nonaligned conferences.

[13] Telegram 1893, Cairo to Washington, May 22, 1961, NSF, box 252A, "Belgrade, Conference of Non-Aligned Nations [1 of 2]" folder, JFKL; Telegram 2022, Cairo to Washington, June 15, 1961, ibid.; Letter 10717/61, Cairo to London, May 16, 1961, FO 371/158874, TNA.

Kenneth Galbraith that he planned to attend, but "without much enthusiasm," hoping to ensure that the conference was "as sensible as possible."[14] Conversations between American and Indian diplomats in Cairo further helped to shape U.S. expectations; the Indian ambassador there, Azim Hussein, emerged as a key conduit of information about the impending conference.

In early June 1961, representatives from states handpicked by Nasser and Tito met in Cairo to plan the Belgrade Conference. The question of attendance proved particularly divisive. India, backed by other Asian states, advocated an inclusive conference, one defining nonalignment in the broadest way possible, encompassing European neutral states. The Indian delegation, however, found itself consistently outvoted on these questions. A more ideologically restrictive schema prevailed, limiting African and Latin American attendance and excluding European neutrals.[15] Nehru's delegation extracted a pledge that the conference would dedicate itself to overarching international issues, not the parochial concerns of individual attendees. Nonetheless, the Cairo meeting represented a setback to Indian foreign policy and underscored to Nehru the need to keep Washington and London informed. He still hoped for a moderate conference and, paradoxically, tried to enlist the help of aligned powers to safeguard his vision of nonalignment.

Despite having entered office determined to improve relations with the nonaligned states, the Kennedy administration's initial reaction to the announced Belgrade Conference resembled Eisenhower's noncommittal response to Bandung, impeded by bureaucratic inertia and expectations that the event would assume a largely anti-Western character. The escalation of the Berlin crisis that summer, however, led the White House to attach increasing significance to Belgrade, eliciting in response a far more direct approach to the conference. During that anxious summer, Belgrade became a critical litmus test of nonaligned opinion on the East-West confrontation and an early gauge of Kennedy's progress in the Third World.

This initial passivity stemmed from the State Department's belief that the conference would inevitably produce an array of resolutions critical of the United States and its allies. The State Department argued for a "hands off approach" toward the Belgrade Conference. Rusk's department had been particularly influenced by a dispatch from Cairo, reporting on Indian concerns about the direction of conference planning.[16] Ironically, India had been trying through informal Indo-American conversations in Cairo to calibrate Washington's expectations of the gathering. Nehru's subsequent communications showed

---

[14] Telegram 2083, New Delhi to Washington, June 23, 1961, NSF, box 106, "India: General, 6/16/61–7/31/61" folder, JFKL.

[15] Jansen, *Nonalignment*, 278–290; Despatch 21, Cairo to London, June 17, 1961, FO 371/161212, TNA; Letter, P. H. Gore-Booth to N. Pritchard, July 25, 1961, FO 371/161215, TNA, Telegram 1151/61, New Delhi to Bonn, June 30, 1961, B34/324, AA.

[16] Telegram 2299, Washington to Vienna, June 19, 1961, NSF, box 252A, "Belgrade, Conference of Non-Aligned Nations [1 of 2]" folder, JFKL; Circular CG-1019, June 6, 1961, NSF, box 439, "Non-Aligned Conferences, 1961–1963, Cairo-Belgrade [2 of 2]" folder, JFKL.

that he wanted Kennedy to aid his own efforts to moderate the conference. Instead, India's initial communication fueled the more fatalistic outlook dominant within the State Department.

Rusk did not mandate an entirely silent response to Belgrade. Over the summer, the State Department opted to work on a bilateral basis to explain American positions on nuclear testing and other disarmament issues to the conference attendees.[17] This did not, however, prevent the U.S. ambassador to Brazil, John M. Cabot, an outgoing Eisenhower appointee, from instigating a minor squall by implying that attendance would violate Brasilia's commitments to Washington. News of Cabot's remarks reverberated well outside of Brazil.[18] Tito's government felt "deeply affected and hurt" by their impression that Washington was acting to undermine the conference, interpreting each subsequent declined invitation as evidence of U.S. pressure.[19]

Alarmed by the strength of the Yugoslav anger, U.S. Ambassador to Yugoslavia George F. Kennan asked the State Department to issue a statement affirming that it did not oppose the gathering. The department replied that such a statement would likely be misinterpreted; the "hands off" policy remained the best available option.[20] As reports of U.S. tampering with the conference continued to reverberate, the administration's response to Belgrade resembled nothing so much as the uneasy silence of its predecessor toward the Bandung meeting.

Here, a helpful contrast may be drawn to the British stance in the months preceding the conference. The government of Harold Macmillan also worried that Belgrade would produce a stream of anti-Western resolutions but concluded that it might be a less inflammatory event if moderate governments were discreetly encouraged to attend. The Cabot affair baffled the British. Philip Ziegler of the Foreign Office complained that the administration was "allowing their obsession with Cuba to intrude" in an instance when "really Cuba is of little significance," bemoaning the American tendency "to draw a distinction between neutralism in Latin America and elsewhere."[21]

The "hands off" policy endured into August, despite growing opposition from Kennedy's White House staff, who were, in turn, galvanized by a wave of setbacks in the Third World. The first of these was the belated announcement of

[17] Circular Telegram 140, Washington to Various Posts, July 22, 1961, ibid.
[18] Memcon, Tito and Kennan, July 17, 1961, Schlesinger White House Files – Classified, box WH-25, "Belgrade Conference" folder, JFKL. See James G. Hershberg, "'High Spirited Confusion': Brazil, the 1961 Belgrade Non-Aligned Conference, and the Limits of an 'Independent' Foreign Policy during the High Cold War," in *Cold War History* 7 (August 2007), 373–388.
[19] Telegram 115, Belgrade to Washington, July 31, 1961, Schlesinger White House Files, WH-25, "Belgrade Conference" folder, JFKL; Telegram 526, Belgrade to London, August 1, 1961, FO 371/161215, TNA.
[20] Telegram 116, Belgrade to Washington, August 1, 1961, NSF, box 209, "Yugoslavia: General, 1/61–8/61" folder, JFKL; Telegram 110, Washington to Belgrade, NSF, box 252A, "Belgrade, Conference of Non-Aligned Nations [1 of 2]" folder, JFKL.
[21] Letter, Philip Ziegler to P. Murray, July 10, 1961, FO 371/161214, TNA; Minutes, WP13/41, Ziegler, July 17, 1961, ibid.

the murder of the popular former Congolese Prime Minister Patrice Lumumba on February 13. Lumumba had embodied the hopes of African nationalists and his death brought fierce cries of outrage directed at the United States and its Belgian ally.[22] Subsequent United States support for a coalition government in the Congo diminished the most stringent criticism, but the memory of Lumumba's killing remained painfully fresh in the minds of nonaligned leaders as they approached the Belgrade Conference.

In April, the failed Bay of Pigs invasion of Cuba marked the second major setback experienced by the United States. The invasion – plainly the handiwork of the CIA – brought scorn and condemnation from the nonaligned leaders. Tito and Nasser sent a joint communiqué promising to take "all available measures" to protect Cuban sovereignty.[23] Nkrumah sent his personal congratulations to Castro.[24] Notably, the Indian response was the most restrained. Nehru abstained from criticism for two days, until Washington's culpability was fully apparent, and then expressed his dismay that the invasion would complicate world tensions, particularly in Laos.[25]

Surveying the scene on April 21, Walt Rostow of the NSC worried that the "greatest problem we face is not to have the whole of our foreign policy thrown off balance" by the Bay of Pigs debacle. The invasion had seemed to set the United States on the same "obsessive" level as the European colonial powers. Worse, it set a dangerous precedent for other powers. The Bay of Pigs had been a response not to overt aggression, but rather to the presence of an ideologically objectionable regime; as such it could legitimate Chinese aggression in Southeast Asia, with results that would be "murderous for Nehru." Forging a grand partnership – one that would somehow incorporate nonaligned, non-communist states such as India – required a distinct change of tactics.[26]

Thirdly, just weeks before the conference, a French clash with Tunisia fostered outrage in Africa and Asia. Tunisia was enmeshed in a dispute with France over French use of the naval base at Bizerte, which lay within Tunisian territory. Tunisia's President Habib Bourguiba blockaded the base during the summer of 1961, and then in July began military action against the French garrison. In retaliation, Paris launched a combination of armored and aerial attacks on the Tunisian forces in and around Bizerte. In a pitched battle, more than a hundred Tunisians – soldiers and civilians alike – were killed.[27] The shock of Bizerte reverberated around the world.

[22] Letter, Sekou Touré to President Kennedy, February 14, 1961, NSF, box 102, "Guinea, General 1/61–5/61" folder, JFKL; Richard Mahoney, *JFK: Ordeal in Africa* (New York: Oxford University Press, 1983), 69–73.

[23] Jay Walz, "Nasser and Tito Vow Aid to Cuba," *NYT*, April 20, 1961, 13.

[24] "Nkrumah Praises Castro," *NYT*, April 24, 1961, 2.

[25] Nehru, *India's Foreign Policy*, 587–588; Andrew J. Rotter, *Comrades at Odds: The United States and India, 1947–1964* (Ithaca: Cornell University Press, 2000), 70.

[26] Memorandum, Rostow to Kennedy, April 21, 1961, NSF, box 303, "Policy Planning, 2/11/61–5/61" folder, JFKL.

[27] See Matthew Connelly, *A Diplomatic Revolution: Algeria's Fight for Independence and the Origins of the Post-Cold War Era* (New York: Oxford University Press, 2002), 249–254.

The event dismayed Washington. Bourguiba was no anti-Western radical – he seemed, if anything, the ideal Middle Eastern leader. His government was credibly nationalistic but also staunchly anticommunist. Bourguiba had emphasized internal development over regional prestige and the Kennedy administration hoped to make Tunisia an economic example for Africa and the Middle East. Komer termed Tunisia "one of the bright little spots in the Afro-Arab world," deserving of "rather special treatment."[28] Perhaps recalling the Suez crisis, Bourguiba hoped that such sentiment would bring support from the Kennedy administration and pleaded for American assistance in securing the removal of French forces from Tunisian soil.[29]

If Bourguiba vested serious hope in American intervention, he was to be disappointed. The Berlin crisis highlighted France's vital contribution to Western security. Moreover, French President Charles de Gaulle's domestic position seemed uncertain throughout 1961, as he faced the possibility of a right wing coup by officers disgruntled with his policies in Algeria. His perseverance in office represented the only hope of ending the war in Algeria – another irritant on relations between the West and the postcolonial states. De Gaulle skillfully exploited Kennedy's fears of a coup in Paris, warning that the future of NATO and his own hold on power would depend on Washington's reaction to Bizerte.[30] Kennedy was inclined to accept this explanation, remarking:

With all his defects, de Gaulle represents the only hope of gaining a solution in Algeria. Our sympathy continues to be with the nations throwing off the bond of colonialism; but the cause of anti-colonialism will not be helped by the overthrow of de Gaulle.[31]

Consequently, when Tunisia repeatedly raised the Bizerte question in the UN Security Council, the United States opposed resolutions that would humiliate France and weaken de Gaulle.[32] Bizerte cast a long shadow over the upcoming Belgrade meeting.

Finally, and most critically, the escalating Berlin crisis gave the Kennedy administration particular cause to worry about the character of the deliberations at Belgrade. Policymakers in the White House and State Department came to see international opinion as a vital factor in the standoff and feared that the nonaligned states might accept and promulgate the Soviet interpretation of the crisis and extend diplomatic recognition to East Germany. Paradoxically, however, Berlin preoccupied policymakers to the exclusion of almost all else; although it gave some observers cause to be concerned with Belgrade, it also made reversal of established policy more difficult.

[28] Memorandum, Komer to Rostow, July 12, 1961, NSF, box 444, "Tunisia: 1/61–11/63, White House Memoranda" folder, JKFL.
[29] Telegram 106, Tunis to Washington, July 22, 1961, NSF, box 444, "Tunisia: 1/61–11/63 2 of 2" folder, JFKL.
[30] Editorial Note, DOS, *FRUS 1961–1963, Vol. 21: Africa* (Washington: GPO, 1995): 254–255.
[31] Memorandum, Schlesinger to Stevenson, August 23, 1961, ibid.
[32] See Contingency Paper, undated, NSF, box 70, "France, General, 10/61" folder, JFKL.

As these crises and setbacks built upon one another, impatience with the "hands off" policy grew within the White House. Presidential aide Arthur M. Schlesinger worriedly noted to National Security Advisor McGeorge Bundy that the State Department had failed to assign anyone to design a strategy for responding to the conference. If the administration failed to plan for the conference, Schlesinger wrote, "We will repeat the Bandung situation where everything was ignored till the last minute."[33] Komer also argued for a more active posture. Objecting to the pessimism he perceived in the State Department's stance, he asked Rostow and Bundy:

What do we have to lose if we make a try and fail? Will the conference be any more anti-American than otherwise? Will the emergence of a neutralist bloc with anti-US overtones be thereby facilitated? (If this is the way things are going, they'll do so anyway). In sum, I'm afraid we have a typical example of foreign policy caution outweighing the possibilities of influencing a key conference.[34]

Komer perceived a real need to inform attendees of American positions on core issues such as Southeast Asia, the troika question, a nuclear test ban, and Berlin. The alternative, as he saw it, was a *greater* risk that the conference would go beyond the expected denunciations of colonialism and endorse a broadly anti-American document. A month later, with the "hands off" policy still in place, Komer again wrote his colleagues to ask whether it could be revised, citing the concerns of West Berlin Mayor Willy Brandt that the conference could endorse Soviet proposals for the divided city. In frustration, he proposed a run around the secretary of state, suggesting that Kennedy could ask Rusk pointedly if the "hands off" policy was really worthwhile.[35]

Yet even while the "hands off" policy remained the State Department's preferred response to Belgrade, the worsening Berlin crisis drove Rusk and his peers ever closer to making some kind of effort to minimize the harm done by the conference. By the middle of July, Rusk was thinking actively about the role of world opinion in the standoff. In a paper outlining Western objectives, the secretary explored the possibility of using Berlin as a wedge issue, specifying the need to seek "maximum support of world public opinion to make aggressive moves by Khrushchev as costly as possible in other areas in which he was interested."[36]

Such thinking was on display in early August when Rusk met with his French and British counterparts. Rusk stressed that the Berlin crisis stood to affect both the U.S. and Soviet positions elsewhere in the world. Khrushchev believed that he had the sympathy of a number of neutral non-communist countries;

---

[33] Memorandum, Schlesinger to Bundy, July 31, 1961, NSF, box 252A, "Belgrade, Conference of Non-Aligned Nations [1 of 2]" folder, JFKL.

[34] Memorandum, Komer to Rostow and Bundy, June 21, 1961, NSF, box 439, "Non-Aligned Conferences, 1961–1963, Cairo-Belgrade [White House Memoranda]" folder, JFKL.

[35] Memorandum, Komer to Bundy and Rostow, July 25, 1961, ibid.

[36] Paper, Rusk, "Outline on Germany and Berlin," July 17, 1961, in DOS, *FRUS, 1961–1963, Vol. 14: Berlin Crisis, 1961–1962* (Washington: GPO, 1993): 207–209.

deprived of that support, the Soviet premier would be less confrontational and more willing to compromise. Rusk wanted to ensure that the allies had a coherent message for the world, preferably before the Belgrade conference convened. Absent efforts by the Western powers to clarify their position, there was a real risk that the September UN session would endorse Moscow's position – particularly in the wake of Bizerte.[37] Rusk, in short, sought to force a choice upon Khrushchev: abandon his brinksmanship or face a loss of prestige throughout the Third World. Policymakers also wanted to avert the risk that critical UN resolutions might damage the Western position.

This concern for neutral opinion was but one component of the multipronged White House strategy during the crisis, but it mandated, in turn, a reconsideration of the "hands off" policy toward Belgrade. Swaying world opinion on Berlin reinforced Komer's logic that there was good cause to dispatch a message to the conference. Within the White House, a clear consensus emerged for stating a coherent Western stance on the crisis – particularly a willingness to negotiate with Moscow – before the nonaligned leaders convened.[38] The East German construction of a physical barrier between the Allied and Soviet halves of Berlin on the morning of August 13, 1961, heightened Kennedy's interest in using the crisis as a "good propaganda stick" in the battle for world opinion.[39] He recognized that this, in turn, required demonstrating a real commitment to negotiate with the Soviets.[40] He held to this stance, despite the opposition of de Gaulle, who doubted the value or impartiality of world opinion and worried that offering to talk would only encourage Khrushchev and demoralize West Germany.

During August Kennedy grew particularly interested in world opinion on the crisis. He accepted Rusk's reasoning that if Moscow were perceived as acting recklessly, that perception could be employed against the Soviet Union. Kennedy became increasingly frustrated when this did not occur. When the nonaligned states accepted the division of Berlin without outrage, his brother, Attorney General Robert F. Kennedy, complained: "Assume the tables were turned and we were responsible for what the Russians have just done. The hue and cry, the riots and disturbances around the world, would be echoing and reechoing at this very moment."[41] Days later, the president wrote to Kennan, Bowles, and Stevenson: "I have read recently that the neutral nations have been unimpressed by our arguments about our rights and obligations in West Berlin." Why, the president asked, was it impossible to gain support on this fundamental issue? Giving voice to a sense that he was damned either way, Kennedy observed:

We seem to be caught between two unsatisfactory alternatives. If we respond vigorously to Khrushchev's pressure, we are regarded as beligerant [sic] and saber-rattling and we

[37] Memcon, Ministerial Consultations on Berlin, August 5, 1961, ibid., 269–280.
[38] Memorandum, Bundy to Kennedy, "Berlin Negotiations and Possible Reprisals," August 14, 1961, *FRUS, 1961–1963*, 14: 330–331.
[39] Memorandum, Kennedy to Rusk, August 14, 1961, ibid.: 332.
[40] See Letter, Kennedy to de Gaulle, August 24, 1961, Digital National Security Archive.
[41] Memorandum, Robert F. Kennedy to Kennedy, August 17, 1961, NSF, box 82, "Berlin, 8/17/61" folder, JFKL.

lose support. If we attempt to work out our difficulties by negotiation, as in Laos, we are regarded as weak and on the decline.[42]

Kennedy's liberal advisors rushed to seize the opportunity offered by the telegram. Bowles advised Kennedy to approach Berlin as an issue of self-determination, to take more steps consonant with African and Asian opinion on colonial disputes such as Bizerte, and to do so with a public statement to the Belgrade Conference. Stevenson echoed these points, emphasizing the importance of colonial questions.[43]

The president's concern with world opinion gave an added salience to the urgings of both the White House staff and nonaligned governments to address the Belgrade Conference. On August 21, Galbraith, circumventing State Department channels, directly cabled the White House from New Delhi, noting that it had been "informally suggested" that a presidential message to the conference would make a "very good impression" on the attendees.[44] Three days later, Komer urged Schlesinger to approach Kennedy on the issue, observing that the Soviet Union was now prepared to send its own message to the conference. This, at long last, tipped the balance. On August 25, after speaking to Schlesinger, Kennedy abruptly overruled the "hands off" policy and called for the drafting of a presidential message to the conference.[45] The text of Kennedy's statement was distributed to the embassies of the conference attendees on August 29 and issued at a press conference the next day.

The final statement was laudatory, brief, and general. It stressed the shared values of the United States and the conference attendees. Invoking the American Revolution, it explicitly likened the nonaligned states' struggle for self-determination, development, and peace, with America's own historical struggles. The statement made no direct mention of Berlin or the question of a test ban, stating instead that whereas the attendees did not consider themselves committed on Cold War issues, they were undoubtedly committed to the principles of the UN Charter.

With this sudden shift in policy toward Belgrade came, ineluctably, heightened hopes and expectations. The summer-long crisis placed extraordinary stress upon the president and his aides, as they faced the real possibility of war over Berlin. Under such circumstances, it is understandable that the White House clutched at the hope that the message emerging from Belgrade might

---

[42] Telegram HYWH2, Kennedy to Stevenson, Bowles, and Kennan, August 20, 1961, NSF, box 86a, "Berlin, Neutral Nations Support" folder, JFKL.

[43] Memorandum, Bowles to Kennedy, August 22, 1961, NSF, box 82, "Berlin, 8/22/61" folder, JFKL; Memorandum, Stevenson to Kennedy, August 23, 1961, NSF, box 86a, "Berlin, Neutral Nations Support" folder, JFKL.

[44] Letter, Galbraith to White House, August 21, 1961, NSF, box 252A, "Belgrade, Conference of Non-Aligned Nations [1 of 2]" folder, JFKL.

[45] Memorandum, Schlesinger to Charles Johnson, August 25, 1961, ibid.: Arthur M. Schlesinger Jr., *A Thousand Days: John F. Kennedy in the White House* (Boston: Houghton Mifflin, 1965), 518–519.

restrain Khrushchev. The fate of Berlin, Kennedy believed, should be an issue of concern to nonaligned states: was this not a fundamental question of freedom and self-determination? Here, he felt, was an opportunity for the nonaligned states to demonstrate that they applied their principles impartially. This seemed all the more true after Khrushchev, on the eve of the conference, broke his three-year atomic test moratorium, exploding a massive nuclear device at the Semipalatinsk test range, in present-day Kazakhstan.

The Soviet test resumption abruptly transformed both the atmosphere surrounding the conference and Washington's expectations for the gathering. The Soviet test was a dangerously provocative act, providing further opportunity for the conference attendees to prove that they were what Kennedy deemed "truly nonaligned." It gave even Rusk, who still fretted that it was undignified for Washington to address a conference to which it had not been invited, cause to hope for positive statements. He abandoned his own "hands off" policy, proposing to ask a friendly delegation to propose the observance of a minute of silence over the Soviet test.[46]

Washington did not succumb to unfettered optimism. Attendees such as India, Burma, and Afghanistan continued to signal low expectations for the event. Kennan cautioned that much of the conference rhetoric would not be friendly to the West. By this point it was too late; the perceived mix of dangers and opportunities had driven the White House to invest far more importance in the conference than it had previously. As the proceedings commenced, on August 31, 1961, they were scrutinized exactingly by an exhausted president and staff, torn between their anxieties and their hopes.

INDECISION AT BELGRADE

The nonaligned states perceived heightened tensions and expectations as their delegations gathered in Belgrade, but the divisions within their ranks had not disappeared. The discussions at Belgrade further widened the chasm between India and other attendees, marring the image of nonaligned unity. Whereas a number of delegations arrived at Belgrade determined to discuss colonial issues – even after the Soviet nuclear test – Nehru felt otherwise. He was in transit to Yugoslavia when the news from Semipalatinsk broke. Upon disembarking, he received word of the test from Indian journalists, who asked him for his response. Tito, Nehru's erstwhile host, attempted to intercede, dashing between the journalists and Nehru, exclaiming, "Later, later!" Unfazed, Nehru stated that he opposed nuclear testing under any circumstances.[47] This fleeting

---

[46] Transcript, Rusk and Edward R. Murrow, August 29, 1961, RG-59, Records of Secretary of State Dean Rusk, Transcripts of Telephone Calls, box 45, 8/1/61–8/31/61" folder, NA; Telegram 253, Washington to Belgrade, September 1, 1961, NSF, box 252A, "Belgrade, Conference of Non-Aligned Nations [1 of 2]" folder, JFKL.

[47] Jansen, *Nonalignment*, 294–295.

episode at the airport offered observers an early indication of the conference's fundamental divisions.

Nehru's speech to the conference reflected his desire to steer the meeting in a more cautious, strictly neutral direction and to emphasize questions of war and peace over those of colonialism and poverty. It proved to be most satisfying to U.S. observers and most disappointing to their communist counterparts. Nehru declared that he deeply regretted the Soviet decision to resume testing, observing that it had "enhanced" the danger of war. He termed this danger the most immediate issue facing the delegations at Belgrade. "Nothing is more important or has more priority to us," Nehru declared, "than this world situation of war and peace." He confined discussion of colonialism to the end of his speech, touching briefly on Bizerte. Even Nehru's remarks on Germany were mild; while he called for recognizing the "facts of life," this entailed accepting both two German states *and* access routes to West Berlin.[48] An East German analysis of his speech observed disappointedly: "Nehru has not recognized the danger emanating from West Germany and West Berlin."[49]

Tito's speech, on the other hand, proved the most frustrating to Western observers. The Yugoslavian leader seemed to accept wholly Khrushchev's rationale for the resumption of nuclear testing. His proposals for resolving the Berlin crisis hewed closely to Moscow's line, as he called for recognizing two German states, and he favorably contrasted socialist East Germany with West Germany, which he deemed "fraught and interwoven with remnants of fascist and revanchist conceptions and tendencies."[50] Sitting in the chamber, Kennan was appalled to find Tito's reaction to the Soviet tests "weaker and even more pro-Soviet than those of Nasser and Nkrumah," and that his statement on Germany contained "no word that could not have been written by Khrushchev."[51]

Other speeches by nonaligned leaders similarly disappointed Kennan and the administration. Nkrumah expressed his shock at the testing resumption, but he also called for the recognition of both German states and the admission of the Peoples Republic of China to the United Nations. It seemed to Kennan that Nkrumah had "reproduced [the] straight Soviet line" on Berlin. Sukarno avoided any mention of the test resumption and focused on condemning colonialism. Like Nkrumah, he demanded an end to colonialism within two years and called for the recognition of two German states side by side.[52]

[48] *The Conference of Heads of State or Government of Non-Aligned Countries* (Belgrade: 1961), 107–117; Telegram 372, Kennan to Rusk, September 3, 1961, NSF, box 252A, "Belgrade, Conference of Non-Aligned Nations [1 of 2]" folder, JFKL.
[49] Bericht, Außereuropäische Abteilung, September 15, 1961, MfAA, A 13966, AA.
[50] *Belgrade Conference*, 153–156.
[51] Telegram 377, Belgrade to Washington, September 4, 1961, NSF, box 252A, "Belgrade, Conference of Non-Aligned Nations [1 of 2]" folder, JFKL.
[52] *Belgrade Conference*, 25–39, 98–107; Telegram 372, Belgrade to Washington, September 3, 1961, NSF, box 252A, "Belgrade, Conference of Non-Aligned Nations [1 of 2]" folder, JFKL.

Nasser's speech, however, proved to be far less radical than expected. Predictably, the Egyptian leader assailed colonialism in Africa, but he spoke carefully on the German question, stopping short of recommending the recognition of the status quo. Additionally, Nasser expressed dismay at the resumption of testing by Khrushchev.[53] Like his colleagues, he appealed for negotiation at the highest levels between the superpowers, but he prudently refrained from offering a particular solution to the Berlin crisis. This apparent moderation impressed Washington, as did the role Nasser played in the critical negotiations that preceded the conference's final resolution.

Nehru had been nearly alone in his emphasis on global issues of war and peace, an emphasis that was submerged in a torrent of anticolonial rhetoric from other attendees. Behind the scenes, India proved a far stronger voice, if only because any final conference declaration required a stamp of approval from the largest of the nonaligned states. Nehru staunchly and successfully opposed any declaration that took a stance on the German question. Bitter discussions raged between India and its Asian allies, on the one hand, and the more radical West African states and Indonesia, on the other, over whether to include a deadline for the end of colonialism; again, the Indians prevailed and no deadline was issued. The latter group resolved to raise the issue again at a later date.[54]

Nehru also prevailed on another key demand: that the conference issue a document, separate from its main communiqué, that would warn of the dangers of war. This separate document ultimately took the form of letters to both Khrushchev and Kennedy. Following the conference, Nehru and Nkrumah conveyed one copy to Moscow; Sukarno and President Modibo Keita of Mali carried another to Washington (prompting Kennedy to muse that Khrushchev had gotten "the pick of the litter"). Perhaps venting some of his pent-up frustration, Nehru rebuffed Nkrumah's request to share a flight to Moscow, telling the Ghanaian to find his own plane.[55]

The Belgrade Conference was marred by discord within its meeting halls and overshadowed by superpower brinksmanship. Favoritism by the planners limited the number of attendees. Unsurprisingly, despite the best efforts of the Yugoslav government to promote the affair, it failed to live up to the idealism of Bandung. If nonalignment offered a more inclusive uniting principle than Afro-Asian identity, the concept failed to stave off serious disagreements among the attendees. The acrimony within the conference hall put to rest the specter of Khrushchev's troika proposal; no effective voting bloc could be forged from such a group. Despite this, Belgrade marked a

---

[53] *Belgrade Conference*, 40–51.

[54] Jansen, *Nonalignment*, 299–303. See also Vijay Prashad, *The Darker Nations: A People's History of the Third World* (New York: Free Press, 2007), 100–102.

[55] Jansen, *Nonalignment*, 299–305; Telegram 671, Belgrade to London, FO 371/161224, TNA; Schlesinger, *A Thousand Days*, 521; Telegram 418, Belgrade to Washington, September 5, 1961, NSF, box 252A, "Belgrade, Conference of Non-Aligned Nations [2 of 2]" folder, JFKL.

signal moment in the history of nonalignment: though fundamental debates about the goals and traits of nonalignment raged through the 1960s, the conference came to represent the formal emergence of the Non-Aligned Movement.

THE AFTERMATH

Having elevated its hopes on the eve of the conference, the White House now reaped the wages of disappointment. Frustration raged over the general failure to condemn the Soviet test resumption. Schlesinger wrote that Kennedy "spoke with great and acrid profanity about the neutrals," believing that they would have reacted far less mildly to an American nuclear test. Reflecting bitterly on the counsel he had received from his liberal advisors, the president remarked, "Do you know who the real losers were at Belgrade? Stevenson and Bowles."[56]

Washington's allies differed significantly in their assessments of the Belgrade Conference. The British Foreign Office regarded the conference as a "modest success" for the West – the vague appeal to Kennedy and Khrushchev avoided any specific endorsement of Soviet positions. When added to the "built-in antipathies" to the West felt by the attendees, Bizerte had made pro-Western resolutions unlikely to pass. Nehru had played a decisive role in moderating the conference, ensuring a "colorless" final resolution. London was even inclined to discount Tito's recourse to pro-Moscow rhetoric, noting that the Yugoslav leader would never have been inclined to align with the West at such a meeting. In sum, the nonaligned states seemed to have quietly asserted their independence from both East and West.[57]

More pessimistic analyses came from the continental allies. France's de Gaulle scoffed at the conference, wondering at the Anglo-Saxon interest in public opinion. "What is world public opinion?" he asked. "Is it the favorable opinion and support of uncommitted countries?" Belgrade, in his view, showed that it was "useless" to seek their support; they were only "motivated by fear" and feared the strongest power – the Soviet Union. Hence, they would not criticize Moscow, even when it broke the test moratorium.[58] The West German Foreign Ministry opined that more states had sided with the communist bloc than with the West. Attendees had "unanimously" rejected

[56] Arthur M. Schlesinger Jr., *Journals 1952–2000* (New York: Penguin, 2007), 133; Schlesinger, *A Thousand Days*, 520.

[57] Telegram 1037, London to Washington, September 11, 1961, NSF, box, "Non-Aligned Conferences, 1961–1963, Cairo-Belgrade [2 of 2]" folder; "UK Views on the Conference," September 12, 1961, FO 371/161225, TNA; Despatch 98, Belgrade to London, September 20, 1961, FO 371/161226, TNA.

[58] Telegram 2810, Paris to Washington, November 28, 1961, NSF, box 70, "France, General, 11/61–12/61" folder, JFKL; Circular Telegram 147, September 9, 1961, in MAE, DDF, 1961, Tome II (Paris: Imprimerie Nationale, 1998): 374–376.

the West German claim to be the sole legitimate German state, revealing a "fundamental separation" between the West and the neutralists. In Belgrade, Bonn's policy of denying recognition to East Germany had just faced its "most severe endurance test." In Bonn's view, the Soviet tests had cowed the neutrals into a pro-Moscow tilt.[59] An East German analysis agreed, noting with satisfaction that "the majority of participants recognized the reality of two German states."[60]

Kennedy's assessment of the conference remained sour in the days that followed its adjournment. It fell to Komer to sound a characteristically optimistic note amid the gloom permeating the White House. When the State Department recommended that Kennedy politely receive the message and confine any discussion with Sukarno and Keita to the business at hand, Komer fired off a series of memoranda, objecting to the "slightly standoffish" recommendations that the State Department had given Kennedy. In his words, Rusk's department was more concerned "with how to fob off these neutrals, rather than maximize the opportunity of using them." The guests would inevitably want to talk about Berlin or bilateral issues such as West New Guinea; why not utilize the meeting as a chance to communicate U.S. views?[61] Seizing on a suggestion communicated by Nasser, Komer recommended that Kennedy's reply to the conference declaration be issued to *all* conference attendees – not just to Sukarno and Keita.[62] Rostow also advised Kennedy to use the meeting to advance bilateral ties with both countries.[63]

Kennedy, surmounting his annoyance with the meeting, acted upon Komer's advice and seized a parting victory from the ambiguous outcome of the conference. He made a point of conversing privately with Keita, who had remained silent while the garrulous Sukarno spoke incessantly; the Malian appreciated the attention.[64] For his part, Sukarno was as charmed as ever by Kennedy. Some bitterness intruded on the visit, however. Rusk told Keita and Sukarno over dinner that the United States might have to imitate Khrushchev, since

[59] Telegram 532, Bonn to Washington, September 6, 1961, JFKL, NSF, box 252A, "Belgrade, Conference of Non-Aligned Nations [2 of 2]" folder; Telegram 189, Hermann Voigt, "Belgrader Gipfelkonferenz nichtgebundener Staaten," September 29, 1961, B34/324, AA; William Glenn Gray, *Germany's Cold War: The Global Campaign to Isolate East Germany, 1949–1969* (Chapel Hill: University of North Carolina Press, 2003), 124–131.

[60] See Memorandum, "Vorläufige Information über die Belgrader Konferenz," undated, MfAA, A 14375, AA.

[61] Memorandum, Komer to Kennedy, September 8, 1961, NSF, box 439, "Non-Aligned Conferences, 1961–1963, Cairo-Belgrade [White House Memoranda]" folder, JFKL; Memorandum, Komer to Rostow, September 8, 1961, ibid.

[62] Memorandum, Komer to Rostow, September 8, 1961, NSF, box "Non-Aligned Conferences, 1961–1963, Cairo-Belgrade [White House Memoranda]" folder, JFKL.

[63] Memorandum, Rostow to Kennedy, September 10, 1961, in DOS, *FRUS 1961–1963, Vol. 23: Southeast Asia* (Washington: GPO, 1994): 423–425.

[64] Walt W. Rostow, *The Diffusion of Power: An Essay in Recent History* (New York: Macmillan, 1972), 192–193.

he seemed to have been able to impress the conference attendees with his pre-conference show of force.[65]

Belgrade might have posed a setback to the administration's hopes, but Kennedy's reception of Sukarno and Keita showed that he had no intention of abandoning engagement. The conference underscored the depth of anticolonial sentiment in Africa and Asia and the apparent reluctance of nonaligned leaders to criticize Moscow. Discredited for the moment was the stratagem of forcing Khrushchev to pay a political cost in the Third World for his policies in Europe. Nonetheless, as Komer and Rostow argued, energetic, bilateral diplomacy still stood to keep nonaligned leaders from drifting into the Soviet camp. Together, the two men continued to advocate engagement, convincing Kennedy to continue on his prior course. More realistic, less grandiose goals emerged from their efforts.

At the end of September, Rostow sent the president a memorandum making the case for maintaining the policy. Nonaligned states were important, he asserted, because the United States retained a crucial interest in their developing along non-communist lines and pursuing foreign policies that would not aid the communist bloc. Their votes in the UN represented a third, "marginally important" concern. Repudiating recent strategy, Rostow observed that uncommitted states "can't really help us much nor should they hinder us much" on questions like Berlin. As Keita had observed, they consistently operated from a position of weakness, lacking military security and political stability and being overwhelmingly concerned with local issues.[66]

Critically, Rostow offered Kennedy an operational strategy for pressing forward with engagement, one seemingly based on sound statistical observation. Discounting ideology, he stressed that nonaligned states took positions based on their own calculation of national interest – and this could be altered over time. Attendees receiving U.S. aid, he argued, had generally taken more moderate positions. As evidence, he positively correlated aid received from Western sources with stances taken at Belgrade. This, as Schlesinger, later wrote, made "great sense" to Kennedy.[67]

Operating in tandem, Komer and Rostow provided Kennedy with rationales and strategies for persisting with engagement in Belgrade's wake. They deflated the exaggerated expectations he had held of influencing Soviet behavior through diplomacy in the Third World. Komer's arguments about diplomatic engagement and Rostow's case for the positive effects of aid offered seemingly sound, tested methods. Simultaneously, they reinforced the ongoing shift toward engagement as an almost exclusively bilateral enterprise, concerned with individual relationships and region-specific policies. Such a shift naturally placed more emphasis on the three largest nonaligned states: India, Egypt, and Indonesia.

---

[65] Telegram 524, Washington to London, September 15, 1961, FO 371/161223, TNA.
[66] Memorandum, "Neutralism and Foreign Aid; or Belgrade Reconsidered," Rostow to Kennedy, September 27, 1961, DDRS.
[67] Ibid.; Schlesinger, *A Thousand Days*, 521–522.

THE BILATERAL ANTIDOTE

The Kennedy administration's experience with conference diplomacy reinforced the opinion that the United States was at an inherent disadvantage when the nonaligned states congregated. Dealing with them individually offered hope for progress on separate fronts. Bilateral diplomacy, employing energetic ambassadors, offers of aid, and the calculated use of presidential diplomacy afforded the administration a chance to sound out the nonaligned powers, inform or "educate" them about the bases of American policies, and gradually sway them toward a more cooperative relationship.

The United States was well represented in the nonaligned capitals. Ambassadors such as Galbraith in India, John S. Badeau in Egypt, Howard P. Jones in Indonesia, William Mahoney in Ghana, and William Attwood in Guinea were consummate New Frontiersmen. A number of them – notably Galbraith, Badeau, Mahoney, and Attwood – were not career diplomats. Howard Jones, although a State Department veteran, had an established rebellious streak; after his arrival in Jakarta in 1958, he compellingly argued against the policy of subverting Sukarno.[68] Their informality and enthusiasm aided them; they were able to cast themselves as non-career diplomats, freethinkers, and straight shooters. Galbraith, Mahoney, and Attwood were friends of Kennedy, which bolstered their credibility to their hosts. Nkrumah, Sukarno, Nehru, Touré, and Nasser all seemed to have warm places in their hearts for their American ambassadors. Ambassadorial success was, however, dependent on presidential action. Ambassadors needed to demonstrate that they could influence policy, that their cables were not being consigned to somewhere in State Department cubbyholes. To that end, presidential diplomacy was necessary to cement relations with the nonaligned world.

When he entered office, Kennedy already had substantial experience in conversing with nonaligned leaders. In 1951, as a young congressman, he had met Nehru, but not entirely auspiciously – after a few minutes, the visibly bored Indian prime minister began staring at the ceiling.[69] Kennedy experienced greater success as he neared the presidency. In 1959, upon hearing that Guinean President Sekou Touré was visiting the United States, the senator flew to meet him outside Disneyland. John Morrow, the first United States ambassador to Guinea, wrote later of the meeting:

The Guineans ... were not more enthusiastic in their reactions to any other American than they were to Kennedy. They praised his youth, his courage, his astonishing knowledge of world affairs in general, and of the problems of developing countries in particular.[70]

---

[68] See George McT. Kahin and Audrey Kahin, *Subversion as Foreign Policy: The Secret Eisenhower and Dulles Debacle in Indonesia* (New York: Norton, 1995), 160–182.

[69] See Robert Dallek, *An Unfinished Life: John F. Kennedy 1961–1963* (New York: Little, Brown, and Co., 2003), 168.

[70] John Morrow, *First American Ambassador to Guinea* (New Brunswick: Rutgers University Press, 1968), 108; Schlesinger, *A Thousand Days*, 568; "Meet at Disneyland" Associated Press Wirephoto, *NYT*, November 3, 1959, 3.

Sukarno, too, had a favorable meeting with Kennedy while the latter was in the Senate; he expressed hope for improved relations as Kennedy took office.[71]

Kennedy proved to be an enthusiastic practitioner of presidential diplomacy. He preferred to act as his own secretary of state, as his advisors often observed. Foreign affairs engaged him more than domestic issues; consequently, he frequently impressed foreign visitors with his mastery of detail.[72] He tended to ask detailed questions of his guests, eliciting their views of world events and the domestic challenges they faced. Kennedy's April 1961 conversation with Sukarno was a case in point. Opposite his loquacious visitor, Kennedy made his points firmly and candidly, without papering over the real differences between the United States and Indonesia. When Sukarno asked, with some emotion, why the United States never supported the Indonesian claim to West New Guinea, Kennedy admitted that he had to weigh NATO relations in the equation. Sukarno had hoped for U.S. support on this question, yet was deeply impressed by his host. He remarked, "The Americans have a very well-informed President. He is charming and was very gracious to me. I feel that he can be ruthlessly practical when the situation calls for it."[73]

In many cases, nonaligned leaders felt a real rapport with Kennedy. They viewed themselves as dynamic and idealistic and saw in Kennedy a kindred spirit. His commitment to advancing civil rights for African-Americans especially impressed African leaders (however belatedly Kennedy pursued this goal). These factors enabled Kennedy, in turn, to speak with candor. When meeting Keita, Kennedy remarked that U.S. national security sometimes required it to side with European powers on colonial questions, such as Portugal's refusal to leave its African colonies, although he desired the end of colonialism itself. Keita expressed his appreciation for Kennedy's frankness. This was among the most charged international issues for the Malian leader, but Kennedy's presentation of the U.S. perspective helped to assuage significant differences and to make the meeting as a whole a success.[74] Kennedy was similarly candid during his concurrent meeting with Sukarno, speaking emphatically about the Berlin crisis. Sukarno and his foreign minister told Adlai Stevenson the following day that they were "particularly impressed by [Kennedy's] sincerity" on Berlin.[75] To these guests, Kennedy's candor was a sign of respect.

---

[71] Telegram 2176, Jakarta to Washington, January 27, 1961, NSF, box 113, "Indonesia, General, 1/61–3/61" folder, JFKL.

[72] First Interview, Robert Komer, June 18, 1964, OH, JFKL; Theodore Sorensen, *Kennedy* (New York: Harper & Row, 1965), 509–512.

[73] Memcon, Kennedy and Sukarno, April 24, 1961, in *FRUS, 1961–1963*, 23: 382–390; Editorial Note, ibid., 390–391; Memorandum to Kennedy, May 3, 1961, NSF, box 113, "Indonesia, General, 5/61–7/61" folder, JFKL.

[74] Memcon, Kennedy and Keita, September 13, 1961, NSF, box 140, "Mali, General, 8/61–9/61" folder, JFKL.

[75] Memcon, Kennedy and Sukarno on Belgrade and Germany, September 13, 1961, NSF, box 113, "Indonesia, General, Sukarno-Keita Visit" folder, JFKL; Telegram 774, New York to Washington, September 16, 1961, DSCF, 656.9813/9–1661, NA.

Kennedy's personal style constituted a sturdy pillar supporting engagement. His meetings with nonaligned leaders established strongly amicable bonds, amplifying the benefits of some policies and limiting the harm done by others. Posthumous tributes to Kennedy offered by nonaligned leaders were doubtless meant as political signals, but they also mirrored what these leaders had said about Kennedy during his lifetime.

Personal rapport must be eliminated as a factor when examining the remarkably warm regard that Egypt's Gamal Abdel Nasser held for Kennedy. The two men never met during Kennedy's term in office. Although the possibility of a meeting was broached several times, it seemed to risk serious domestic complications for JFK. Kennedy and his advisors desired a Nasser visit, but only after the groundwork for such a bold event had been carefully laid. The circumstances were never ripe; however, Nasser came to regard Kennedy warmly. He enjoyed cordial relations with U.S. Ambassador John Badeau, contributing to his perceptions about the Kennedy administration. More fundamentally, however, Kennedy's willingness to correspond frequently with Nasser had a remarkable impact. The Egyptian leader was fond of sending long, expressive letters, and Kennedy began his own correspondence with Nasser in the spring of 1961. The two leaders argued over the Bay of Pigs, but Nasser clearly appreciated the gesture. In May, Kennedy dispatched a letter to the leaders of the Arab world stating his desire for a peaceful solution to the Arab-Israeli conflict. To his vexation, he received some startlingly uncivil replies – notably from Saudi Arabia, a notional ally. Nasser's reply was, however, remarkably courteous, conveying his "immense satisfaction and appreciation" that Kennedy had raised the issue.[76] This exchange set the mold for an ongoing dialogue between Kennedy and Nasser that helped to improve relations between the United States and Egypt over time.

Kennedy's one apparent failure in the realm of presidential diplomacy came, ironically, in the one case in which shared interests were strongest. Among the nonaligned states, India best practiced what Kennedy saw as true nonalignment. By the 1960s, Nehru clearly desired favorable ties with Washington and was increasingly fearful of China; he also perceived Kennedy as more sympathetic to India than Eisenhower had been. With such broad areas of agreement, Kennedy and Nehru might have been expected to have especially productive talks when the latter visited the United States in November 1961.

The visit proved a great disappointment to the White House. Accounts of their meeting by administration sources allude to long silences and Nehru's impenetrable lethargy. Galbraith wrote that "Nehru simply did not respond"

[76] Letter, Nasser to Kennedy, August 22, 1961, POF, box 127, "United Arab Republic, General, 1961–1962" folder, JFKL. For more on the Kennedy-Nasser relationship, see Bass, *Support Any Friend*, 64–143; John A. Badeau, *The Middle East Remembered* (Washington: Middle East Institute, 1983), 174–177. Mohammed Heikal, *The Cairo Documents: The Inside Story of Nasser and his Relationship with World Leaders, Rebels, and Statesmen* (New York: Doubleday, 1973), 188–224, is also worth examining.

to Kennedy's questions, offering only "monosyllables or a sentence or two at most." This reticence shocked Kennedy; it was utterly contrary to his other experiences with nonaligned leaders. In the first ten months of 1961 he had met with a rather garrulous set of nonaligned leaders: Nkrumah, Tanganyika's Julius Nyerere, twice with Sukarno, and Keita (once Sukarno had left). His relatively succinct letters to Nasser had brought effusive, verbose replies. Kennedy felt most comfortable asking questions, letting his guest take center stage, and using comments and follow-up questions to direct the conversation. With a tired, disinterested, or uncommunicative Nehru, this technique failed. Kennedy and his advisors concluded that Nehru was a man past his prime, likening his vague replies to wisps of fog. Kennedy later called the encounter "a disaster ... the worst head-of-state visit I have had."[77] He may have been unduly critical of his guest; reports from the Indian side allude to a productive meeting.[78]

Whether Nehru's health, Kennedy's brashness, the generation gap between the two men, or some other unfathomable factor was at work, the Nehru meeting stood as a conspicuous anomaly amid Kennedy's interactions with nonaligned leaders. In any event, the president met with numerous other visiting Indian officials – almost always to better effect – and dispatched his wife on a successful trip to India the following year. Subsequent events in 1962 gave the United States good cause to see a bright future for Indian-American ties as well as relations with most other nonaligned states.

THE CAIRO ECONOMIC CONFERENCE

The first nonaligned gathering to occur after Belgrade represented one sign of progress to the New Frontiersmen. In July 1962, the nonaligned states held the Cairo Economic Conference of Developing Countries to address a serious shared economic predicament. Largely exporters of raw materials, the nonaligned states faced low export revenues stemming from a glut of their goods on the world market. The economic integration of Western and Eastern Europe into the respective Common Market and COMECON blocs left many former colonies with diminished access to what had once been their best markets. While the European Common Market continued to deepen, tariff barriers,

---

[77] Schlesinger, *A Thousand Days*, 522–526; Sorensen, *Kennedy*, 578; John K. Galbraith, *Ambassador's Journal: A Personal Account of the Kennedy Years* (Boston: Houghton Mifflin, 1969), 247–253. See also Andrew J. Rotter, *Comrades at Odds*, 23–24, 215–217; and Dennis Kux, *Estranged Democracies: India and the United States, 1941–1991* (Thousand Oaks, CA: Sage, 1994), 193–196.

[78] Most accounts have been based largely on American recollections of the meeting. However, on a subsequent stop in Paris, Nehru pronounced himself "satisfied" with his meeting with Kennedy and happy to see that the American people did not view the world with an "aggressive psychosis." See Telegram 2121–2128, Paris to New Delhi, November 22, 1961, in *DDF, 1961, Tome II* (Paris: Imprimerie Nationale, 1998): 621–622. The Japanese ambassador in New Delhi made a similar observation to his French colleague. See Telegram 1404, New Delhi to Paris, November 28, 1961, Inde 1956–1967, 224, MAE.

agricultural subsidies, and import restrictions obstructed commerce from outside its borders.[79]

As before, the nonaligned leaders had distinctly different agendas as they approached the conference. The 1962 Cairo Conference sought to address the economic uncertainties facing the nonaligned states. Yugoslavia was again a prime backer of the conference, feeling itself excluded from the economic blocs of Western Europe. Tito resented Yugoslavia's exclusion from the Common Market, which he blamed directly on German opposition. The previous fall, he had inserted language into the Belgrade conference declaration, decrying rising economic barriers and fluctuating commodity prices.[80] Tito hoped that an economic association of the nonaligned countries might revive declining export revenues and alleviate a worsening balance of payments. Nasser was receptive to the idea and eager to host a nonaligned meeting. For his part, Nehru had lost none of his concern about the tone of nonaligned gatherings but, seeking to maintain his and India's influence, elected to act as a sponsor of the event. His cosponsors were more conciliatory to him than they had been the preceding year, and India won what it had failed to gain in the preparations for the Belgrade Conference: a remarkably broad pool of invitees, including European neutrals and Latin American states. As before, Indian diplomats acted to keep their American counterparts informed about the conference's format and likely attendees.[81]

Concern in Washington focused on the role of Yugoslavia. Worrisome reports from Belgrade of Tito's animus against the Common Market prompted Komer to write to his colleague Carl Kaysen, on February 23, 1962, "We are damned fools if we don't take forestalling action before this snowballs."[82] Rusk, however, approached the conference with characteristic pessimism. Keeping the experience of Belgrade in mind, Rusk informed ambassadors from countries attending the conference that it would "almost certainly become a platform for attacking the economic policies of the West." He worried that the conference could ultimately endorse Khrushchev's call for the creation of a world trade organization to counter the ECM.[83] Once again, U.S. policymakers were caught between European and nonaligned opinion, without sharing a common view on the nature of nonalignment and how it might be approached. The

[79] Jansen, *Nonalignment*, 308–311; Sidney Dell, *Trade Blocs and Common Markets* (New York: Knopf, 1963), 168–208.

[80] Jansen, *Nonalignment*, 312; *Belgrade Conference*, 17–23.

[81] Telegram CA-3085, Ball to Various Embassies, June 20, 1962, NSF, box 439, "Non-Aligned Conferences, 1961–1963, Cairo-Belgrade [1 of 2]" folder, JFKL; Memorandum, Hilsman to Rusk, May 16, 1962, ibid.; Airgram A-456, Belgrade to Washington, May 12, 1962, ibid.; Jansen, *Nonalignment*, 314–315.

[82] Memorandum, Komer to Kaysen, February 23, 1962, NSF, box 439, "Non-Aligned Conferences, 1961–1963, Cairo-Belgrade [White House Memoranda]" folder, JFKL.

[83] Telegram 2189, Rusk to Various Embassies, June 29, 1962, NSF, box 439, "Non-Aligned Conferences, 1961–1963, Cairo-Belgrade [1 of 2]" folder, JFKL; Telegram 40, Washington to Cairo, New Delhi, July 5, 1962, ibid.

absence of a crisis atmosphere comparable to that of the preceding summer ensured that the Cairo Conference received less attention than its predecessor.

Nasser's opening address to the conference helped to set the event's moderate tone. The Egyptian leader emphasized the need for economic development, without unduly criticizing the Common Market.[84] As the State Department's E. S. Little noted,

It was a nine minute speech which in comparison to Nasser's usual style was remarkable not only for its restraint but also for its positive tone. Not once did the word 'imperialism' or 'neo-colonialism' appear, nor do any of the customary clichés and shibboleths which Nasser has used in the past to attack the West.

As the State Department's William Brubeck wrote, the conference was notably restrained on political matters. Ghana, Guinea, Mali, and Indonesia had attempted to introduce the topic of neocolonialism, only to be thwarted by other attendees. The result was dramatic: "a final declaration devoid of political invective," which did not "lash out at past grievances."[85] The Egyptian government deserved the lion's share of credit for this outcome, and Rusk thanked the Egyptian leader for the positive, constructive character of the final declaration.[86]

To advocates of engagement, the Cairo meeting offered real grounds for encouragement. Reports of a restrained conference focused entirely on economic development signified substantial improvement when compared to what they saw as the tiresome anticolonial theatrics on display at Belgrade.[87] To policymakers like Komer and Rostow, who believed that difficulties with the nonaligned states would pass with the age of colonialism, yielding to an era of development and cooperation, an event like the Cairo Economic Conference marked a real sign of progress, further anchoring the sense that, after the tumult of 1961, 1962 was to be a year of accomplishment.

1962: THE TURNING OF THE TIDE?

Kennedy's second year in office seemed a watershed year in U.S.–nonaligned relations. For much of that year, the White House perceived that real political gains were accruing in the Third World, products of prudent policy and communist blunders. Reflecting this new optimism, Kennedy wrote in early 1963: "Future historians, looking back at 1962, may well mark this year as the time

---

[84] *The Conference on the Problems of Economic Development* (Cairo: Ministry of Information, 1962), 19–22.

[85] Memorandum, Brubeck to Bundy, August 2, 1962, NSF, box 439, "Non-Aligned Conferences, 1961–1963, Cairo-Belgrade [1 of 2]" folder, JFKL.

[86] Circular Telegram 111, Rusk to Various Embassies, July 21, 1962, NSF, box 439, "Non-Aligned Conferences, 1961–1963, Cairo-Belgrade [1 of 2]" folder, JFKL; Memorandum, Brubeck to Bundy, August 3, 1962, NSF, box 445, "UAR 1961–1962 1 of 4" folder, JFKL.

[87] Memorandum, E. S. Little to Bundy, July 13, 1962, NSF, box 445, "United Arab Republic, 1961–1962 2 of 4" folder, JFKL; Memorandum, Komer to Bundy, July 19, 1962, ibid.

when the tide of international politics began at last to flow strongly toward the world of diversity and freedom."[88]

The expansion of U.S. aid to the nonaligned world, and its immediate effect on bilateral relations, provided one source of confidence to the United States. In December 1961 Kennedy approved, with considerable reluctance, funding for Ghana's Volta River Dam, and this seemed, in the near term, to improve relations.[89] After three successive six-month food aid agreements with Egypt, Kennedy authorized a grandiose three-year sale in October 1962, offering some $431 million in U.S. surplus grain to Cairo at concession prices. These grain sales were vital to the continued health of the Egyptian economy, and Nasser signaled his gratitude.[90] India was the largest aid beneficiary among the nonaligned states, receiving food and technical aid, a three-year grain sale of its own, and a pledge of $1 billion to stabilize its balance of payments.[91] After the summer resolution of the West New Guinea dispute, Indonesia also stood to receive a robust assistance package. The dispatch of Peace Corps volunteers across Africa and Asia earned Kennedy additional gratitude from nonaligned states.[92]

Additionally, by autumn Kennedy had earned considerable goodwill for positions he had adopted on colonial issues. U.S. policies on the questions of West New Guinea, the Congo, and Portuguese Africa pleased nonaligned leaders, fostering an image of Kennedy as a man sympathetic to the anticolonial struggle. In time, these feelings of satisfaction gave way to urgent pleas for further action, but 1962 marked a high-water mark for the administration on questions of national liberation. Khrushchev's challenge seemed to have been met.

Symbolic victories on nonaligned battlegrounds also fueled administration optimism. One such triumph occurred in Guinea – once again seemingly a bellwether of nonaligned opinion. In early 1961, the West African nation seemed on the cusp of allying with the Soviet bloc, and Khrushchev spoke of it as a key Soviet friend in the Third World.[93] As he prepared to depart for his assignment, Kennedy's ambassador to Guinea, William Attwood, observed in Washington a "widespread disposition to 'write Guinea off'" as lost to communism.[94]

---

[88] *PPP: John F. Kennedy, 1962* (Washington: GPO, 1963), v–vi.

[89] NSC Paper, "Ghana: Assessment Since Volta," June 13, 1962, in *FRUS, 1961–1963*, 21: 375–377.

[90] Memorandum, Komer to Kennedy, October 5, 1962, in DOS, *FRUS, 1961–1963, Vol. 18: Near East, 1962–1963* (Washington: GPO, 1995): 161; William J. Burns, *Economic Aid and American Policy Toward Egypt, 1955–1981* (Albany: SUNY Press, 1985), 121–134.

[91] Robert J. McMahon, *The Cold War on the Periphery: The United States, India, and Pakistan* (New York: Columbia University Press, 1994), 276–277.

[92] See Telegram 423, Jakarta to Washington, September 4, 1962, NSF, box 114, "Indonesia, General, 9/62–10/62" folder, JFKL. See also Elizabeth Cobbs Hoffman, *All You Need Is Love: The Peace Corps and the Spirit of the 1960s* (Cambridge, MA: Harvard University Press, 1998).

[93] Telegram 2365, Moscow to Washington, April 1, 1961, in *FRUS, 1961–1963*, 5: 119–120.

[94] William Attwood, *The Reds and the Blacks: A Personal Adventure* (New York: Harper & Row, 1967), 22.

Attwood rejected this pessimism; once installed in Conakry, he worked tire-lessly to reach out to Touré's government, while urging Washington to offer aid to Guinea. Touré responded favorably to these initial contacts.[95]

External circumstances further advanced Guinean-American relations. During the fall of 1961, Touré became increasingly agitated by a rise in left-wing opposition to his government. After a series of violent clashes with the opposition, Touré came to believe that Moscow was seeking to undermine him; objecting to contacts between some of his opponents and the Soviet and Czechoslovakian embassies, he expelled the Soviet ambassador in December. The entire episode occurred without any U.S. involvement or encouragement: Attwood had been hospitalized for polio in the United States, and Rusk pru-dently chose to neither publicize the fallout nor urge any course of action on Touré.[96]

By the fall of 1962, Attwood observed a definite change of atmosphere in Guinea. Government organs that had once publicized the Soviet line on various world disputes now observed stringent neutrality. Aid from the United States and other Western countries began to fill the vacuum left by the Soviets, who had dramatically reduced their contributions to Conakry. Touré, grateful for the new aid, now made a point of attacking "all the imperialisms" – a choice of phrase that had been employed by the pro-Western attendees at Bandung. Noting the changes in Conakry, Roger Hilsman of the State Department, wrote:

Guinea occupies a symbolic position which gives it a political importance out of all pro-portion to its size. Perhaps more than any country in Africa, it has become a testing ground for conflicting hypotheses about Africans and their relations with the non-African world.

As a state that had seemingly embraced and then rejected affiliation with the Soviet bloc, it stood as a powerful refutation of Moscow's claims to represent and understand the aspirations of the postcolonial world. With Guinea, the Kennedy administration experienced the type of victory that Dulles had sought with Aswan: the discrediting of Soviet promises. Kennedy called Guinea "a big small country."[97] His sentiment was further reinforced by Touré's reaction to the Cuban Missile Crisis that autumn.

Nonaligned reactions to the October crisis offered evidence of the progress made since the Belgrade Conference – none more so than in the case of Guinea.

---

[95] On Guinea's course after independence, see Mairi Stewart MacDonald, "The Challenge of Guinean Independence, 1958–1971," Ph.D. dissertation, University of Toronto, 2009.

[96] Attwood, *The Reds and the Blacks*, 60–66; Telegram 406, Washington to Conakry, January 3, 1962, in *FRUS, 1961–1963*, 21: 401. See Sergey Mazov, *A Distant Front in the Cold War: The USSR in West Africa and the Congo* (Stanford: Stanford University Press, 2010), 181–197.

[97] Attwood, *The Reds and the Blacks*, 66, 101–102; Memcon, Kennedy and Guinean ministe-rial delegation, May 10, 1962, in *FRUS, 1961–1963*, 21: 402–404; Telegram 24, Conakry to Washington, July 14, 1962, NSF, box 102, "Guinea, General 7/62–9/62" folder, JFKL; Research Memorandum, Roger Hilsman to George Ball, October 5, 1962, NSF, box 102, "Guinea, General 10/62" folder, JFKL; Memorandum, "Reflections on Egypt," Hubert Humphrey, October 22, 1961, NSF, box 445, "UAR, 1961–1962 3 of 4" folder, JFKL.

Poised along the westernmost tip of Africa, Guinea lay astride direct air routes between the Soviet Union and Cuba. Well before Soviet missiles were discovered on Cuba, the State Department worried about Guinea facilitating aerial linkages between the USSR and the island nation. Kennedy's decision to quarantine Cuba accorded real urgency to the question of a Guinea-Cuba air link. On October 23, one day after he announced the presence of the missiles, Kennedy cabled a letter to Touré imploring him not to grant landing rights to Soviet flights. Although the decision must have been difficult, Touré made it quickly. The next day Touré served notice that Guinea would not allow Soviet resupply flights to use its airfields.[98]

Although no response to the Cuban crisis could be quite as satisfying as Guinea's, the general reactions of the nonaligned states proved heartening to the administration. Sukarno's measured rhetoric about the crisis brought him a letter of thanks from Kennedy in early November.[99] Although Cairo formally opposed the blockade of Cuba, it spoke carefully and moderately. Following the crisis, Nasser sent Kennedy a graciously written letter that credited the administration with acting "in a manner devoid of aggressive incitement." One Egyptian official observed that, notwithstanding the tone taken by the official press, some 90 percent of the Egyptian population understood the reasons for the blockade.[100] India expressed sympathy, but was entirely concerned with its unfolding war against China. The crisis even brought a rare degree of moderation from Nkrumah.[101]

During the crisis, the nonaligned powers typically showed comprehension of U.S. policy. They largely enjoyed favorable relations with Cuba, a Belgrade Conference attendee, but also acted on a pragmatic desire to appease Washington in its hour of crisis. As states with their own profound concerns about security, they could fathom Washington's preoccupation with missiles in Cuba, and Kennedy's pledge not to invade Cuba showed him to be sensible in their eyes – comprehending, perhaps, their convictions about self-determination. The change in tone from their reaction to the Berlin crisis the previous year seemed striking.

Just as Kennedy confronted the Soviet Union, another major crisis was unfolding on the other side of the world. Over the previous several years Mao Zedong's insistence on redefining China's boundaries had led him inexorably into conflict with India over a barren, windswept stretch of terrain on the fringes of the Tibetan Plateau. The Indian army fared poorly in the initial days of fighting, and a desperate Nehru appealed to the United States for help. Meeting on October 26 with India's Ambassador B. K. Nehru (a distant cousin

[98] Telegram 331, Washington to Conakry, October 23, 1962, NSF, box 102, "Guinea, General, 10/12/62–10/31/62" folder, JFKL; Attwood, *The Reds and the Blacks*, 108–111.

[99] Letter, Kennedy to Sukarno, November 2, 1962, in *FRUS, 1961–1963*, 23: 648–649.

[100] "Blockade of Cuba is Opposed by U.A.R.," *NYT*, October 25, 1962, 22; Memorandum, Phillips Talbot to Rusk, November 2, 1962, NSF, box 445, JFKL; Telegram 698, Cairo to Washington, November 1, 1962, NSF, box 445, "UAR, 1961–1962, 1 of 4" folder, JFKL.

[101] Memorandum, Kaysen to Kennedy, October 29, 1962, in *FRUS, 1961–1963*, 21: 379–383.

of the prime minister), Kennedy pledged to aid India in its hour of crisis.[102] This
seemed a watershed event to the policymakers of the Kennedy administration,
validating their belief that communist expansionism would ultimately threaten
the nonaligned powers, compelling them into a closer relationship with the
West. As the United States and Britain began a sizable airlift to India, men like
Komer optimistically envisioned a realignment of the American relationship
with India and the consummation of an anti-Chinese alliance in South Asia.[103]

With these two autumn events foremost in mind and perceiving their policy of bilateral diplomacy to have been successful, advocates of engagement
entered 1963 believing that the previous year had witnessed remarkable progress. Komer wrote to Bundy in November:

> For my money, our real gains in [the] Afro-Asian world over last year have been with
> Nasser, Sukarno, Nehru, even Touré, not with our so-called allies.... All things considered,
> we're putting some real spokes in the Soviet wheel. That Moscow no longer has a free hand
> in such places as Jakarta and Cairo is alone worth all of our efforts to date.[104]

Rusk, usually less optimistic, reinforced this assessment in an annual report
on the just-concluded session of the UN, noting that the Sino-Indian War and
the Cuban crisis had made a deep impression on a number of nonaligned delegations, prompting them to conduct "agonizing reappraisals" of their prior
stances. Although colonialism remained an issue of key concern, potentially
dividing the United States from African and Asian delegations, the secretary
predicted, "As the number ... of colonial issues declines, the Soviet empire
stands out more and more prominently on the horizon."[105]

Kennedy shared this optimism. In his January 1963 message to Congress, he
spoke at length about the transformation of U.S.–nonaligned relations:

> What of the developing and nonaligned nations? They were shocked by the Soviets' sud-
> den and secret attempt to transform Cuba into a nuclear striking base – and by Communist
> China's arrogant invasion of India. They have been reassured by our prompt assistance
> to India, by our support through the United Nations of the Congo's unification, by our
> patient search for disarmament, and by the improvement in our treatment of citizens and
> visitors whose skins do not happen to be white. And as the older colonialism recedes, and
> the neo-colonialism of the Communist powers stands out more starkly than ever, they real-
> ize more clearly that the issue in the world struggle is not communism versus capitalism
> but coercion versus free choice.[106]

---

[102] Telegram 1677, Washington to New Delhi, October 27, 1962, in *FRUS, 1961–1963, 19*: 352–
353; Telegram 1687, Washington to New Delhi, October 28, 1962, ibid.: 360; Telegram 1443,
New Delhi to Washington, October 29, 1962, ibid.: 361.

[103] Memorandum, Komer to Bundy, November 6, 1962, NSF, box 322, "Robert Komer, 11/62–
12/62," JFKL. See also McMahon, *Cold War on the Periphery*, 286–296.

[104] Memorandum, Komer to Bundy, November 1962 (undated), NSF, box 322, "Robert Komer,
11/62–12/62" folder, JFKL.

[105] Memorandum, Rusk to Kennedy, "The 17th General Assembly," undated, in DOS, *FRUS,
1961–1963, Vol. 25: Organization of Foreign Policy; Information Policy; United Nations;
Scientific Matters* (Washington: GPO, 2002): 509–514.

[106] PPP: John F. Kennedy, 1963 (Washington: GPO, 1964), 16.

These assertions designated the high-water mark for the Kennedy administration's policy of engagement. The two crises of the previous autumn had seemingly confirmed JFK's belief that communist aggression and the waning of colonialism would eventually transform the outlooks of the nonaligned states – compelling them finally to realize that communism posed the greatest threat to them.

Such confidence was to prove short-lived. Colonial disputes in Africa and Asia that seemed quiet at that moment stood poised to intensify dramatically. Regional conflicts in Africa, the Middle East, Southeast Asia, and South Asia also flared anew as 1963 dragged onward. The Kennedy administration faced increasing difficulty persuading skeptical legislators of the value of aiding the nonaligned world, even as the nonaligned leaders themselves came to doubt the political and economic utility of receiving Washington's aid. Finally, the consequences of the violent November 1963 overthrow of South Vietnam's President Ngo Dinh Diem dragged the United States into an unrelenting quagmire in Southeast Asia, which further divided it from the nonaligned states. The progress of 1962 proved ephemeral and the optimism of the beginning of 1963 came at the sight of a false dawn. The overwhelming emphasis on bilateral action impeded the ability of senior policymakers to grasp the full force of these trans-regional factors or to avoid repeating the same mistakes in their responses, particularly after the Kennedy presidency came to its tragic, traumatic end. In no case would this be more true than in Kennedy and Johnson's response to the rising tide of anticolonial sentiment in the Third World.

4

"Getting the Worst of Both Worlds": The United States and Colonial Conflicts

From its inception, the policy of engagement forced the Kennedy administration to confront the problem of imperial remnants. Decolonization had advanced remarkably in the 1940s and 1950s, but significant areas of the globe remained under the formal or informal control of a colonial power. The Netherlands retained the western half of New Guinea; Belgian troops were ensconced in the Congo; and Portugal swore to retain its overseas empire for another five hundred years. Although Britain had led the way with decolonization, its lingering presence in Africa, on the Arabian Peninsula, and on the islands of Cyprus and Borneo marked it, too, as an imperial power. To the postcolonial states of Africa and Asia, the endurance of empire was intolerable, representing a far more ominous threat than the Cold War.

Without exception, the colonial disputes of the 1960s pitted Western European states against African or Asian peoples. These conflicts imposed delicate dilemmas upon the White House, as NATO allies demanded solidarity and nonaligned leaders implored the United States to demonstrate its support for decolonization. Caught between rival imperatives, policymakers were forced to debate the core principles of U.S. policy, often in the midst of a crisis. Clear answers were rarely forthcoming. The Kennedy administration both benefited and suffered from the heightened expectations that the nonaligned world placed on the president's shoulders. Having declared the age of colonialism over in 1957, Kennedy now bore direct responsibility, in the eyes of Third World leaders, for expediting the arrival of the post-imperial age he had heralded.

Simultaneously beset by a number of these disputes, the White House sought to devise strategies and rhetorical themes that might articulate the role of the United States in a decolonizing world. Debate centered on two courses: either defining a neutral middle course for United States foreign policy or actively expediting the end of the colonial era. Pragmatists like the NSC's Robert Komer favored the latter approach. In an April 21, 1961, memorandum to National Security Advisor McGeorge Bundy, entitled "Getting the Worst of Both Worlds," Komer noted:

It should now be clear to most observers that the US has made a significant change toward a more openly anti-colonial policy. But we have made this change through a series of pragmatic steps which both expose us to recriminations in detail and make it hard to reap the full benefit.

This change, as Komer saw it, came with real costs to existing alliances. U.S. policy toward colonial conflicts had sparked discord with NATO allies such as the Netherlands, Portugal, and Belgium. Komer advocated a dramatic change of course:

Instead of dealing ad hoc with each of these problems as they come along, we also need to explain our overall rationale to our allies. We should point out bluntly that the loss of these vestigial colonial remnants is inevitable, and could not be stemmed even if we intervened. The only result would be that we, along with our allies, would go down to defeat after having wasted money and lives and used up what good will we still have in the Afro-Asian world. Thus we have to inform our allies that we can no longer afford to follow such a policy.

Komer dismissed concerns that an anticolonial stance would jeopardize NATO unity, arguing that no member would withdraw from the alliance over colonial issues.[1]

An envisioned end of colonialism, moreover, figured prominently in the administration's grand strategy. Walt Rostow of the State Department's Policy Planning Council (PPC) believed that this transition was likely to usher in a new age of global cooperation. Throughout the Kennedy years, Rostow advanced the notion that the United States, acting with its Western European partners, should take the lead in forming a "community of free nations," fostering Third World development and shielding its members from communism. This vision depended upon the timely resolution of colonial disputes and the amelioration of antagonistic relationships between former colonizers and the postcolonial states. Rostow's vision of a cooperative community was shared by liberals in the State Department, such as Chester Bowles and G. Mennen Williams. They viewed support of decolonization as both a natural extension of traditional American ideals and a geopolitical necessity for the anticommunist struggle. Adlai Stevenson's work at the UN led him to recognize the critical importance of colonial issues to the body's numerous African delegations.

Along with the liberals, Komer argued that a public stance in favor of liquidating these colonial vestiges would enable the United States to redirect the attention of the nonaligned states toward what he termed "the 'neo-colonialism' of the Bloc." This was not a new goal. The Truman and Eisenhower administrations had implored nonaligned leaders to recognize Soviet behavior in Eastern Europe as a far more insidious and threatening form of colonialism. Communist rule represented the "far more iron tyranny" to which Kennedy

---

[1] Memorandum, Komer to Bundy, April 21, 1961, NSF, box 321, "Robert Komer, 4/17/61–5/15/61" folder, JFKL.

had alluded in his inaugural address. The advance of decolonization gave this
old argument new viability. Komer suggested that Kennedy frame his conversations with nonaligned leaders to argue that "the miseries of colonial disengagement are almost over." This was, of course, an optimistic statement that
badly underestimated the tenacity of pro-colonial sentiment in Europe and the
depths of anger in Africa and Asia over the endurance of foreign empires.[2]

More anxious analyses emerged from elsewhere in the State Department.
Observing the changing demographics of the UN and the increased weight
that body accorded to colonial issues, George McGhee of the PPC worried
that decolonization augured efforts to seek redress against the Western nations
to settle grievances of an economic or racial character. One of McGhee's colleagues from the Bureau of Intelligence and Research (INR), Allan Evans, wondered if the UN was destined to become "a vehicle for the underprivileged and
pigmented to get back at the privileged and white."[3] These were some of the
same anxieties that had haunted the Eisenhower administration on the road to
Bandung. In a less visceral, more prescient INR analysis, Thomas L. Hughes
questioned whether the United States could truly continue on its middle course
between its European allies and the postcolonial states. "In Asia we are really
dealing with two dilemmas," Hughes observed:

1.) our desire to engage the aid and support of our European allies in the area versus
the existing views of Asian nations toward colonialism, neo-colonialism, and big power
domination and 2.) the desire to have responsible regional allies firmly on our side versus the desire to make friends with the neutrals. Can we really hope, in the foreseeable
future, to have it both ways? Or will the determination to pursue both facets simultaneously be mutually destructive? Take, for example, our dilemma in the West New
Guinea dispute.[4]

This debate remained in the background, as crises over Berlin, Southeast Asia,
and Cuba dominated the attention of policymakers. Thus preoccupied, the
Kennedy administration proved unwilling to make any comprehensive declarations about colonies. In the absence of a Kennedy Doctrine on decolonization,
policy toward individual crises was determined on an ad hoc basis. The NSC
and State Department each shaped policy but neither enjoyed a free hand. The
pragmatists of the NSC and their liberal allies in the State Department held a
relative advantage during the crisis years of 1961 and 1962 but found frequent
cause to complain that the State Department's leadership was undermining
their efforts. Subsequently, a more cautious outlook associated with Secretary
of State Dean Rusk prevailed. Taking stock of the friction that anticolonial

---

[2] Memorandum, Komer to Bundy and Rostow, May 16, 1961, ibid.
[3] Memorandum, Jenkins to Walter McConaughy, June 1, 1961, in DOS, *FRUS, 1961–1963, Vol.
25: Organization of Foreign Policy; Information Policy; United Nations; Scientific Matters*
(Washington: GPO, 2002): 346–349.
[4] Memorandum, "Comment on the Basic National Security Strategy Paper," Thomas Hughes
to Rostow, March 6, 1962, in DOS, *FRUS, 1961–1963, Vol. 8: National Security Policy (MS)*
(Washington: GPO, 1997): doc. 182.

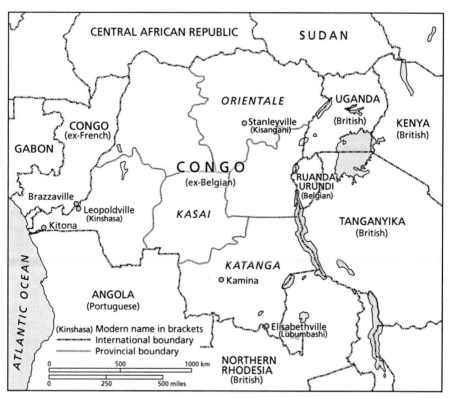

MAP 1. The Congo at Independence.

policies had added to relations with European allies, Kennedy and Johnson edged away from explicit opposition to colonialism from 1963 onward.

The Kennedy administration's initial support of decolonization brought short-term successes but long-term challenges. The policies of 1961 and 1962 fueled anticipation among nonaligned leaders that a greater commitment to decolonization was forthcoming – even as Washington grew increasingly chary of the costs of alienating European opinion. This cycle of action and raised expectations proved unsustainable. As the stakes and violence of colonial conflicts rose, the chasm between United States policy and nonaligned opinion became increasingly unbridgeable. Policies that seemed beneficial in the first months of the New Frontier ultimately became insufficient in the eyes of the nonaligned world. The full trajectory of U.S. policy toward colonial conflicts can be traced by examining four key cases: the Congo, Goa, West New Guinea, and Portuguese Africa.

"THIS UNSPEAKABLE CRIME": THE CONGOLESE CATACLYSM

The Congo crisis of 1960–1961 presented the Kennedy administration with its first hard choice between nonaligned and European opinion. The international furor that erupted after the killing of popular Congolese Prime Minister Patrice Lumumba posed the greatest threat to the position of the United States among the uncommitted states since the Suez crisis of 1956. Faced with an international uproar, Kennedy made a significant break from Eisenhower's policy and cultivated the support of nonaligned states, notably India, in restoring stability in the former Belgian colony. The Congo thus became a decisive early proving ground for his promises to deal differently with the nonaligned world, and, for a time, it was a success story.[5] His efforts to obtain and retain nonaligned support tried the patience of Kennedy's European allies.

No issue posed a greater challenge to the U.S. position in the Third World as the Kennedy administration took office. Growing African impatience with U.S. policy on Congolese issues facilitated the emergence of a coherent nonaligned faction, even before word broke of Lumumba's murder. In January 1961, Presidents Gamal Abdel Nasser of Egypt, Kwame Nkrumah of Ghana, Sekou Touré of Guinea, and Modibo Keita of Mali met in Casablanca, Morocco, where they proclaimed the establishment of a joint organization: the African Charter of Casablanca. The four presidents appealed for the release of Lumumba by his Congolese government captors, the withdrawal of all Belgians from the Congo, and unequivocal UN support of the central government. The Casablanca group also declared its willingness to struggle for the liquidation of colonialism throughout the African continent, a promise made good by Nasser's repeated efforts to ship Soviet-made weapons to Lumumba's supporters.[6] Touré and Nkrumah saw the Congolese leader as an ideological brother, committed to their dream of a unified Africa. Alarmed by Lumumba's detention, Nkrumah warned that his death would have "a most serious effect" on relations between Africa and the West.[7]

The crisis engulfed the new administration as soon as it took office. Threatened with the withdrawal of Casablanca group detachments from the United Nations Operation in the Congo (ONUC), the White House perceived a need to act rapidly to preserve the UN mission. A hastily convened Congo Task Force submitted, with Rusk's approval, a proposal for a reversal of policy. Turning their back on the Eisenhower policy of supporting Congolese President Joseph Kasavubu, the task force recommended seeking a broad-based government including supporters of Lumumba. Rusk wrote, "One of the principal purposes of the new policy is to reorient the United States position so that it will have the support of world opinion generally, and in particular the support

---

[5] Accounts of U.S. policy toward the Congo include Richard Mahoney, *JFK: Ordeal in Africa* (New York: Oxford University Press, 1983); Madeleine G. Kalb, *The Congo Cables: The Cold War in Africa – From Eisenhower to Kennedy* (New York: Macmillan, 1982); and John Kent, *America, the UN and Decolonisation: Cold War Conflict in the Congo* (New York: Routledge, 2010).

[6] W. Scott Thompson, *Ghana's Foreign Policy, 1957–1966: Diplomacy, Ideology and the New State* (Princeton: Princeton University Press, 1969), 152–157; "Casablanca Powers," *International Organization*, Vol. 16, No. 2 (Spring 1962), 437–439.

[7] Telegram 839, Accra to Washington, January 25, 1961, POF, box 117, "Ghana" folder, JFKL.

of principal segments of opinion in Africa and Asia." States like India, Nigeria, and Ghana were to be encouraged to "take the lead." Although the task force distrusted Lumumba, it considered his exclusion from the government dangerous, calling instead for a power-sharing arrangement that would include his followers.[8]

These recommendations had been crafted in an effort to balance the goal of excluding communist influence from the Congo with that of preserving the cooperation of moderate nonaligned states. Most critically, however, they were based on the assumption that Lumumba still lived. News of his death, when it broke in mid-February, enraged the more radical nonaligned states. In a letter to Kennedy, Touré declared, "This unspeakable crime destroys the hope that African nationalism had placed in your government."[9] Nkrumah termed Lumumba's death proof of the ends to which "imperialism and colonialism are prepared to go."[10] Nonetheless the two pan-Africanists hinted at the possibility of some accord with Washington. Nkrumah's condemnations were followed by entreaties that Kennedy should "take a new initiative" in the Congo, since "our ideas seem fundamentally so much the same."[11]

Moscow, meanwhile, worked to exploit the aftermath of Lumumba's death. Khrushchev sought to involve himself in the Congo, viewing it as a critical test of his approach to wars of national liberation. He had cultivated Lumumba as an ally and responded enthusiastically to the Congolese leader's request for military support in the summer of 1960. Lumumba's ouster, abduction, and execution incensed Khrushchev, who believed that the UN mission and Secretary General Dag Hammarskjold had been complicit in the act. Well before February 10, the Soviet leader had made the Congo a rallying call in his "troika proposal" to alter the governing structure of the UN.[12]

Khrushchev's full-throated denunciations of the UN served to escalate the situation, but paradoxically they helped Kennedy salvage the ONUC by appealing to India, one of its leading backers. Here, too, New Delhi stood at some distance from its African peers in the nonaligned movement. Nehru's paramount concern with the Congo, he told Undersecretary of State Chester Bowles before Lumumba's death, was keeping it from becoming a Cold War battleground.[13] Nehru was alarmed at the prospect of Soviet arms flowing into the territory. To Nehru the Congo represented a vital test case of the effectiveness of the UN.

[8] Memorandum, Rusk to Kennedy, February 1, 1961, in DOS, *FRUS, 1961–1963, Vol. 20: Congo Crisis* (Washington: GPO, 1995): 40–45.

[9] Letter, Touré to Kennedy, February 14, 1961, NSF, box 102, "Guinea, General, 1/61–5/61" folder, JFKL.

[10] Telegram 980, Accra to Washington, February 18, 1961, POF, box 117, "Ghana" folder, JFKL.

[11] Letter, Nkrumah to Kennedy, February 22, 1961, NSF, box 99, "Ghana, General, February 22–28, 1961" folder, JFKL.

[12] Aleksandr Fursenko and Timothy Naftali, *Khrushchev's Cold War: The Inside Story of an American Adversary* (New York: W. W. Norton, 2006), 292–322; William Taubman, *Khrushchev: The Man and His Era* (New York: W. W. Norton, 2003), 477, 488.

[13] Bowles to Kennedy, Notes, undated, POF, box 118a, "India, General, 11/60–5/61" folder, JFKL.

In January, Nehru was beginning to despair, declining a request by Hammarskjold for reinforcements to the ONUC.[14] He changed course in February, however, committing 4,700 troops to the mission – India's largest post-1947 external deployment of soldiers. Khrushchev's vehement attacks on the UN played a key role. Days after learning of Lumumba's murder, Nehru told an Indian audience, "The future of the UN is in doubt and if it fails, the future of humanity is in doubt."[15] Khrushchev unwittingly made Indian-American accord on the Congo far more likely with his assault on the UN.[16]

Nehru would not, however, have renewed his commitment to the ONUC without assurances that it could succeed. Here Kennedy's volte face on the Congo, specifically his shift toward support of a broad-based government, held critical importance. After Lumumba's death was announced, Nehru refrained from the more accusatory statements of his nonaligned peers, laying culpability at the feet of the Katangan separatists without castigating Kennedy. Instead, he stated that the United States, "under the new regime ... had definitely decided to change the old policies and do several things which we and others had been asking for."[17] He indicated that he would assent to the dispatch of combat troops to the Congo "if our views could be accepted." Indar Rikhye, the head of India's detachment in the Congo, attributed Nehru's change of heart to the messages he had received from Kennedy.[18]

In this turbulent atmosphere, the mandate of the just-salvaged ONUC remained a matter of debate. The nonaligned nations advanced a new resolution before the Security Council, which authorized the peacekeepers to use force to restore the sovereignty of the Congolese government. Heeding the objections of European allies, Rusk objected to the resolution, as did the State Department's European Bureau, but Stevenson succeeded in convincing Kennedy that excluding communism from the Congo required bolstering the ONUC, particularly as further Katangan atrocities came to light. Consequently, to the evident pleasure of African and Asian delegations, Kennedy decided to vote in favor of the resolution, which passed the Security Council.[19]

The passage of the UN resolution and the Indian deployment shored up the ONUC and induced relative moderation in the more radical nonaligned states. Nkrumah reaffirmed his support of the UN mission and implied that he now expected Kennedy to act forthrightly to preserve the country's territorial

---

[14] Telegram 2010, New York to Washington, January 26, 1961, RG-59, DSCF, 770G.00/1–2661, NA.

[15] "Nehru Demands Action," *NYT*, February 14, 1961, 16; "Nehru Calls for Strong UN Action in the Congo," *Chicago Tribune*, February 18, 1961, 4; Subimal Dutt, *With Nehru in the Foreign Office* (Calcutta: Minerva Associates, 1977), 272–273.

[16] Sarvepalli Gopal, *Jawaharlal Nehru: A Biography, Vol. 3, 1956–1964* (Cambridge, MA: Harvard University Press, 1984), 152–157.

[17] See Mahoney, *JFK: Ordeal in Africa*, 66; Rajeshwar Dayal, *Mission for Hammarskjold: The Congo Crisis* (Delhi: Oxford University Press, 1976), 227.

[18] Jawaharlal Nehru, *India's Foreign Policy; Selected Speeches, September 1946-April 1961* (New Delhi: Ministry of Information and Broadcasting, 1961), 525.

[19] Mahoney, *JFK: Ordeal in Africa*, 74–77; Kalb, *The Congo Cables*, 230–236.

integrity.[20] Once a critic of the ONUC, Nasser offered belated support to the mission. Touré, too, admitted that he had overreacted to Lumumba's murder and promised to assume a more moderate posture.[21]

Confronting the vacuum left by Lumumba's death, the Kennedy administration sought to avoid any further fragmentation of the Congo. Against the opposition of Rusk and the French and British governments, Kennedy proceeded to seek a broad Congolese government, one incorporating the faction of Lumumba's former deputy Antoine Gizenga, whom Rusk and the Europeans regarded as a dangerous radical. Kennedy held little more regard for Gizenga than did the Europeans but believed that he could be neutralized within a broader Congolese government. A combination of diplomacy and outright bribery ultimately resulted in the selection of the White House's favorite, labor leader Cyrille Adoula, as the Congo's premier.[22]

Apparent progress toward the formation of a Congolese government helped to placate nonaligned leaders. The change in attitude toward Washington's Congo policies was apparent at Belgrade – not so much in what was said, but in what was not said and in who was allowed to speak. While decrying apartheid and Portuguese colonialism, Nkrumah made no substantive mention of the Congo. Nor did Guinean Foreign Minister Louis Beavogui. Nasser merely mentioned Lumumba's murder and said nothing of events after February. Signifying broad acceptance of the new Congolese government, the conference allowed speeches by both Gizenga and Adoula. The final conference declaration addressed the Congo question in a moderate manner entirely acceptable to the Kennedy administration, declaring that the tragic events of early 1961 must never be repeated and calling for full Congolese self-determination.[23]

The problem of separatist Katanga remained unsolved. The nonaligned world demanded the restoration of government authority over the breakaway region. Bankrolled and armed by the Belgians, Tshombe's province seemed a neocolonialist cancer menacing not only the Congolese state, but all of free Africa. Adoula implored the United States to help him return Katanga to federal control. If he failed to defeat the separatists, Adoula risked overthrow by Gizenga. Establishing Adoula as a national leader required helping him to reintegrate Katanga, preferably without igniting civil war.

The project gained a tragic urgency after Hammarskjold died in an air crash on September 17, 1961. Despite a lack of support from Washington, Hammarskjold had committed the UN to the restoration of federal authority in Katanga. Shortly before his death, he had ordered UN units into the renegade

[20] Memcon, Kennedy and Nkrumah, March 8, 1961, in DOS, *FRUS, 1961–1963, Vol. 21: Africa* (Washington: GPO, 1996): 344–347.

[21] Telegram 3318, New York to Washington, June 13, 1961, in *FRUS, 1961–1963*, 20: 144–146; Airgram G-30, Ougadougou to Washington, May 13, 1961, RG-84, Guinea, Classified General Records, box 2, "320 – Guinea-U.S. Relations" folder, NA.

[22] Kalb, *The Congo Cables*, 240–281.

[23] *Conference of Heads of State or Government of Non-Aligned Countries* (Belgrade: Publicisticko-Izdavacki Zavod, 1961), 40–51, 98–106, 220–225.

province; stiff resistance by Katanga's mercenary defenders ground the UN offensive to a halt. Rusk objected to Hammarskjold's action; the communist leanings of Gizenga preoccupied the secretary of state more than Katanga did. With Hammarskjold now dead and the UN offensive stalled, Adoula's position seemed increasingly imperiled by the Gizengists and Katanga.[24]

Solving the latter problem was essential to solving the former. This, in turn, required the United States to support the Congolese government and the ONUC in their drive to bring Katanga to heel – over the vehement objections of European allies. Britain, France, and Belgium each viewed the UN operation with concern, reacting sharply to (often fabricated) reports of atrocities committed by UN soldiers against the Katangan civilian population. The European allies, moreover, held considerable investments in the mineral-rich province, giving them further reason to balk at any course of action threatening their commercial interests. France saw a particular need to demonstrate solidarity with its Belgian ally.[25] As one British diplomat remarked, the diplomats of the Foreign Office and the heads of the mining companies entrenched in Katanga had attended the same elite schools; they spoke to each other "in unfinished sentences."[26] Mindful of Britain's economic stake in Katanga and concerned about the dangers that prolonged fighting could pose to his neighboring colonies, British Prime Minister Harold Macmillan argued against military action, believing "no good could come of destroying Tshombe."[27]

Katanga proved a vexing question, not merely in late 1961 but throughout the next year. The Congo crisis elicited mercurial behavior on the part of the president and a number of his advisors. The chaotic situation on the ground and a chorus of cautioning voices mired Kennedy in frustrated indecision. Men like George Ball, who had advocated a hard line on the renegade province in the wake of Hammarskjold's death, drew away from confrontation after taking stock of European objections. Rusk and the CIA regarded Gizenga as their main problem in the Congo. Repeatedly overruled by Ball and Rusk on the Katanga question and fearful of the future of U.S.-African relations, Williams considered resigning.[28]

Tshombe sensed the State Department's hesitance; he knew when to feign conciliation and proved an expert at dragging his heels when actual concessions were demanded of him. Bankrolled by the Belgian mining concern

[24] Telegram 624, Washington to Leopoldville, October 13, 1961, in *FRUS, 1961–1963,* 20: 248–250.
[25] Note de la Direction d'Afrique-Levant, "France, Belgique et Congo," May 18, 1961, in *MAE, DDF, 1961, Tome I* (Paris: Imprimerie Nationale, 1997): 603–605.
[26] David Newsom, *The Imperial Mantle: The United States, Decolonization, and the Third World* (Bloomington: University of Indiana Press, 2001), 164.
[27] Harold Macmillan, *At the End of the Day, 1961–1963* (New York: Macmillan, 1973), 279–285; Nigel Ashton, *Kennedy, Macmillan, and the Cold War: The Irony of Interdependence* (New York: Palgrave Macmillan, 2002), 112–114.
[28] Thomas J. Noer, *"Soapy": A Biography of G. Mennen Williams* (Ann Arbor: University of Michigan Press, 2005), 254.

Union Minière du Haut Katanga and supported by the authorities of British Rhodesia, Tshombe was able to wait out the unstable Congolese government. Tshombe succeeded in further muddying the waters through his sponsorship of a highly effective lobbying effort in the United States. U.S. legislators, notably Connecticut Senator Thomas Dodd, lionized Tshombe as Africa's most ardent anticommunist, raising the domestic costs of an anti-Katanga policy.[29]

Adoula's weakness and the renewed threat of a UN withdrawal fostered a sense of crisis at the end of 1962, as the White House contemplated the near-term prospects of deeper entanglement in the Congo or a Soviet presence in Central Africa. Fighting between Adoula's and Gizenga's factions occurred throughout 1962; despite CIA action against the Gizengists, Adoula's hold on power continued to weaken. In December 1962, Adoula tearfully told U.S. Ambassador Edmund Gullion of Moscow's repeated offers of military assistance and his fears that the Congolese parliament and military would accept them.[30] As in 1961, the fate of the UN mission also hung in the balance, with the large Indian detachment likely to be withdrawn in early 1963 and the funding for ONUC near exhaustion. These factors played to the administration's anxieties. As Carl Kaysen of the NSC observed, the prospect of a Soviet presence in the heart of Africa was "the gut issue."[31]

Kennedy doubted the capacity of ONUC to defeat the Katangans and worried about being drawn into an African quagmire, particularly as his advisors urged him to commit U.S. aircraft in support of the UN forces. Kaysen, the NSC staff member most involved with the Congo, informed Kennedy that the United States faced a choice between involvement in the near-term reintegration of Katanga or witnessing the collapse of the UN mission, coupled with a severe blow to the organization's prestige.[32] George Ball agreed with this assessment, forcefully arguing to Kennedy during a lengthy meeting of the NSC's Executive Committee on December 17 that the administration faced the risk of "a substantial Soviet Union presence in a place which is about as strategically well-centered as any in Africa ... for the infection of the rest of the continent." Stevenson and Assistant Secretary of State Phillips Talbot argued that U.S. prestige in Africa hinged on a resolution of the Katanga problem.[33]

Facing a nearly united front among his advisors, Kennedy warily approved the use of U.S. equipment in support of the UN mission but held back on committing U.S. military forces. Events on the ground, however, contrived to bring the end of Katanga sooner than anyone in Washington had expected. As the administration watched uneasily, a UN offensive, arising haphazardly out of a

[29] Kalb, *The Congo Cables*, 310–312.

[30] Telegram 1321, Leopoldville to Washington, December 6, 1962, in *FRUS, 1961–1963*, 20: 708–710.

[31] Editorial Note, ibid.: 716–717.

[32] Memorandum, Kaysen to Kennedy, December 17, 1962, ibid.: 364–365.

[33] Draft Transcript, Executive Committee Meeting, December 17, 1962, JFK Library Transcripts, Tape 68, MC.

skirmish with the Katangans at the end of 1962, gathered steam, finally shattering the Katangan defenses in January 1963.[34]

Washington's middle path on the Congo led to not only a general improvement in its relations with African states but also a heightening of expectations. The U.S. stand on Katanga had bought it some credibility with leaders such as Touré of Guinea, who told an American diplomat in the spring of 1963 that the United States had come a long way in Africa, owing to Kennedy's "dynamic personality" and opposition to Katangan secession. It could, however, "lose everything" if Kennedy did not take a "forthright stand" on the Portuguese and South African questions.[35]

Washington's European allies were less pleased; indeed, the Congo emerged as a major source of trans-Atlantic discord. The first Katanga offensive was a source of contention between London and Washington. In December 1962, when he met the president at Nassau, Macmillan asked Kennedy to forestall UN action. He was concerned about British investments in Katanga and fearful of the fallout of prolonged fighting. Kennedy disregarded Macmillan's advice, dealing a blow to British prestige on the African continent. This in turn contributed toward what the historian Nigel Ashton has termed "a crisis of interdependence": an undermining of trust between London and Washington at the end of 1962. Anglo-American friction over the Congo compounded the damage done to bilateral ties by graver events, such as the U.S. cancellation of the Skybolt missile program.[36]

France was also disgruntled by U.S. policy. President Charles de Gaulle had made no secret of his opposition to the UN mission. Paris was angered by U.S. actions undertaken with minimal consultation in a Francophone area of the world, particularly the suppression of Katanga.[37] This added to frustrations over divergences of policy elsewhere in the world, notably Guinea, Algeria, and Indochina. Although de Gaulle's subsequent rejection of the Anglo-Americans, expressed in his January 1963 veto of Britain's European Economic Community application, stemmed primarily from European causes, the general chafed at Kennedy's policies in Africa.

Such defiance of allies was possible only because of the Congo's perceived Cold War significance. Kennedy did not act in the Congo with the primary intention of appeasing nonaligned opinion. Kennedy and Eisenhower approached the fractious new nation with the same objective: to deny communism access to one of the largest, most mineral-rich, and populous states in Africa. This goal drew both men, to varying degrees, to employ covert action; Eisenhower plotted against Lumumba, Kennedy worked to undermine Gizenga. Nonetheless,

[34] Kent, *America, the UN and Decolonisation*, 132–144.
[35] Telegram 854, Conakry to Washington, June 22, 1963, NSF, box 102, "Guinea, General, 6/63–7/63" folder, JFKL.
[36] See Ashton, *Kennedy, Macmillan and the Cold War*, 109–126, 223–226; Kalb, *The Congo Cables*, 302–322.
[37] See, for example, Telegram 1766–1777, Paris to London, February 4, 1961, in *DDF, 1961*, 1: 148–150; Telegram 548–558, Washington to Paris, February 5, 1961, ibid.: 151–154.

the Congo emerged as a fundamental test of Kennedy's belief in the intrinsic importance of working constructively with the nonaligned states. The choice of Adoula reflected and successfully met this objective. It is here that the distinction should be drawn. A combination of realism and careful diplomacy forged an Indian-American partnership that advanced both Cold War goals and the position of the United States in nonaligned capitals. Other nonaligned states could have played a spoiling role in the territory after Lumumba's death by opposing Adoula; that they did not testifies to the extent to which the Kennedy administration's policies satisfied them, at least for the time being. Declarations of victory in the Congo, however, invariably proved premature. The excruciating experience of crafting policy toward the fractured ex-colony over a period of two years offered a powerful cautionary tale as the administration confronted other colonial conflicts.

MORE REGRET THAN ANGER: THE CASE OF GOA

At midnight, on December 17, 1961, the Indian army unleashed Operation Vijay, dispatching 30,000 soldiers into three Portuguese colonial enclaves along the Arabian Sea: Goa, Daman, and Diu. Enjoying clear numerical superiority, India secured control of Goa, the largest enclave by far, within 36 hours. Portuguese resistance, although steep in places, fell short of Prime Minister Antonio Salazar's decree that his soldiers either "conquer or die." The 450-year Portuguese presence in South Asia, dating back to the age of the great explorer Vasco da Gama, had come to a swift, inglorious end.[38]

The fall of Goa represents an important and overlooked milestone in the development of anticolonial sentiment around the world. Although primarily studied for its effects on Indo-American relations, Goa had more profound consequences for a range of other colonial conflicts thousands of miles away. More than a brief crisis, Goa was a critical precedent for anticolonial action, auguring a broader intensification of nonaligned efforts against imperial remnants. Goa's fall was, in short, a sign of things to come.

Portugal's dominion over Goa dated to the early-sixteenth century, and Lisbon opted to retain its South Asian enclaves after India gained independence in 1947.[39] India objected vociferously to the perpetuation of colonial rule on the subcontinent but the challenges and traumas of partition preoccupied the government in New Delhi, making the Portuguese enclaves a secondary problem in the post-independence years. India hinted in the 1950s that it might resort to force if Portugal refused to offer Goa self-determination.[40] Salazar's dictatorial

---

[38] P. D. Gaitonde, *The Liberation of Goa: A Participant's View of History* (New York: St. Martin's Press, 1987), 157–169; Tom Gallagher, *Portugal: A Twentieth-Century Interpretation* (Dover: Manchester University Press, 1983), 155–156.

[39] Gallagher, *Portugal*, 4–8; M. N. Pearson, *The Portuguese in India* (New York: Cambridge University Press, 2006), 131–154.

[40] See, for example, Telegram 536, New York to Washington, January 11, 1957, in DOS, *FRUS, 1955–1957: Vol. 8, South Asia* (Washington: GPO, 1987): 110–113.

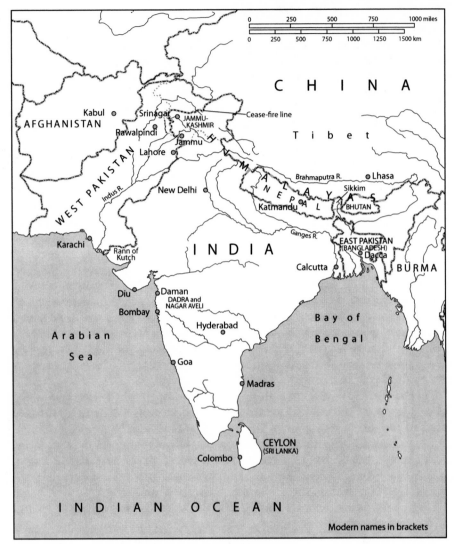

MAP 2. South Asia, 1961.

regime, however, belonged in spirit to another era, haunted by the ghosts of the
Portuguese imperial past. After a 1963 visit to Lisbon, George Ball mused that
Portugal seemed to be ruled by "a triumvirate of Vasco da Gama, Henry the
Navigator, and Salazar."[41] Accordingly, the Portuguese disdained suggestions
that Indian independence necessitated their departure from South Asia.

[41] George W. Ball, *The Past Has Another Pattern: Memoirs* (New York: W. W. Norton, 1982),
277.

Distracted by myriad crises around the world, the incoming Kennedy administration remained unaware that it would soon witness the liquidation of Portugal's Indian empire. The Goa dispute hardly appeared to be a problem requiring immediate attention. NSC planning documents from the first half of 1961, which identified West New Guinea and Portuguese Africa as potential areas of concern, omitted any mention of Goa.[42] India did very little to signal any escalating concern with the Portuguese enclave. Consequently, in crafting their India policy, the White House and the State Department focused on the question of economic aid, on New Delhi's policies toward crises in Laos and the Congo, and on Nehru's view of the Berlin crisis. Goa was simply not on the radar.[43]

This did not mean that the issue had receded from the Indian political arena or among the nonaligned states. Increasing unrest in Angola spurred Goans and their sympathizers in India to step up their efforts against the increasingly beleaguered Portuguese.[44] India's peers in Africa and Asia meanwhile regarded New Delhi's response to this continued colonial indignity as a litmus test of Nehru's credibility as a nonaligned leader and foe of colonialism.[45] The significance of this factor, according to Nehru's leading biographer Sarvepalli Gopal, cannot be overstated.[46] Nehru's domestic opposition, meanwhile, attacked the government for its failure to resolve the issue.[47]

This combination of international and domestic pressure and Nehru's own frustration shifted Indian policy gradually, although not imperceptibly, after the early summer of 1961. India denounced Portugal's conduct in Angola and formally annexed two inland South Asian enclaves, Dadra and Nagar Aveli, which Portugal had controlled until revolts in 1954, after which India had asserted effective albeit informal control. Lisbon's irate response to the annexations drew a warning from Nehru that he would not rule out the use of military action against the other enclaves.[48] In October, Nehru held an international conference on the subject of Portuguese colonialism. Encountering

---

[42] See, for example, Report, "Key National Security Problems," February 10, 1961, NSF, box 303, "Policy Planning, General, 1/61–2/10/61" folder, JFKL; Memorandum, Rostow to Kennedy (with attachment), February 23, 1961, "Policy Planning, General, 2/11/61–5/31/61" folder, JFKL; Memorandum, Komer to Bundy and Rostow, May 15, 1961, ibid.; Memorandum, Rostow, May 30, 1961, ibid.

[43] On the U.S. response, see Robert J. McMahon, *The Cold War on the Periphery: The United States, India, and Pakistan* (New York: Columbia University Press, 1994), 281–282; John K. Galbraith, *Ambassador's Journal: A Personal Account of the Kennedy Years* (Boston: Houghton Mifflin, 1969).

[44] "Goan Extremists Exploiting Troubles in Angola," *NYT*, May 21, 1961, 2.

[45] See Unnumbered Telegram, Bombay to Washington, September 18, 1961, RG-59, DSCF, 753D.00/9-1861, NA.

[46] Gopal, *Nehru*, Vol. 3, 194–195.

[47] Airgram A-168, New Delhi to Washington, October 31, 1961, NA, DSCF, 753D.00/10–3161, NA.

[48] "Paul Grimes, Nehru Threatens Force on Goa; Bars Portuguese from 2 Areas," *NYT*, August 18, 1961, 4.

criticism from African attendees, he hinted in his address that he planned to take action.[49]

Tension over Goa strained Portuguese-American relations, as Salazar began to press the Kennedy administration for a pledge of military support. On two separate occasions, Lisbon protested to the United States about India's rhetoric, prompting the State Department to inquire about the probability of an Indian invasion.[50] Ambassador John Kenneth Galbraith reported that Indian action remained improbable, while cautioning that Nehru would likely resent any U.S. "intrusion" in the matter.[51] Accordingly, Rusk informed Lisbon that Indian action seemed unlikely; hence, any warning to India would be "unproductive and unjustified by the situation."[52] For its part, New Delhi was determined not to raise the issue with the United States. During his November 1961 visit, Nehru scarcely mentioned Goa in his conversation with Kennedy.[53] The Indian government perceived no need to involve the United States in what it regarded as a purely regional affair; Washington had no desire to trouble New Delhi with Portuguese complaints. Galbraith continued, for vital days, to insist that military action remained unlikely.

Tensions on the ground escalated in the final week of November, as the Indian press reported that Portuguese soldiers had shot at Indian boats from the enclaves. Although reluctant, Nehru was driven by nonaligned peers and domestic foes to take action.[54] Mounting evidence of Indian preparations to assault the enclaves drove Galbraith to embark on an eleventh-hour effort. He sought to shift Washington from a stance of passive disapproval of Portugal's colonial empire toward active efforts to promote immediate self-determination. Aside from holding the strategically valuable Azores, a group of islands in the North Atlantic, Portugal was a negligible contributor to Western security, Galbraith argued. In Africa and elsewhere, "its hour" was fast approaching and the United States needed to avoid being, once again, seen as defending a colonial power. Even the loss of the Azores, Galbraith contended, could not do more damage than the "world-wide weakening of the United States because of the inability of our services to circumvent the need for a few acres of asphalt."[55] The ensuing debate highlighted deep internal divisions within the State Department more than it shifted policy. C. Burke Elbrick, the ambassador

---

49 Indian Council for Africa, Report of the Seminar on the Problem of the Portuguese Colonies (New Delhi: Indian Council for Africa, 1961), 3–28.

50 Telegram 460, Lisbon to Washington, October 10, 1961, NSF, box 155, "Goa, 10/11/61–12/10/61" folder, JFKL.

51 Telegram 1277, Washington to New Delhi, October 12, 1961, DSCF, 753D.00/10–1061, NA; Telegram 1093, New Delhi to Washington, October 13, 1961, DSCF 753D.00/10–1361, NA; Telegram 1220, New Delhi to Washington, October 27, 1961, DSCF 753D.00/10–2761, NA.

52 Telegram 424, Washington to Lisbon, October 18, 1961, DSCF 753D.00/10–1361, NA.

53 Memcon, Kennedy and Nehru, November 7, 1961, in DOS, *FRUS, 1961–1963, Vol. 19: South Asia* (Washington: GPO, 1996): 128–135.

54 Gopal, *Nehru*, Vol. 3, 190–203.

55 Telegram 1611, New Delhi to Washington, December 5, 1961, in DOS, *FRUS, 1961–1963, Vol. 13: West Europe and Canada* (Washington: GPO, 1994): 908–910.

in Lisbon, took offense to Galbraith's tartly written telegram. Writing with apparent irritation, Elbrick cited a recent governmental finding that the Azores constituted the "single most valuable facility" leased to Washington by a foreign government.[56]

The imminence of Indian action, the overwhelming likelihood of its success, and the value accorded to relations with New Delhi and the nonaligned world drove the White House to apply unprecedented pressure on Lisbon. In early December, Rusk urged the Portuguese to reconsider their stance on their colonies, regardless of whether Goa faced an immediate threat. Portugal should not count on the United States to oppose hostile actions against its colonies, Rusk added, if Lisbon proved unwilling to accede to one of the "historical imperatives of [the] day and accept and proclaim self-determination as the goal for its overseas territories." The United States could not allow itself to be seen protecting the status quo in Goa or elsewhere.[57] U.S. entreaties to Portugal continued until the very eve of the Indian invasion, although the State Department held little hope that they would succeed.[58] Instead, the urgings brought Lisbon to apply its own pressure. Portugal's foreign minister warned that if Washington did not support his government's stance on Goa, Portugal would have to "reconsider" its relationship with the United States.[59]

A similar degree of stress befell relations with India. As much as advocates for engagement scorned Salazar's quixotic desire to retain the colonies, they recognized that the administration would be publicly obliged to deplore military action against the enclaves. With tensions over West New Guinea escalating, a successful Indian invasion of Goa seemed likely to spur Sukarno to attempt his own military solution. If Washington failed to act before an invasion, India could easily achieve a fait accompli, yet preventive action stood to position the United States as Portugal's defender.[60] Kennedy wrote to Nehru on December 13, entreating him not to take action that would set a "grievous example for the world." Galbraith pleaded with Nehru, going so far as to invoke the ghost of Gandhi, but to no avail.[61] The era of nonviolent resistance to colonialism was passing from the scene.

The United States was obliged to condemn India's action before the UN Security Council. Stevenson decried the Goa operation as a violation of both the UN Charter and the Gandhian principles upon which modern India had

---

[56] Telegram 617, Lisbon to Washington, December 8, 1961, ibid.: 911–912.

[57] Telegram 532, Washington to Lisbon, December 9, 1961, RG-59, DSCF, 753D.00/12–961, NA.

[58] See, for example, Telegram 72, Washington to New Delhi, December 14, 1961, in *FRUS, 1961–1963*, 19: 157–158.

[59] Telegram 654, Lisbon to Washington, December 18, 1961, RG-59, DSCF, 753D.00/12–1861, NA.

[60] Memorandum, Robert Johnson to Carl Kaysen, December 12, 1961, NSF box 155, "Goa, 12/11/61–12/13/61" folder, JFKL.

[61] Telegram 1767, New Delhi to Washington, December 15, 1961, in *FRUS, 1961–1963*, 19: 160.

been founded. To the aged statesman, this was a remarkably dangerous precedent, one that stood to endanger international institutions still being tested in
the Congo.[62] Stevenson drew the ire of India's representative, L. K. Jha, who
noted that the United States had avoided taking a position on the validity of
Portugal's claim to Goa. "Does not that statement," Jha asked, anticipating
the torrent of criticism that would befall the United States in three short years,
"show some kind of disregard, some kind of indifference," toward "the motivations, the feelings" of people striving for freedom?[63]

The Goa episode played on Kennedy's intermittent exasperation with nonaligned leaders. Belgrade remained a recent memory, Indonesia was set on a
dangerous course in its dispute with the Netherlands, and Kennedy had just
reluctantly approved funding for Ghana's Volta River Dam. The Goa action
evoked real frustration from the president. Nonetheless, Kennedy's interest in
India stemmed from his appreciation of its potential role in the world, not from
any blind adulation of Nehruvian principles. He regarded Goa as an unfortu-
nate setback, not as cause to rethink policy toward India. Kennedy remained
focused on New Delhi's potential role as a counterweight to China, as a moderating force within the nonaligned movement, and a model of non-communist
development. As such, Kennedy reacted to Goa with regret, not outrage.[64]

In his reply, Nehru expressed his hopes that relations with the United States
would soon recover, pledging himself to continue to seek "the friendship and
cooperation of the United States."[65] Kennedy responded cordially on January
18, observing that Goa had made it more difficult to oppose forcible revisions
of boundaries elsewhere in the world and that it had strengthened domestic
foes of aid to India. He added that he was writing:

in no mood of self-righteousness, and with no feeling that our own policy is above reproach.
Indeed I trust that you will continue to make clear in equal candor your views on matters
of common concern. Meanwhile, you can count on me to do all that I can to ensure that
any damage to our common interests is temporary. Good and fruitful relations with India
have been a matter of great concern to me for many years, and I have taken satisfaction in
the progress we were making together before this episode. I believe we can and must get
back on this high road, and I shall work steadily toward this end.[66]

Private communications thus assured India that Kennedy remained intent
on improving relations. Disappointed as he was, Nehru seems to have
grasped this.[67]

---

[62] United Nations, *Security Council Official Records*, Sixteenth Year, 987th Meeting, 15–18.

[63] United Nations, *Security Council Official Records*, Sixteenth Year, 988th Meeting, 13–18.

[64] Telegram 1918, New Delhi to Washington, December 28, 1961, in *FRUS, 1961–1963*, 19:
    164–166; Arthur M. Schlesinger Jr., *A Thousand Days: John F. Kennedy in the White House*
    (Boston: Houghton Mifflin, 1965), 526–530.

[65] Letter, Nehru to Kennedy, December 29, 1961, DDRS.

[66] Letter, Kennedy to Nehru, January 18, 1962, in *FRUS, 1961–1963*, 19: 197–199.

[67] See Jawaharlal Nehru, *Letters to Chief Ministers, 1947–1964*, Vol. 5, 1958–1964 (New York:
    Oxford University Press, 1989), 507–508.

Even so, Goa damaged India's image within the United States. Within the administration, it prompted sardonic remarks; even proponents of engaging New Delhi, like Kennedy, thought the operation hypocritical and felt a bit of schadenfreude. The impact outside the White House, however, was more serious. Foes of aid to India, particularly Missouri Senator Stuart Symington, cited Goa as evidence of India's perfidy in subsequent debates over foreign aid.[68]

Beset by Cold War crises through 1961, the Kennedy administration was slow to awaken to the risk of a clash over Goa. If the danger of Indian action was abstract at the beginning of the year, it surely should have seemed more concrete once Nehru's rhetoric shifted. In the absence of NSC discussion of the issue, Rusk's cautious middle-of-the-road approach remained dominant. Yet the likelihood of Indian action pushed Rusk and his colleagues closer to a strong anticolonial message than they reached on other, more nettlesome questions. He never again came this close to the liberal position as he had on the eve of the Indian operation.

Portugal's reaction to the loss of Goa forced this retreat. Lisbon responded to Goa with a mix of grief, rage, and grim resolve. Elbrick reported the following January that Salazar had staked his future on preserving whatever remained of the empire, regardless of the cost.[69] Goa deepened Salazar's anger toward the United States and inclined him toward greater acts of rhetorical brinksmanship in his relations with Washington.

Indeed, Goa's consequences outside the Indo-American relationship proved far more significant. The same African movements and states that had prodded Nehru toward action thereafter considered Goa a valuable precedent for military action against empire. The short crisis had demonstrated both the necessity and efficacy of military action against the Portuguese Empire, encouraging the Africans in their own efforts to support spreading rebellions in Lisbon's colonies. More immediately, however, the event also offered an ill omen for the resolution of another colonial dispute: the ongoing Dutch-Indonesian conflict over West New Guinea.

THE "HOLDING OPERATION": WEST NEW GUINEA

There, another dangerous dispute over a remnant of empire threatened to pit a European ally against a pivotal nonaligned state. In 1961, the western half of New Guinea represented the last remaining fragment of the centuries-old Dutch empire in the East Indies. Dutch politicians and colonialist organizations spoke solemnly of their duty to administer and prepare it and its native Papuan population for independence, while Indonesia claimed the territory.[70] Upon

---

[68] Felix Belair Jr., "Senate Unit Cuts Aid to India 25%," NYT, May 12, 1962, 1.

[69] Telegram 728, Lisbon to Washington, January 6, 1962, RG-59, DSCF, 641.537/1–662, NA.

[70] Arend Lijphart, The Trauma of Decolonization: The Dutch and West New Guinea (New Haven: Yale University Press, 1966), 25–27.

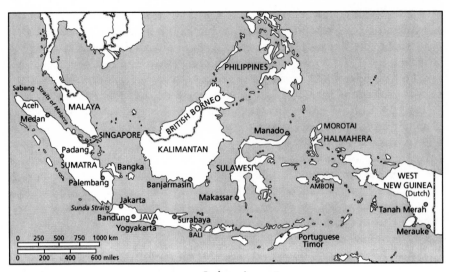

MAP 3. Indonesia, 1961.

the ensuing dispute rested the U.S. position in Indonesia and, by extension, Southeast Asia.[71]

Like Goa, this was a lingering colonial dispute dating back to the 1940s. The West New Guinea crisis tested policymakers through 1961 and into the summer of 1962. Over this span, U.S. policy passed through four distinct phases. For much of 1961, the NSC and the State Department alternated in setting policy. An initial period of sounding out the combatants, with some tentative steps toward the Indonesian position, gave way, in the autumn of 1961, to a more pro-Dutch stance of seeking a UN-mediated solution. Increased violence in early 1962, however, led the administration to press the Dutch to negotiate directly with the Indonesians. Difficulties in these negotiations, however, brought the fourth phase: direct U.S. mediation of the dispute, during which time Washington secured grudging Dutch acquiescence to Indonesian demands. Indonesian intransigence raised a fundamental question about engagement: how far could the White House go in challenging an ally on behalf of a nonaligned state?

Surprisingly far, it turned out. The dispute marked a milestone in the White House's approach to colonial conflicts. Here the White House not only ignored the counsel of an ally, it pressured the ally on behalf of a nonaligned state. Nowhere was the break from Eisenhower-era policy so apparent.

---

[71] On the West New Guinea dispute, see the excellent Matthew Jones, *Conflict and Confrontation in South East Asia, 1961–1965* (Cambridge: Cambridge University Press, 2002), 31–60; also Bradley Simpson, *Economists with Guns: Authoritarian Development and U.S.-Indonesian Relations, 1960–1968* (Stanford: Stanford University Press, 2008), 37–61; C. L. M. Penders, *The West New Guinea Debacle: Dutch Decolonization and Indonesia, 1945–1962* (Honolulu: University of Hawaii Press, 2002).

Simultaneously, however, the frustrations accumulated during the long crisis fostered a growing weariness in Washington, helping to ensure that the drastic actions undertaken over West New Guinea would not be replicated elsewhere.

Early in 1961, the West New Guinea dispute appeared to enter a dangerous new phase. Having severed relations with the Netherlands the previous year, Indonesia announced the acquisition of Soviet-supplied arms. The military balance continued to tip away from the Dutch. Indonesian sources reported to the CIA that Khrushchev had agreed to a massive $520 million military assistance program, including arms clearly intended to support amphibious operations: landing craft, warships, and amphibious tanks.[72] An alarmed Komer wrote to Rostow and Bundy, "Anyone who doesn't believe that the Indonesians are planning something eventually in West New Guinea need only look at the Soviet aid agreements."[73]

The administration first needed to decide whether Sukarno was even worth engaging. Only a few years before, Eisenhower and Dulles had tried to undermine the fiery Indonesian. The CIA, the State Department's Bureau of European Affairs, and several noted academic experts on Indonesia all believed that Sukarno could not be reasoned with; any attempts to resolve the West New Guinea crisis in Indonesia's favor would merely encourage further adventurism. The Jakarta embassy, the Bureau of Far Eastern Affairs, and several key members of the NSC believed Indonesia was not yet lost to communist influence, perceiving the field still open for a new approach to Sukarno. The dispute pitted skeptics like Rusk against both pragmatists and liberals, shedding light on the broader motivations and outlooks of both sides. No other nonalignment-related issue in Kennedy's term sparked as much internal acrimony.

Unlike Goa, the West New Guinea dispute received early attention at the highest levels of the government, not least because of the administration's intense concern with Southeast Asia. The NSC staff in February 1961 deemed it "the chief remaining colonial issue in Asia" and argued that the United States could no longer eschew action.[74] Policymakers contemplated two options: a shift toward an outwardly pro-Indonesian posture or establishing some form of international trusteeship over the disputed territory. The latter appealed to Rusk, who distrusted Sukarno and feared the precedent that would be set by a transfer of the territory. Others, such as Komer, disparaged the trusteeship idea, arguing that Sukarno would accept nothing less than full control of the territory.[75] Rusk wanted a solution consistent with international law; the

---

[72] Current Intelligence Weekly Summary, February 16, 1961, NSF, box 113, "Indonesia, General, 1/61–3/61" folder, JFKL.

[73] Memorandum, Komer to Bundy and Rostow, March 2, 1961, NSF, box 423, "West New Guinea, White House Memoranda" folder, JFKL.

[74] Report on Key National Security Problems, February 10, 1961, NSF, box 303, "Policy Planning, General, 1/61–2/10/61" folder, JFKL.

[75] Memorandum, Robert Komer, February 17, 1961, NSF, box 423, "West New Guinea, White House Memoranda" folder, JFKL.

NSC and Ambassador Howard Jones in Jakarta wanted one consistent with Indonesian demands.

To many in Washington, Sukarno seemed a menacing figure whose external policies threatened American allies and whose internal policies seemed to favor the large Communist Party of Indonesia (PKI). The veteran CIA analyst Richard Bissell warned in March that Sukarno was irredeemably anti-Western, susceptible to Soviet manipulation, and increasingly dependent on the PKI. "Like Hitler," Bissell wrote, "he is an open book, there to be read." Only his "removal from power" could salvage the Western position in Indonesia.[76] Foy Kohler of the State Department's European Bureau, citing entreaties from other European allies, feared that failing to support the Dutch would damage the NATO alliance to no good end.[77]

Advocates of engagement read the situation differently. They were primarily concerned with keeping Indonesia from allying with the Soviet Union, thereby endangering the U.S. position in the entire region. To them, Indonesia's geopolitical significance was incontrovertible and Sukarno was a nationalist, not a crypto-communist. As Komer wrote,

[I have] never understood proposition that Sukarno's 'global orientation' makes him necessarily pro-Communist and is incompatible with our own goals. Over long run precise opposite seems true. Indonesian nationalism will sooner or later run afoul of ChiComs (of whom they [are] already scared) if only we play it right.[78]

Komer instead called for taking strong action to preserve the Western position in Indonesia. Citing reports from Jones, he argued that "[w]hat we need now is a holding operation" to preserve U.S. influence in Indonesia for the present time. A shift on West New Guinea, coupled with an aid program for Jakarta, were essential to that end.[79] Komer specifically cited the warnings of Jones, who had been in Indonesia since 1958 and had befriended Sukarno. By 1961, the ambassador worried that the ongoing crisis was jeopardizing his ability to attain even his "minimum objective" – keeping the country out of the communist bloc – or, moreover, to avert a Dutch-Indonesian war that would force Washington to choose between NATO and ANZUS allies and the nonaligned states.[80]

Caught between a NATO ally and the second largest nonaligned state, the Kennedy administration hoped to play an informal mediating role: encouraging the two parties toward talks, while avoiding direct involvement. During

---

[76] Memorandum, Bissell to Bundy, March 27, 1961, in DOS, *FRUS, 1961–1963: Vol. 23, Southeast Asia* (Washington: GPO, 1995): 328–333.

[77] See Memcon, Kohler and others, February 1, 1961, DSCF, 656.9813/2–161, NA; Memorandum, Kohler to Parsons, February 6, 1961, DSCF, 656.9813/2–661, NA; Telegram 1042, The Hague to Washington, February 17, 1961, DSCF, 656.9813/2–1761, NA.

[78] Memorandum, Komer to Bundy, March 27, 1961 in *FRUS, 1961–1963*, 23: 333–334.

[79] Ibid.

[80] Telegram 2154, Jakarta to Washington, January 25, 1961, in *FRUS, 1961–1963*, 23: 302–304; Telegram 1952, Jakarta to Washington, January 4, 1961, RG-59, DSCF 656.9813/1–461, NA.

the first phase of U.S. policy toward the conflict, Kennedy and Rusk sounded out both Sukarno and his Dutch adversary, Foreign Minister Joseph Luns, but found little in the way of middle ground. Policy in the first phase represented in microcosm policy throughout the crisis: although the administration valued its relations with the Netherlands, concern about its position in Indonesia and Southeast Asia proved dominant.

The first litmus test of priorities in the crisis came in March, when the Netherlands invited Washington to dispatch a representative to the convening of the West New Guinea legislative council. Although the invitation was initially accepted, Jones and Komer campaigned vehemently in favor of declining it, the latter asking Bundy how the United States could credibly oppose Portuguese colonialism in the UN and then recognize Dutch sovereignty over West New Guinea.[81] This debate coincided with mounting U.S. anxiety about the situation in Laos, where communist forces were engaged in a sustained offensive against the U.S.-backed government. Against this backdrop, it seemed imperative to avoid additional trouble in Southeast Asia. Kennedy chose to renege on his earlier acceptance, citing Laos as the reason for the reversal. The act was symbolic but important: Washington had stepped back from prior support of Dutch policy. This marked the White House's first step toward a pro-Indonesian policy on the West New Guinea dispute and reflected the deep linkage between this issue and administration objectives in mainland Southeast Asia.[82]

Predictably, the cancellation elicited anger in the Netherlands. Luns, a stalwart defender of The Hague's policy toward West New Guinea, wasted no time in registering his "shock, dismay, and deep disappointment."[83] When Luns visited Washington in April, he rebuffed Rusk's inquiries about an international solution for the territory and complained about what he saw as a long-standing U.S. betrayal of a faithful ally. The soft-spoken Rusk had to tell his agitated guest that no useful purpose could be served by rehashing questions predating Indonesian independence. Luns's tirade failed to secure his chief objective: an unequivocal U.S. warning to Sukarno not to act against West New Guinea.[84]

Soon afterward came Sukarno's visit. Sukarno stuck firmly to his prior stance on the West New Guinea question, rejecting a proposed plebiscite. Notably, his foreign minister, Subandrio, indicated a willingness to offer face-saving measures to The Hague, specifically a one- or two-year trusteeship. Still, the outcome of this trusteeship needed to be clear at the outset: a case of

[81] Memorandum, Komer to Bundy, March 24, 1961, NSF, box 321, "Robert Komer, 3/15/61–3/29/61" folder, JFKL; Notes for Meeting, Komer, March 28, 1961, ibid.; Telegram 2735, Jakarta to Washington, March 23, 1961, NSF, box 143, "Netherlands, General 2/15/60–4/30/61" folder, JFKL.

[82] Telegram 1296, Washington to the Hague, March 31, 1961, NSF, box 143, "Netherlands, General 2/15/60–4/30/61" folder, JFKL; Memcon, March 27, 1961, RG-59, DSCF, 656.9813/3–2761, NA.

[83] Telegram 1223, The Hague to Washington, March 27, 1961, NSF, box 143, "Netherlands, General 2/15/60–4/30/61" folder, JFKL.

[84] Memcon, Rusk and Luns, April 10, 1961, in *FRUS, 1961–1963*, 23: 352–360.

borrowing the hand of the United Nations to facilitate the transfer of the territory, as Sukarno put it.[85] The Indonesians confirmed what Komer, Jones, and
others had insisted: they would settle for nothing less than acquiring West New
Guinea and would not be disarmed by any offers of a plebiscite or trusteeship.
With Indonesia implacable and continually increasing pressure on the territory,
engagement's advocates were obligated to whittle down the Dutch position to
a point wherein the possibility of independence was merely symbolic.

By the summer of 1961, this hardly seemed impossible, as the White House
had ample evidence that Dutch public opinion was far from united on the colonial question. Opponents of The Hague's policy, including a group of prominent industrialists and the royal consort, Prince Bernhard, made it clear to
Washington that Dutch opinion was not nearly as unyielding as Luns claimed
and could accept the loss of the territory.[86] Rusk, however, continued to hope
for an international solution to the crisis, even as his counterparts on the NSC
warned that any formula likely to please the Dutch would only alienate the
Indonesians. As the Berlin crisis escalated, distracting the White House, internationalization became the de facto preference. Indonesia regarded such proposals warily, believing internationalization a Dutch ploy to either stall for
time or enlist other countries to their side.[87] Faced with a choice between an
ally and a nonaligned state, Rusk still desired a middle course that would limit
disruptions to either relationship and stay consistent with his sense of legality.

This shift toward internationalization in the latter half of 1961 brought
tensions within the administration to the surface. Komer and the NSC staff
thought this strategy shortsighted. He warned Kennedy on September 11, "We
must bear in mind that we are heading almost inexorably toward a major crisis over [West New Guinea], unless it can be forestalled." "Like Angola," he
wrote, "this is a case where European interest must be subordinated; unlike
Portugal, however, Holland would be unlikely to cut off its nose to spite its
face."[88] Bowles agreed, in light of the fragile U.S. position in the region, arguing: "A stable anti-Communist Indonesia is absolutely vital to whatever hope
there may be for a secure Southeast Asia."[89]

On September 26, the Dutch submitted a draft resolution to internationalize West New Guinea for consideration before the United Nations General
Assembly.[90] When the Dutch resolution proved stillborn, Rusk directed

[85] Memcon, Kennedy and Sukarno, April 24, 1961, ibid.: 382–390.
[86] Memorandum, Rostow to Kennedy, April 6, 1961, NSF, box 143, "Netherlands, General,
    5/61–9/61" folder, JFKL; Memcon, Kennedy and Prince Bernhard, April 25, 1961, ibid.;
    Memorandum, Willem Oltmans to Rostow, undated, ibid.; Lijphart, *The Trauma of
    Decolonization*, 145–150, 227. Bernhard made this point directly to Kennedy.
[87] Memcon, Rusk and Howard Beale, August 22, 1961, in *FRUS, 1961–1963*, 23: 412–414;
    Memorandum, Johnson to Rostow, September 2, 1961, ibid.: 416–418.
[88] Memorandum, Komer to Kennedy, September 11, 1961, ibid.: 426.
[89] Telegram SECUN 6, Jakarta to Washington, November 17, 1961, RG-59, DSCF, 656.9813/11–
    1761, NA.
[90] Telegram 226, The Hague to Washington, September 3, 1961, RG-59, DSCF, 656.9813/
    9–261, NA.

Stevenson to back a compromise measure somewhat closer to the Indonesian stance, albeit one that still left the fate of the territory to an international commission. He pressed ahead with it, even after Subandrio indicated that it was unacceptable to Indonesia and warned that the United States risked turning West New Guinea into a "Cold War issue."[91] Neither resolution succeeded in the General Assembly, although the U.S.-backed resolution won a majority of votes. To Luns and Rusk, this show of support seemed to represent a moral victory of sorts. The Indonesians complained that it signified effective U.S. support of the Dutch.[92]

Over the autumn, as the international option foundered, the NSC staff became increasingly critical of Rusk, who seemed to be giving particular weight to Australian concerns about Indonesian expansionism and his own misgivings about Sukarno.[93] Carl Kaysen of the NSC observed that Rusk was "still concerned with the rightness or wrongness of Sukarno's behavior," rather than the likely outcome of continuing to pursue the present course.[94] Citing reports from Jakarta of growing Indonesian frustration with U.S. policy, the NSC staff signaled their disquiet in memos to Kennedy.[95] Significantly, Bundy also began to weigh in, writing to Kennedy that Rusk's "respect for the Australians and dislike of Sukarno" was damaging the U.S. position in Indonesia.[96]

This focused criticism of Rusk ultimately shifted U.S. policy away from internationalization. Until this point, Kennedy had stayed distant from the debate, making only occasional comments on the issue. In October, he had advised his staff to "lean gently on the Dutch"; yet in the wake of the UN resolutions the Dutch seemed to feel they enjoyed U.S. support.[97] Subsequently, in November, following Bundy's advice, Kennedy appointed veteran diplomat Averell Harriman, an advocate of engaging Sukarno, to head the State Department's Far East Bureau. JFK stated his preferences clearly before the NSC in early 1962. West New Guinea, he said was "most unsuitable" for a war. Although he did not want to humiliate the Dutch, the government needed to recognize that the territory was likely to go to Jakarta. At stake, Kennedy emphasized, was Indonesia itself: "the most rich and populous country in [Southeast Asia]" and the target of "energetically pursued Soviet ambitions."[98]

---

[91] Telegram 1269, Washington to New York, November 16, 1961, RG-59, DSCF, 656.9813/11–1661, NA; Telegram 807, Jakarta to Washington, November 1, 1961, RG-59, DSCF, 656.9813/11–161, NA.

[92] Telegram 1014, Jakarta to Washington, December 7, 1961, NSF, box 113, "Indonesia, General, 10/61–12/61" folder, JFKL.

[93] See, for example, Memcon, Rusk and others, January 27, 1961, RG-59, DSCF, 656.9813/1–2761, NA.

[94] Memorandum, Kaysen to Bundy, January 12, 1962, in *FRUS, 1961–1963*, 23: 504–506.

[95] Memorandum, Rostow to Kennedy, October 13, 1961, ibid.: 440–442.

[96] Memorandum, Bundy to Kennedy, December 1, 1961, ibid.: 462–463.

[97] Memorandum, Robert Johnson, to Bundy, November 6, 1961, ibid.: 447–452.

[98] Summary of President Kennedy's Remarks to the 496th Meeting of the National Security Council, January 18, 1962, in FRUS, 1961–1968, 8: 241; Jones, *Conflict and Confrontation*, 46–50.

Henceforth, the United States increasingly applied concerted diplomatic pressure on the Netherlands to negotiate directly with Indonesia. In the wake of a Dutch-Indonesian naval clash in January, Washington rejected a Dutch request to cease military assistance to Indonesia. The United States also withheld landing rights to several chartered flights transferring military personnel from the Netherlands to the beleaguered colony. The Dutch looked on with growing dismay.[99]

Kennedy now sought direct negotiations between the Dutch and the Indonesians. To signal this, he sent his brother Robert to visit both Indonesia and the Netherlands in February. In Jakarta, the attorney general won Sukarno's agreement to negotiate by hinting that he would likely obtain the territory.[100] Negotiations in The Hague proved more difficult, as RFK spoke quite forcefully to his hosts. His apparent disdain for the Dutch position convinced many, including Prime Minister Jan de Quay, that their hopes for U.S. assistance were in vain. A reluctant Luns conceded his government's willingness to negotiate.[101]

Luns made one last attempt to gain U.S. pledges of support in a March visit to Washington. He announced his government's decision to dispatch four naval vessels to reinforce West New Guinea. Alarmed, Kennedy, Rusk, and Bundy told Luns in no uncertain terms that Papuan self-determination was not a Cold War concern and that it paled in importance next to the struggle against communism in Indonesia and mainland Southeast Asia. Defeated, the Dutch signaled their willingness to engage in direct, mediated negotiations with Jakarta. Indonesia agreed to mediated talks as well.[102] Internal bickering had run its course; the administration now spoke with one voice.

This was far from the end of the dispute. Over the next six months, the Dutch and Indonesians engaged in a sporadic set of negotiations under the supervision of veteran U.S. diplomat Ellsworth Bunker. Negotiations began in March, amid a backdrop of continuing clashes around the territory, but broke up over an Indonesian demand to assume administrative control of the territory.[103] The White House was now in a far more watchful mood, and pro-Dutch voices had been defeated. Washington applied continual pressure on The Hague to concede the colony, knowing that prevailing winds in Dutch politics were eroding domestic support for retaining the colony.

Impartial mediation having proven insufficient, Washington now advanced a specific plan for the resolution of the dispute. Known as the Bunker formula,

[99] Memcon, William Tyler and J. V. van Roijen, February 28, 1962, RG-59, DSCF, 656.9813/2–2862, NA; Editorial Note, *FRUS, 1961–1963,* 23: 546n.

[100] Telegram 1445, Jakarta to Washington, February 14, 1962, in *FRUS, 1961,* 23: 523–526.

[101] Telegram 4044, Paris to Washington, February 27, 1962, ibid.: 544; Memorandum, Komer to Kennedy, February 28, 1962, ibid.: 545–547; Penders, *The West New Guinea Debacle,* 351–356.

[102] Memcon, Kennedy and Luns, March 2, 1962, in *FRUS, 1961–1963,* 23: 549–552.

[103] Howard Schaeffer, *Ellsworth Bunker: Global Troubleshooter, Vietnam Hawk* (Chapel Hill: University of North Carolina Press, 2003), 95–98.

the plan called for the transfer of West New Guinea to a UN administrator, who would govern it for a period of one to two years. Following the period of UN control, Indonesia would administer West New Guinea for a number of years, finally staging a popular plebiscite to determine the region's ultimate status. The formula essentially favored the Indonesian side, with the UN administrator provision representing only a fig leaf for the Dutch. The Hague disliked the Bunker formula, but the Dutch political consensus on the colony was unraveling. Parties of the left did not wish to fight for the colony, and business interests hoped to resume lucrative commercial relations with Indonesia. At the end of June, the Dutch signaled their willingness to return to negotiations. They had effectively acceded to the Indonesian demands.

Only the fine print of a settlement remained to be negotiated, yet this task proved remarkably difficult. In the months preceding the final agreement, Sukarno continued to engage in military brinksmanship. At the last minute, the Indonesian leader objected to transferring the territory in 1963, citing a promise made to his people that Indonesia would govern West New Guinea in 1962. This, on top of everything else, upset Rusk, who declared, "We don't let Khrushchev get away with such tactics." The United States could not press the Dutch to yield "without surrendering our own integrity and self respect."[104]

The situation seemed darkest before the dawn. Even as the two delegations neared a final agreement, Komer wrote gloomily that Indonesian military action seemed certain.[105] Kennedy dispatched a last-minute presidential letter to Sukarno, massaging the Indonesian's ego and informing him that the world would not understand an act of war with an agreement so near. Sukarno, concluding that he could afford to be magnanimous, agreed to the Bunker plan. The West New Guinea crisis was at an end, and the terms of the settlement brought a mood of "awed wonderment" to Sukarno's government.[106] Advocates of engagement expressed elation; the dispute had been the primary obstacle to a broader improvement of relations with Indonesia.[107]

The ensuing settlement went far beyond anything that Kennedy's predecessors would have countenanced. The West New Guinea agreement did, indeed, buy time for the United States to forge a stronger tie with Indonesia – albeit significantly less time than the administration wanted. It delighted Sukarno, convincing him that he had a friend in Kennedy. It also outraged domestic critics of the White House, who deemed it appeasement.[108] British observers stopped short of condemning the settlement, but lacked the optimism of their American counterparts. R. W. Selby of the British embassy in Jakarta wrote

---

[104] Telegram Secto 52, Geneva to Washington, July 25, 1962, RG-59, DSCF, 656.9813/ 7–2562, NA.
[105] Memorandum, Komer to Bundy, July 26, 1962, NSF, box 423, "West New Guinea, White House Memoranda" folder, JFKL.
[106] Telegram 281, Jakarta to Washington, August 16, 1962, NSF, box 113, "Indonesia, General, 7/62–8/62" folder, JFKL.
[107] Memorandum, Komer to Kennedy, August 15, 1962, in *FRUS, 1961–1963*, 23: 626.
[108] Simpson, *Economists with Guns*, 60–61.

that Indonesians regard the settlement as a validation of their "application of forceful measures." He predicted:

Things should be easier for the Western Powers now and I am sure that it should be their endeavor to regain the ground they have lost during the course of this struggle. But it will not be easy. The struggle has lasted too long and produced a set of slogans from which it will be difficult to rid this slogan-riddled land.[109]

Britain recognized the importance of mainland Southeast Asia to Kennedy's policy but worried at the precedent being set. Recalling Hitler's annexations in the interwar years, Permanent Under Secretary Harold Caccia fretted presciently that if "strong-arm methods are seen to succeed" they would not be applied only to colonial remnants.[110] Indeed, Sukarno had cause to think that confrontation was a viable strategy, applicable to future disputes.

These concerns were not lost within Washington. The U.S. debate over policy toward West New Guinea had, itself, been a deliberation over whether Sukarno's behavior should be rewarded. The pragmatists of the NSC and their liberal allies won a sizable victory on this question, arguing that Sukarno, however distasteful, needed to be placated. The broader arc of U.S. concerns in Southeast Asia, ranging from the shoring up of nervous or shaky regimes, such as the South Vietnamese government, to the containment of Chinese influence, undermined the force of arguments predicated on international legality or the duty owed a distant ally.[111] These concerns far outweighed Kennedy's fears that a coercive policy would jeopardize his relationship with The Hague, which generally supported British and U.S. policy objectives within European organizations.[112] In any event, the unraveling of the Dutch domestic consensus on the colonial issue limited the damage inflicted upon bilateral relations.

At the same time, this achievement came at a real human cost. The Dutch had lobbied sincerely on behalf of the Papuan people, as much out of a genuine sense of human obligation as any lingering imperial ideology. They were correct in predicting an unhappy future for the Papuans under Indonesian rule, even if that future can largely be attributed not to Sukarno but to his successor, Suharto. The Kennedy administration may have averted a divisive war. It did so at a cost to the future of a people, having given little thought at all to the well-being of the Papuans, regarding them as ill-prepared for independence.[113]

In another sense, as well, the victory was Pyrrhic. The crisis underscored difficulties of coordination in the informal Kennedy White House, as the NSC and State Department alternated in setting policy. For much of 1961, the NSC

---

[109] Despatch, Selby to Home, September 7, 1962, PREM 11/4870, TNA.
[110] Memorandum, "American Policy Over West New Guinea," May 30, 1962, FO 371/166553, TNA.
[111] Memorandum, Komer to Rostow, April 20, 1961, NSF, box 113, "Indonesia, General, 4/61" folder, JFKL.
[112] See Memcon, Kennedy and Bundy, March 22, 1962, in *FRUS, 1961–1963, 13*: 834.
[113] David Webster, "Regimes in Motion: The Kennedy Administration and Indonesia's New Frontier, 1960–1962," *Diplomatic History 33*, No. 1 (January 2009), 95–123.

sat by in frustration as the internationalization option was vainly pursued. Kennedy's intervention proved decisive, but the president had failed to make himself heard earlier. After Kennedy's intervention, Sukarno's constant resort to threats and refusal to compromise reinforced a growing weariness with colonial issues within the administration, particularly on the part of Rusk and his fellow skeptics. For Komer and his peers, on the other hand, the resolution of the crisis and the seeming opening of Indonesia to U.S. influence validated the holding strategy. For most within the administration, however, the West New Guinea dispute was a marathon, an ordeal leaving the White House with little appetite for further intervention in colonial conflicts – even as the intensity of anticolonial sentiment in Africa and Asia continued to grow.

EVADING THE "FACTS OF LIFE": PORTUGUESE AFRICA

For all the trouble they had caused, the disputes over West New Guinea and Goa paled in severity and duration next to the turmoil witnessed in Portugal's extensive African empire. These vast possessions, considered essential to Portugal's economic health, were far more strongly garrisoned than the Indian enclaves. Sustained warfare in Angola, Mozambique, and Portuguese Guinea posed a long-standing problem for United States foreign policy.[114] Of the colonial conflicts of the 1960s, these proved the most consequential and damaging to the U.S. position in the nonaligned world.

March 1961 brought the first stirrings of revolt in Angola, triggered in part by growing unrest in Portugal itself.[115] Portuguese Guinea was next to erupt, and there the rebel movement, Amilcar Cabral's PAIGC, enjoyed greater success, controlling significant parts of the colony by the summer of 1963.[116] Mozambique was the last of the three to ignite, beginning with the autumn of 1964 uprising by the FRELIMO movement.[117]

The timing of the Angolan revolt could scarcely have been worse. Unrest in Portuguese Africa evoked serious concern in a White House already facing the fallout from the death of Lumumba. Angola represented exactly the kind of anachronistic colonialism that Kennedy had denounced in his Algeria speech. Liberia sponsored a resolution before the UN Security Council calling for self-determination in the colonies and an international inquiry into Portugal's actions. Confronted with the bloodshed in Angola while it strove

[114] Essential works on the Portuguese question include Thomas J. Noer, *Cold War and Black Liberation: The United States and White Rule in Africa, 1948–1968* (Columbia: University of Missouri Press, 1985); Mahoney, *JFK: Ordeal in Africa*; Thomas Borstelmann, *The Cold War and the Color Line: American Race Relations in the Global Arena* (Cambridge, MA : Harvard University Press, 2001).

[115] Gallagher, *Portugal*, 143–154.

[116] Gallagher, *Portugal*, 176–178; Russell Howe, "A War of Nerves Jangles Africa in Fight for Freedom," *The Washington Post*, August 18, 1963, E4.

[117] Adrian Hastings, "Some Reflections Upon the War in Mozambique," *African Affairs* 73 (July 1974), 263–266.

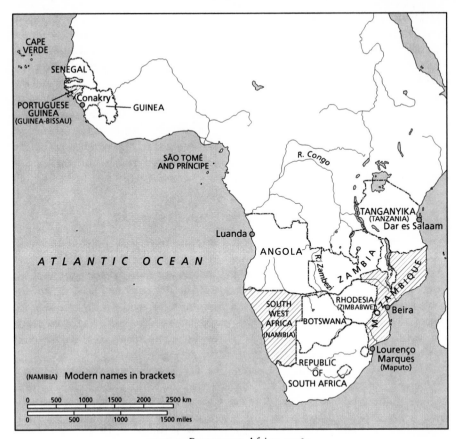

MAP 4. Portuguese Africa, 1961.

to stabilize the Congo, the United States voted in favor of the resolution, on March 15, 1961. Rusk dispatched a telegram to Lisbon, imploring Salazar to set his colonies on a path to self-determination.[118]

With this action and its subsequent denunciations of Portuguese policy in Africa, the administration purchased itself valuable political capital among Asian and African leaders, as well as the expectation that further action was imminent. Egypt's Nasser declared that he was "very pleased" with the leadership the United States was displaying on the Portuguese question.[119] So, too, was Mali's President Modibo Keita, who added, however, that continued support for decolonization would be needed to encourage the neutrality of Africa in the Cold War.[120] The Belgrade Conference, where

---

[118] Noer, *Cold War and Black Liberation*, 67–71; Mahoney, *JFK: Ordeal in Africa*, 187–191.

[119] Memorandum, Hubert H. Humphrey to Kennedy, October 23, 1961, NSF, box 445, "UAR: 1961–1962 3 of 4" folder, JFKL; also Interview, April 21, 1961, FO 371/157388, TNA.

[120] Telegram 56, Bamako to Washington, July 22, 1961, NSF, box 140, "Mali, General, 7/61" folder, JFKL.

Portuguese colonialism was condemned with unequaled intensity, reinforced this message.[121] If Washington's early steps were applauded by nonaligned states, they were appreciated more as portents of future policy than in their own right.

Salazar, predictably, was flabbergasted at the seeming betrayal, and also alarmed by contacts between the United States and Portuguese dissidents. Portugal refused to answer Rusk's entreaty; moreover, it took the offensive against the administration. Lisbon retained the services of an American public relations firm, Selvage and Lee, to lobby on its behalf. The campaign was remarkably effective, working alongside well-choreographed Portuguese efforts to depict its colonies as harmonious, multiracial paradises. Southern opponents of the Kennedy administration's civil rights policies were happy to support the Portuguese, just as they praised Tshombe and the Katangans. Taken together, these efforts created a formidable domestic obstacle for the administration as it sought to ease Salazar out of Africa.[122]

With Angola smoldering, liberals and pragmatists alike hoped that Portugal could be convinced to abandon its colonies. Komer wondered if the administration had yet explained the "grim fact of the anti-colonial revolution" to Portugal, observing: "Over the long run, they have no better chance of holding on to their colonies than French, Belgians, or British did."[123] Williams warned that the Portuguese had yet to realize the depth of discontent in their colonies after an August 1961 visit to Angola.[124] In August 1961, William Attwood, the United States ambassador in Guinea, wrote to Kennedy,

It is not enough to express sympathy and extend aid to maintain the progress we have made in Africa since your inauguration. We must also convince nationalist leaders like Touré that our African policies are no longer cleared in Paris or Lisbon.... If we look at Africa in political terms – as we should – we can see that there is a winning issue, nationalism, and a losing issue, colonialism, and that neither can be straddled.[125]

In June 1961, Williams, seeking to capitalize on shifts in African policy achieved thus far, submitted a broad proposal to prod Portugal toward allowing self-determination in its colonies. He proposed working with NATO allies, Brazil, and the Vatican to persuade Salazar to establish a timetable for Angolan independence.[126]

Here, however, the liberals ran headlong into the Department of Defense. The Pentagon was alarmed by the prospect of jeopardizing NATO use of the Azores, which constituted a vital refueling stop for trans-Atlantic flights and a

[121] *Conference of Non-Aligned Countries* (Belgrade: 1961), passim.
[122] Mahoney, *JFK: Ordeal in Africa*, 214–215; Noer, *Cold War and Black Liberation*, 74–76.
[123] Memorandum, Komer to Rostow, March 28, 1961, NSF, box 321, "Robert Komer, 1/161–3/14/61" folder, JFKL.
[124] Report of G. Mennen Williams on his Second Trip to Africa, undated, NSF, box 2, "Africa, General, 9/1/61–9/10/61" folder, JFKL.
[125] Letter, Attwood to Kennedy, August 7, 1961, NSF, box 102, "Guinea, General, 6/61–8/61" folder, JFKL.
[126] Noer, *Cold War and Black Liberation*, 78–79.

military staging area. The Joint Chiefs of Staff stated forcefully that the bases were a military necessity and that their loss would pose "a very considerable hardship to the security measures of the United States."[127] This was an exceedingly powerful concern in the midst of the Berlin crisis. Additionally, fears of communist gains on the European continent counterbalanced concern about communism in Africa. In July 1960, the Lisbon embassy had warned that the loss of any of Portugal's African colonies would likely topple the Salazar regime, conceivably bringing a "leftist or neutralist" government to power in its place. Such a regime would likely terminate NATO basing rights in the Azores and withdraw from the alliance altogether.[128] Under such circumstances, a 1961 study by the INR division concluded, "it would be difficult to prevent the world Communist apparatus from intervening."[129]

When Kennedy and his advisors addressed the question, in July 1961, the Berlin crisis was reaching its height. Needing to preserve alliance solidarity, the White House declined to endorse any specific deadlines for Angolan self-determination or any direct measures to pressure Salazar, but did indicate an interest in working with allies to lobby the Portuguese. Addressing one of the most vexing complications of the Angolan crisis, Kennedy directed the State Department to take steps to prohibit the use of U.S.-made weaponry in Portuguese counterinsurgency operations.[130] This marked the utmost extent of the pressure he was willing to apply.

Even in 1961, Kennedy's thinking was dominated by concern over the Azores, and the ongoing crisis allowed him scant opportunity to forget their military value. "Have we considered," he asked in July, "(1) whether we can be successful in persuading the Portuguese ... or (2) whether this will have an adverse effect upon the use of the Azores base. I wonder if we should perhaps content ourselves with a public statement." Rusk, replying, opined that a public statement would only further enrage the Portuguese.[131] Kennedy sought to dampen African expectations of further changes in policy, asking the State Department to remind its UN delegation of the value of the Azores bases and to explain United States policy to African delegations.[132] United States policy moved toward managing, rather than meeting, the expectations of Africans. This shift in policy was abetted by the waning influence of the liberals,

[127] Memorandum, Earle Wheeler to White House, July 3, 1961, NSF, box 155, "Azores Base, 4/3/61–3/9/62" folder, JFKL; Memorandum, Maxwell Taylor to Kennedy, January 27, 1962, ibid.

[128] Memorandum, Robert McBride to Foy Kohler, July 21, 1960, RG-59, Bureau of European Affairs (BEA), Office of Western European Affairs (OWEA), Portugal 1956–1963, box 1, "16.1 African-Portuguese Relations, 1959–1960" folder, NA.

[129] Memorandum, February 8, 1961, RG-59, BEA, OWEA, Portugal 1956–1963, box 1, "16-A. Portuguese Overseas Possessions, General" folder, NA.

[130] NSAM 60, July 18, 1961, in *FRUS, 1961–1963*, 13: 901–902.

[131] Memorandum, Bundy to Kennedy, August 31, 1961, in DOS, *FRUS, 1961–1963, Vol. 21: Africa* (Washington: GPO, 1995): 548–549.

[132] Memorandum, Bundy to U. Alexis Johnson, July 28, 1961, NSF, box 2, "Africa, General, 8/61," folder, JFKL.

particularly after the demotion of Bowles in November 1961. His successor, Ball, was significantly more sympathetic to the Salazar government. Both he and Rusk opposed taking any coercive steps toward a NATO ally and feared that a Portuguese withdrawal would merely serve as a prelude for another Congo-like implosion of a former colony.

With the United States lease on the Azores due for renewal in 1962, the Portuguese indicated that renewal could occur only if Washington afforded them greater consideration on African issues. Lisbon directed its ire at Stevenson's votes in favor of Angolan self-determination and tentative contacts between the United States and rebel groups. Rebel groups in all three colonies looked to Washington for either humanitarian or political assistance. Some of these groups were well regarded in the administration. Robert F. Kennedy, upon meeting the Mozambican rebel leader Eduardo Mondlane, termed him "a terrifically impressive fellow." His brother responded by asking of Mozambique: "That's Portuguese?"[133] Rusk, nonetheless, acted to curtail U.S. contacts with all rebel movements, fearing Lisbon's reprisals should they be uncovered.[134]

The rebel groups could be disavowed; the entreaties of their African patrons were harder to ignore. Mounting frustration with the perseverance of white rule in sub-Saharan Africa spurred African states to establish the Organization of African Unity (OAU) in May 1963. The establishment of the OAU allowed African nations to make a concerted demand for Western action on the Portuguese question. Expecting that diplomatic appeals might prove fruitless, the OAU also established the African Liberation Committee to coordinate military efforts on the continent. The burden of expelling the Portuguese could not, however be shared evenly. Nations bordering the embattled colonies stood to bear much of the cost and risk of hosting rebel groups. Consequently, two of these states, Guinea and Tanganyika, strove to shift U.S. policy on the Portuguese question.

Working in tandem in the spring and summer of 1963, Touré and Tanganyika's Julius Nyerere attempted to convince Kennedy to provide, in Touré's words, "concrete assistance to Africa" in resolving the problem of Portuguese colonialism. Touré wrote JFK frequently, convincing Thomas Cassilly, the U.S. chargé in Conakry, that he hoped to establish a "direct and special relationship" with Kennedy.[135] Nyerere visited Washington in July 1963. Both Africans stressed the urgency of the moment, telling Kennedy that U.S. action was needed to stave off a violent confrontation akin to the recent Algerian war.[136] Nyerere highlighted the case of Goa, both as a demonstration

---

[133] Draft Transcript, John and Robert Kennedy, Undated, JFK Library Transcripts, Kennedy Dictabelts, Conversation 18B.3, MC.

[134] Memorandum, Averell Harriman to Rusk, July 1, 1964, in DOS, FRUS, 1964–1968, Vol. 24: Africa (Washington: GPO, 1999): 742; Noer, Cold War and Black Liberation, 84–94.

[135] Airgram A-449, Conakry to Washington, June 20, 1963, RG-59, CFPF: 1964–1966, box 2258, "POL 15–1 GUIN, 2/1/63" folder, NA.

[136] Letter, Touré to Kennedy, June 17, 1963, NSF, box 102, "Guinea, General, 8/63" folder, JFKL.

of Portuguese intransigence and as a positive precedent the Africans might follow.[137] "Events are moving in [a] way to make US, fairly or no, critical factor in African view for [the] resolution [of the] Mozambique problem," warned the U.S. ambassador in Tanganyika.[138]

Kennedy, however, had already decided to avoid further drastic action on Portuguese Africa. During 1962, he sought to moderate African expectations, explaining his predicament at length to visiting African leaders. Domestic pressures, which could only be worsened by the loss of the Azores, and growing concern with Soviet behavior led Kennedy to ignore the entreaties of the liberals, instead heeding the more cautious counsel of Rusk.[139] That stance solidified by the summer of 1963. Meeting with his advisors on July 15, the same day as his conversation with Nyerere, Kennedy stated that his central aim in policy toward Portuguese Africa was to maintain access to the Azores and to avoid being the primary target of African pressure to resolve the issue. He was unwilling to consider the use of economic sanctions against Portugal, although he could consider their use against South Africa.[140] As a result, the White House foreswore its most effective means for preventing the use of U.S.-made weaponry in Portuguese Africa. Consequently, Kennedy responded to both Nyerere and Touré by stating that he believed he could gain little from directly pressing Portugal.[141] Kennedy instead tried to offer Lisbon carrots. During a 1963 trip to Lisbon, Ball attempted to persuade the Portuguese to grant self-determination, offering financial incentives to do so; when that failed, he did not recommend stronger inducement.[142]

The African states, meanwhile, escalated their diplomatic initiatives against Portugal. In July, they pressed the offensive at the UN, proposing an arms embargo against Portugal. This was stronger medicine than the Kennedy administration could contemplate. Against the objections of the liberals, Kennedy directed the UN delegation to abstain, marking the first major public indication of the new policy in place.[143] Reflecting the new policy in Washington

[137] Telegram 107, Dar es Salaam to Washington, July 25, 1963, RG-59, CFPF: 1963, box 4056, "POL 1: General Policy Background" folder, NA; Memcon, Kennedy and Nyerere, July 15, 1963, in DOS, *FRUS, 1961–1963: Vol. 21: Africa* (MS) (Washington: GPO, 1996): doc. 682; Memcon, Rusk and Nyerere, July 15, 1963, RG-59, CFPF: 1963, box 4057, "POL-Political Affairs & Relations" folder, NA.

[138] Telegram 690, Dar es Salaam to Washington, April 5, 1963, DSCF, CFPF: 1963, box 4022, "POL Port-T" folder, NA.

[139] See, for example, Memcon, Kennedy and Félix Houphouët-Boigny, May 24, 1962, in *FRUS, 1961–1963: 21* (MS): doc. 527; Memcon, Kennedy and Olympio, March 21, 1962, ibid.: doc. 688; Mahoney, *JFK: Ordeal in Africa*, 209–222.

[140] Memorandum for the Record, July 15, 1963, box 3, "Africa, General, 7/63" folder, JFKL.

[141] Letter, Kennedy to Touré, August 23, 1963, NSF, box 102, "Guinea, General, 8/63" folder, JFKL; Memcon, Kennedy and Nyerere, July 15, 1963, in DOS, *FRUS, 1961–1963: 21* (Supplement) (Washington: GPO, 1997): doc. 682; Memcon, Rusk and Nyerere, July 15, 1963, RG-59, CFPF: 1963, box 4057, "POL-Political Affairs & Relations" folder, NA.

[142] Noer, *Cold War and Black Liberation*, 105–106; Ball, *The Past Has Another Pattern*, 276–282.

[143] Noer, *Cold War and Black Liberation*, 102–104.

in the autumn of 1963, the NSC's William Brubeck opined that the time had arrived to focus less on satisfying the African states and more on appeasing the Portuguese and South Africans.[144]

Kennedy had not, however, concluded that Portugal's position in Africa was tenable. Meeting with his new ambassador in Lisbon, George W. Anderson, he stressed that world events "made it necessary in his opinion for the Portuguese to take a positive and affirmative attitude" toward the question of self-determination. Washington had to retain use of the Azores; it also needed to "use its best influences to support the moderate elements in Africa and restrain the more radical ones." Although stymied by Portuguese threats and his own hesitance, Kennedy perceived the importance of the colonial question to U.S. standing in Africa. His withdrawal was more likely tactical than strategic, but any conclusions about how he might have acted had he not been assassinated must remain speculative.[145]

The shift away from the African position consolidated in 1964. Johnson inherited two wars in Portuguese Africa, with a third – in Mozambique – only months away from erupting. The altered internal dynamics of the new administration combined with Johnson's concern with his reelection to thwart any further initiatives to sway the Portuguese. Other African crises and deepening concern with Vietnam ensured that, as the NSC's Ulric Haynes Jr. later recalled, Portuguese Africa *"really* fell by the wayside."[146] Policy calcified in the middle position, as the rebels and their nonaligned supporters became increasingly embittered toward the United States. Cabral began to denounce the United States openly, while Mondlane's FRELIMO – once primarily focused on gaining Western support – turned its attention east, moving beyond initially tentative conversations with communist governments.[147] These shifts augured a broader African disillusionment with the United States as the wars raged on. Events in the Congo in the summer and autumn of 1964, however, built upon existing frustrations, bringing U.S.-nonaligned relations to an unprecedented state of acrimony. This, in turn, shaped the next major nonaligned conference, held in Cairo that October.

FALL FROM GRACE: THE CAIRO CONFERENCE AND STANLEYVILLE

The confidence felt by engagement's proponents at the end of 1962 had much to do with their success in facing a wide range of colonial issues. At that point, Katanga was on its last legs, the West New Guinea dispute had been resolved, Indian-American relations were riding high in the wake of the Sino-Indian War, and the United States still enjoyed the esteem of African states for its stance

---

[144] Memorandum, William Brubeck to Bundy, October 29, 1963, in *FRUS, 1961–1963*, 21: 505–507.

[145] Memcon, Kennedy and George Anderson, September 12, 1963, in *FRUS, 1961–1963*, 13: 982–983.

[146] Ulric Haynes Jr., Interview with the author, April 17, 2007.

[147] See, for example, Aktenvermerk, Cairo, March 10, 1963, MfAA, A 16052, AA.

on Portuguese colonialism. The situation changed dramatically in 1963 and 1964. The shock of the Kennedy assassination reverberated around the world. In August of the following year, Johnson authorized air strikes against North Vietnam, retaliating for a naval clash in the Gulf of Tonkin. A spreading wave of regional conflicts divided the United States from nonaligned states, particularly Indonesia and Egypt. Washington's wavering position on Portuguese colonialism steadily eroded its image in Africa. Most damaging in the months preceding the pivotal October 1964 meeting of the nonaligned movement was the resumption of hostilities in the Congo.

Much as Bizerte shaped the Belgrade Conference, events in the Congo loomed over the proceedings in Cairo. The perennial crisis entered a brief lull after the fall of Katanga. Adoula's hold on power, however, remained tenuous. His nonalignment and support of the anticolonial struggle established him as a credible leader to his African peers, but Adoula lacked a strong domestic base and his tenure was marred by army unrest, strikes, and regional revolts. In July 1964, facing another rebellion in the east of the country, the exhausted Adoula resigned. President Kasavubu appointed Moise Tshombe in his place.

The Johnson administration, preoccupied with matters elsewhere, considered it an internal matter of the Leopoldville government and saw no suitable alternative. This view was not shared by the nonaligned nations. Tshombe's responsibility for the death of Lumumba made him the most hated man in Africa. His return to power brought exclamations of outrage from nonaligned capitals – some of it directed at the United States – and an intensification of the rebellion in the eastern Congo. Tshombe abandoned Adoula's tacit support for Angolan rebels and engaged the services of South African mercenaries against the revolt. This only reinforced the conviction of Nkrumah and other African nationalists that the Congo remained a central front in their struggle against empire.[148] Although Washington hoped for help from moderate African states and urged Tshombe to seek rapprochement with his African peers, it came to view the mercenaries as an indispensable tool for defeating the insurgency. Perceiving no other options, the Johnson administration decided to support Tshombe, seeing him as the alternative to chaos in the Congo and the spread of communist influence into the vast territory.[149]

Anger at Tshombe's return combined with other events to shape the Cairo Conference in October, the first official general gathering of the nonaligned nations since Belgrade. India and its fellow Asian moderates were now squarely outnumbered by newer African members, whom the Indian delegation considered more radical and less interested in the Nehruvian concept of nonalignment, with its attending concern for grand issues of war and peace. Colonialism and

---

[148] Kwame Nkrumah, *Challenge of the Congo* (New York: International Publishers, 1967), 235–239.

[149] Kent, *America, the UN and the Congo*, 185–187; Noer, "*Soapy*," 280–285; Piero Gleijeses, *Conflicting Missions: Havana, Washington, and Africa 1959–1976* (Chapel Hill: University of North Carolina Press, 2002), 60–74.

the fight against it rose to the top of the agenda, and the United States reaped far more criticism than it had received at Belgrade.

Sukarno, now in the heady throes of his confrontation with Britain and Malaysia, declared that the United States and its allies were the implacable foes of the Afro-Asian world.[150] Others echoed him. Mali's Modibo Keita – whom Kennedy had carefully welcomed three years before – also declared the state of the world *worse* in 1964:

Since Belgrade, in spite of the apparent relaxation of the situation between the two great Powers ... never have specific peoples been the object of ... so many acts of aggression and extreme violence against their sovereignty and their sacred right to self-determination.... Never since Belgrade has imperialism been so violently aggressive.[151]

Echoing Keita, Nkrumah decried "neo-colonialism" in the Congo, and condemned the Western powers for abetting Portugal's retention of its colonial empire.[152] The Cairo Conference produced a final resolution primarily concerned with colonialism and imperialism, which declared, "The forces of imperialism are still powerful, and they do not hesitate to resort to the use of force." Particular emphasis fell on the Congo, the Portuguese colonies, Rhodesia, and neocolonialism in Latin America.[153]

Komer found the outcome of the conference disappointingly one-sided. In 1961, he had predicted a waning of anticolonial sentiment as decolonization continued to advance. Now, in the wake of Cairo, he seemed at a loss to explain the nonaligned movement's continued preoccupation with imperialism:

The process of decolonization is practically over (though we'll be coping with the problems it's created for the next 100 years). Yet to listen to the din you'd think it had hardly begun. While the problem will be easier once such vestigial remnants as the Portuguese hangers-on, etc. are disposed of, we ought to start now vigorously proclaiming that the period of colonialism is indeed over – so why all the shouting?[154]

On one level Komer grasped – as well as anyone in Washington – the concerns of nonaligned elites. He recognized that the traumas of colonialism still lingered, yet he recommended a policy of denying that they existed. The "Portuguese hangers-on" that he mentioned so offhandedly were, along with the crisis in the Congo and the dogged perseverance of racist regimes in Rhodesia and South Africa, the most pressing geopolitical issues for African elites. The aggravation caused by minority rule could not be minimized by forceful, early declarations of the end of colonialism. The "shouting" came from genuine anger, not mere political opportunism.

[150] United Arab Republic, Second Conference of Non-Aligned Countries (Cairo: Ministry of Information, 1964), 18–32.
[151] Cairo Conference, 247–256.
[152] Cairo Conference, 85–94.
[153] Cairo Conference, 334–357; G. H. Jansen, *Nonalignment and the Afro-Asian States* (New York: Praeger, 1966), 384–392.
[154] Memorandum, Komer to Bundy, October 9, 1964, RWKP, box 44, "Nonaligned Conference Cairo" folder, LBJL.

Worse followed in subsequent weeks. In the eastern city of Stanleyville, Congolese rebels took hostage hundreds of Belgian citizens and a group of U.S. diplomats from the local consulate. Alarmed by reports that the rebels planned to massacre their prisoners, moved by Belgian entreaties, and finding the OAU too antagonistic to Tshombe to act as a viable mediator, the Johnson administration, on November 23, authorized the use of U.S. aircraft in a bid to free the hostages.[155] The ensuing rescue operation, carried out by Belgian paratroopers, succeeded in freeing most of the captives but produced a firestorm of African condemnation.[156]

The Stanleyville operation further enflamed African frustration over the Congo and the West's failure to act against the Portuguese. To the nonaligned world, the U.S.-Belgian operation, undertaken in conjunction with the use of mercenaries, represented manifest neocolonialism: an active effort to regain effective control of the Congo, with Tshombe's collaboration. Washington's willingness to employ force to free the captive Europeans was contrasted with its unwillingness to assist the colonized peoples of Portuguese Africa – or to cease arms deliveries to Portugal. For its part, the Johnson administration was incensed by African unwillingness to condemn the hostage-taking and by African support of the rebels; it had assisted the operation with no illusions that it would escape criticism.[157]

In the subsequent UN debate, nonaligned nations directed an unprecedented volume of criticism at the United States. Guinea's foreign minister, Louis Beavogui, compared the activities of the mercenaries to the deaths of black Americans in Mississippi during the Freedom Summer of 1964 and the U.S. blockade against Cuba. "Not so long ago the 'new frontier' raised a great wind of hope in Africa," Beavogui observed. "We must ensure that this wind does not become a capricious breeze." Mali's Ousman Ba termed Stanleyville "a premeditated, cold-blooded act." Improbably, Ba implied that Stanleyville had been perpetrated by "the same imperialist forces" that bore responsibility for "the dastardly assassination of John Kennedy ... the fighter for freedom."[158] Ghana's Kojo Botsio wondered how the United States could offer military assistance to Tshombe's regime, when it had recently denied Cuba's right to seek protection from the Soviet Union.[159] These charges incensed Stevenson. "I have served in the United Nations from the day of its inception off and on for seven years," he declared in his defense of the Stanleyville operation. "But

---

[155] Memorandum, Brubeck, "The Congo," Undated, NSF, CF, box 84, "Congo, Vol. 9, Memos" folder, LBJL.

[156] See Memorandum, Carl Rowan to Johnson, November 27, 1964, ibid.; Note 526, Paris, December 3, 1964, in MAE, DDF, 1964, Tome II (Paris: Peter Lang, 2002): 522–524.

[157] Memorandum, "Dragon Rouge," Hughes to Rusk, November 18, 1964, NSF, CF, box 83, "Congo, Vol. 7, Memos (2)" folder, LBJL.

[158] United Nations, Security Council Official Records, 1171st Meeting, December 10, 1964, 2–17.

[159] United Nations, Security Council Official Records, 1170th Meeting, December 9, 1964, 17–33.

never before have I heard such irrational, irresponsible, insulting, and repugnant language in these Chambers."[160]

This was a watershed moment in relations between the United States and the nonaligned world. Stanleyville evoked far more outspoken criticism of the United States than had the death of Lumumba, nearly four years earlier. This change in rhetoric mirrored a sea change in perceptions of the United States. Less than two years before, Washington had been widely perceived as having a separate agenda from that of the European colonists. Now it seemed to share the neocolonialist mission.

The African reaction to the Stanleyville operation must be placed within the broader context of continental politics. At that moment, warfare in Portuguese Africa represented the main concern of the OAU. Events in the Congo tapped an existing well of accumulated anger and frustration, sowing the seeds for an unprecedented degree of suspicion where the United States was concerned. Had the Kennedy or Johnson administrations taken what Touré deemed concrete action against the Portuguese, the African leaders might have listened to the NATO allies when they explained the purpose of the Stanleyville operation. In the absence of such concrete action, however, the operation could only evoke deep-seated fears of racism and neocolonialism. This, in turn, helped to set the tone for the subsequent polarization of U.S.-African relations.

Protracted warfare in Africa continued to amplify tensions. Portugal threatened "legitimate retaliation" against states supporting the insurgencies in its colonies. East African states aided the Congolese rebels, although the insurrection waned after Stanleyville, as the mercenaries advanced into the rebel region. These threats fed African fears of neocolonialist plots. The presence of South African mercenaries close to his border left Nyerere visibly distraught – and suspicious. The U.S. embassy in Tanzania was dogged by accusations of complicity in plots against Nyerere, leading to the expulsion of two of its diplomats in 1965. Guinea, too, harbored similar worries, and in 1965 charged that the CIA sought Touré's overthrow (although here Soviet forgeries were at work).[161]

The failure to take concrete action against Portuguese Africa, of all the colonial disputes, caused the greatest damage to the U.S. position in the nonaligned world. The United States could not have offered much aid to the African rebels. It could, however, have reduced the leverage of the Portuguese. As Bowles and others suggested, it could have taken steps to declare the Azores the jurisdiction of the entire NATO alliance, it could have restricted arms exports to Salazar's government, and it could have continued to vote in favor of condemnatory

---

[160] United Nations, *Security Council Official Records*, 1174th Meeting, December 14, 1964, 10–25.
[161] Telegram 1150, Dar es Salaam to Washington, November 26, 1964, NSF, CF, box 84, "Congo, Vol. 9, Memos" folder, LBJL; Christopher Andrew and Vasili Mitrokhin, *The World Was Going Our Way: The KGB and the Battle for the Third World* (New York: Basic Books, 2005), 435–438.

resolutions after 1962.[162] The New Frontiersmen grasped that Portugal could not retain its colonies but, even so, they vainly sought a middle course between Salazar and the Africans. Washington's retreat from the principles of 1957 and 1961 came at a real, foreseeable cost to its prestige in Africa. Brushfires were left to burn for succeeding administrations to handle. Concerned with near-term Cold War imperatives, Kennedy and Johnson inadvertently drew the United States toward another, more dangerous confrontation in Africa in the following decade. In the process, they squandered the credibility they had endeavored to establish on the continent, poisoning U.S.-African relations for years to come.

"GETTING THE WORST OF BOTH WORLDS"

Since 1961, the United States had waded into a number of dangerous colonial conflicts, achieving decidedly mixed results. Washington's successes proved dismayingly short-lived, and its failures became more damaging over time. In 1961 and 1962 Kennedy had been willing to side with nonaligned states against allies. This policy drew real criticism in the domestic arena: Nehru's seizure of Goa, the UN campaign against Katanga, and the West New Guinea settlement all aroused criticism of the administration's foreign policy, leading to a severe attack on JFK's policy in 1963.

Kennedy's halfway steps toward a consistent policy on decolonization had come at a real cost to European alliances. The colonial issue inflamed relations with Portugal, imperiling NATO's access to the Azores. The Congo conflict complicated already troubled relations with France and Britain. West New Guinea drove a wedge between Washington and The Hague. By 1963, the cumulative cost of these early quarrels, particularly the Congo and West New Guinea, made Washington wary of further intra-alliance squabbling, even as the intensity of the anticolonial struggle escalated. As Rusk wrote to Williams, "What are the prudent and practical limitations on our traditional view of colonialism? One or two more Congos – and we've had it."[163] "We always have to be proving ourselves," Kennedy complained, while contemplating intervention in the Congo in December 1962.[164]

United States policymakers truly believed, in 1961, that the age of colonialism was coming to an end. The vast majority of colonial territories had either received or been promised their independence. Nonetheless, it proved a profound error to think that concern about colonial issues would be proportionate to colonialism's reach: that it would naturally decline over time. This assumption fundamentally failed to understand African and Asian fears

---

[162] Memorandum, Bowles to Kennedy, June 4, 1962, in *FRUS, 1961–1963*, 13: 930–931.

[163] Letter, Rusk to Williams, January 8, 1962, in RG-59, Records of G. Mennen Williams, box 29, "Correspondence with Secretary" folder, NA.

[164] Draft Transcript, Executive Committee Meeting, December 17, 1962, JFK Library Transcripts, Tape 68, MC.

of neocolonialism. The specter of neocolonialism took palpable form with the Congolese crisis and the death of Lumumba and haunted Africans and Asians ever after. Indians described Goa as an imperialist beachhead that endangered their state. Sukarno viewed West New Guinea in much the same fashion. Along with Rhodesia and South Africa, Portuguese Africa evoked the same fears across sub-Saharan Africa. African and Asian governments acted against the specter of neocolonialism not merely out of deep-seated belief, but also out of a profound sense of threat.[165] The depth of their concern was lost in Washington, as policymakers remained intent on convincing the Third World that communism represented the greatest neocolonialist menace of all.

During this time as well, the changing dynamics of nonalignment increased the likelihood that the postcolonial states would take matters into their own hands. African nonaligned leaders came from a continent only partly free. Events in Africa, from Guinean independence onward, conditioned these leaders to expect conspiracies against them. African states formed a large bloc within the nonaligned caucus, and other governments sought to court them. India battled to shape the agenda at Belgrade; afterward, Nehru's move on Goa was broadly interpreted as a bid to restore his prestige in Africa. The seizure of Goa encouraged Sukarno to raise the ante with West New Guinea and lent encouragement to rebels in Portuguese Africa. A complex intercontinental chain of events intensified the anticolonial struggle and ensured that nonaligned states would attach ever greater importance to its resolution. This escalation was driven by ideology, threat perception, and the quest for national prestige.

This, too, was not fully understood in the United States. In all cases, Washington focused on the imperative of combating communism. In some instances this pursuit dovetailed with engaging the nonaligned states. Support for the ONUC and for Indonesia's position in the West New Guinea dispute simultaneously advanced the goals of containment and engagement. Arguments about Portuguese Africa, on the other hand, pitted these goals against one another. Anticommunist priorities, in short, overruled the agendas of the regional bureaus of the State Department. As engagement was itself a project driven by Cold War concerns, it could hardly have been otherwise. This focus, however, left policymakers unprepared to fathom the depth of Third World anticolonial sentiment, leading them to regard it often as an irrational emotional disorder.

At stake in these crises was the credibility of the United States as a friend to the nonaligned world. When Washington took affirmative steps to address the residual problem of colonialism, it received plaudits from nonaligned leaders. Failures in the Congo and Portuguese Africa, on the other hand, produced disillusionment and a sharpening of nonaligned rhetoric toward the United States, as occurred at Cairo. Communist solidarity with the nonaligned states on these

---

[165] On South Africa and a parallel process of African disaffection, see Ryan M. Irwin, "A Wind of Change? White Redoubt and the Postcolonial Moment, 1960–1963," *Diplomatic History* 33, No. 5 (November 2009), 897–925.

questions was received with gratitude – and one form of this came in a tendency by nonaligned states to refrain from criticism of their erstwhile allies. A vicious cycle was at work: the diminishing of U.S. prestige spurred increased reliance on communist support, producing, in turn, greater U.S. disaffection toward the nonaligned states. Rising disenchantment with U.S. policies in Africa spurred a growing willingness in 1964 to describe Washington's growing entanglement in South Vietnam as a colonial project. Nkrumah made the comparison explicit in a 1965 book, arguing that the United States had informally replaced French colonial rule in South Vietnam with its own indirect imperial control, and calling Washington "the world's leading imperial power."[166] Others would soon echo that charge.

By themselves, however, colonial conflicts did not doom the policy of engagement. Pragmatic considerations for nonaligned leaders, especially their desire for financial assistance from the United States, exerted a powerful countervailing influence. If the conflicts of the 1960s had solely been colonial in nature, the United States might have fared better in its dealings with the nonaligned world. Regional conflicts, however, did greater damage to the goal of engagement. To their lasting regret, U.S. leaders would learn that enmities rooted in recent events could be at least as venomous as those dating from the high age of imperialism.

---

[166] Kwame Nkrumah, *Neo-Colonialism: The Last Stage of Imperialism* (New York: International Publishers, 1965), x–xi.

5

The "Diffusion of Power" and the Spread
of Regional Conflicts

For some it was a time of hope; for others, it was an era of confrontation. The twenty-seven months between the October 1962 resolution of the Cuban Missile Crisis and the initiation of the U.S. Rolling Thunder bombing campaign against North Vietnam witnessed two fateful trends. East-West tensions ebbed substantially over the spring and summer of 1963, as the two superpowers drew back from the brink of calamity. Kennedy's "Peace Speech," delivered on June 10, 1963, at American University, and the subsequent conclusion of the Test Ban Treaty seemed to herald a new era of superpower détente. Simultaneously and paradoxically, however, regional conflicts and rivalries intensified through the postcolonial world: in the Middle East, West Africa, South Asia, and Southeast Asia. These concurrent developments were not unrelated to each other; ironically, the relaxation of Moscow-Washington tensions acted as an accelerant to conflicts elsewhere in the world.

For all the problems they posed, colonial conflicts had seemed to be a relatively impermanent phenomenon. The regional conflicts that festered in the postcolonial world offered no such reassurance. In the 1960s, as localized fault lines deepened through the Third World, Washington faced a new, more complex set of challenges. Influential nonaligned states such as Ghana, Indonesia, Egypt, and India remained embroiled in divisive, violent regional conflicts. U.S. policymakers hoped that economic aid and preventive diplomacy would encourage national leaders to focus on internal development. Localized rivalries thwarted those hopes, and left policymakers facing an unenviable set of dilemmas that tempered and limited their ambitions.

The Kennedy and Johnson administrations attempted to ameliorate localized conflicts, offering to serve as an honest broker between combatants, providing aid to both parties and believing that the menace of communism would eventually render regional feuds moot. Defending these tactics, Robert Komer of the NSC staff observed:

Problems arise from the simple fact that the policies of Nasser or Sukarno cut across those of many other US friends; hence we are constantly being put in the position of being asked to choose between them. It would be simpler, for example, to choose sides in Yemen than to take the present middle road. Yet to do so would cost us more with one side than we would gain with the other.[1]

Nonaligned states, however, resented the continued association between the United States and their adversaries, providing an image of Washington as a friend of reaction and neocolonialism. Once enflamed, regional conflicts added an insupportable burden to U.S.-nonaligned relations.

Simultaneously, Kennedy's policy of engagement contributed to a growing crisis of confidence felt by allies, some already uneasy about U.S.-Soviet détente. Washington's efforts to engage major nonaligned powers reinforced growing doubts in governments already fearful that they had erred in entrusting their security to the United States. Moscow's new vigor in the Third World and the strains imposed by the Berlin and Cuban crises further underscored these concerns. This crisis of confidence was felt around the world. France and Germany increasingly questioned their safety under the U.S. nuclear umbrella, alarmed by Kennedy's willingness to deny Bonn a nuclear capability or a meaningful stake in NATO's deterrent force. Britain nursed its own worries, born of a wide range of issues, about the reliability of its special partnership. Washington's policies toward colonial conflicts in Africa and Asia further exacerbated tensions with a number of European allies. Elsewhere, engagement contributed to the disquiet of major regional allies. Iran and Pakistan, conscious of their proximity to the Soviet Union, felt profound unease as Eisenhower and then Kennedy began serious efforts to engage Egypt and India. Kennedy's efforts at defusing potential Cold War battlegrounds furthered this trend. The neutralization of Laos evoked serious doubt in Thailand, the Philippines, and South Vietnam, while the West New Guinea settlement left Australia fretful about future Indonesian intentions. Beset by quarrels with nonaligned states, friends and allies made sharp, public appeals for Washington's solidarity; they also proved less willing to heed their ally's calls for restraint.

These anxieties mounted as Cold War tensions ebbed in 1963. As presidential advisor Walt Rostow reasoned, a "diffusion of power" was occurring, as the reduction of Cold War tensions allowed the release of centrifugal stresses within alliances, in particular NATO and the Sino-Soviet alliance.[2] By 1964, a new wave of conflicts threatened the position of the United States in the nonaligned world. They came as the United States increasingly entangled itself in Southeast Asia, while facing major crises in Panama and Cyprus, and as Lyndon Johnson plunged into the 1964 presidential election. The harried Johnson had little patience for the added frustration posed by nonaligned states and their regional conflicts.

He felt differently toward the complaints of friends. With U.S. resources increasingly strained and as Vietnam's shadow lengthened, Johnson sought to

---

[1] Memorandum, Komer to Kennedy, January 19, 1963, in DOS, *FRUS, 1961–1963*, Vol. 8: *National Security Policy* (Washington: GPO, 1996): 456–457.
[2] Memorandum, "State of the World," Rostow to Rusk, September 17, 1963, in *FRUS, 1961–1963*, 8: 507–511.

both reassure and obtain assistance from a broad range of allies. None was more important than Great Britain, which held primary responsibility for the Persian Gulf and Indian Ocean and which acted as a valued collaborator in Europe, Africa, and Asia.[3] Of the allies, London was ubiquitous: virtually every Third World regional conflict had an Anglo-American dimension. U.S. dependence on Britain held profound consequences for engagement.

Although localized in nature these conflicts came to hold significant Cold War implications. This escalation of regional conflicts coincided with the deepening of the Sino-Soviet rivalry and the emergence of a more assertive Chinese foreign policy directed at displacing Moscow's influence in the Third World. African and Asian issues substantially drove and accelerated the schism. The Chinese Communist Party charged its Soviet rival with being insufficiently supportive of Third World liberation movements.[4] From late 1963 to February 1964, Premier Zhou Enlai embarked on an African tour, bolstering the image of Chinese dynamism in the Third World. China's diplomatic offensive brought growing involvement in regional conflicts ranging from South Asia, to the heart of Africa, to the island of Borneo. "The Chinese want people in Afro-Asian and Latin American countries to adopt militant, aggressive and revolutionary attitudes," Nehru warned Kennedy in an August 1963 letter. "They have been exploiting local quarrels between the countries in various regions all over the world to maintain an atmosphere of tension and conflict."[5]

The Sino-Soviet battle was mirrored by a similar contest between China and India. New Delhi sought, with mixed results, to rally its nonaligned partners to its side during and after its border war with China. Sino-Indian antagonism spurred Mao to support a model of nonalignment predicated on Afro-Asian and anticolonial solidarity, not Nehruvian ideas. The nonaligned movement, too, suffered from the ongoing fragmentation of blocs and the emergence of newer geopolitical rivalries, as regional quarrels and its ongoing doctrinal dispute became intermeshed.

Facing this destructive interaction between U.S. policies, the aspirations of major nonaligned states, the insecurities of allies, and the growing Sino-Soviet competition, advocates of engagement emphasized the need for preventive action, for engaging both sides of regional disputes. "I fully appreciate how our frustrations over Indonesia, the UAR, India, Ghana, Algeria, etc. may tend to force our hand," wrote Komer in 1964:

But a hard line now may increase the chances that – in addition to the Vietnam, Cuba, Cyprus, Panama, and other current trials – will be added come summer Indonesia/

---

[3] See Thomas A. Schwartz, *Lyndon Johnson and Europe: In the Shadow of Vietnam* (Cambridge, MA: Harvard University Press, 2003), 66–86.

[4] Lorenz M. Lüthi, *The Sino-Soviet Split: Cold War in the Communist World* (Princeton: Princeton University Press, 2008), 224–339; Odd Arne Westad, *The Global Cold War: Third World Interventions and the Making of Our Times* (New York: Cambridge University Press, 2006), 160–165.

[5] Letter, Nehru to Kennedy, August 11, 1963, POF, box 118A, "India Security" folder, JFKL.

Malaysia, Arab/Israeli, India/Pak crises which may be even more unmanageable. Their emergence may be inevitable, no matter how skillful our preventive diplomacy, but I see a real case for trying to short circuit them.

He suggested that he and his colleagues were "victims of our own success" forced to live with "secondary troubles in an increasingly pluralistic world."[6] This was, at best, a saccharine gloss on deep and lasting problems, and it reflected the administration's preoccupation with the Cold War, a deeply exaggerated estimation of its own ability to resolve regional troubles, and its lasting belief that the struggle against communism was *the* defining feature of global politics. To all too many states in Africa and Asia, however, this hierarchy was entirely inverted: regional disputes were central and the exhortations of the superpowers secondary. The Johnson administration suffered heavily for this misperception.

GHANA CONFRONTS ITS NEIGHBORS

Just after daybreak on the morning of January 13, 1963, U.S. Ambassador Leon Poullada drove through Lomé, the capital of the small West African state of Togo. His embassy stood on the same block as the residence of Togolese President Sylvanus Olympio. Upon his arrival, Poullada observed soldiers standing along the street, some on embassy property. Poullada was joined by his vice consul, Richard Storch. At 7:10 A.M., Storch observed the soldiers guarding a barefoot man in shorts and a shirt. Noting the man's subdued demeanor and casual dress, Storch assumed he was an employee of Olympio's household. Storch abandoned his vigil for a few minutes to get a glass of water; while in the kitchen, he heard three evenly spaced shots. Returning, he saw the man now lying dead in the road. When Poullada examined the corpse, he found it was no servant, but Sylvanus Olympio, the first president of Togo and a strong ally of the United States. Olympio had died seeking refuge in the embassy. He had been shot three times and bayoneted for good measure. Poullada and Storch carried Olympio's body within the embassy complex to protect it against further depredations and to free a path out of the driveway.[7]

Olympio's assassination bore tragic implications for Togo and Africa; it also held broad ramifications for the Ghanaian-American relationship. Ghana's President Kwame Nkrumah was the single most prominent leader in sub-Saharan Africa; his stature within the nonaligned movement and involvement in the Congo made the improvement of relations with Ghana a significant priority for Kennedy. Ghana's geopolitical ambitions in Africa, including its policies toward neighbors like Togo, however, posed an insurmountable obstacle. Like Egypt's President Nasser, Nkrumah espoused an ideology founded

---

[6] Memorandum, Komer to Bundy, February 25, 1964, NSF, CF, box 246, "Indonesia, Vol. I, Memos 11/63/3/64" folder, LBJL.

[7] Airgram A-215, Lomé to Washington, January 23, 1963, NSF, box 165, "Togo, General, 1/23/63–1/31/63" folder, JFKL.

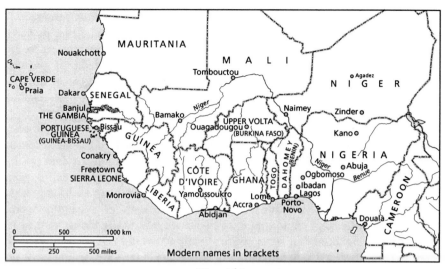

MAP 5. West Africa, 1961.

upon his own prestige as a national leader, aimed at regional unification. This inexorably brought him into conflict with a number of his neighbors.[8]

Nkrumah had few friends on the African continent. Guinea's Sekou Touré and Mali's Modibo Keita were his principal allies, although their regional policies frequently diverged from his. Three enmities merit particular attention. Nigeria, led by Prime Minister Abubakar Balewa, was the most populous country in Africa and a natural rival to Ghana's leadership. Cote d'Ivoire, governed by President Félix Houphouet-Boigny, was the leading state of the Union Africain et Malagache, a group of Francophone states retaining close ties to Paris. Finally, little Togo had consistently tense relations with Ghana, which claimed much of its territory.

Of Nkrumah's three main foes, Nigeria was the most important to Kennedy's African strategy – more so than even Ghana. Nigeria represented the focal point of the administration's political goals of demonstrating the applicability of Western programs of economic modernization to sub-Saharan Africa. Rostow deemed it a "key state"; in June 1961, he listed it, along with India and Brazil, as a worthwhile target of long-term development aid.[9] Rusk regarded

---

[8] On the intersection of Ghana's struggle for influence and the Cold War, see W. Scott Thompson, *Ghana's Foreign Policy, 1957–1966: Diplomacy, Ideology and the New State* (Princeton: Princeton University Press, 1969); Richard Mahoney, *JFK: Ordeal in Africa* (New York: Oxford University Press, 1983), 157–186; David Rooney, *Kwame Nkrumah: The Political Kingdom in the Third World* (London: Tauris, 1988).

[9] Memorandum, Walt Rostow to Kennedy, June 17, 1961, NSF, box 405, "Memos to the President, 6/61" folder, JFKL; Memorandum, Rostow to Kennedy, July 21, 1961, in DOS, *FRUS, 1961–1963, Vol. 21: Africa (MS)* (Washington: GPO, 1996): doc. 582. See also, Robert B. Shepard, *Nigeria, Africa, and the United States: From Kennedy to Reagan* (Bloomington: Indiana University Press, 1991), 20–25.

Balewa as a force for moderation and was impressed by Lagos's careful policy toward the Congo.[10] Kennedy shared these views, telling Balewa in 1961
that Nigeria's development and leadership were of the greatest interest to the
United States.[11] Accordingly, foreign aid to Nigeria far exceeded that given to
any other sub-Saharan African state, totaling nearly thirty percent of the dis-
bursements made to the continent by 1963.[12] Nigeria represented the African
proving ground for Kennedy's development policies.

Simultaneously, the White House needed to keep a close eye on Ghana.
The demands of its regional strategy forced the Kennedy administration in
December 1961 to grudgingly support Nkrumah's plan to build a dam on the
Volta River, affirming a commitment made by Eisenhower the preceding year.
Paradoxically, the resentments raised by such a large program and the threats
perceived by Ghana's neighbors demarcated the limits of engaging Accra.
Having made one large commitment to Nkrumah, the White House wished to
reassure his neighbors that *their* political support would not go unrewarded.
This, in turn, shackled U.S.-Ghanaian relations to Ghana's worsening position
in West Africa.[13]

In December 1961, after weeks of difficult deliberation, Kennedy elected to
offer funding in support of Ghana's planned dam on the Volta. On its surface,
this decision was puzzling. Although Nkrumah had ceased active opposition to
Kennedy's policy in the Congo, he had done little else to reassure the administration. After his unsatisfactory speech at Belgrade, the Ghanaian pledged
to send 400 of his officers to the Soviet Union for training and dismissed all
remaining British officers still serving in his army.[14]

Nkrumah's behavior vexed the Kennedy administration and might have
spurred it to deny Ghana funding for the dam, had a range of allies not urged
otherwise. British Colonial Secretary Duncan Sandys warned that reneging
would damage the standing of the United States throughout Africa, even in
sympathetic states such as Nigeria.[15] The CIA shared this assessment, observing that most African and Asian leaders believed the United States was morally obligated to fund the dam. African moderates, although distrustful of
Nkrumah, would likely interpret a denial of funding as signaling "a reluctance

---

[10] Memcon, Rusk and Maurice Couve de Murville, August 7, 1961, in DOS, *FRUS, 1961–1963,*
Vol. 20: Congo Crisis (Washington: GPO, 1995): 186–187.

[11] Memcon, Kennedy and Balewa, July 25, 1961, in *FRUS, 1961–1963,* 21 (MS): doc. 583.

[12] Memorandum, Ralph Dungan to Kennedy, March 6, 1963, in *FRUS, 1961–1963,* 21:
329–330.

[13] See Thomas J. Noer, "The New Frontier and African Neutralism: Kennedy, Nkrumah, and
the Volta River Project," *Diplomatic History* 8, No. 1 (January 1984), 61–80; Mahoney, *JFK:
Ordeal in Africa,* 162–179.

[14] Memorandum, Rostow to Kennedy, September 13, 1961, in DOS, *FRUS, 1961–1963, Vol. 21:
Africa* (Washington: GPO, 1995): 352–353; Memcon, Kennedy and Ball, September 29, 1961,
ibid.: 358.

[15] Telegram 1455, London to Washington, October 10, 1961, NSF, box 99, "Ghana, General,
10/61" folder, JFKL.

to contribute substantively to African development."[16] Embassies in both Togo and Nigeria reported that a reversal of policy would embarrass both the United States and friendly local governments.[17]

Simultaneously, Ghana's receipt of such sizable support was bound to prompt resentment among its rivals. A number of embassies registered their unease at the extent of U.S. support for Nkrumah. A U.S. diplomat in Cote d'Ivoire observed:

I must point out [the] steadily growing belief [in] this part [of the] world that bad boys are invited to the banquet and good boys get scraps. If this feeling persists it can lead only to bad boys remaining bad and good boys turning naughty.[18]

Kennedy absorbed both sides of this debate, and approached the decision with ambivalence. He reasoned: "If it is cancelled, they will blame everything on us. On the other hand, if we go through with it, everybody will think we are crazy in the Congress and every place else."[19]

It seemed to the administration that the die had already been cast: reneging on the offer now would only damage the United States position across the African continent. When the NSC met, on December 5, 1961, to make a final decision on the dam, Rusk and Secretary of Defense Robert McNamara offered guarded support, citing the prior commitment, while Attorney General Robert F. Kennedy advised against the project. Facing the "hot breath" of his brother's opinion, JFK nevertheless approved the loan, announcing the decision in a letter to Nkrumah. Kennedy's letter underscored his concerns about Ghana, clearly implying to Nkrumah that the continuation of U.S. support would depend on Ghanaian moderation.[20]

Bilateral issues, however, were not the sole irritant vexing Washington and Accra. Relations between Ghana and its neighbors were fractious during Kennedy's first two years in office. Togo accused Ghana of involvement in a December 1961 attempt on Olympio's life, and Olympio characterized Nkrumah as a "Black Hitler."[21] Ghana's isolation was confirmed when a regional conference in Lagos elicited broad denunciations of Nkrumah.[22] Even

[16] Memorandum, Sherman Kent to John McCone, "Likely Consequences of Various US Courses of Action on the Volta Dam," November 16, 1961, NSF, box 99, "Ghana, General, 11/61" folder, JFKL.

[17] Telegram 79, Lomé to Washington, October 6, 1961, Record Group 59 (RG-59) DSCF, 845J.2614/10-661, NA; Telegram 351, Lagos to Washington, September 30, 1961, RG-59, DSCF, 845J.2614/9-2861, NA.

[18] Telegram 314, Abidjan to Washington, December 18, 1961, NSF, box 99, "Ghana, General, 12/16/61-12/31/61" folder, JFKL.

[19] Memcon, Kennedy and Ball, September 21, 1961, in FRUS, 1961-1963, 21: 355-356.

[20] Notes for the Record, "NSC Meeting on Volta Dam," December 5, 1961, ibid.: 369-370; Letter, Kennedy to Nkrumah, December 14, 1961, ibid.: 371-372.

[21] Telegram 171, Lomé to Washington, December 29, 1961, NSF, box 165, "Togo, General, 1961" folder, JFKL.

[22] Research Paper, "Ghanaian Subversion in Africa," February 12, 1962, NSF, box 99, "Ghana, General, 1/62-3/62" folder, JFKL.

Guinea seemed to be turning its back on Nkrumah; Touré delivered an implicit rebuke when he spoke before the UN in September.[23] Most fatefully, however, relations between Ghana and Togo worsened dramatically.

Acrimonious exchanges between the two African states brought occasional expressions of concern in Washington but no direct action. Rusk expressed concern at the prospect of conflict between the two states and wrote that Togo, as a "moderate and essentially pro-Western neutral state," deserved U.S. support. Upon consideration, it still seemed preferable to entrust Togo's security to its regional allies.[24] Washington was not blameless in stoking the fire. It maintained contacts with Ghanaian exiles in Togo, in meetings facilitated by Olympio's government.[25] During 1962 and 1963, anti-Nkrumah dissidents staged a bombing campaign in Ghana, including an attempt on the president's life. Nkrumah, convinced that he was facing a CIA-sponsored insurgency staged out of Togo, threatened to expel the Peace Corps. He retaliated for West German economic support of Togo by announcing he would open a trade office in East Berlin.[26]

Ghana's neighbors watched the situation anxiously, seeing Nkrumah's actions toward Togo as a litmus test of his intentions toward them as well. In December 1962, Balewa expressed his concern and asked repeatedly if the United States could support him if he came to Togo's defense.[27] Olympio's death seemed the final straw, panicking other African governments, even in the absence of direct evidence of Ghanaian involvement.[28] The British Commonwealth Relations Office noted that the assassination, the first sub-Saharan coup d'etat, had evoked more alarm on the continent than the recent Cuban Missile Crisis or the Sino-Indian War.[29] In the weeks following the assassination, both Nigeria and Cote d'Ivoire complained of Ghanaian plots to subvert their governments.[30] Faced with a new government in Lomé that they regarded as a Ghanaian puppet regime, other African governments withheld recognition and requested that the United States do so as well. A second regional conference in Lagos resulted in a declaration that the new government would not receive recognition until the coup had been investigated and

[23] Thomson, Ghana's Foreign Policy, 198–262. Touré called for African unity on the basis of "honest cooperation," not the "doctrinal theories" associated with Nkrumah.

[24] Telegram CA-574, Rusk to Various Posts, December 2, 1961, FRUS, 1961–1963, 21 (MS): doc. 684.

[25] See, for example, CIA Telegram, September 19, 1962, NSF, box 100, "Ghana, General, 9/62" folder, JFKL; Telegram 61, Lomé to Washington, August 15, 1962, NSF, box 165, "Togo, General, 6/62/12/62" folder, JFKL.

[26] Telegram 752, Accra to Washington, December 8, 1962, NSF, box 100, "Ghana, General, 11/62–12/62" folder, JFKL.

[27] Telegram 860, Lagos to Washington, December 28, 1962, NSF, box 100, "Ghana, General, 11/62–12/62" folder, JFKL; Bassey E. Ate, Decolonization and Dependence: The Development of Nigerian-U.S. Relations, 1960–1984 (Boulder: Westview, 1987), 141–146.

[28] See Thompson, Ghana's Foreign Policy, 308–312; Atsutsé Kokouvi Agbobli, Sylvanus Olympio: Un Destin Tragique (Abidjan: LivreSud, 1992).

[29] Memorandum, November 1963, DO 193/37, TNA.

[30] Telegram 1167, Lagos to Washington, February 13, 1963, in FRUS, 1961–1963, 21 (MS): doc. 586; Memcon, Wayne Fredericks and Konan Bedie, February 19, 1963, ibid.: doc. 530.

new elections held. These substantial preconditions made immediate recognition infeasible for the United States.[31]

Nkrumah's seeming complicity in the Togo coup damaged his already battered image in Washington. Kennedy, long exasperated by the Ghanaian leader, asked, "What is this guy – some kind of a nut?"[32] Dismay with Nkrumah and the Africans' united front drove the decision to delay recognition. This was by no means a unanimous decision. The embassy in Lomé pleaded for Washington to support the post-coup government, reasoning that it was the best available under the circumstances.[33] George Ball thought delaying recognition "a very bad posture for us to get ourselves into."[34] Nonetheless the White House waited until it received a green light from other African states. Here the administration made a clear choice, favoring states such as Nigeria and Cote d'Ivoire over Ghana.

In the spring, further proof of Nkrumah's tenuous status among his peers came when the Organization of African Unity (OAU) held its first summit in Addis Ababa. Ghana had approached the conference with an ambitious set of proposals for a centrally governed African union. The Ghanaian state press had, meanwhile, also denounced other attendees as pawns of the imperialists. Upon his arrival, Nkrumah found his proposals stillborn and himself marginalized.[35] To U.S. Ambassador William Mahoney, Nkrumah appeared "tired and depressed" upon his return.[36]

Nkrumah's relations with his neighbors remained tense in succeeding months. In the summer, the Ghanaian embroiled himself in a dispute with a number of East African states, most notably Tanganyika, when he opposed the East African Federation, a proposed economic and political union of Uganda, Kenya, and Tanganyika, which had been praised by the United States as a positive step for African development.[37] Ghana's interference prompted U.S. suspicions that the communist bloc was acting through Nkrumah. Ghana, in turn, took umbrage at Washington's stance, charging that the United States opposed African unity.[38]

---

[31] Circular Telegram 1329, Washington to Various Embassies, January 29, 1963, NSF, box 165, "Togo, General, 1/23/63–1/31/63," JFKL.

[32] Mahoney, *JFK: Ordeal in Africa*, 186.

[33] Telegram 326, Lomé to Washington, January 18, 1963, NSF, box 165, "Togo, General, 1/16/63–1/22/63" folder, JFKL.

[34] Conversation between George Ball and George McGhee, February 19, 1963, GWBP, box 8, Togo File, JFKL; Conversation between Ball and Fredericks, February 19, 1963, ibid.

[35] Thompson, *Ghana's Foreign Policy*, 316–323; Circular Telegram 2032, May 28, 1963, in FRUS, 1961–1963, 21: 332–334.

[36] Telegram 1323, Accra to Washington, May 29, 1963, NSF, box 3, "Africa General, Addis Ababa Conference, 5/63–6/63" folder, JFKL; Note, "Conférerence d'Addis-Abeba," June 11, 1963, in MAE, DDF, 1963, Tome I (Paris: Imprimerie Nationale, 2000): 614–620.

[37] See Opoku Agyeman, *Nkrumah's Ghana and East Africa: Pan-Africanism and African Interstate Relations* (Teaneck, NJ: Fairleigh Dickinson University Press, 1992).

[38] Telegram 192, Dar es Salaam to Washington, August 17, 1963, NSF, box 100, "Ghana, General, 8/63–11/63" folder; Telegram 97, Washington to Accra, August 9, 1963, ibid.; Memcon, Williams and Kojo Botsio, September 26, 1963, ibid.

For much of 1963, the U.S.-Ghana relationship appeared to be in a state of flux, as the Ghanaian leader made sporadic efforts to improve his ties with the United States. After visiting Accra, Assistant Secretary G. Mennen Williams reported that Nkrumah genuinely liked Kennedy, particularly after the president's June 11 address on civil rights. Nonetheless, "suspicion and some distrust of US is prevalent," stemming from fears of CIA plots against Nkrumah, perceived support of colonialism and neocolonialism, and the "sincere belief [that] US is actively opposing Nkrumah's Pan-African policies."[39] Such mixed signals engendered ambivalence in Washington to the end of the Kennedy administration. In his final meeting with Mahoney, on November 19, 1963, Kennedy still seemed baffled by Nkrumah.[40] It is debatable how viable the relationship was at this point. The forces that doomed Washington's policy toward Ghana had been set in motion long before Johnson took office. Confronting a myriad of other issues, bereft of both Kennedy's interest in Africa and any rapport with Nkrumah, Johnson kept a wary distance from the Ghanaian, shifting further toward support of his rivals.

Faced with a choice between Nkrumah and much of the rest of West Africa, Washington was bound to choose allies like Nigeria and Cote d'Ivoire and to heed their counsel after events like the coup in Togo. Unlike Egypt, India, or Indonesia, Ghana lacked strong partisans in Washington or the local embassy. Williams battled long and hard on behalf of intervention in Katanga and confronting Portuguese colonialism but saw no reason to abstain from criticism of Nkrumah's rhetoric or of his policies toward his neighbors. Turmoil in Ghana, moreover, made Nkrumah's overthrow seem increasingly possible; both the State Department and CIA undertook contingency planning for the event of a successful coup.[41] Nkrumah reacted to domestic unrest by undertaking actions that alienated Washington: suppressing Ghana's judiciary, dismissing British officers from his army, and centralizing power. Even had Kennedy found Nkrumah's foreign policy more agreeable, political uncertainty and increasing authoritarianism in the country made him chary of further investments in Ghana.

Ghana's regional agenda and the broad African policy of the United States proved to be mutually incompatible. Without intending to, by supporting a broad range of African governments, the White House waded into a complex and baffling set of regional quarrels, ultimately dooming its efforts to forge a stable rapport with Nkrumah. Although they proved less durable than their Middle Eastern or South Asian equivalents, the enmities within West Africa were a formidable obstacle to the goals of the Kennedy and Johnson

[39] Telegram 283, Libreville to Washington, July 1, 1963, NSF, box 100, "Ghana, General, 5/63–7/63" folder, JFKL.

[40] Memcon, Kennedy and Mahoney, November 19, 1963, in *FRUS, 1961–1963*, 21: 390–391.

[41] See Memorandum, William Brubeck to Bundy, October 4, 1962, NSF, box 100, "Ghana, General, 10/62" folder, JFKL; Telegram, CIA, September 30, 1962, NSF, box 100, "Ghana General, 9/62" folder, ibid.

administrations; the disparity between sides in this particular quarrel made the final choices somewhat simpler than they would be elsewhere.

THE MALAYSIAN CONFRONTATION

Alliance commitments exerted an even more profound influence in the case of another dangerous regional conflict: Indonesia's clash with Malaysia. Whereas the combined weight of African opinion helped to steer U.S. policy away from engaging Ghana, traditional U.S. deference to its British ally and London's sharp exhortations after the beginning of the confrontation drew the Johnson administration into its conflict with Jakarta in the autumn of 1964. Lyndon Johnson's own reservations about Sukarno contributed to the effective collapse of U.S.-Indonesian relations by the end of that year.

This collapse was all the more striking because it came unanticipated. As the Kennedy administration emerged from the final tumultuous negotiations over West New Guinea, it felt it had turned a corner in its approach to Sukarno. The "holding operation" had been a success. Accordingly, in August 1962, Kennedy endorsed the promotion of "a new and better relationship with Indonesia," to be founded upon expanded economic and developmental assistance.[42] In succeeding months, U.S.-Indonesian dialogue largely focused on the type and extent of economic and military aid Jakarta would receive, a question made urgent by Indonesia's dire economic situation.

Simultaneously, however, the archipelago's next crisis was quietly taking root. During 1962, the project of Malaysia – the creation of a federation encompassing both the independent peninsular republic of Malaya and Britain's colonial holdings on the island of Borneo – moved toward fruition. London hoped to lighten its overseas defense budget by entrusting its remaining Southeast Asian colonies to Malaya and its ruler, Tunku (Prince) Abdul Rahman. Despite initially receiving the project mutedly, Sukarno came to fear that the north of Borneo might soon host U.S. or British military facilities.[43] Such fears drew him to outwardly support a brief, ill-fated rebellion in British-held Brunei and, as 1963 dawned, to assail the Malaysia project as a neo-colonial enterprise.[44]

Lacking Kennedy's belief that the Indonesian leader could be coaxed toward less confrontational policies, the British were unsurprised by Sukarno's opposition to Malaysia. An autumn 1962 intelligence report forecast vehement

---

[42] Memorandum, Komer to Kennedy, August 15, 1962, in DOS, *FRUS, 1961–1963, Vol. 23: Southeast Asia* (Washington: GPO, 1994): 626; NSAM 179, August 16, 1962, ibid.: 627. See also Bradley R. Simpson, *Economists with Guns: Authoritarian Development and U.S.-Indonesian Relations. 1960–1968* (Stanford: Stanford University Press, 2008), 63–112.

[43] J. A. C. Mackie, *Konfrontasi: The Indonesia-Malaysia Dispute, 1963–1966* (New York: Oxford University Press, 1974), 37–77; Telegram 592, Jakarta to Washington, September 28, 1962, NSF, box 114, "Indonesia, General, 9/62–10/62" folder, JFKL; Intelligence report, CIA, October 4, 1962, ibid.

[44] Mackie, *Konfrontasi*, 113–125; Telegram 951, Jakarta to Washington, December 18, 1962, NSF, box 114, "Indonesia, General, 11/62–12/62" folder, JFKL.

opposition to Malaysia, observing of Sukarno, "His talent is for the revolutionary and destructive, and not for constructive action." The Indonesian leader remained "antagonistic" to Western ideals and institutions, and more inclined to tilt toward the Soviet bloc.[45] A cabinet-level analysis the following spring held no hope of compromise, averring that nothing would make Sukarno abandon his hostility.[46] Britain saw no real prospect of reaching a modus vivendi with the unpredictable Indonesian leader; all that could be done was to forge ahead and establish Malaysia, while treating Indonesian objections as stalling tactics. To that end, Washington's support of Malaysia and cessation of aid to Indonesia were essential. So long as the United States aided Jakarta, Foreign Secretary Alec Douglas-Home reasoned, it was subsidizing Sukarno's aggression.[47]

An aid cutoff was far stronger medicine than the White House was ready to contemplate. Instead, from January 1963 onward, the United States made it clear to Sukarno that it expected him to address his concerns about Malaysia peacefully. Kennedy publicly announced his support of the Malaysia proposal. U.S. Ambassador Howard Jones told the Indonesians that Malaysian federation would offer them a buffer against Chinese expansionism.[48] Michael V. Forrestal, the NSC's Far East specialist, visited Indonesia in January. Meeting with Sukarno, he spoke primarily of economic aid, adding that it behooved Indonesia not to engage in external adventures. Sukarno quickly assured his guest that Indonesia "had no plans for adventures."[49]

Behind these messages to Sukarno was the sense, through the critical first eight months of 1963, that the crisis had not and should not endanger Washington's critical investment in Indonesia. After a visit to Jakarta in March, Assistant Secretary of State Averell Harriman advised maintaining aid programs, including military assistance. "If Indonesia can survive short run," he wrote, "we should be able [to] assure ourselves of a neutral, independent and non-Communist nation."[50] Kennedy and the NSC staff shared this assessment and forged ahead with seemingly more immediate bilateral questions: negotiating the terms of Indonesia's aid package and lobbying on behalf of U.S. oil companies in a nettlesome dispute over the distribution of revenue.

As before, however, policy took on a two-headed character. While Washington resisted British pressure to suspend aid to Indonesia, it also declined to act to defuse the crisis – particularly by urging Britain to negotiate seriously with Indonesia. While London regarded Sukarno's objections as spurious, the Tunku felt otherwise. Over the spring and summer of 1963, he

[45] JIC report draft, undated, DO 169/67, TNA.
[46] Memorandum, Burke Trend to Macmillan, April 23, 1963, CAB 21/4849, TNA.
[47] Aide memoire, Alec Douglas-Home, January 11, 1963, NSF, box 114, "Indonesia, General, 1/63–3/63" folder, JFKL.
[48] Telegram 682, Washington to Jakarta, January 16, 1963, in *FRUS, 1961–1963*, 23: 658–659.
[49] Telegram 1117, Jakarta to Washington, January 20, 1963, NSF box 114, "Indonesia, General, 1/63–3/63" folder, JFKL.
[50] Telegram 1333, Jakarta to Washington, March 1, 1961, in *FRUS, 1963–1963*, 23: 659–662.

engaged in serious negotiations with Sukarno and the Philippine government (which also had some objections to Malaysia). Tripartite meetings in May and June of 1963 between the respective leaders and their foreign ministers seemingly illuminated a path forward. In the June 1963 Manila Accord, Sukarno indicated that he could be amenable to Malaysia if some effort was made to ascertain the wishes of the people of Borneo. Setting aside his rank hypocrisy – he had rejected the use of plebiscites during the West New Guinea dispute – this still offered grounds for hope.

London, however, forced the issue to a head. Subsequent to the Manila Accord, the British insisted on setting a definite date for the establishment of Malaysia, regardless of Jakarta's desire to ascertain the inclinations of the Borneans. Along the way, the Tunku gave ample notice of his frustration with London's directives. During an August 27 meeting with Colonial Secretary Duncan Sandys, Abdul Rahman complained bitterly that British criteria were making compromise with Indonesia impossible. Relations between Malaya and Indonesia, he told Sandys, represented "*his* 'cold war' which he must handle as he thought best." What concern was it to London how he negotiated with the Indonesians?[51] Unmoved, Sandys pressed home and won the Tunku's grudging acquiescence to a September 16 date, with or without an ascertainment. Two days later it was announced.[52]

Here the Kennedy administration failed to avert disaster. Through much of 1963, the State Department deferred to London on all Malaysia-related questions. Rusk informed Home on April 8 that he perceived the issue as "primarily a UK-Malayan responsibility." The only role he perceived for United States policy was "to commend Malaysia to Indonesia and [the] Philippines."[53] Understandably, Rusk did not wish to inflame ties with London over Borneo, but he also had ample evidence that Indonesia would not respond lightly to a fait accompli.

As early as February, Jones wrote: "It will not repeat not be possible [to] cram Malaysia down [the] throats [of] Indonesia ... with anything but adverse results for US position [in] this area." Premature action on London's part could only aid the Indonesian communists, offering them an "enormous boost."[54] Despite this prescient warning, as Komer later recalled, "We didn't really begin stepping into the Malaysian situation until after Malaysia was formed."[55] Two

[51] Telegram 62, Kuala Lumpur to Commonwealth Relations Office, August 27, 1963, CAB 21/5520, TNA. See also Matthew Jones, *Conflict and Confrontation in South East Asia, 1961–1965: Britain, the United States and the Creation of Malaysia* (Cambridge: Cambridge University Press, 2002), 187–191.

[52] Jones, *Conflict and Confrontation*, 172–199; Roger Hilsman, *To Move a Nation: The Politics of Foreign Policy in the Administration of John F. Kennedy* (New York: Doubleday, 1967), 399–405.

[53] Telegram Secto 8, Paris to Washington, April 8, 1963, NSF, box 171, "UK, General, 4/1/63–4/18/63" folder, JFKL.

[54] Telegram 1242, Jakarta to Washington, February 12, 1963, NSF, box 114, "Indonesia, General, 1/63–2/63" folder, JFKL.

[55] Fourth Oral History Interview, Robert Komer, October 31, 1964, 4, OH, JFKL.

factors, in addition to alliance considerations, impeded an administration response to the crisis. For the first half of the year, the dispute with Jakarta over petroleum export revenue distracted the White House. Congressional assaults on Indonesia aid policy in the summer also put Kennedy on the defensive. The most significant U.S. intervention was an August letter from Kennedy to Macmillan, asking for a brief postponement to provide Sukarno a "fig leaf." Macmillan replied that it would do little good to humor a man like Sukarno.[56] Little more was done.

Malaysia came into being on September 16, before the completion of the UN's ascertainment, which Britain had acted to delay. On September 18, 1963, Sukarno raised the stakes. A large mob assaulted and set fire to the British embassy. Similar attacks were perpetrated against other British properties in Jakarta.[57] Indonesia increased guerrilla incursions into North Borneo, while Britain escalated its own military response.

Once again, the United States was caught between rivals. Britain had lost patience with U.S. policy well before September; Macmillan derided Kennedy's approach as a "policy of unsuccessful bribery."[58] Indonesian criticism of Washington heightened with the deepening of the crisis. Sukarno was particularly angry at Congressional proposals to strip Indonesia of aid and complained to Jones that the CIA was plotting against him. A pro-American Indonesian diplomat lamented that the United States had squandered its opportunity to exploit the West New Guinea settlement.[59]

The Kennedy administration sought to keep relations with Jakarta open during the autumn, although Congressional and allied pressure obliged it to curtail economic and military aid. Komer urged Kennedy to send a personal envoy to meet with Sukarno; while recognizing a need to support Malaysia, he feared that further escalation might push Sukarno into the arms of the communist bloc.[60] Nor was the president eager to abandon the U.S. position in Indonesia. In an October meeting, Kennedy cited Jones's report from Jakarta in defense of continuing aid to Indonesia.[61]

Jakarta and Washington clung to hopes that the relationship was salvageable. Sukarno still aspired to host a Kennedy visit; he told Jones that the president would be welcomed with "the grandest reception anyone ever received here." Jones met with Kennedy on November 19 and discussed a "package

56 Telegram CAP 63419, Kennedy to Macmillan, August 3, 1963, in *FRUS, 1961–1963*, 23: 725, 725n.
57 Telegram 382, State Department to Jakarta, September 26, 1963, NSF, box 114, "Indonesia, General, 9/63" folder, JFKL; "10,000 in Jakarta Attack and Burn British Embassy," *NYT*, September 19, 1963, 1.
58 Telegram 1097, Jakarta to Foreign Office, September 13, 1963, PREM 11/4870, TNA.
59 Telegram 320, Jakarta to State Department, November 16, 1963, NSF, box 320, "Michael Forrestal, 11/62–11/63" folder, JFKL; Telegram 1012, Jakarta to Washington, November 4, 1963, in *FRUS, 1961–1963*, 23: 692–694.
60 Memorandum, Komer to Bundy, October 9, 1963, in *FRUS, 1961–1963*, 23: 742–743.
61 Memcon, Kennedy and Sir Garfield Barwick, October 17, 1963, ibid.: 750–753.

deal" for Sukarno, offering aid in exchange for an Indonesian pledge to settle the dispute peaceably. Indonesia's General Abdul Haris Nasution, due to visit Washington in the following week, was to be told that the White House viewed Malaysia as "a temporary problem which should not be permitted to interfere with our [cooperative] long range objectives."[62]

Had the president survived his trip to Dallas, U.S. policy would likely have sought to coax Indonesia out of confrontation with Malaysia, playing upon Sukarno's affinity for Kennedy. Nasution arrived, however, less as an Indonesian emissary than as his nation's representative to Kennedy's funeral. Although Johnson assured his guest that he would continue his predecessor's policies, Kennedy's last Indonesian initiative proved stillborn.

In this case, the presidential transition had a decisive, immediate effect on policy. Johnson brought his own outlook to the increasingly tense relationship with Indonesia. He distrusted the Indonesian leader as a deceitful bully. When Jones urged him to meet Sukarno, Johnson replied that it seemed that "the closer we get to Sukarno the more difficult he becomes."[63] "I don't trust him. I don't think he's any good," he remarked in a January 1964 phone call to his friend and mentor, Georgia's Senator Richard Russell. As Johnson saw it, any aid to Sukarno while he confronted Malaysia "just shows weakness on our part."[64] Whereas Kennedy, albeit halfheartedly, had emphasized the potential role of the United States as an intermediary, Johnson approached the dispute believing that it was incumbent upon him to avoid offering any further encouragement to Sukarno.[65] Strong Congressional opposition to aid to Indonesia only reinforced the new president's reluctance to involve himself with the Indonesian.

Consequently, Johnson never invested very much in the diplomatic option. He declined entreaties from Sukarno for a meeting. On the advice of Bundy, but with some skepticism, he dispatched Attorney General Robert F. Kennedy to Tokyo again to play the role of crisis mediator. Kennedy's discussions with Sukarno seemed to bear fruit.[66] At a follow-up meeting in Jakarta, however, Sukarno seemed to renege on commitments he had made in Tokyo, prompting RFK to reargue several issues he had thought concluded.[67] The Kennedy mission helped to facilitate subsequent meetings in Bangkok in March and Tokyo in June, but neither brought significant progress.

---

[62] Notes from meeting with Kennedy, November 19, 1963, Howard Jones Papers, box 92, first folder, Hoover Institution; Telegram 1012, Jakarta to Washington, November 4, 1963, in *FRUS, 1961–1963*, 23: 692–694; Memcon, Kennedy, Jones, and others, November 19, 1963, ibid.: 694–696.

[63] Memcon, Johnson and Nasution, November 29, 1963, in *FRUS, 1963–1963*, 23: 699–701; Memcon, Johnson and Jones, December 18, 1963, ibid.: 704–705.

[64] Memcon, Johnson and McNamara, January 2, 1964, in DOS, *FRUS, 1964–1968, Vol. 26: Indonesia; Malaysia-Singapore; Philippines* (Washington: GPO, 2001): 1–2.

[65] See Simpson, *Economists with Guns*, 126–127.

[66] Memorandum, Komer to Johnson, January 18, 1964, in *FRUS, 1964–1968*, 26: 42.

[67] Telegram 1510, Jakarta to Washington, January 23, 1964, ibid.: 45–49.

At the same time, Johnson drew nearer to both Britain and Malaysia. In February, Johnson agreed to endorse Britain's defense of Malaysia. In making their case, the British had stressed the inseparability of the defense of Malaysia from the defense of South Vietnam, which was in a precarious state, having undergone two coups d'etat in the previous three months.[68] Concern about Vietnam had compelled Kennedy to support Indonesia in 1962; ironically, less than two years later that same imperative drove a wedge between his successor and Sukarno. Bolstered by Johnson, London remained convinced that Sukarno, above all, needed to be taught a lesson. As guerrilla warfare raged in Borneo, the chasm between the United States and Indonesia widened inexorably.

The United States held some carrots where Sukarno was concerned, but could not hope to monopolize his attention. Indonesia was too large and Sukarno too prominent for Washington's reduction of aid and strong words about the confrontation to be decisive. Jakarta had reasonable hopes of harnessing political support from fellow nonaligned states, playing to Sukarno's belief that he should lead the uncommitted world. He was also receiving the competing attentions of both the Soviet Union and China. Peking's party chairman, Liu Shaoqi, had already visited Jakarta in April 1963, just days after a trip by Soviet Field Marshal Rodion Malinovsky. The Liu visit helped to cement bilateral ties; Indonesia endorsed China's position against India in the Himalayan border dispute, and Liu condemned the creation of Malaysia as "neocolonialism."[69]

Amicability in 1963 became outright alliance in 1964, as Sukarno sought to internationalize the Malaysia dispute with considerable aid from Peking. In Sukarno, Mao found an eager partner for his project of redefining the non-aligned movement and a vocal supporter of his ally, North Vietnam. China and Indonesia jointly promoted a second Afro-Asian conference, espousing a view of nonalignment oriented around shared anticolonialism and Afro-Asian solidarity. Moscow made its own diplomatic entreaties to Sukarno, motivated as much by fear of spreading Chinese influence as by opportunism; its entreaties were sweetened by the sale of advanced MiG-21 fighters to Jakarta.[70]

Washington had assumed that Indonesia ultimately had the most to fear from China. In the immediate term, this proved fundamentally wrong; indeed, during 1964, Indonesian rhetoric increasingly treated the United States as the greatest threat to its security. U.S. support of Britain and a friendly July visit by

---

[68] Jones, *Conflict and Confrontation*, 258–263.

[69] Telegram 1797, Hong Kong to Washington, April 23, 1963, NSF, box 114, "Indonesia, General, 3/63–4/63" folder, JFKL; Telegram, DDR Generalkonsulat in Jakarta to Berlin, May 5, 1963, MfAA, A 16071, AA.

[70] Telegram, DDR Generalkonsulat in Jakarta to Berlin, May 27, 1964, ibid.; Intelligence Cable 314/00634, July 25, 1964, NSF, CF, box 246, "Indonesia, Vol. II, Cables and Memos" folder, LBJL.

the Tunku to the White House incensed Sukarno, who had in vain sought his own meeting with LBJ.[71] Increasingly, Sukarno condemned the growing U.S. military commitment to South Vietnam, culminating with his August 1964 diplomatic recognition of North Vietnam.

With Sukarno's tacit acceptance, the PKI waged a violent campaign against U.S. property in Indonesia. On August 15, a mob seized a USIS library in the city of Jogjakarta. Two days later, Sukarno criticized the U.S. deployment of advisors to South Vietnam. He derided U.S. claims that it sought friendship with both Indonesia and Malaysia. This, Sukarno declared, was patently impossible; these statements, he claimed, were intended to mask the hostility of the United States. He implied that U.S. businesses in Indonesia would soon be nationalized.[72] Simultaneously, Indonesia escalated the confrontation, initiating guerrilla operations against the Malayan peninsula.

By the autumn of 1964, as the confrontation raged on, U.S.-Indonesian relations had entered a state of crisis. Sukarno, regarding the United States as his most powerful neocolonialist foe, was moving into unabashed alliance with China. Americans in Indonesia faced the same harassment that their British counterparts had endured the previous year. Most alarmingly, Sukarno's age and increasing volatility fueled fears that the emboldened PKI would soon be in a position to assume control of Indonesia.

A conflict that policymakers had scarcely imagined two years before had thoroughly wrecked the Kennedy administration's Indonesian endeavor and now threatened the broader position of the United States in Southeast Asia. It came as no small irony that the only Western nation left with substantial influence in Jakarta was now the Netherlands, which had quietly reopened relations with Sukarno's government. Rusk opined to the (presumably bemused) Dutch Foreign Minister Joseph Luns that the Dutch could soon become "the only Western presence in Indonesia."[73]

Much of the blame for the confrontation and the decline of United States-Indonesian relations must rest with Sukarno. Even if one concedes that his fears were legitimate, he chose policies that only exacerbated the situation. His behavior encouraged the belief that he was confronting Malaysia to distract his population from Indonesia's widespread economic difficulties – Nasution said as much in private.[74] As Jones later wrote, Sukarno seemed to have yielded his judgment to an "addiction to the politics of excitement," reasserting his self-image as a bold revolutionary leader.[75]

---

[71] Telegram 241, Jakarta to Washington, August 10, 1964, DSCF, CFPF, 1964–1966, box 2327, "POL INDON-US, 1/1/64" folder, NA; Telegram 187, Jakarta to Washington, July 31, 1964, ibid.

[72] Current Intelligence Memorandum, August 20, 1964, in FRUS, 1964–1968, 26: 134–136.

[73] Memcon, Rusk and Luns, October 24, 1964, RG-59, CFPF, 1964–1966, box 2326, "INDON-MO" folder, NA.

[74] Telegram 1943, Jakarta to Washington, March 19, 1964, in FRUS, 1964–1968, 26: 80–82.

[75] Howard Jones, Indonesia: The Possible Dream (Palo Alto: Hoover Institution, 1971), 272.

Nevertheless, despite Sukarno's recklessness and irresponsibility, the path to confrontation was not preordained. When Indonesians and Malayans met they tended to make headway. Sukarno showed a greater willingness to concede ground in these negotiations than he had displayed in the case of West New Guinea. British interference with the negotiating process aggravated the Indonesians and pushed Malaya away from previously concluded compromises – to disastrous consequences.

Caught between the two sides, U.S. policy deferred too long to the preferences of the British. Although Johnson's desire to distance his government from Indonesia contributed to the rupture, the pivotal decisions came before Kennedy's death. Earlier involvement might have allowed Sukarno the fig leaves he wanted. Given the importance that the Kennedy administration assigned to Indonesia, it could have done more during 1963 to assert its own preferences, perhaps working to bolster the Tunku against pressure from London. As Matthew Jones has written, the Malayan leader seemed to be seeking such support.[76] Johnson's apparent disinterest in ties to Jakarta convinced Sukarno to seek aid elsewhere. Consequently, the United States drifted into outright antagonism with Indonesia. Reflexive deference to an alliance helped to doom the project of engagement, with far-reaching repercussions for the position of the United States in the nonaligned world.

OUT OF THE ICEBOX, INTO THE FIRE: KENNEDY, JOHNSON, AND EGYPT

Whereas the Malaysian conflict brought the U.S.-Indonesian rupture of 1964, the simultaneous decline in relations between Washington and Cairo could claim no single predominant cause. Instead, an interrelated set of conflicts and disputes ranging from the horn of Arabia to the heart of Africa steadily undermined progress made by the Kennedy administration in 1961 and 1962. Three powerful forces were at work: the Arab-Israeli conflict, rivalry between Egyptian President Gamal Abdel Nasser and his Arab rivals, and Nasser's broader aspirations to lead the nonaligned world. Taken together, these factors combined to halt Kennedy's forward momentum in 1963, leading to a serious near-breach in U.S.-Egyptian ties at the end of the following year.

The Arab-Israeli conflict represented the most obvious source of Egyptian-American conflict in 1961. Nasser regarded the 1948 creation of Israel as a hostile act against the Arab nation, and Israel considered Egypt its most dangerous foe. Basic (although still nominal) U.S. support of Israel seemingly stood between Kennedy and any betterment of ties to Cairo. By 1961, however, Cairo was sending, through its ambassador, Mustafa Kamel, signals that it sought fruitful relations with Washington. Kamel liked to remark that the Israel question could be kept "in the icebox." The two governments would agree to disagree about Israel and endeavor not to inflame the issue, while

[76] See Jones, *Conflict and Confrontation*, 188.

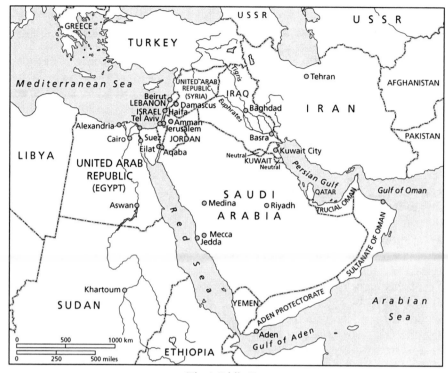

MAP 6. The Middle East, 1961.

striving to work constructively on other questions. Kamel expressed particular interest in obtaining economic assistance, particularly food aid through the Food for Peace program.

Other governments and organizations, however, opposed any rapid improvement of U.S.-Egyptian relations. The United Arab Republic, as Nasser's Egypt was commonly known, suffered from poor relations with a number of Western-aligned monarchies, especially Saudi Arabia and Jordan. With Suez a recent memory and Britain still ensconced in Aden, a strategically valuable colony on the tip of the Arabian Peninsula, Anglo-Egyptian relations remained uneasy. American oil companies shared the anxiety of their Arab business partners over Nasser's Pan-Arabism. Finally, supporters of Israel in the United States opposed any improvement of ties to the UAR.

These obstacles loomed far larger in 1961 than any comparable factors in cases such as India or Indonesia. The Egyptian leader's prominence and Pan-Arab ambitions made the task of seeking accommodation with him both important and difficult. Concern about domestic fallout kept Kennedy from holding an early meeting with Nasser, as he did with Nehru, Nkrumah, and Sukarno. Nonetheless, there seemed little alternative to rapprochement with the face of Arab nationalism. A June 1961 National Intelligence Estimate depicted Nasser as the present and probable future leader of the Arab world, describing the outlook for Arab conservative regimes as "bleak." Citing it, Komer observed, "Nationalism will remain the most dynamic force in the Arab world and Nasser will remain its foremost leader. His influence is likely to grow rather than decline." Komer argued for staying "in the game with Nasser, not deluding ourselves with any idea that we can bring him into the Western camp, but merely that we can live with him and he must live with us."[77] These were comparatively modest goals compared to the case of India; here merely reducing the points of friction seemed a substantial accomplishment.

The first major test of the administration's policy toward Egypt came in the early autumn of 1961, when Syria – then a part of the UAR – revolted against Cairo's rule. The White House had strong reason to accord recognition to the new Syrian government. Allies such as Turkey, Iran, and Jordan had done so quickly, and these nations believed U.S. recognition necessary to avert an Egyptian effort to recover Syria.[78] Some in Washington regarded the episode as a welcome comeuppance for Nasser's Pan-Arabist project.[79] U.S. policy moved in a different direction, however. Having received stern warnings from Egypt that early recognition would entail "endangering its own interests and antagonizing the biggest country in the area" and following suggestions made by Bowles and Komer, Kennedy moved slowly, only urging Nasser to address the crisis through "peaceful means."[80] Washington waited for Nasser to concede Syria its independence before issuing its own statement of recognition, giving Cairo early notice.[81]

This decision had fateful consequences for the administration's standing in the region. Nasser gave every indication that he appreciated Kennedy's restraint and hinted to the visiting Senator Hubert Humphrey that, with this distraction removed, it was time to focus on the economic development of Egypt.[82] Forwarding Humphrey's account to Kennedy, Komer commented, "The time has come for us to make a gesture toward Nasser designed to reassure him that we are not really sitting back and chortling over his discomfiture in Syria." Nasser remained the "most powerful leader in the Arab world," yet now it seemed that his setback in Syria might "lead him to turn inward," forsaking grandiose geopolitical ambitions.[83] Kennedy agreed. On October 16,

---

[77] Memorandum, Komer to Rostow, June 30, 1961, in DOS, *FRUS, 1961–1963, Vol. 17: Near East, 1961–1962* (Washington: GPO, 1994): 173.

[78] See Telegram 181, Amman to Washington, October 1, 1961, ibid.: 273–276.

[79] Memorandum, "What Policy in Syria?" Komer to Bundy and Rostow, October 10, 1961, in DOS, *FRUS, 1961–1963, Vol. 17 (MS)* (Washington: GPO, 1996): doc. 243.

[80] Circular Telegram 629, October 2, 1961, ibid.: 276–280; Circular Telegram 636, October 3, 1961, ibid.: 279–280; Telegram, Washington to Cairo, October 3, 1961, ibid.: 281.

[81] Memorandum, Komer to Bundy and Rostow, September 30, 1961, in *FRUS, 1961–1963*: 17: 272–273; Memorandum, Rusk to Kennedy, October 7, 1961, ibid.: 289–290.

[82] Memorandum, "Reflections on Egypt," Hubert Humphrey, October 22, 1961, NSF, box 445, "UAR: 1961–1962 3 of 4" folder, JFKL.

[83] Memorandum, Komer to Kennedy, October 26, 1961, NSF, box 445, "UAR, 1961–1963, White House Memoranda" folder, JFKL.

1961, he directed the State Department to examine seriously whether Nasser would "turn his energies more inward" generating "opportunities for bettering US-Egyptian relations via US developmental assistance."[84]

This remained the bedrock assumption behind U.S. engagement of Egypt during the Kennedy years. It was, however, woefully misguided. Increased economic assistance, particularly food aid, strengthened ties to Cairo but had little effect in persuading Nasser to adopt a more introspective foreign policy. Nasser invested real importance in his newfound tie to the United States but also – in spite of the loss of Syria – retained his own grand ambitions for Egypt's regional and global roles.

Simultaneously, growing U.S.-Egyptian ties seemed to sharpen regional tensions. Nasser's conservative rivals grew fearful of being abandoned by Washington. In April 1962, Jordan's King Hussein cautioned, "As a friend, I must warn you that your current UAR policy will have disastrous consequences for you and your friends in the Eastern Arab states."[85] Envoys from the Saudi monarch asked angrily if Kennedy regarded Nasser as the leader of the Arab world.[86] Israel, too, was visibly alarmed at growing ties between Washington and Cairo. Citing continuing Egyptian purchases of advanced Soviet weaponry, Israeli diplomats successfully argued for the sale of HAWK missiles to Jerusalem. Nasser received news of the HAWK sale unhappily but kept his response muted. The sale marked the first direct provision of U.S.-made weaponry to Israel, preparing the ground for future sales as the Arab-Israeli conflict intensified.[87]

Despite these thunderheads on the horizon, optimism about the U.S.-Egyptian relationship peaked in the summer of 1962. "Our policy is paying off," Komer wrote to Bundy in July, citing Nasser's moderate role at the Cairo Economic Conference and his speech the preceding autumn at Belgrade; he would later term those months the "high point" of relations with Cairo.[88] Nasser seconded the verdict, terming the state of the relationship "good."[89] Washington signaled its satisfaction by concluding a generous multi-year food aid agreement with Cairo. Kennedy also made his own attempt to resolve

---

[84] NSAM 105, October 16, 1961, in *FRUS, 1961–1963*, 17: 302.

[85] Telegram 463, Amman to Washington, April 2, 1962, in *FRUS, 1961–1963*, 17: 571–575; Airgram A-215, Amman to Washington, in *FRUS, 1961–1963: 17* (MS): doc. 169; Telegram 825, Amman to Foreign Office, August 4, 1962, FO 371/163970, TNA; Uriel Dann, *King Hussein and the Challenge of Arab Radicalism: Jordan, 1955–1967* (New York: Oxford University Press, 1989), 118–126.

[86] Telegram 711, Jidda to Washington, May 12, 1962, in *FRUS, 1961–1963*, 17 (MS): doc. 229; Letter, Parker Hart to Robert Strong, June 9, 1962, ibid.: doc. 231; Memorandum, William Brubeck to Bundy, July 10, 1962, ibid.: doc. 232.

[87] On this, see Warren Bass, *Support Any Friend: Kennedy's Middle East and the Making of the U.S.-Israel Alliance* (New York: Oxford University Press, 2002), 145–185.

[88] Memorandum, Komer to Bundy, July 19, 1962, NSF, box 445, "UAR, 1961–1962 (2)" folder, JFKL; Second Oral History Interview, Robert Komer, July 16, 1964, OH, JFKL.

[89] Memorandum, Brubeck to Bundy, July 18, 1962, in DOS, *FRUS, 1961–1963, Vol. 18: Near East, 1962–1963* (Washington: GPO, 1994): 20–21.

the region's primary conflict, dispatching envoy Joseph Johnston in an effort to ease the Palestinian refugee problem. Although unsuccessful, the Johnston initiative reflected the administration's sense of progress in the region and its belief that it could successfully mediate local conflicts.[90]

The idyll did not last. The fall of the monarchist government in Yemen in a military coup at the end of September 1962, followed by the establishment of the Yemen Arab Republic (YAR), brought the inter-Arab conflict to a critical stage. The YAR proclaimed its support of Nasserism and appealed to Cairo for assistance in pacifying the countryside, where the royalists enjoyed considerable support. Nasser responded favorably, not out of any great faith in his would-be allies, but rather seeking to rebuild his international and domestic prestige.[91] Even as he began dispatching soldiers, Nasser informed Kennedy that he had no desire to fight a proxy war with his Arab rivals.[92] His wishes notwithstanding, he soon had one. Alarmed, his Saudi and Jordanian foes retaliated by aiding the Yemeni monarchists. As the fighting escalated, Egyptian forces began staging attacks into Saudi Arabia; the frightened Saudis demanded immediate U.S. assistance.

Seeking to break the logjam, the United States proposed a mutual drawdown in Yemen: an Egyptian withdrawal paired with the termination of Saudi aid to the royalists. Disengagement was more easily proposed than carried out. Each side placed responsibility for breaking the stalemate on its foe, even as Egyptian aircraft and commandos continued to raid Saudi territory. This compelled the White House to come to the Saudi monarchy's defense; on the advice of Komer and Assistant Secretary for Near East Affairs Phillips Talbot, Kennedy deployed a fighter squadron to Saudi territory.[93] Kennedy also sought to mediate the conflict, sending Ellsworth Bunker into the fray. Although he secured an initial agreement on disengagement, the veteran diplomat was unable to resolve the conflict, as disputes over implementation rendered the accord moot.[94]

The Yemen war gradually added another state to the roster of Nasser's foes: Britain. As in the case of Malaysia, demands from London exerted an increasing tug on U.S. policy.[95] Macmillan, although briefly engaged in his own effort to build ties with Cairo, harbored deep suspicions of Nasser, at one point writing, "For Nasser, read Hitler and it all rings familiar."[96] Nasser's deployment

[90] Bass, *Support Any Friend*, 165–177.

[91] Robert Stephens, *Nasser: A Political Biography* (New York: Simon & Schuster: 1971), 393–396.

[92] Telegram 655, Cairo to Washington, October 18, 1962, in *FRUS, 1961–1963, 18*: 184–186.

[93] Memorandum for the Record, February 25, 1963, ibid.: 363–367.

[94] Howard B. Schaffer, *Ellsworth Bunker: Global Troubleshooter, Vietnam Hawk* (Chapel Hill: University of North Carolina Press, 2003), 110–127.

[95] See Robert McNamara, Britain, *Nasser and the Balance of Power in the Middle East* (Portland, OR: Frank Cass, 2003); Nigel Ashton, *Kennedy, Macmillan and the Cold War: The Irony of Interdependence* (New York: Palgrave Macmillan, 2002), 90–108; and W. Taylor Fain, *American Ascendance and British Retreat in the Persian Gulf Region* (New York: Palgrave Macmillan, 2008), 111–140, 150–152.

[96] Quoted in Ashton, *Kennedy, Macmillan and the Cold War*, 102–103.

to Yemen brought a new point of friction between London and Cairo: Aden. The colony served as a vital link in the line of communications between the United Kingdom and the Far East. Before the Yemen War, it had not been a major source of discord with Cairo, but the sudden proximity to Aden of tens of thousands of Egyptian troops brought an inexorable rise in tensions with the UAR and the YAR. Alarmed by the rhetoric of the new Yemeni government, Macmillan urged Kennedy to obtain an Egyptian withdrawal, while declining the president's request that he recognize the YAR.[97] This early disagreement augured broader arguments between London and Washington on policy toward the conflict.

Nasser's embroilment in a Yemeni proxy war did not entirely derail the Kennedy administration's project of engaging him. Komer and other advocates of engagement remained cautiously optimistic through the year.[98] It did, however, halt the forward progress made during 1962 and precluded any prospect of a Kennedy-Nasser meeting. Yemen helped to make economic aid to Cairo a politically charged issue in Congress. Above all, it cost the White House the momentum achieved earlier, paving the way for a crisis in U.S.-Egyptian relations during 1964.

Despite the strains imposed by Yemen, Komer was still convinced of the value of U.S. ties to Cairo, noting Nasser's seeming disavowal of a military solution to the Arab-Israeli conflict in his December 1963 Port Said speech. "He's the one major Arab leader who may make sense," Komer wrote, adding prophetically: "The Near East will be quite a test of our policy (and nerves) in '64."[99] Indeed, Johnson's first full year in office witnessed its own arc of Middle East crises. Each involved Cairo and most involved London. Nasser seemed increasingly inclined to clash with U.S. allies, even as Johnson sought, with growing reluctance, to maintain Kennedy's policy toward Nasser.

Nasser did not set out to wreck the relationship he had established with the United States during the Kennedy administration. Both he and Johnson faced a bewildering range of crises that pushed their respective regional agendas further and further apart. Most critically, a number of factors drew the Arab-Israeli conflict from Kamel's proverbial icebox. Egypt was alarmed at Israel's continued pursuit of atomic power. Israel, in turn, feared Egypt's acquisition of surface-to-surface missiles and advanced Soviet tanks and sought its own equivalent systems. A dispute over Israeli plans to divert the waters of the Jordan River further compounded the region's arms race. To Talbot, the water question was *the* most critical regional problem.[100] Johnson, moreover,

---

[97] Telegram 4351, Washington to London, February 14, 1963, in DOS, *FRUS, 1961–1963, 18 (MS)* (Washington: GPO, 1996): doc. 304; McNamara, *Britain, Nasser and the Balance of Power*, 177–182.

[98] This is argued in Bass, *Support Any Friend*, 133–143.

[99] Memorandum, Komer to Bundy, December 30, 1963, in *FRUS, 1961–1963*, 18: 860.

[100] Memorandum, Talbot to Rusk, November 18, 1963, in *FRUS, 1961–1963*, 18: 792–793. On the water issue, see Peter L. Hahn, *Caught in the Middle East: U.S. Policy toward the Arab-Israeli Conflict, 1945–1961* (Chapel Hill: University of North Carolina Press, 2004), 170–174.

felt both an instinctive sympathy for Israel and a political need to show strong support for it.[101]

Nasser made clear his unequivocal opposition to unilateral Israeli action on the Jordan waters question, and, in a January 1964 Arab summit, sought to ease his tensions with Saudi Arabia and Jordan while building a united Arab front in opposition to Israel's diversionary plan.[102] "Under the magic rubric of uniting against Israel, the contesting Arab leaders will paper over their differences," Komer predicted. "The hell of it is that all this Arab 'unity' will be at the expense of Israel, which will put us on the spot."[103]

In the immediate term, however, Nasser seemed more intent on driving the British from their remaining bases in the Middle East. Although the Johnson administration expected difficulties over heightened Arab-Israeli tensions and the ongoing Yemeni morass, it was surprised when Nasser urged Libya to close air bases that it had leased by treaty to Britain and the United States. Komer and Bundy concluded that Nasser's actions had been stimulated by growing Arab-Israeli tensions.[104] Another point of conflict emerged when Nasser offered military assistance to the Greek-majority government of Cyprus, then embroiled in an increasingly tense standoff with the island's Turkish minority (a situation that risked a broader war between NATO allies Greece and Turkey). Nasser believed himself obliged to aid a fellow nonaligned state and, here too, objected to the presence of British bases on the island.[105] In so doing, he strengthened the hand of the Greek Cypriots, while angering Turkey, Britain, and the United States.

The Yemen War also intensified in the new year, as hostilities grew between London and Cairo. Further tensions erupted in March, when London bombed a fort in Yemeni territory, at Harib, in retaliation for cross-border raids. Britain suspected Egypt and Yemen of sponsoring rebels in Aden; in turn, it offered covert assistance to the Yemeni royalists.[106] Komer urged that the United States avoid being linked to the UK's "foolish Sandys style Arab policy." "There are ample signs," he wrote, "that Home government is going to launch an attack on our Arab policy quite analogous to the one on Malaysia." He mused that the British thought the Johnson administration "an easier mark" than

[101] See Warren I. Cohen, "Balancing American interests in the Middle East: Lyndon Baines Johnson vs. Gamal Abdul Nasser," in Cohen and Tucker eds., *Lyndon Johnson Confronts the World: American Foreign Policy, 1963–1968* (New York: Cambridge University Press, 1993), 281–282.

[102] Telegram 1493, Cairo to Washington, January 7, 1964, in DOS, *FRUS, 1964–1968, Vol. 18: Arab-Israeli Conflict, 1964–1967* (Washington: GPO, 2000): 9–10.

[103] Memorandum, Komer to Bundy, January 2, 1964, NSF, CF, box 158, "UAR, Vol. 1, Memos [2 of 2]" folder, LBJL.

[104] Memorandum, Bundy and Komer to Johnson, March 17, 1964, in DOS, *FRUS, 1964–1968, Vol. 24: Africa* (Washington: GPO, 1999): 72.

[105] Telegram 1995, Cairo to Washington, March 10, 1964, RG-59, CFCP: 1964–1966, box 2767, "POL UAR-US, 2/1/64" folder, NA.

[106] McNamara, *Britain, Nasser and the Balance of Power*, 191–194.

its predecessor.[107] On Rusk and Ball's advice Washington abstained on a UN Security Council resolution condemning the raid, further distancing itself from Nasser.[108]

Nasser's rhetoric stood to undermine the Anglo-American position in the region, alarming engagement's skeptics in the State Department. Rusk stated angrily in April 1964 that he believed that the United States had yet to realize any benefits from engaging Nasser. The Egyptian leader's actions in Yemen, threats against Aden, arms purchases, and rhetoric about the Libyan bases all argued for reevaluating the administration's approach.[109] "Rusk is beset just now by all the anti-Arabs," Komer wrote to Johnson, alluding to Iranian, British, and Turkish complaints about Nasser.[110] In Cairo, Badeau adopted an increasingly stern tone in his conversations with Nasser, telling the Egyptian leader that the United States wondered if the UAR truly sought cooperative relations. In reply, Nasser noted his sense that the United States was siding with Israel. Badeau reported to Rusk, "Nasser believes something new is in the making between the United States and Israel."[111]

To Britain, however, the problem was that the United States had not changed its policy sufficiently. Prime Minister Home sought closer coordination, opining that, as in the case of Indonesia, a joint policy toward Egypt should be formulated.[112] British Foreign Secretary R. A. Butler deemed Nasser a "major enemy" of both Britain and the United States when he met with Rusk on April 27, telling the secretary that any aid or further attempts to court Cairo were counterproductive. Rusk, although "a bit wobbly" on the issue in Komer's eyes, defended existing U.S. policy as providing a channel of communication to Cairo.[113] British pressure on the United States continued, however, spurred by increasing Anglo-Egyptian friction.[114]

Nasser reacted to these changing winds by shoring up his ties to the Soviet Union. In May 1964 he welcomed Nikita Khrushchev on a state visit to Cairo. Although clear differences were apparent between the two leaders – particularly

[107] Memorandum, Komer to Bundy, March 30, 1964, in DOS, *FRUS, 1964–1968, Vol. 21: Near East Region; Arabian Peninsula* (Washington: GPO, 2000): 620; Memorandum, Komer to Bundy, April 2, 1964, NSF, CF, box 161, "Yemen, Vol. 1, Memos" folder, LBJL.
[108] Telegram 2581, Washington to New York, April 1, 1964, in *FRUS, 1964–1968*, 21: 621–622; Memorandum, Bundy to Johnson, April 9, 1964, ibid.: 623–624; Telcon, Stevenson and Ball, April 9, 1964, GWBP, box 6, "Yemen [4/9/64–2/23/66]" folder, LBJL.
[109] Memorandum for the Record, April 2, 1964, in *FRUS, 1964–1968*, 18: 80–81.
[110] Memorandum, Komer to Johnson, April 27, 1964, NSF, CF, box 206, "UK, Vol. 1, Cables" folder, LBJL.
[111] Telegram 2316, Cairo to Washington, April 5, 1964, NSF, CF, box 158, "UAR, General, Vol. I, Cables [2 of 2]" folder, LBJL.
[112] Telegram 4910, Foreign Office to Washington, April 10, 1964, PREM 11/5199, TNA.
[113] Memorandum, Komer to Johnson, April 27, 1964, NSF, CF, box 206, "UK, Vol. 1, Cables" folder, LBJL; Memcon, Rusk, R. A. Butler, and others, April 27, 1964, in *FRUS, 1964–1968*, 21: 130–135; Telegram 1587, Washington to Foreign Office, April 28, 1964, FO 371/178583, TNA.
[114] McNamara, *Britain, Nasser and the Balance of Power*, 191–203.

as the Soviet leader praised Arab socialism but not Arab nationalism – they
struck a common tone on a number of questions. Their joint communique
espoused a common view on issues including Cyprus, Taiwan, foreign military
bases, and Palestine. Komer bluntly asked Kamel whether the UAR was still
endeavoring to keep difficult issues in the icebox.[115]

Arab-Israeli tensions continued to ferment over the summer. King Hussein
had joined the proposed United Arab Command in January. Although this
contributed to a Jordanian-Egyptian rapprochement, the UAC also obligated
Hussein to coordinate defense strategy with Nasser. During the summer, Nasser
pressured Hussein to expand his arsenal, suggesting that the king purchase
fighter aircraft from the Soviet Union. Hussein, in turn, asked Washington if it
could sell him F-104 jets; otherwise he would have to buy from Moscow.

Up to this point, the United States had tried to remain aloof from the Middle
East's arms race. Hussein's request threatened to spur a competing request for
arms from Israel. For much of the year, Israel had pressed the Johnson administration to supply it with M-48 tanks, arguing that its arsenal was outclassed
by the advanced armor Egypt was receiving from the Soviets. A sale to Jordan
would inevitably require Washington to arrange a compensating sale to Israel,
preferably through a European proxy.[116] This, in turn, could not go unnoticed
by other Arab states. What then?

The long, slow slide in bilateral relations unnerved and bewildered the pragmatists in the NSC. In a July 1964 memorandum to Talbot, Komer observed,
"As I follow the traffic these days, I'm struck by the increasing number of
points at which UAR policies are coming into contact with ours.... If the Arabs
want to force us wholly to Israel's side," Komer wrote, "they could hardly take
a better way to do so."[117] Policymakers in each state believed that the other
was fundamentally changing its policy. In Washington, Kamel kept stressing
the benefits of maintaining the relationship. Bundy – who deemed himself "a
determined 'icebox' man" – replied that the UAR needed to treat the relationship as a "two-way street."[118]

The single most damaging conflict between Washington and Cairo that year,
however, came over Egyptian support for rebels in the Congo. For Nasser, the
Congolese conflict represented an alluring opportunity to expand his influence
within the nonaligned caucus. In his eyes, Egypt's illustrious history, its position at the junction of Africa and Asia, and its dynamic leadership and successful defiance of the colonial powers in 1956 marked it as a natural leader of the
continent.[119] Moreover, he worried at the breadth of Israeli influence below

---

[115] Telegram 5538, Washington to Cairo, May 27, 1964, NSF, CF, box 158, "UAR. Vol. 1, Memos
[1 of 2]" folder, LBJL.

[116] Memorandum, Talbot to Rusk, July 22, 1964, in *FRUS, 1964–1968, 18*: 182–184.

[117] Memorandum, Komer to Talbot, July 28, 1964, RG-59, NE/SA, UAR Affairs, box 3, "POL –
US-UAR" folder, NA.

[118] Memcon, Bundy, Kamel, and others, August 10, 1964, in *FRUS, 1964–1968, 18*: 199–202.

[119] Stephens, *Nasser*, 303–308; Anthony Nutting, *Nasser* (London: Constable & Co., 1972),
289–292.

the Sahara. Becoming an active member of the OAU promised to improve his continental standing.[120] Nasser's focus on sub-Saharan Africa increased substantially after the first meeting of the OAU, in May 1963. His Congo policy shifted, however, after Adoula's fall and Tshombe's return. Along with its nonaligned peers, Cairo vociferously denounced the Stanleyville operation, but Nasser soon went beyond rhetoric, providing political and military support to the Congolese insurgents.[121] Complicating the matter, on November 26, a mob of enraged African students attacked and vandalized the U.S. embassy in Cairo, burning the embassy's attached USIS library.

In response, Johnson directed his ambassador in Cairo to deliver an oral message to Nasser. The message had been written carefully, with some "Kennedy-style" revisions made by Komer. It spoke to a shared U.S.-Egyptian interest in keeping communism and the Cold War out of Africa and solicited Nasser's views on how the Congo might be resolved.[122] By itself, this demarche might have stemmed the growing chasm between Nasser and Johnson, but external events once again intruded. On December 19, the Egyptian air force shot down an aircraft owned by a personal friend of President Johnson. The incident upset U.S. Ambassador Lucius Battle. When he met with the Egyptian agricultural minister, he declared himself unable to talk about the day's topic: food aid for Egypt. Nasser, believing Battle's response signaled an imminent withdrawal of U.S. food aid, delivered a fiery speech on December 23. He declared he would gladly support the rebels in the Congo; if the United States disapproved, it could drink from the Red Sea. This was his sharpest denunciation of the United States in years, and it shocked the White House, sending relations to a low unseen since the Eisenhower years.

Taking the broad view, the U.S.-Egyptian relationship that Nasser, Kennedy, and Johnson tried to forge always faced long odds. Preexisting U.S. commitments to allies clashed inexorably with Nasser's own need – driven by both foreign and internal pressures – to demonstrate his leadership of the Arab world. From the very outset of the endeavor, the White House faced a chorus of criticism for its Egyptian enterprise from domestic critics, but also from its many allies in the region. The bedeviling turbulence of Middle East politics deprived the two administrations of any sustained quiet during which U.S.-Egyptian ties could be focused around constructive questions.

Having lost Syria in 1961, Nasser felt obliged to vie for his revolution elsewhere: the horn of Arabia and then in the heart of Africa. Increasingly, his policy goals involved not only raising the stakes in the Arab-Israeli conflict, but also challenging the United Kingdom and gradually the United States, in places such as Libya, Cyprus, and the Congo – all areas that bore strategic

---

[120] See Note, Cairo to Foreign Office, August 22, 1963, FO 371/172864, TNA.

[121] Memorandum, Jernegan to Palmer, December 28, 1964, RG-59, NE/SA, UAR 1961–1966, box 3, "POL UAR-Congo, 1963" folder, NA.

[122] Telegram 3429, Washington to Cairo, December 12, 1964, NSF, RWKP, box 51, "UAR December 1963–1964 [1 of 4]" folder, LBJL; Memorandum, Komer to Jernegan, December 9, 1964, ibid.

significance in the Cold War. Battling various foes, Nasser found his prestige inextricably opposed to U.S. regional policy, and every step the Kennedy and Johnson administrations took to reassure their anxious allies carried them further away from their goal of reaching detente with the most prominent leader in the Arab world. Some disputes, such as the Congo, Cyprus, and the Libyan bases, faded in the coming year. Others – notably Yemen and the Arab-Israeli conflict – steadily undermined what remained of President Kennedy's outreach toward Nasser.

AYUBS OR NEHRUS?: THE UNITED STATES AND SOUTH ASIA, 1961–1964

Were any nonaligned state to defy the trend of faltering relations in 1964, it should have been India. Among the nonaligned states, India held a singular importance to the Kennedy administration. It was the largest nonaligned state, solidly democratic, and New Frontiersmen such as Walt Rostow saw it as the essential proving ground for their models of non-communist economic development. Nehru's concept of nonalignment was the one most compatible with the administration's understanding of the phenomenon, and he stood as the movement's most moderate voice. Finally, India assumed a particular value to United States policymakers as a counterweight to Chinese power, a state that might check Beijing's influence in the nonaligned councils and in Southeast Asia. What had been a nascent policy goal under Eisenhower became a capital objective under Kennedy.[123]

Reaching out to India risked, however, jeopardizing relations with its foe Pakistan, an avowed ally. In the early 1950s, Pakistan's willingness to stand up and be counted as a friend of the West had made it a more promising ally than the larger but implacably nonaligned India. Nonetheless, ambivalence gradually crept into the U.S.-Pakistani relationship as Eisenhower began to revisit his earlier assessment, offering substantial economic aid to India in the last years of his presidency.

Kennedy consequently inherited an increasingly uneasy relationship with Pakistan. Pakistan's president, Mohammed Ayub Khan fretted openly at the apparent pro-India views of a number of Kennedy's advisors.[124] A January 1961 State Department assessment, warning of a growing trend toward neutralism in Pakistan, reported that the Ayub government needed visible signs of support

---

[123] The single best account of the U.S. approach to South Asia in this period is Robert J. McMahon's *The Cold War on the Periphery: The United States, India, and Pakistan* (New York: Columbia University Press, 1994), 272–336; also McMahon, "Toward Disillusionment and Disengagement in South Asia" in Cohen and Tucker eds, *Lyndon Johnson Confronts the World*, 135–172. Also insightful are H. W. Brands, *India and the United States: The Cold Peace* (Boston: Twayne, 1990), 99–113; and Dennis Kux, *The United States and Pakistan, 1947–2000: Disenchanted Allies* (Baltimore: The Johns Hopkins University Press, 2001) 115–158.

[124] Telegram 1374, Karachi to Washington, February 16, 1961, in DOS, *FRUS, 1961–1963*, Vol. 19: *South Asia* (Washington: GPO, 1996): 8–10.

from Washington.[125] Pakistan tried, to no avail, to shift United States foreign policy during 1961 and 1962. Ayub approached his crisis of confidence with more patience and tact than his Saudi counterparts. He shied away from condemning outright aid to nonaligned states, implying instead that allies should merely continue to receive preferential treatment.[126] When he met Kennedy in July 1961, Ayub implored the president to press India to settle the question of Kashmir. He alluded to popular pressure for closer ties to China, adding quickly that he, personally, thought China could "go to hell."[127]

India, for its part, witnessed a warming of relations with Washington in 1961 and 1962, but remained deeply concerned by U.S. arms shipments to Pakistan. Ayub's seeming technological advantage fostered feelings of insecurity in New Delhi, encouraging it to enhance its own arsenal. Moscow was happy to assist. In 1962, with the reluctant assistance of the British government, Kennedy tried unsuccessfully to forestall an Indian purchase of Soviet MiG-21 fighters. Seeking to court both states, Washington stood by in a partial state of paralysis: wary of being a bystander to an influx of Soviet technical advisors in India but also chary of either sharing advanced weaponry with a nonaligned state or of contributing to a dangerous military escalation in South Asia.[128]

Komer believed that alleviating regional disputes could help to forge a united South Asian front against communist expansion, but once again he did not rule out the possibility of having to choose an ally on the subcontinent. "If we must choose among these countries, there is little question that India (because of its sheer size and resources) is where we must put our chief reliance," he wrote. "Are we more interested in a Western-oriented weak ally or a strong neutralist India able to defend its own national interests (which happen to broadly coincide with ours)."[129]

The alternative to picking sides would have been working to resolve the major source of conflict between India and Pakistan: the disputed region of Kashmir. Throughout 1962, Washington made sporadic attempts to spur India and Pakistan toward substantive negotiations on Kashmir. These efforts not only failed to narrow the gap between the two rivals but also served to damage the Indo-American relationship. In the spring of 1962, the United States voted in favor of a UN Security Council resolution urging negotiations on the issue, believing it mildly worded. Nehru still took offense, asking whether the United States really bore India goodwill, in light of its votes on both Goa and Kashmir and its sale of jets to Pakistan.[130] This incident boded ill for future attempts to resolve the conflict, even after China's attack on India that autumn.

---

[125] Memorandum, G. Lewis Jones to Rusk, January 31, 1961, ibid.: 2–3.
[126] See Telegram 1622, Karachi to Washington, March 22, 1961, in *FRUS, 1961–1963, 19*: 26–30.
[127] Memcon, Kennedy and Ayub, July 11, 1961, ibid.: 66–74.
[128] Position Paper, "Indian Military Purchase from the United States," November 1961, POF, box 118A, "Nehru Trip Security" folder, JFKL.
[129] Memorandum, Komer to Bundy, January 6, 1962, in *FRUS, 1961–1963, 19*: 179–181.
[130] Telegram 4351, Washington to New Delhi, June 24, 1962, ibid.: 291–292.

The Sino-Indian War of October 1962 seemed a fundamental turning point, not merely in terms of relations with India, but also within the international system. China's simmering border dispute with India erupted into open warfare during October 1962, coinciding with the Cuban Missile Crisis. Meeting with Ambassador B. K. Nehru on October 27, Kennedy was quick to offer assistance, adding that he did not wish it to appear as though New Delhi was being enlisted into a grand anticommunist coalition. The president wondered aloud if there was some linkage between Moscow's decision to place missiles in Cuba and China's invasion. He spoke repeatedly not of "the Chinese" but "the Communists," seemingly expecting that the twin crises would push the two major communist states back into closer alignment.[131]

Emergency military assistance was granted to India with the express purpose of aiding it in its hour of need *and* establishing a long-term foundation for closer ties. Fueling the rush to aid New Delhi were the disastrous performance of Indian armies in the field and a lack of information about Chinese goals: were Beijing's actions merely intended to redraw the border or were they preludes to a broader stroke at India?[132] For that matter, would the Indians accept their losses or seek to reverse them in the near future?[133] This uncertainty militated against unduly limiting aid to India or deferring to Pakistani concerns.

Kennedy's NSC advisors presumed that the war would force Pakistan, however gradually, to confront the reality of communist expansionism in South Asia. "Only Chinese pressure will make Indians and Paks more statesmanlike and less chauvinistic toward each other," Komer wrote in December 1962.[134] This was, as Robert McMahon has written, a dubious forecast. Ayub had hinted of the possibility of closer ties to China in 1961 and had verbally assailed India through 1962. Despite these veiled threats, Kennedy wrote to Ayub on October 28, asking him to understand his decision to aid India, to restrain the Pakistani press, and to offer Nehru private assurances that Pakistan would not seek to exploit the situation.[135]

Pakistan registered its alarm at the new course of United States policy. Replying on November 5, Ayub politely but firmly doubted that India was the victim of Chinese aggression, refusing to send the requested message to Nehru.[136] After a visit to South Asia, Bundy's deputy, Carl Kaysen, warned that U.S. aid to India had fostered outrage in Pakistan. If the United States

[131] Ernest May and Philip Zelikow eds., *The Presidential Recordings: John F. Kennedy, The Great Crises*, Vol. 3 (New York: Norton, 2001), 337–344; Theodore Sorensen, *Counselor: A Life at the Edge of History* (New York: Harper & Row, 2008), 9.

[132] Memorandum for the Record, November 19, 1962, in *FRUS, 1961–1963*, 19: 394–396.

[133] Memorandum, Komer to Bundy, November 14, 1962, NSF, box 322, "Robert Komer, 11/62–12/62" folder, JFKL.

[134] Memorandum, Komer to Kennedy, December 1, 1962, NSF, box 109, "India: General, 12/1/62–12/4/62" folder, JFKL.

[135] Telegram 681, Washington to Karachi, October 28, 1962, in *FRUS, 1961–1963*, 19: 358–359.

[136] Telegram 759, Washington to Karachi, November 13, 1962, in *FRUS, 1961–1963*, 19: 377–380.

offered arms to India, it needed to reassure Pakistan through military aid and a commitment to resolving Kashmir.[137] Ayub saw no evidence that Kennedy was making real demands on India in return for aid. Instead, Pakistani influence in Washington was at its lowest ebb since the partition. "One thing is becoming quite clear," Ayub remarked in January 1963 in a televised interview, "the line between friends and those that have not been friends is now getting obliterated."[138]

The British evinced a similar skepticism. In spite of a number of disagreements, London enjoyed civil relations with India and served as New Delhi's Western arms supplier. After the Chinese offensive, London also perceived a "great opportunity to influence the future course of Indian foreign policy." Prior experience with Nehru still engendered a bemused skepticism in Macmillan, who wrote in October of "the transformation of Nehru from an imitation of George Lansbury into a parody of Churchill."[139]

Consequently, Macmillan approached the endeavor with wariness. London retained control of Hong Kong, off the Chinese mainland, and was reluctant to jeopardize its colony by needlessly provoking Peking. When he met with Kennedy at Nassau, the prime minister, although agreeing to aid India, worried about issuing the wrong message:

Prime Minister Macmillan said that what worries him is that, as so often before, we support the people who are troublesome, such as Nehru and Krishna Menon, and abandon the people who support us. He was sure it would be dangerous if we let Ayub feel we are abandoning him. ... He liked the idea that we should start slowly and not go ahead building up armies of the people who for 12 years or more have attacked us, have trumpeted the benefits of being non-aligned, have helped build up the neutralist Afro-Asian Bloc, and who have been, how should he say it, contemptuous – like a camel looking down his nose at you.

Macmillan agreed on the necessity of aiding India but also thought it essential to press Nehru to make concessions on Kashmir. Failure to insist on reciprocity would lead the Indians to "slide back into their same old arrogance and beautifully detached view."[140] Kennedy and Macmillan thus agreed to make long-term aid to India – particularly in the field of air defense – contingent on progress on Kashmir.

After a promising start, Kashmir negotiations began to stall the following month. The administration primarily blamed Pakistan, particularly after Ayub dispatched his foreign minister, Zulfikar Ali Bhutto, to China to sign a border

---

[137] Memorandum, "Main Conclusions on the India-Pakistan Trip," Kaysen to Kennedy, December 3, 1962, NSF, box 109, "India, General, 12/1/62–12/7/62" folder, JFKL.

[138] Transcript, ABC Special Report, Interview with Ayub Khan, January 6, 1963, NSF, box 441, "Pakistan, General, 1961–1963, 2 of 3" folder, JFKL.

[139] Letter, Ormsby Gore to Rusk, November 2, 1962, NSF, box 170, "United Kingdom, General, 10/15/62–11/12/62" folder, JFKL; Harold Macmillan, At the End of the Day, 1961–1963 (New York: Harper & Row, 1973), 228. Lansbury was a famous British pacifist.

[140] Memcon, Kennedy and Macmillan, December 20, 1962, in FRUS, 1961–1963, 19: 448–454.

demarcation treaty.[141] Rostow observed, after an April 1963 visit to India and
Pakistan, that neither side believed that the process would truly resolve the
question.[142] Against such fatalism, hopes for a settlement withered.

As they did so, the administration deliberated whether to take the leap
toward offering India long-term military assistance in spite of Nehru's failure to compromise. On April 25, when Kennedy met with his senior advisors
to discuss the question, Rusk, usually a voice of caution on such matters,
advised going ahead. Following advice he had received from Komer, the president was unmoved by British reluctance, asserting that London should not be
allowed to restrain the endeavor. Efforts were to be made to keep Macmillan
on board but, as Kennedy remarked, "India is the important thing, not the
UK." Congress, he reasoned, would be far madder if India turned toward the
communist bloc than it would be if he aided Nehru.[143] With his own administration united, Kennedy succeeded in winning the reluctant Macmillan's
acquiescence, although the prime minister warned that Washington overestimated the threat from China and underestimated the extent of Pakistani
alienation.[144]

Pakistan's disappointment became increasingly apparent over the successive months. Ayub's ambassador in Washington, Aziz Ahmed, remarked to
Kennedy in July that the situation in South Asia was "gloomy verging on
tragic."[145] Signaling its discontent, Ayub's government denied a U.S. request
to expand an electronic intelligence-gathering installation in the northwest-
ern city of Peshawar, alarming the CIA, which regarded the facility as critical.
Sino-Pakistani ties continued to broaden during 1963, and Bhutto stated that
he expected Chinese support in a confrontation with India.[146] Kennedy sent
Undersecretary of State George Ball to meet with Ayub. Armed with offers of
additional U.S. military aid well in excess of anything India had received to
date, Ball sought to arrest Pakistan's drift and explain U.S. policy to Ayub. Ball
left convinced that Ayub could, with a countervailing offer of military supplies,
accept some level of aid to India. He had also gained a pledge to allow continued use and the possible expansion of the Peshawar facility.[147]

[141] Memcon, Rusk, Ambassador Ahmed, and Talbot, February 23, 1963, ibid., 510–515.

[142] Memorandum, Rostow to Kennedy, April 8, 1963, ibid.: 538–541.

[143] Memorandum for the Record, April 25, 1963, ibid.: 561–565; Memorandum for the Record,
April 26, 1963, ibid.: 566–567; Memorandum, Komer to Kennedy, April 25, 1963, NSF, box
110, "India, General, 4/20/63" folder, JFKL.

[144] Telegram 6016, Washington to London, May 13, 1963, in *FRUS, 1961–1963, 19*: 590–591;
Telegram 6038, Washington to London, May 16, 1963, ibid.: 692–693; Memorandum for the
Record, May 17, 1963, ibid.: 593–596; Telegram 6401, Washington to London, May 29, 1963,
ibid.: 607–608 Memorandum, Commonwealth Relations Office, March 23, 1964, CAB 148/2,
TNA.

[145] Telegram 80, Washington to Karachi, July 11, 1963, in *FRUS, 1961–1963, 19*: 617–619.

[146] Memorandum, August 7, 1963, NSF, box 444, "Pakistan, 1/61–11/63 [1 of 3]" folder, JFKL.

[147] Telegram 526, Karachi to Washington, September 9, 1963, NSF, box 441, "Ball Mission, 9/63"
folder, JFKL; Telegram 236, Tehran to Washington, September 5, 1963, in *FRUS, 1961–1963,
19*: 661–668; Memorandum for the Record, September 9, 1963, ibid.: 675–678.

From the summer onward, the Kennedy administration perceived itself on the defensive on the question of India policy. The failure of Kashmir mediation increased Congressional pressure on economic aid to New Delhi, and Pakistani alienation had collectively fostered a sense of caution in Washington. Kennedy became increasingly concerned with the possibility of a Sino-Pakistani alliance.[148] Komer advised Kennedy that it was time to "sit back and rethink Pak-Indian matters."[149] By November 1963, the White House found itself engaged in a delicate balancing act, unable to engage India as energetically as it had the previous autumn.

Kennedy had not, however, fundamentally changed his mind on the utility of broader ties to India. During the autumn, his new ambassador in New Delhi, Chester Bowles, sought extensive, multi-year aid commitments to India and received a favorable hearing from Kennedy. Komer wrote on the morning of November 22, 1963, that JFK had a "sense that we should get on with our Indian enterprise. We've been marking time too much because of Congress and the Paks."[150]

Kennedy's last inclination had been to forge ahead with India, but he never had the opportunity to see the effort past the impasses of 1963. His successor, Johnson, held his own views of South Asia. The new president was particularly impressed by Ayub, whom he called "a very good guy."[151] On November 30, Johnson expressed his belief that more could be done to bring the Pakistani leader around. Moreover, he approached South Asia with more bounded expectations than Kennedy, remarking in 1964 that he did not see how "ancient feuds" like Kashmir could be resolved through U.S. action. The new president's outlook set back the influence of pro-India advocates in the White House. Komer did not think Johnson "sufficiently clued on India/Pakistan to see the opportunity and the stakes we're playing for." As Komer saw it, LBJ preferred "Ayubs to Nehrus."[152]

Consequently, U.S. policy toward the subcontinent moved toward the back burner in 1964. Having received favorable nods from Kennedy for a sustained military aid program, Bowles watched in dismay as the plan seemed to fall between the cracks. "Three months have passed with no, repeat, no word whatsoever," Bowles wrote angrily in February 1964, warning of increased Indian interest in further weapons procurement from the Soviet Union.[153] After Bowles asked to speak directly to Johnson, Bundy wrote,

---

[148] Ibid.; Memorandum for the Record, August 12, 1963, ibid.: 635–639.

[149] Memorandum, Komer to Kennedy, September 9, 1963, NSF, box 441, "Ball Mission, 9/63, WHM" folder, JFKL.

[150] Memorandum, Komer to Bundy, November 22, 1963, "India, General, 10/20/63–11/22/63" folder, JFKL. Third Oral History Interview, Robert Komer, September 3, 1964, 21, OH, JFKL. A contrary view emerges in Dennis Merrill, *Bread and the Ballot: The United States and India's Economic Development, 1947–1963* (Chapel Hill: University of North Carolina Press, 1990), 195–203.

[151] First Oral History Interview, Robert Komer, January 30, 1970, 7, OH, LBJL.

[152] Memorandum, Komer to Bundy, December 23, 1963, NSF, CF, box 128, "India, Vol. 1, Memos and Misc" folder, LBJL. See McMahon, *Cold War on the Periphery*, 305–306, 316–317.

[153] Telegram 2457, New Delhi to Washington, February 20, 1964, NSF, CF, box 128, "India, Vol. 1, Cables, 1 of 2" folder, LBJL.

We here have reacted with lively sympathy to your paeans of woe from Delhi, and have been doing all we can to help. For what it's worth, my feeling (and Bob Komer's too) is that we're the victims of an inevitable falling off in US/Indian relations from the high point of Winter 1962.

Bundy asked Bowles for patience, attempted to reassure him that Johnson shared his views, and stressed the unlikeliness of election-year initiatives toward India, observing: "The moratorium on politics is over, and we're going to have to steel ourselves for a lot of silly fuss."[154] Bowles's image as an unrestrained advocate for India did not help his position in the new administration; Komer and Bundy took his cables seriously, but few others did so.[155]

Increased political uncertainty in India further muddled the picture. Nehru suffered a stroke in January 1964, which left him severely incapacitated. Ayub, meanwhile, raised the Kashmir question at the Security Council. Komer observed that India was reportedly "wallowing in self-pity," with pro-American Indians reportedly "moaning how we missed a great opportunity in not continuing to support them against China." "We've lost more momentum than we may have realized with India," he added.[156] Bundy and Komer warned Johnson that "Ayub seems to think he has us on the run." The NSC sought a strong warning to Pakistan, but Johnson demurred, fearful of angering Ayub. LBJ approved sending Talbot to speak with Ayub, but overruled his aides when they suggested linking Pakistani moderation toward India to U.S. military aid.[157]

Johnson wanted strong relations with both South Asian states but felt an instinctive skepticism toward the entreaties of his pragmatist advisors. He enjoyed teasing his NSC staffers about their pro-Indian outlook, telling the visiting Indira Gandhi, at one point, while pointing to Bundy and Komer, that her government had succeeded in "subverting his staff."[158] Such jibes were normal for Johnson, but they made ambitious, position-conscious staffers like Komer wary of overstating their case.[159] Continued frustrations with both Indians and Pakistanis, above all, gave LBJ a healthy distaste for grand designs in the subcontinent. With crises elsewhere, mounting U.S. involvement in Southeast Asia, and his own reelection looming, Johnson wanted no more headaches.[160]

[154] Letter, Bundy to Bowles, March 9, 1964, in DOS, *FRUS, 1964–1968, Vol. 25: South Asia* (Washington: GPO, 2000): 51–52.

[155] Memorandum, Komer to Bundy, June 3, 1964, NSF, CF, box 128, "India, Vol. 2, Memos" folder, LBJL.

[156] Memorandum, Komer to Bundy, March 6, 1964, NSF, CF, box 128, "India, Vol. 1, Memos & Misc" folder, LBJL.

[157] Memorandum, Bundy and Komer to Johnson, March 8, 1964, in *FRUS, 1964–1968*, 25: 49–50; Telegram 47, Rawalpindi to Washington, March 11, 1964, ibid.: 56–62.

[158] Intelligence Information Cable, Undated, NSF, CF, box 128, "India, Vol. 2, Cables" folder, LBJL.

[159] First Oral History Interview, Robert Komer, January 30, 1970, 40–41, OH, LBJL. Years later, Komer remarked, of being called an "India lover," "That was one of the phrases he used that hurt."

[160] Fifth Oral History Interview, Robert Komer, December 22, 1969, 68, OH, JFKL.

Nehru died on May 27, 1964. His successor, Lal Bahadur Shastri, struck the White House as a fortunate choice. The new prime minister was regarded as moderate in outlook and interested in negotiations with Pakistan.[161] India's political paralysis appeared to be at an end and Ayub appeared receptive to his new counterpart. At last, it seemed possible that the South Asian logjam might be cleared. But this, too, proved a brief interlude. After the administration offered India $50 million in arms aid and another $50 million in credits, Ayub sent Johnson an angry letter.[162] The administration found itself in the same pit as before: unable to appease either Pakistani sensibilities or Indian demands, unwilling to cede the role of India's arms supplier to Moscow, but unable to match the Soviets offer for offer, particularly in the key field of fighter aircraft. India's interest in weaponry far exceeded Washington's estimates of what it needed and included items, such as warships, with no conceivable use against China.[163] As the summer dragged on, LBJ, preoccupied with his own reelection, his domestic program, and South Vietnam, had far less time or patience for intractable South Asian matters.

Without the sense of urgency that had animated the Kennedy administration on South Asian questions, policy toward the region moved gradually toward the back burner. Having sought to engage both states, the White House found itself in a truly invidious situation. Failing to provide India with satisfactory military aid gave New Delhi added reason to buy from the Soviets. Pakistan, however, found even what aid Washington could offer India grounds for protest – and an alibi for bolstering its ties with China. His earlier protestations to the contrary, Ayub proved quite comfortable with broadening his ties with Mao's government. In March 1965, capping several years of visits by mid-level officials, he staged a week-long visit to China, providing irrefutable evidence to the world of Pakistan's new bond with the PRC.

Frustration with Washington drew Pakistan, moreover, toward nonalignment. Ayub's government embarked on its own diplomatic offensive toward the nonaligned states, sending envoys as far afield as Guinea. Pakistan built increasingly strong ties with Indonesia, as Sukarno's rhetoric toward the West grew harsher, even offering discreet support against Malaysia. In 1964, Ayub and Bhutto signaled Pakistan's support of a Sino-Indonesian proposal for an Afro-Asian conference in the mold of Bandung.[164] Indeed, at an April 1964 preparatory conference for "Bandung II," Bhutto played a prominent role – more so, some said, than his Indian counterparts.[165] Pakistani-Indonesian friendship

---

[161] Memorandum, Komer to Bundy, June 2, 1964, in *FRUS, 1964–1968*, 25: 114.

[162] Letter, Ayub to Johnson, July 1, 1964, in *FRUS, 1964–1968*, 25: 129–130.

[163] See, for example, Telegram 509, London to Washington, July 30, 1964, NSF, CF, box 128, "India, Vol. 3" folder, LBJL; *FRUS, 1964–1968*, 25: 159n.

[164] Telegram 1793, Karachi to Washington, March 25, 1964, RG-59, CFPF: 1964–1966, box 1830, POL-8 series, NA.

[165] Telegram 2041, Karachi to Washington, April 23, 1964, RG-59, CFPF: 1964–1966, box 1830, "POL 8, 4/1/64" folder, NA.

proved an enduring bond, cemented in place by a shared antipathy toward India and a cooperative relationship with China.

The Soviet Union, on the other hand, benefited from increased Indian insecurity and Washington's inability to furnish New Delhi with the weapons it desired. In 1961, communist diplomats had worried about rising Western influence in India. In successive conversations with East German colleagues, Soviet diplomats expressed concern at Indian dependence on Western economic aid, New Delhi's opposition to the spread of communism in Asia, and the growth of pro-Western sentiment within the country.[166] The East Germans, for their part, were disappointed by Nehru's stance on the Berlin question at the Belgrade Conference.[167] However, beginning with the 1962 MiG sale, Soviet arms shipments to India bolstered Moscow's position. As French diplomats noted, the deepening Sino-Soviet split afforded Moscow greater leeway to aid New Delhi.[168] Soviet military aid to India continued to increase, while the U.S. pipeline dried out in 1964.

Other events in 1965 further shook the U.S. position in South Asia: Indo-Pakistani clashes in the Kashmiri district of Kargil and on a stretch of coastline known as the Rann of Kutch. These events foretold the end of Washington's efforts to build an anticommunist front in South Asia; they bore the seeds of the war that scarred the subcontinent later that year, marking the failure of Kennedy's effort to build an Indo-American partnership. Although Johnson sought his own constructive ties with India after the 1965 war, U.S. hopes never returned to the heights attained in the fall of 1962.

In South Asia, the allied crisis of confidence, the Sino-Soviet rivalry, and regional tensions intertwined, drawing India toward a greater reliance on Soviet arms and Pakistan toward open alliance with China. Pakistan's warming ties with Peking and its growing rivalry with India brought Ayub's government closer to a breach with Washington than any other ally in this period. So, too, did Kennedy's ambitious approach to India, predicated on hopes that it could pose a regional counterweight to China. This fueled Ayub's disaffection and increased his interest in nonalignment. India, on the other hand, felt profound disappointment over the inability of the United States to keep the promises made after the autumn 1962 war. By pinning their hopes on either a Kashmir accord or a Pakistani volte face, Kennedy's advisors deceived themselves into thinking they could transcend the subcontinent's defining rivalry. Indian hopes, once inflated by Kennedy, came crashing down as the contours of Johnson's policy toward New Delhi emerged. Washington's hope of bridging the South

[166] On this see Vermerk über ein Gespräch mit Botschafter der UdSSR Benediktov, New Delhi, August 17, 1961, MfAA, A 13911, AA; Vermerk über ein Gespräch mit dem Sowjetischen Botschafter, New Delhi, August 5, 1961, ibid.; Bericht über indische Haltung zu Laos, New Delhi, May 16, 1961, MfAA, A 13942, AA.

[167] Bericht, Außereuropäische Abteilung, September 15, 1961, MfAA, A 13966, AA.

[168] Telegram 945–949, New Delhi to Paris, August 9, 1963, in MAE, DDF, 1963, Tome II (Paris: Imprimerie Nationale, 2001): 164–165; Note, "Évolution du litige sino-indien," August 12, 1963, ibid.: 174–179.

Asian divide to create a regional anti-Chinese alliance proved farfetched and ultimately disastrous, leaving Pakistan disaffected and India looking elsewhere for the means to its self-defense.

THE DIFFUSION OF POWER

By the end of 1964, regional conflicts in Africa and Asia had severely complicated U.S. relations with both allies and nonaligned states. Washington's reluctance to give allies the backing they desired fostered a crisis of confidence and increasingly strident demands for solidarity. With the partial exception of Pakistan, allies ultimately succeeded in curbing or limiting U.S. aid to nonaligned countries, or in obtaining their own security-related concessions from the Kennedy and Johnson administrations. With more open avowals of solidarity toward allies came significantly worsened relations with nonaligned states. Paradoxically, states claiming a right to nonalignment in the Cold War allowed little middle ground where their own conflicts were concerned. Indonesian, Egyptian, Indian, and Ghanaian leaders scrutinized U.S. statements on local issues as closely as the Kennedy administration had the statements they had made at the Belgrade Conference.

It was no coincidence that the shift back toward allies occurred after Kennedy's death. Lyndon Johnson inherited a number of regional crises from his predecessor, but he was less inclined than Kennedy to stretch the fabric of existing alliances. Komer was right when he wrote that Johnson preferred Ayubs to Nehrus. By the end of 1963 – as the next chapter will detail – aid programs essential to engagement were under attack in the Congress, threatening Democratic control of the White House in the following year's election. It fell to Johnson to beat an orderly retreat. Domestic pressures reinforced his own reluctance to take many risks where the Nassers, Nehrus, Nkrumahs, and Sukarnos of the world were concerned.

No alliance was affected as broadly by the U.S. effort to engage nonaligned states as the Anglo-American alliance. Far more than colonial conflicts, regional conflicts tested the fabric of the special relationship. Like the Kennedy and Johnson administrations, successive British governments accepted the end of formal empire, taking a relative middle ground on colonial disputes. Regional conflicts, however, challenged the postcolonial arrangements that Britain had established. This relationship emerged from these conflicts tested, somewhat worn, but nonetheless intact. Differences of opinion over Indonesia and Egypt initially divided the allies, but such tensions were mollified by changing attitudes in Washington and consequent shifts in U.S. policy. Disputes jeopardizing key regional bases inevitably pushed the British and U.S. positions closer together. The cases of South Asia and West Africa, on the other hand, reveal the depth of Anglo-American collaboration.

Deepening commitments, particularly in Southeast Asia, drove the Johnson administration to exhort its allies to assist elsewhere in the world: none more so than Britain. In December 1964, Rusk and Secretary of Defense Robert

McNamara made an emphatic case to the new Labour prime minister, Harold Wilson, for maintaining Britain's military presence in the Indian Ocean region, pleading that the United States could not bear its present burden indefinitely.[169] London, facing a currency crisis, was reluctant to play this role, and this gave Washington cause to approach the relationship gingerly. As George Ball remarked, with regard to the Malaysia dispute, the United States was asking so much of Britain around the globe that it could not afford to give London the back of its hand.[170] This determination had fateful consequences in the autumn of 1965.

Growing entanglement in regional conflicts came to jeopardize the status of U.S. diplomats and facilities on the ground. In the autumn of 1964, three different USIS libraries – two in Indonesia and one in Egypt – were burned down. *The Washington Post* mused, "Apparently the most dangerous place to be during any mob riot abroad is in the local USIS library."[171] Now the target of angry mobs and government-affiliated presses, Washington could scarcely claim the middle ground in the new conflicts of the Third World. Efforts to defuse the zero-sum nature of regional conflicts had, without exception, failed utterly. U.S.-sponsored mediation sported a dismal track record in cases including Malaysia, Yemen, Kashmir, and the Arab-Israeli conflict.

To some extent, the Soviet Union benefited from these conflicts. The regional conflicts that tortured the Kennedy and Johnson administrations presented the Kremlin with easy choices. Soviet arms exports to Indonesia were made with the full knowledge that they would be employed against Malaysia. Moscow also gained from spiraling Arab-Israeli tensions *and* escalating rivalries among the Arab states, expanding its arms exports to Egypt. Similarly, Moscow substantially expanded its supply of weapons to India as it faced a Sino-Pakistani alliance.[172]

The diffusion of power heightened perceptions of threat and opportunity in the free, communist, and nonaligned worlds. Washington's efforts to evade or mediate regional conflicts weakened ties to nonaligned states and strained existing alliances. Nor did the Soviet Union benefit from the fragmentation of power, as it battled the Chinese for influence across the entire Third World. Moscow's quest for position in the nonaligned world forced it to embrace states such as Egypt, where communists faced constant political repression, or Indonesia, despite reservations about Sukarno's campaign against

[169] Memcon, Talbot and Kamel, December 7, 1964, in DOS, *FRUS, 1964–1968, Vol. 12: Western Europe* (Washington: GPO, 2001): 475–479. See also Fain, *American Ascendance and British Retreat*, 147–152.

[170] Telephone Conversation, Ball and Berger, August 23, 1965, GWBP, box 1, "Britain III" folder, LBJL.

[171] Dan Kurzman, "USIS Libraries a Favorite Spot to Vent Anti-American Venom," *The Washington Post*, December 11, 1964, 17.

[172] Research Memorandum, Hilsman to Rusk, March 1, 1963, NSF, box 432, "Malaysia, 1961–1963" folder, JFKL; Telegram 680, Jakarta to Washington, October 12, 1962, NSF, box 412, "Indonesia, General, 9/62–10/62" folder, JFKL.

Malaysia.[173] Even though Moscow emerged as the main supplier of arms to India, this came as a response to the perceived threat posed by Western aid – a threat that, in turn, exacerbated the Sino-Soviet split. Moscow's effort to court the leading nonaligned state caused significant damage to its most important alliance. Although the Sino-Soviet split stemmed in large part from other causes, the Soviet Union may have paid the highest price of all for its own effort at engagement.[174]

The historian Fredrik Logevall characterizes the time between August 1963 and February 1965 as the "Long 1964," the critical eighteen-month span during which the White House acted to Americanize the war in Vietnam.[175] It bears mentioning that events in South Vietnam during this period commanded far more attention and concern than the regional conflicts discussed here. Critically, the same general period witnessed both a consolidation of these conflicts and a consequent faltering of U.S.-nonaligned relations. The Malaysian Confrontation erupted as Kennedy embarked upon a collision course with the South Vietnamese government of Ngo Dinh Diem. Nasser's Port Said outburst came a mere three days after yet another military coup in Saigon. Border tensions between India and Pakistan accumulated through the early months of 1965, erupting into bloodshed two weeks after Johnson explained his policy in Vietnam in an April speech at The Johns Hopkins University. Even before it elicited action on the part of the nonaligned world, the ongoing crisis in Southeast Asia fostered distraction in Washington.

By 1965, with a second Afro-Asian conference looming on the horizon, possibly to be dominated by the new Sino-Indonesian axis, the position of the United States in the nonaligned world stood at a crossroads – just as the phenomenon of nonalignment itself seemed to be dramatically shifting. The optimism of late 1962 was entirely gone. Washington's growing entanglement in Southeast Asia curtailed its freedom of movement elsewhere. The United States retained one major card – economic aid – but even that proved a difficult one to play in the nonaligned world.

---

[173] See Telegram 1011, Jakarta to Washington, November 4, 1963, NSF, box 114, "Indonesia, General, 10/63–11/63" folder, JFKL.

[174] See Lüthi, *The Sino-Soviet Split*, 224–228; Chen Jian, *Mao's China and the Cold War* (Chapel Hill: University of North Carolina Press, 2001), 79–80.

[175] Fredrik Logevall, *Choosing War: The Lost Chance for Peace and the Escalation of War in Vietnam* (Berkeley: University of California Press, 1999), xiii–xiv.

6

"Our Most Difficult Political Battle": The Question of Aid

The history of U.S. aid to the nonaligned world during the 1960s illustrates a fundamental and intrinsic problem with foreign assistance: despite efforts to depict the purposes of aid as being broadly humanitarian, its distribution remained fundamentally political in nature. The Kennedy administration did much to reinforce the hopes of nonaligned leaders that it would assist them. Kennedy's inaugural address extended the lofty promise of aid given without political strings, of cooperation with nations premised not on fidelity but a shared commitment to the independence of the recipient. "Nothing could be farther from my thought than to make our assistance to India contingent on her acceptance of our particular wishes in foreign or domestic policy," Kennedy wrote to Nehru, in the wake of the Goa invasion, "We seek to help develop independence and independence exists to be used."[1] His administration promised to make the 1960s the "Decade of Development," an historic era in which underdeveloped, postcolonial societies would make vital strides toward prosperity and political stability. This pledge fostered hope in the postcolonial world, but proved difficult to fulfill, in large part because Kennedy's advisors underestimated the intractability of poverty, but also because of the politics of aid.

The New Frontiersmen spoke of a universal humanitarian mission on the part of the industrialized world to aid the poorer countries of the globe, yet political calculi remained inescapable and visible to all. Recalling the case of the Aswan High Dam, Kennedy and his advisors were sensitive to the possibility that they could be accused of using aid to bribe or coerce foreign governments. Even so, neither they, nor Congress, nor the American public could reject the notion that aid should, in turn, bring political concessions from grateful recipients. The clash between this expectation and the disappointing reality of the politics of aid sowed division between Washington and nonaligned states.

[1] Letter, Kennedy to Nehru, January 18, 1962, in DOS, *FRUS, 1963–1963, Vol. 19: South Asia* (Washington: GPO, 1996): 197–199.

The administration's focus on economic aid stemmed directly from its sense of the dangers of communist encroachment in underdeveloped areas of the world: in Africa, Asia, and Latin America. Kennedy's concern about the spread of Cuban-style communism within Latin America drove him to initiate the Alliance for Progress, an ambitious and ultimately unsuccessful effort to foster economic growth throughout Latin America. In a similar vein, the White House established the Peace Corps, dispatching American civilian volunteers to the farthest reaches of the globe. In Africa and Asia, the administration supported high-profile Aswan-like initiatives, such as dams in Ghana and steel mills in India. Through the Food for Peace program it sold, at concession prices, much-needed grain to countries facing poor harvests.

As usual, a variety of motives lay behind U.S. policy. Conceptions about the goals of aid ranged from those of Walt Rostow, who supported long-term projects and balked at tying aid to immediate political objectives, to those of Robert Komer, who viewed aid largely through political lenses. Rostow believed the creation of prosperous societies in the postcolonial world the most important goal of aid programs. His vision of global development was motivated both by Cold War concerns and a broader liberal vision of a universal right to prosperous living.[2] He was consequently reluctant to taint aid programs by making them contingent on political ends, writing in September 1961, "It is crucial that we do not permit our short-term tactics to disrupt the long-term strategy." The establishment of long-term aid relationships with nonaligned states, he argued, would lead to their pursuing more agreeable foreign policies. His analysis of the Belgrade Conference found that aid recipients had, indeed, tended to take more moderate positions.[3]

The Rostovian vision dovetailed broadly with the aspirations of postcolonial governments, which sought rapid economic development as a means to alleviate poverty and secure national independence. In India, he found a receptive audience for his theories in Prime Minister Jawaharlal Nehru, whose Five Year Plans envisioned a steady stream of capital aiding the development of Indian industry. Egypt's President Gamal Abdel Nasser was so impressed by Rostow's theories that he had *The Stages of Economic Growth* translated into Arabic and distributed to his cabinet.[4] In sub-Saharan Africa demand for rapid industrialization was particularly pronounced: Ghana had its planned Volta River project and Guinea's President Sekou Touré espoused his own dream of a dam on the Konkoure River.

[2] On these dual motivations, see Walt W. Rostow, *The Stages of Economic Growth: A Non-Communist Manifesto* (New York: Cambridge University Press, 1960), 165–167. See also Michael Latham, *Modernization as Ideology: American Social Science and Nation Building in the Kennedy Era* (Chapel Hill: University of North Carolina Press, 2000), 56–58.

[3] Memorandum "Neutralism and Foreign Aid; or Belgrade Reconsidered," Rostow to Kennedy, September 27, 1961, DDRS.

[4] Warren Bass, *Support Any Friend: Kennedy's Middle East and the Making of the U.S.-Israel Alliance* (New York: Oxford University Press, 2002), 63.

Considerations of cost and political expediency, however, limited the number of prestige projects the United States could fund. With such constraints, aid was necessarily a tool for immediate-term political use in the eyes of many on the NSC, most prominently Robert Komer. Komer felt no reservations about explicitly linking aid to the policies of recipient countries. He was fond of describing aid using the familiar Arabic word "baksheesh," which equated, in this case, to either charity or bribery, and he approached aid projects expecting that they would make recipients more amenable to U.S. policies. Although Komer accepted development rationales for aid, he did not consider these the sole or most pressing goal of assistance programs. As he wrote to David Bell, the administrator of the Agency for International Development (AID),

Let's face it, Dave – a high proportion of our aid total is for such purposes as buying political leverage, baksheesh, buoying up feeble regimes, preclusion [of communist influence] and the like – hardly "constructive" purposes. But these are essential (though overused) instrumentalities of our cold war policy, and as insurance against worse they are probably worth the cost in gross terms.[5]

At the same time, as a matter of tactics, Komer was generally reluctant to pull the strings when recipients pursued disagreeable policies. He wrote in January 1963:

If we think Nasser is misbehaving in the Yemen or Sukarno is again showing undue territorial appetite, we need merely ask ourselves how much more difficult they would be if they didn't feel a real concern lest they sacrifice actual and prospective aid from us. The trouble is that this is hardly a convincing public rationale for giving aid.[6]

Here, in a rare instance, Komer erred on the side of understatement.

Aid to nonaligned states was a uniquely competitive endeavor. Rostow and his peers had elaborate (often conflicting) plans for the development of states such as India and Indonesia, but so, too, did communist donors. Nonaligned states were consequently battlefields for rival visions of modernization but also were able to impose real limits on the use of aid as a tool for advancing a specifically American vision of progress.[7] Nonaligned states had their own distinct, often state-centered concepts of development, and – unlike allied aid recipients – the freedom to solicit competing bids from their suitors. Visions of development came at least as often as not from nonaligned recipients. Under such circumstances, aid to the nonaligned states frequently represented "baksheesh."

In theory, Washington's financial resources made aid the strongest lever it could wield in support of engagement, provided that it was seen as a generous

---

[5] Memorandum, Komer to David Bell, February 28, 1963, NSF, box 412, "Clay Committee [2 of 2]" folder, JFKL.

[6] Memorandum, Komer to Kennedy, January 19, 1963, in DOS, FRUS, 1961–1963, Vol. 8: National Security Policy (Washington: GPO, 1996): 456–457.

[7] See Bradley Simpson, Economists with Guns: Authoritarian Development and U.S.-Indonesian Relations, 1960–1968 (Stanford: Stanford University Press, 2008), 256–257, on this distinction.

donor, respectful of recipients' sovereignty. Both Kennedy and Johnson strove to convey this message to the world. Ultimately, however, the altruistic image of aid clashed with the strategic goals driving U.S. policy toward the Third World. The White House could publicly disavow the existence of strings, but it could never surmount the problem of reciprocity: the expectation that aid should purchase *something* from its recipients. The two presidents were thus torn between the image and goals of their aid policy.

Equally important was the reality that the White House was not the sole actor within the government on aid-related questions. During the 1960s, foreign aid became an increasingly charged subject in U.S. politics, as the two Democratic administrations encountered increasingly sharp Congressional opposition. The aid debate forced Kennedy and Johnson to confront popular views of the Cold War and of nonalignment. Public views of nonalignment remained closer to those of John Foster Dulles than those of John F. Kennedy. At the grassroots level, anticommunism, racial attitudes, and a fundamental skepticism toward foreign assistance combined to make attacks on the aid budget both appealing and politically advantageous. The growing outflow of currency from the national economy seemed to render aid programs a costly indulgence. Above all, only the executive branch felt any ambivalence about seeking reciprocity. Congress and the public had no reservations about expecting that aid should purchase some degree of allegiance; if it did not, what was the use? Why should the United States aid countries that spurned and criticized it, when it had so many loyal allies in the world? Both presidents struggled to answer this question, as they fought to steer aid appropriation bills through Congress. Kennedy battled an increasingly skeptical Congress on behalf of aid to nonaligned states, suffering a major defeat in 1963. Johnson, tiring of the fight, attached increasingly overt strings to aid – to the profound resentment of nonaligned recipients. This dual struggle, pitting the White House against both Congress and the nonaligned world, ultimately caused significant damage to the international image of the United States.

"THE ROCK-BOTTOM MINIMUM"

Aware of the difficulties his aid program faced, Kennedy addressed the question of foreign aid in one of his first speeches as president, on March 22, 1961. He sought to bolster public support for foreign aid programs, while at the same time both streamlining and adding to them. The speech focused primarily on the first goal: convincing a skeptical public and Congress that foreign aid was in the national interest. Kennedy appealed to notions of American mission and charity and domestic anticommunism as well. Poverty in the Third World, Kennedy argued, "would inevitably invite the advance of totalitarianism into every weak and unstable area."[8] Harnessing Rostovian ideas, he proposed to make the 1960s "the crucial Decade of Development," when

[8] *PPP: John F. Kennedy, 1961* (Washington: GPO, 1962), 204.

"many less-developed nations [could] make the transition into self-sustained growth" – thereby reducing poverty and political instability. Such goals could not be financed on a short-term basis – recipients expected a long-term commitment. Accordingly, Kennedy asked for an aid allotment of $4 billion, "the rock-bottom minimum of funds necessary to do the job." Although a large sum, this did not represent a substantial increase over Eisenhower's final aid budget.

The speech mixed New Frontier idealism and legislative realism. Having served in both houses of Congress, Kennedy clearly understood that he could not count on their unflinching support. Eisenhower, for his part, had faced sharp Congressional criticism for aiding Yugoslavia and for initially proposing to fund Egypt's Aswan High Dam – much of it coming from within his own party.[9] Kennedy was further hampered by his weak reputation within the Senate, where he had been seen as a relative lightweight.[10]

Facing these legislative challenges, Kennedy often described the difficulties facing his aid program to nonaligned leaders. One notably frank reminder came in his post-Goa letter to Nehru. After declaring that he had no desire to make aid "a question of strings," Kennedy continued:

Still, we must both weigh the effects of action by one country on public opinion and political action in another. You are justified in asking that American action be considerate of the problems of Indian democracy.... Similarly I think it reasonable that American public opinion should be a subject of concern to you. Each year our appropriations to help, not India alone, but also the other developing countries of the world, involve our most difficult political battle.... I hope you will agree that we have a common interest in maintaining the political atmosphere and the public attitudes that are sympathetic to this effort.[11]

This was an imperative that nonaligned leaders could fathom but not one to which they could easily commit. They could not subordinate their own political needs to the goal of maintaining the domestic standing of the U.S. president. Inflammatory rhetoric emanating from Congress, moreover, frequently offended them and demanded a vehement response. Meeting Egyptian President Gamal Abdel Nasser in 1966, the veteran diplomat Averell Harriman remarked, "Nothing can be done to control Congressmen." The Egyptian leader replied: "Sometimes it is difficult to control our reaction to their statements."[12] Domestic politics, in short, worked to turn aid from a force for comity to a source of profound acrimony in the relationship between the United States and the nonaligned world.

[9] See H. W. Brands, *The Specter of Neutralism: The United States and the Emergence of the Third World, 1947–1960* (New York: Columbia University Press, 1989), 191–211, 268–275.

[10] Lewis L. Gould, *The Most Exclusive Club: A History of the Modern United States Senate* (New York: Basic Books, 2005), 233–239.

[11] Letter, Kennedy to Nehru, January 18, 1962, in *FRUS, 1961–1963*, 19: 197–199.

[12] Airgram A-567, Cairo to Washington, January 5, 1966, NSF, RWKP, box 51, "UAR, 1965-March 1966 [1 of 3]" folder, LBJL.

APPLYING THE LESSONS OF ASWAN

Two key episodes, standing in almost-perfect contrast, illustrate the dramatic shift in aid policy that began with the New Frontier: the Aswan High Dam fiasco of 1955–1956 and Kennedy's decision to support Ghana's Volta River Dam in 1961. One event came as a direct consequence of the other: Aswan was the event that most haunted policymakers when they considered aid requests from nonaligned leaders. For the New Frontiersmen, the lessons of Aswan were clear. It was far better to vie for influence, bearing the occasional slings and arrows of a Nasser, than to push him toward the Soviet bloc. Not unlike "Munich," "Aswan" also became a historical analogy freighted with meaning.

In the present environmentally conscious age, it is difficult to recall that in the 1960s dams seemed emblematic of modernization itself. Dams seemed to offer a universal solution to problems of underdevelopment, to Americans, Soviets, and nonaligned leaders alike. New Frontiersmen, who had generally come of age politically during the New Deal years, looked to Franklin D. Roosevelt's Tennessee Valley Authority as exemplifying a specifically American and democratic model of development. The iconic importance of dam projects as symbols of U.S. beneficence and expertise added sting to Aswan and critical importance to the Volta decision.[13]

Aswan's specter loomed over the Kennedy administration's consideration of Ghana's request for assistance with the Volta River Dam. Analogies to Aswan flowed freely in the months preceding the decision. During a conversation with George Ball, Kennedy compared the predicament to Aswan.[14] Two months later, in a letter to Kennedy, British Prime Minister Harold Macmillan wrote: "I fear that if you were now to announce that you could not proceed with Volta, there would be a real danger of repeating in West Africa what happened in Egypt when Foster Dulles made a sudden and ill-prepared change of line about the Aswan Dam."[15] The analogy captivated London long after Kennedy's decision. In a February 1964 discussion about Ghana, Macmillan's successor, Alec Douglas-Home, committed a Freudian slip, uttering "Aswan" when he meant to say "Volta."[16]

As he extended his offer to Ghana, Kennedy sought a reciprocal commitment from Nkrumah: to rhetorical moderation and "true" nonalignment. Kennedy felt caught in a bind. On the one hand, he risked discrediting his promise to offer aid without strings; on the other, he feared a Congressional

[13] See David Ekbladh, *The Great American Mission: Modernization and the Construction of an American World Order* (Princeton: Princeton University Press, 2010), 153–189; Nick Cullather, *The Hungry World: America's Cold War Battle Against Poverty in Asia* (Cambridge, MA: Harvard University Press, 2010), 108–133.

[14] Memcon, Kennedy and Ball, September 21, 1961, in DOS, *FRUS, 1961–1963, Vol. 21: Africa* (Washington: GPO, 1995): 355–356.

[15] Telegram 8413, Foreign Office to Washington, November 16, 1961, CAB 21/5511, TNA.

[16] Memcon, LBJ, Home, and others, February 12, 1964, in DOS, *FRUS, 1964–1968, Vol. 24: Africa* (Washington: GPO, 1999): 417–418.

backlash.[17] His request to Nkrumah was both moderate and discreet. In spite of this, Ghana's subsequent behavior proved dissatisfying to Kennedy. Despite U.S. efforts to revitalize the relationship, Ghanaian criticism of the United States continued. By December 1962, the embassy in Accra recommended that Washington avoid extending any new aid commitments to Ghana and approach any new proposals with an "initially negative attitude."[18]

Volta, the Kennedy administration's largest commitment to a single project within the nonaligned world, came to mark a countervailing example to Aswan. Committing aid to the dam had not satisfactorily changed Nkrumah's policy or rhetoric, but it *did* arouse resentment in other West African states that felt more deserving of aid. Within Congress, moreover, the Volta decision contributed to a mounting tide of criticism against foreign aid, particularly aid to the nonaligned states.

THE BACKLASH: 1961–1962

The Congressional assault against Kennedy's foreign aid program began in 1961, gained critical momentum the following year, and crested in 1963. It rose in opposition to engagement, seizing upon the conflicts in the Congo, Goa, West New Guinea, Yemen, Kashmir, and Malaysia, as justification for penalizing disagreeable nonaligned states. The backlash derived in large part from conservative disaffection with the Kennedy administration's foreign policy outlook, although it also received considerable support from moderate and liberal Democrats. A steadfast anticommunism drove critics of foreign aid, alienating them from policies that seemed tolerant of nonalignment or the statist economic policies of nonaligned leaders.

Trips overseas by members of Congress were a key factor in shaping opinions. Allies, in general, were better prepared to welcome visiting legislators. They knew the value of charming their guests and espousing fervent anticommunism and staunch support of the United States. India and Pakistan formed a telling contrast in this regard: accounts of visits to the two South Asian rivals invariably credited the Pakistanis with superior hospitality and clear allegiance to Washington.[19] Such ties continued long after trips had concluded. A number of allied states proved adept at using their embassies to maintain contact with legislators on Capitol Hill. India's ambassador in Washington, B. K. Nehru, complained of his Pakistani colleague's sway in Congress. Israel enjoyed very strong support on Capitol Hill and among the electorate. Saudi Arabia, too, had a dedicated constituency within the oil industry. Portugal and

---

[17] See also Thomas J. Noer, "The New Frontier and African Neutralism: Kennedy, Nkrumah, and the Volta River Project," *Diplomatic History* 8, No. 1 (January 1984), 61–80.

[18] Telegram 739, Accra to Washington, December 3, 1962, NSF, box 100, "Ghana, General, 11/62–12/62" folder, JFKL.

[19] On this see Andrew J. Rotter, *Comrades at Odds: The United States and India, 1947–1964* (Ithaca: Cornell University Press 2000), 217–219.

the Katangan separatist government each mounted highly effective lobbying operations. Other states, such as Britain and the Netherlands, enjoyed the sympathy of the public as NATO allies.

States that did not hew to the U.S. line, however, won far less sympathy in Congress and the public arena. The case of Yugoslavia in 1961 and 1962 provides a pivotal early example of the growing backlash against aid to uncommitted states. Although Yugoslavia, as an European state, stood apart from the rest of the nonaligned movement, it nonetheless faced the same pressures from both the White House and Congress. Kennedy and his advisors expected that U.S. aid would moderate Yugoslavian foreign policy. When it did not, Belgrade ran afoul of the legislature.

Critical to this case and others was U.S. food aid. In 1954, Eisenhower had signed into law Public Law 480 (PL-480), the Agricultural Trade and Development Assistance Act. The bill represented an innovative attack on two problems: world hunger and domestic grain surpluses. Title I of PL-480 authorized the government to buy U.S. surplus grain and sell it to foreign governments experiencing agricultural shortfalls, with the sales priced in local currency. Later renamed "Food for Peace," the program was substantially revitalized by Kennedy, who envisioned it as another potent weapon in the battle for the Third World.[20]

Alone among the states of Europe, Yugoslavia had adopted nonalignment wholeheartedly, while remaining concerned with the ideological direction of the communist bloc. Entering the 1960s, Tito observed several interconnected challenges and opportunities: the widening split between the Soviet Union and China, Khrushchev's desire to revive relations with Belgrade, and the increasing weight of anticolonial sentiment in Africa and Asia. Perceiving a vital interest in backing the Soviets against the Chinese, Tito softened his criticism of Moscow – most notably at the Belgrade Conference when he declined to criticize Khrushchev's resumption of nuclear testing.

His new direction placed Tito on a collision course with the United States. Kennedy was especially irked by Tito's speech at Belgrade; afterward, he directed Rostow to report to him on the nature of U.S. aid to Yugoslavia.[21] With Kennedy's approval, Secretary of State Dean Rusk sent Tito an unusually sharp message. The Yugoslav leader's speech, Rusk wrote, had been "so patently in support of positions taken by [the] Soviet Union as to raise doubt ... regarding validity of Yugoslavia's status of nonalignment." The administration felt obliged to "give continuing study" to the implications of Tito's conduct

---

[20] On the background of the Food for Peace program, see Kristin L. Ahlberg, *Transplanting the Great Society: Lyndon Johnson and Food for Peace* (Columbia: University of Missouri Press, 2008), 1–31; Peter A. Toma, *The Politics of Food for Peace: Executive-Legislative Interaction* (Tucson: University of Arizona Press, 1967); Mitchel B. Wallerstein, *Food for War – Food for Peace: United States Food Aid in a Global Context* (Cambridge, MA: MIT Press, 1980).

[21] Memorandum, Rostow to Kennedy, September 8, 1961, NSF, box 209, "Yugoslavia: General, 9/61–10/61" folder, JFKL.

at the conference for U.S.-Yugoslav relations.[22] Several days later Kennedy ordered a halt to export licenses for products destined for Yugoslavia.

The president acted in response to mounting domestic criticism of U.S. aid to communist countries. A week after the conference, the House of Representatives voted to authorize an investigation into aid given to communist countries, citing in particular jet sales to Yugoslavia.[23] These concerns meshed with growing conservative doubt over the administration's handling of the Berlin crisis and anger at the perceived pro-Moscow cast of the Belgrade Conference, which, the Republican opposition argued, had exposed the "utter bankruptcy" of Kennedy's foreign policy.[24]

Having made his point to Tito, following the NSC's recommendation, Kennedy removed the ban on export licenses in the middle of October.[25] Rusk subsequently affirmed that, despite Washington's disappointment, its aid to Belgrade was "not designed to purchase agreement with us" but, rather, intended to strengthen Yugoslav independence.[26] However frustrating Tito's speech had been, no real reason existed to think that Yugoslavia was losing its independence.

Tito was not reassured; indeed, Yugoslavia seemed to think that the Kennedy administration was denying it needed grain sales through the PL-480 program. Speaking on November 14, Tito declared that U.S. pressure was being brought to bear on Yugoslavia, even as his country faced a severe drought. Yugoslavia, he said, would acquire wheat, even if it bought not a single grain from the United States. Far from abandoning his earlier statements about Germany, Tito amplified them, charging that Washington planned to arm Bonn with nuclear weapons.[27] Kennan dubbed the address the "most unbalanced and anti-Western" speech given by Tito in recent memory.[28] The speech startled Kennedy as well, particularly Tito's statements on food; he worried that providing Yugoslavia with food aid would now prove far more difficult.[29]

The administration did not seriously entertain punishing Yugoslavia through a reduction in food aid, but the troubled climate of U.S.-Yugoslav relations made any proposed adjustments to the program seem punitive. Try as it might, the Kennedy administration could not dispel the notion in Belgrade that it was using aid as leverage – not while Congress pilloried Yugoslavia. Nor, however, could it resolve a key ambivalence within its own halls. The White House had

[22] Telegram 323, Washington to Belgrade, September 13, 1961, ibid.
[23] Editorial, "The House Finally Acts," *Los Angeles Times*, September 12, 1961, B4; "Last 20 Jets for Tito Due this Month," *Los Angeles Times*, September 2, 1961, 12.
[24] Willard Edwards, "GOP Leaders Voice Fears of Appeasement," *Chicago Tribune*, September 28, 1961, 1.
[25] National Security Council Record of Action No. 2439, in DOS, *FRUS, 1961–1963, Vol. 16: Eastern Europe; Cyprus; Greece; Turkey* (Washington: GPO, 1994): 96.
[26] DOSB, Vol. XLV, No. 1167, November 6, 1961, 750.
[27] Telegram 752, Belgrade to Washington, November 14, 1961, NSF, box 209, "Yugoslavia: General, 11/61–12/61" folder, JFKL.
[28] Telegram 771, Belgrade to Washington, November 17, 1961, ibid.
[29] Memorandum, Kennedy to Rusk, November 17, 1961, ibid.

publicly declared that it did not intend to use aid as leverage against Yugoslavia but *had* implied strongly to Tito that a reevaluation of the U.S.-Yugoslav relationship was imminent. This reevaluation would almost certainly affect the aid Yugoslavia received. Kennan had delivered the demarche forcefully; as the Department moved away from the implications of its earlier message, the ambassador grew increasingly frustrated, like Jonah overlooking Nineveh. He wrote to Washington,

> It is true that we should not demand of the recipients of our aid that they agree with us on all international questions. But we may demand of them a reasonable degree of objectivity at least in the treatment of our differences with the Soviet Union; and we may demand from them the evidence that they feel some concern for the preservation of our power and influence in world affairs. These things we do not receive from the Yugoslavs.[30]

Kennan expressed a recurrent belief among policymakers that, even if they were not buying solidarity with aid, they were at least paying for *some* kind of consideration. The problem of reciprocity – this tension between the image of beneficence and the need for leverage – was never satisfactorily resolved.

Rusk was loath to confirm Tito's claims that the United States was seeking to use food aid for leverage and saw real value in maintaining Yugoslavia's independence from the communist bloc, even if it meant enduring Tito's criticism on occasion. Rusk successfully argued these points to Kennedy when he requested approval for PL-480 sales to Yugoslavia.[31] Even so, some bitterness lingered. When he met Yugoslav Ambassador Marko Nikezic the following year, Rusk remarked that Yugoslavia needed to know that it could not take the United States for granted. Nikezic retorted that Yugoslavia had learned that much after the conference.[32]

Congressional action the following year signaled a new phase in both U.S.-Yugoslav relations and the administration's foreign aid program. On June 6, 1962, the Senate voted to bar communist-dominated countries from receiving any form of U.S. aid. The sponsor of the measure, Wisconsin Democrat William Proxmire, cited Tito's speech as cause to cease aid to Yugoslavia.[33] Few senators were willing to support aid to communist states in an election year.

The vote was perceived as the White House's first foreign policy defeat at the hands of Congress, and it rankled. Bundy had, to no avail, appealed for rejecting the Proxmire amendment.[34] In advance of a presidential press conference, an irate Komer wrote in vintage sarcasm to his colleague Carl Kaysen:

> Kaysen – I'm through being polite, and it's about time you quit being polite too. I'm telling you, and I want you to tell the President that he's got to tell the Nation – this afternoon – that we LOVE the neutrals, that INDIA, YUGOSLAVIA, POLAND, INDONESIA, AND

---

[30] Letter, Kennan to Foy Kohler, October 27, 1961, in *FRUS, 1961–1963,* 16: 222–230.

[31] Memorandum, "Proposed PL 480 Sales to Yugoslavia," Rusk to Kennedy, November 21, 1961, ibid.: 238–241.

[32] Memcon, Rusk and Marko Nikezic, January 8, 1962, ibid.: 252–253.

[33] Letter to the Editor, William Proxmire, *NYT,* June 22, 1962, 18.

[34] McGeorge Bundy, "Letter on Aid to Yugoslavs," *NYT,* June 7, 1962, 16.

THE UAR are our ONLY true allies and that we can't conduct foreign policy if we won't help those who hate us.[35]

This too, was – alas – hardly a convincing public rationale for giving aid.

A similar assault next befell aid to India, with Nehru's invasion of Goa providing the same impetus as Tito's speech at Belgrade. Legislators cited India's assault on a NATO ally when, in the spring of 1962, the Senate Foreign Relations Committee voted to reduce aid to India by 25 percent, despite Rusk's protests that the aid was entirely economic in nature. Missouri Senator Stuart Symington replied that economic aid to India enabled it to maintain a very large military and to purchase Soviet-made MiGs. Symington called Nehru "probably one of the most aggressive persons in the world."[36]

Symington brought almost unparalleled national security credentials to the debate over aid. He was a well-known Democrat, a former secretary of the Air Force, a prominent nemesis of Joseph McCarthy, and a candidate for the presidency in 1960. He did not seek to undermine the White House – indeed, Symington respected Kennedy – but rather to redirect its Cold War strategy.[37] Writing to Kennedy, he cited the contributions to U.S. security made by allies such as Turkey, Iran, and Pakistan, and the trepidation those allies felt as Washington aided a country espousing "pro-Soviet neutralism." Symington and his colleagues espoused a more traditional view of the Cold War world; not unlike Dulles, they favored clear, universal distinctions between allies and neutrals. Symington's letter cited the Shah of Iran's remark that no country could afford to stay neutral in the Cold War. He warned:

Our friends and allies and supporters in the Middle East are patient; but their patience is not inexhaustible. They ask, 'Why should we not be neutral – or pro-Soviet neutral? If we changed ... we would receive more support from you than we do now.'[38]

Several factors sparked the Congressional attack on aid to India: a desire to support allies such as Pakistan, irritation with New Delhi's views, and anger over India's invasion of Goa. Nehru's decision to buy MiGs from the Soviet Union allowed critics to argue that U.S. funds were indirectly subsidizing arms purchases from Moscow.[39] The Sino-Indian War did not change matters. Symington remained opposed to aiding India. "All is not forgiven," warned *National Review*, the conservative flagship magazine, citing India's continued support for seating the PRC at the UN and the threat India posed to Pakistan.

---

[35] Memorandum, "Press Conference Notes," Komer to Kaysen, June 7, 1962, NSF, box 322, "Robert Komer, 6/62" folder, JFKL. Poland, another PL-480 recipient, had also been targeted by the Congressional resolution.

[36] Robert Allen and Paul Scott, "Huge Military Buildup by India Caused Slash in Foreign Aid Fund," *Los Angeles Times*, May 28, 1962, A5.

[37] On Kennedy and Symington, see Linda McFarland, *Cold War Strategist: Stuart Symington and the Search for National Security* (Westport, CT: Praeger, 2001), 108–118.

[38] Letter, Symington to Kennedy, May 11, 1962, POF, box 118A, "India, General, 4/62–12/62" folder, JFKL.

[39] Felix Belair, "Foreign Aid Rise for India Barred by Senate Group," *NYT*, May 22, 1962, 1.

It was time, *National Review* suggested, to press for a Kashmir solution, adding:

There is nothing improper in our using our aid to India in her time of troubles to exert a political pressure of this sort. Our traditional sin has been our failure to employ such strength to such responsible purposes.[40]

In this, the magazine expressed an outlook common to most Americans.

1963: THE DELUGE

Entering the third year of his presidency, Kennedy apprehended the trouble his foreign aid budget would face. Preparing for the next year's aid debate, the president replaced Fowler Hamilton, the head of the Agency for International Development, with David Bell, who was believed to be a more persuasive advocate for aid programs. Kennedy anticipated a pitched battle in the House over the fiscal year (FY) 1964 aid budget, which was intended to cover the period between July 1963 and June 1964.

Lying in wait for the FY 1964 bill was Congressman Otto Passman, the chair of the House Appropriations Subcommittee on Foreign Aid and an implacable foe of foreign aid. The Louisiana Democrat considered aid to be "ill-conceived, badly executed, unrealistic, and enormously wasteful." By his reckoning, aid weakened the dollar by contributing to the nation's dangerous balance of payments gap and made the U.S. currency "a symbol of international charity." Aid had "inculcated in less-favored nations the belief that the United States is morally responsible for bringing the whole world up" to an American standard of living. Passman hoped a major legislative victory in 1963 might help him toward his ultimate goal of eliminating foreign aid.[41]

Seeking to head off Passman's next assault, Kennedy planned preventive action. He convened a panel of noted policy experts under the chairmanship of General Lucius Clay, the widely respected hero of the 1948 Berlin airlift. Although the general and most other members of the committee stood on the political right, Kennedy hoped that Clay would produce a strong endorsement for the principle of foreign aid, buttressed by specific recommendations for refining the program.[42]

In its deliberations, held in January 1963, the Clay Committee extensively interviewed policymakers from the State Department and NSC. Komer and others were alarmed by the tone and thrust of the questions they received. He later referred to his testimony before the committee as "that ghastly half-hour."

---

[40] Memorandum, Harriman to Bundy, December 10, 1962, NSF, box 109, "India, General, 12/8/62–12/16/62" folder, JFKL; "All Is Not Forgiven," *National Review*, December 4, 1962, 423–424.

[41] Otto Passman, "Why I Am Opposed to Foreign Aid," *NYT*, July 7, 1963, SM9; Passman, Untitled Article, *Los Angeles Times*, June 16, 1963, K2.

[42] Arthur M. Schlesinger Jr., *A Thousand Days: John F. Kennedy in the White House* (Boston: Houghton Mifflin, 1965), 595–597.

Clay's questions to committee witnesses made plain his preconceptions about foreign assistance. Clay opined that aid to former European colonies in Africa was unnecessary; if the United States withdrew its assistance, the Europeans would fill the vacuum. To Clay, the rationales for aiding Francophone Africa "would appear to justify an aid program in every single country of the Free World."[43]

Komer informed Kennedy that the Clay Committee was proving unfriendly to the aid program, seeming to believe that aid should be given only to those countries best able to use it, with much of the burden being shifted to European states.[44] These warnings proved prescient. Kennedy's first glance at the draft report alarmed him. "It looks pretty much like an attack on the program," he remarked, "and I think therefore, it will contribute to greater difficulties in moving the program through."[45]

The general added more fuel to the fire when his committee's report was released to the public in March. Clay's criticisms of the excesses of foreign aid seemed more heartfelt than his defense of the program in principle. He declared Indonesia unprepared to receive U.S. aid. In a clear reference to India's proposed Bokaro steel mill, for which New Delhi sought extensive U.S. funding, the report declared that the United States should not financially support state-owned industries. Clay reinforced this point in a press conference. The administration's proposal to fund Bokaro had come on the heels of a comprehensive study of the plant and the exhortations of Ambassador John Kenneth Galbraith, who warned that Washington needed to be seen supporting state industry in India.[46] Kennedy defended Bokaro emphatically in a May 1963 press conference, heightening Indian expectations and raising the political stakes of this allotment. Apprehending that Clay had done far more to damage than bless the administration's case, the president sought to limit the fallout. Kennedy obtained Clay's endorsement for the basic contours of his FY 1964 aid budget.[47] Before the Clay report, he had sought an allotment of $4.9 billion for foreign aid; afterward, to preempt charges of profligacy, the proposed budget was trimmed to $4.5 billion.[48]

[43] Summary of Proceedings, Clay Committee, Meeting 1, Summary 6, January 23, 1963, NSF, box 297, "Clay Committee, Summaries of Proceedings" folder, JFKL; Memorandum, Komer to Bell, February 28, 1963, NSF, box 412, "Clay Committee [2 of 2]" folder, JFKL.

[44] Memorandum, Komer to Kennedy, March 2, 1963, NSF, box 412, "Clay Committee [2 of 2]" folder, JFKL.

[45] Conversation, Kennedy and Robert Lovett, March 7, 1963, Presidential Recordings, Dictabelt 11C.3, MC.

[46] Press Briefing, Clay Committee, March 22, 1963, David E. Bell Papers, box 19, "Memos to JFK – Legislation, 1963" folder, JFKL; Simpson, *Economists with Guns*, 95–96; John K. Galbraith, *Ambassador's Journal: A Personal Account of the Kennedy Years* (Boston: Houghton Mifflin, 1969), 215.

[47] Conversation, Kennedy and Eugene Black, April 2, 1963, Presidential Recordings, Dictabelt 17A.3, MC.

[48] Memorandum, Komer to Bundy, July 17, 1963, NSF, box 297, "Foreign Aid, General, 7/1/63–8/23/63" folder, JFKL.

However inadvertently, Clay had provided cover for foes of foreign assistance, and the summer of 1963 witnessed a dramatic attack on Kennedy's aid budget. In addition to partisan motivations, Robert Johnson's excellent account of the battle identifies three political factors motivating legislative critics: increased conservative hostility toward foreign aid, liberal unease about funding authoritarian governments, and the collapse of the legislative coalition supporting the Alliance for Progress, the administration's expansive Latin American aid program.[49]

Several other elements were also apparent in the ensuing debate. One was a deep skepticism of the visions of development presented by Kennedy and his advisors, particularly when applied in Third World settings. Pejorative racial views of African, Asian, and Latin American peoples inevitably contributed to the belief that aid programs were an inherent waste of money. Southern conservatives opposed civil rights at home and aid to African countries abroad – particularly because of African opposition to white minority rule.[50] Traditional views of the Cold War also drove the legislative attack. The legislators leading the charge had generally been in Congress since the 1950s. Many shared the convulsive anticommunism of that decade, holding the Dulles-like belief that neutrality in a global struggle was immoral and likely impossible. Overseas trips reinforced the perception that aid should exist principally to reward allies. Concern about the growing balance of payments gap – the net outflow of dollars from the national economy – also broadly advanced skepticism toward aid. Finally, as Robert Johnson observes, Congress as a body sought to enhance its influence in foreign affairs. The power of the purse provided the legislature its best opportunity to shape foreign policy.[51]

Facing the likelihood of further cuts, Kennedy approved another preemptive reduction. Accordingly, on June 13, a group of Democratic representatives from the House Foreign Affairs Committee reduced the aid budget by another $400 million to $4.095 billion.[52] Kennedy hoped these cuts might suffice to prevent deeper attacks. "Where do you think they're going to end up?" he asked Ohio Congressman Wayne Hays on June 18. "Well, I would think from the way Passman talks, below three billion," Hays answered. "Holy Jesus," the president replied.[53] After successive cuts, Kennedy's foreign aid budget emerged from the House committee nearly 10 percent smaller. On the floor

[49] Robert David Johnson, *Congress and the Cold War* (New York: Cambridge University Press, 2006), 91–95.

[50] On these see Rotter, *Comrades at Odds*; Thomas Borstelmann, *The Cold War and the Color Line: American Race Relations in the Global Arena* (Cambridge, MA: Harvard University Press, 2001); Douglas Little, *American Orientalism: The United States and the Middle East Since 1945* (Chapel Hill: University of North Carolina Press, 2004), 9–43.

[51] Johnson, *Congress and the Cold War*, 91–104.

[52] Memorandum, Bell to Kennedy, June 17, 1963, NSF, box 297, "Foreign Aid, General, 12/62–6/63" folder, JFKL.

[53] Conversation, Kennedy and Wayne Hays, June 18, 1963, Presidential Recordings, Dictabelt 22B.2, MC.

of the House, disregarding Kennedy's appeals, a coalition of Republicans and Southern Democrats voted to strip *another* $585 million from the bill. Kennedy termed the cut "a shortsighted, irresponsible, and dangerous partisan action," contrary to the bipartisan tenets of postwar U.S. foreign policy.[54]

Such deep cuts imperiled the crown jewel of the 1963 budget: Bokaro. The Clay report had damned the Indian steel mill by inference. U.S. financing of Bokaro would represent the administration's most ambitious commitment to a single project. Three factors militated against Congressional acceptance of Bokaro: the sheer size of the commitment, popular dislike of India and Nehru, and the fact that the plant would be state operated, presumably competing against privately owned facilities. Harnessing this sentiment, Republican William Broomfield of Michigan proposed an amendment specifically targeting Bokaro, requiring Congressional approval for all loans or grants toward any project in excess of $100 million. India watched the debate over Bokaro with concern, and Bowles warned of a "very serious setback" should Washington renege on this commitment.[55]

By mid-August, Congressional opposition and the overwhelming likelihood of severe cuts doomed Bokaro. To spare Kennedy further embarrassment, Nehru retracted his request for financing of the plant at the end of August. The retraction was not acrimonious. Kennedy reaffirmed his support for Indian economic development and Nehru reassured Kennedy of his continuing gratitude for U.S. assistance.[56] Besides, Nehru had other willing financiers; within weeks, intelligence reached Washington of Indian requests to Moscow for assistance with Bokaro.[57] Ultimately, the Kremlin elected to finance the plant.[58]

Congress also targeted aid to Indonesia. So deep was Indonesian President Sukarno's unpopularity within the United States that Bundy remarked to a British diplomat in August that Indonesia was "the only country with which the American people would willingly go to war."[59] During the West New Guinea dispute, popular sympathies had overwhelmingly been on the side of the Dutch. Sukarno's subsequent campaign against Malaysia played on decades-old public sentiment against militant nationalism. Broomfield conveyed the popular image of the Indonesian leader and of Third World nationalism when he declared that: "Instead of curbing Sukarno, our nation's foreign policy appears to be to placate him. Some 11,000,000 Americans learned during

54 *PPP: John F. Kennedy, 1963* (Washington: GPO, 1964): 629–637, 641–642.
55 Telegram 656, New Delhi to Washington, August 13, 1963, NSF, box 420, "Bokaro [1 of 2]" folder, JFKL.
56 Telegram 525, Washington to New Delhi, September 4, 1963, NSF, box 420, "Bokaro [1 of 2]" folder, JFKL; Telegram 828, New Delhi to Washington, August 29, 1963, ibid.
57 Memorandum, Komer to Bundy, September 20, 1963, NSF, box 111, "India, General, 9/63–11/63" folder, JFKL.
58 See Padma Desai, *The Bokaro Steel Plant: A Study of Soviet Economic Assistance* (New York: American Elsevier, 1972); Dennis Merrill, *Bread and the Ballot: The United States and India's Economic Development, 1947–1963* (Chapel Hill: University of North Carolina Press, 1990), 200–202.
59 Letter, Denis Greenhill to Frederick Warner, August 16, 1963, TNA, FO 371/169888.

World War II that it doesn't pay to appease a dictator suffering from delusions of grandeur."[60] On July 18, Broomfield proposed an amendment prohibiting aid to Indonesia, unless it was certified by the president as serving the national interest.[61] Broomfield's Indonesian amendment remained in the aid bill when the House approved it, gaining a companion amendment in the Senate. The amendment placed all U.S. aid to Indonesia under an intense legislative spotlight on the eve of the 1964 election.

Unsurprisingly, Egypt also received the unfriendly attention of the Congress. In November, while the aid bill still languished on Capitol Hill, Alaska Senator Ernest Gruening proposed a further amendment – targeted at Egypt – that would deny aid to any state deemed to be engaged in or preparing for aggression against another recipient of U.S. aid.[62] The depth of anti-Nasser sentiment made passage certain.

Nonaligned governments watched this situation with alarm. Nasser complained that he could not trust the West. He had thought differently after Kennedy's election, but the Gruening Amendment convinced him that he had to "'go back' to 1957": that is, to his post-Suez policy of self-reliance.[63] Congressional rhetoric added insult to injury. Broomfield likened Sukarno to Hitler. Democrat Clement Zablocki said the Indonesian leader was "emotionally unstable."[64] Senator Thomas Dodd termed Ghana "the first Soviet satellite in Africa."[65] These statements received broad publicity in the nonaligned world.

Kennedy's battle for his foreign aid budget raged on into the late autumn, raising the question of whether *any* economic assistance programs would survive. In the final months of his life, Kennedy was deeply preoccupied with the impasse.[66] In his last press conference, on November 14, he criticized Congress at length, remarking, "This is the worst attack on foreign aid that we have seen since the beginning of the Marshall Plan.... I can't imagine anything more dangerous than to end this program." Speaking about aid to Egypt, but also about the broader question of leverage, he said:

These threats that the United States is going to cut off aid [provide] a great temptation to Arabic countries to say, 'Cut it off.' They are nationalist, they are proud, they are in many cases radical. I don't think threats from Capitol Hill bring the results which are frequently hoped ... [as] at the time the Aswan Dam was cut off.

---

[60] "House Unit Votes Jakarta Aid Cut," *NYT*, July 26, 1963, 1.

[61] Norman Cornish, "Indonesia Aid Cut Off by House Committee," *The Washington Post*, July 26, 1963, A17.

[62] Memorandum, Harold Saunders, November 13, 1963, NSF, box 407, "Foreign Aid" folder, JFKL.

[63] Telegram 1092, Cairo to Washington, November 9, 1963, NSF, box 407, "Foreign Aid" folder, JFKL.

[64] Telegram 1012, Jakarta to Washington, November 4, 1963, *FRUS, 1961–1963*, 23: 692–694.

[65] Telegram 25, Accra to Washington, July 12, 1963, NSF, box 100, "Ghana Senate Judiciary Committee" folder, JFKL.

[66] See, for example, Recording, Kennedy, November 12, 1963, Dictabelt 29, John F. Kennedy Presidential Recordings, MC.

When he flew to Dallas, his aid bill remained mired in the Senate. Kennedy's written remarks for the afternoon of November 22 – never delivered – included a protracted defense of foreign aid.[67]

In his final months, Kennedy faced intense pressure to curtail aid to non-aligned states. Nonetheless, he refrained from capricious aid cuts. As one of his final decisions, he approved a large shipment of PL-480 rice to Indonesia. Komer later remarked that Kennedy "was always very resistant to too many useless, punitive measures involving aid."[68] Sensitive to the risk of seeming to infringe on the sovereignty of aid recipients, Kennedy had been determined to avoid another Aswan-like debacle. Although he did not believe that aid came free of strings, he was unwilling to be seen tugging at them. His successor demonstrated an altogether different approach in this realm of policy.

"THE LIMITS OF THE POSSIBLE": AID UNDER JOHNSON

Lyndon Johnson entered office with far greater pull on Capitol Hill. With his wealth of friendships in the legislative branch, he was far better equipped to steer the wayward aid bill toward passage, while averting further reductions. Despite efforts to sway the stubborn Passman, however, LBJ was forced to settle for a much reduced FY 1964 appropriation of $3 billion.

With the 1964 election looming, envisioning the expenses of his proposed Great Society legislation, Johnson fretted that foreign aid would prove a political liability. Like some critics, he also thought the United States was receiving poor returns for its aid. Strings made intuitive sense to him, a former legislative leader, accustomed to trading favors and the perennial task of cudgeling wayward senators into line. Nonaligned states needed to understand how their behavior affected votes in Congress and that U.S. generosity was neither limitless nor unconditional. Looking ahead, Johnson felt a need to limit the expectations of aid recipients. He took the unusual step of writing to Bowles, in January 1964, after the ambassador had implored the White House to approve a sizable multi-year aid commitment:

> You – and all of our key ambassadors – must bear with the limits of the possible in terms of what I can get the Congress to back here. The attack on foreign aid restricts our freedom of maneuver until we can get the aid tangle straightened out.... We will simply have to stretch the resources of diplomacy to restrain Indian appetites, while still getting the forward movement we seek.[69]

Events in 1964 confirmed LBJ's sense that the United States was getting little reward for its aid. The first major aid policy decision to confront Johnson concerned Indonesia. After the West New Guinea settlement, Kennedy had

---

[67] *PPP: John F. Kennedy, 1963* (Washington: GPO, 1964): 849–859, 890–894.
[68] Fourth Oral History Interview, Robert Komer, October 31, 1964, 3, OH, JFKL.
[69] Letter, Johnson to Bowles, January 21, 1964, in DOS, *FRUS, 1964–1968, Vol. 25: South Asia* (Washington: GPO, 2000): 13–14.

approved a broad aid program for Jakarta, including PL-480, technical assistance, Military Assistance Program (MAP) aid, and a currency stabilization loan. In the face of legislative pressure and the confrontation with Malaysia, Kennedy had reduced aid in September 1963, generally approving the delivery of non-military funds or goods in the pipeline, while deferring negotiation or implementation of future agreements.[70] The State Department's Far East Bureau argued for maintaining a basic aid program to keep a "long-term foothold" in Indonesia. Against emphatic British pressure, Kennedy supported this rationale for aid to Jakarta, hoping to offer Sukarno a large incentive, including a substantial increase in PL-480, to make peace with Malaysia.[71]

When Johnson addressed the issue in January 1964, he faced an added political constraint. The Broomfield amendment, now law, required an executive determination that aid to Indonesia was in the national interest – which LBJ personally doubted. In the preceding autumn, Kennedy had reduced the funding available for Jakarta from $85 million to $15 million. Rusk and Bundy both argued against a total aid cutoff; the latter cited the inescapable case of Aswan.[72] Although his advisors urged him to come to a quick decision, Johnson felt reluctant to make any public determination about aid to Indonesia.[73] He remained wary of the political cost he would incur by aiding Sukarno and was essentially distrustful of the Indonesian leader.[74]

Faced with the halt in aid, Sukarno felt betrayed. After a U.S. newsweekly implied that Indonesia would collapse without U.S. aid, he erupted in a memorable blast, with Jones a few feet away:

We receive aid from many countries and we are grateful for such aid. But we will never accept aid with political strings attached. When any nation offers us aid with political strings attached, I will tell them 'Go to hell with your aid!'[75]

Consistent with his aspiration of achieving the impossible, Sukarno had found a new way to lift American outrage to previously unknown heights of indignation. Although Johnson approved continuing existing aid (without a determination) in July, Sukarno's increased anti-American invective the following

---

[70] NSAM 195, October 26, 1962, in DOS, *FRUS, 1961–1963, Vol. 23: Southeast Asia* (Washington: GPO, 1994): 647; Telegram 363, Washington to Jakarta, September 24, 1963, ibid.: 688–689.

[71] Department Telegram 1031, Washington to Tokyo, October 22, 1963, NSF, box 114A, "Indonesia, 10/63–11/63" folder, JFKL; Memcon, Jones, Kennedy, and others, November 19, 1963, in *FRUS, 1961–1963*, 23: 696–698. See also the definitive Simpson, *Economists with Guns*, 122–125.

[72] Memorandum, Rusk to Johnson, January 6, 1964, in DOS, *FRUS, 1964–1968, Vol. 26: Indonesia; Malaysia-Singapore; Philippines* (Washington: GPO, 2001), 5–10; Memorandum, Bundy to Johnson, January 7, 1964, ibid.: 13–14.

[73] Summary Record of 521st NSC Meeting, January 7, 1964, ibid.: 16–20.

[74] Matthew Jones, *Conflict and Confrontation in South East Asia, 1961–1965: Britain, the United States and the Creation of Malaysia* (Cambridge: Cambridge University Press, 2002), 238–242; Howard P. Jones, *Indonesia: The Possible Dream* (Stanford: Hoover Institution, 1971), 298–300.

[75] Jones, *Indonesia*, 320–321.

month, his attacks on mainland Malaysia, and pressure from Congress compelled the White House to strip the aid program down to bare essentials.[76] Aid to Indonesia was maintained only to keep Sukarno from politically exploiting a full cutoff and to retain ties to the Indonesian military.

LBJ faced another key early decision on aid to a nonaligned state when, in April, he approved the continuation of U.S. support for Ghana's Volta dam. Dissatisfaction with Nkrumah had grown during 1964, as the Ghanaian president made repeated accusations of American plots against him. LBJ acted on the recommendation of Harriman and the State Department, who argued that terminating the project would merely throw away the money invested thus far and that the dam remained promising on its own merits.[77] Johnson, however, could not have been happy about the decision.

Over the president's first year, his reluctance to act boldly on aid-related issues prompted concern among his advisors. Confronting multiple crises in the Third World, foreign aid seemed to be a receding political priority for the administration. Komer worried in an October memorandum to Rostow that aid would "get lost in the shuffle" if Johnson's top advisors did not "carry the case to LBJ" himself. "This is the one area in which the Kennedy/Johnson Administration has actually lost ground in the last four years," he wrote. "And the omens are still bad."[78] In September, Congress reauthorized Food for Peace, due for renewal a decade after its inception, but for only an additional two years and with added restrictions.

The October 1964 Cairo Conference further called into question the Kennedy approach to aid. After Belgrade, Rostow had persuaded Kennedy that the more moderate attendees had been aid recipients and that assistance programs would produce more favorable outcomes at future conferences.[79] The Cairo Conference wholly discredited this theory. "Here were 44 countries and 11 observers (virtually all recipients of US aid in one form or another) and not a really friendly reference to the US," an angry Komer wrote to Bundy.[80]

The experiences of 1964 had clearly validated Johnson's hesitancy to continue with aid as before; other shifts in outlook emerged the following year. He requested $3.5 billion for the FY 1965 budget, thirty percent less than Kennedy's first request for FY 1964.[81] Johnson also moved away from funding large individual projects in nonaligned states. Kennedy had committed to

---

[76] Memorandum, Bundy to Johnson, August 31, 1964, in *FRUS, 1964–1968*, 26: 144–148.

[77] Summary Record of 526th NSC Meeting, April 3, 1964, in *FRUS, 1964–1968*, 24: 436–437; Memorandum, Harriman to Johnson, April 3, 1964, ibid.: 438–440.

[78] Memorandum, Komer to Rostow, October 13, 1964, NSF, RWKP, box 10, "AID" folder, LBJL.

[79] Memorandum "Neutralism and Foreign Aid," Rostow to Kennedy, September 27, 1961, DDRS.

[80] Memorandum, Komer to Bundy, October 9, 1964, RWKP, box 44, "Nonaligned Conference Cairo" folder, LBJL.

[81] Memorandum, David Bell to Johnson, October 7, 1964, in DOS, *FRUS, 1964–1968, Vol. 9: International Development and Economic Defense Policy; Commodities* (Washington: GPO, 1997): 28–29.

two large prestige projects: Volta and Bokaro. The former had failed to change Nkrumah's behavior; the latter had become a lightning rod for Congressional attacks on the foreign aid budget. These two experiences conditioned the NSC staff against endorsing major increases in development aid, especially after the acrimonious final months of 1964.

This determination provoked some infighting between different advocates of engagement in the spring of 1965. Seeking to counter increased communist aid to Africa and the ongoing Chinese diplomatic offensive, Assistant Secretary of State G. Mennen Williams argued for a doubling of U.S. development aid to the continent. His proposal was out of step with Johnson's budgetary priorities, public opinion, and even the evolving views of the NSC staff. The pragmatists were unwilling to go out on a limb; Bundy wrote Johnson, "Great big aid programs simply do not do what we want them to do. The whole Ghana project is a case in point." The White House rejected Williams's proposal, favoring instead a set of recommendations by Edward Korry, the U.S. ambassador to Ethiopia, which called for reducing overall aid and focusing on a few key recipient states.[82]

With aid being concentrated in fewer baskets, it was doubly important to choose the right recipients. Memories of the Volta decision remained potent, as pro-Western states in Africa continued to complain about the amounts of aid being sent to Ghana and Guinea.[83] In November 1965, Ulric Haynes Jr. of the NSC staff, wrote:

The retention of our minimal AID programs and major Peace Corps contingent in Ghana, in the face of frequent insults to US national dignity, continues to baffle friendly African governments. It also reinforces N'Krumah's mistaken conception of his own importance in Africa and to the US.[84]

Consistent with Johnson's own preferences, aid strategy was shifting from the imperative of wooing influential nonaligned states toward rewarding allies.

Advocates for engagement strove to adapt themselves to the new circumstances of the Johnson White House, defined by a hostile legislature and a skeptical executive. Advisors who had thrived under Kennedy were unnerved by Johnson's views on aid to nonaligned states. Komer lamented in May 1965, "I have a nagging worry that there's more to LBJ's reluctance than just Congress."[85] His concerns were validated as Johnson confronted the two most critical aid issues of his tenure: food aid to Egypt and India.

---

[82] Memorandum, Bundy to Johnson, June 21, 1965, NSF, MTP, box 3, "Vol. 11, 6/65" folder, LBJL; Memorandum, Komer to Johnson, June 19, 1965, in *FRUS, 1964–1968*, 24: 306–307; Thomas J. Noer, *"Soapy": A Biography of G. Mennen Williams* (Ann Arbor: University of Michigan Press, 2005), 287–291.

[83] See, for example, Memcon, Komer, Haynes, and Konan Bedie, July 29, 1965, NSF, UHP, box 1, "Chron, 3/1/65–6/15/66 [2 of 3]" folder, LBJL.

[84] Memorandum, Haynes to Komer, November 6, 1965, NSF, Edward Hamilton Papers, box 2, "Ghana" folder, LBJL

[85] Memorandum, Komer to Bundy, May 29, 1965, NSF, Name File, box 6, "Robert Komer, Vol. 1 [2 of 3]" folder, LBJL.

FEEDING "THE HAND THAT BITES": EGYPT AND FOOD AID

During the Kennedy years, food aid constituted the most important form of economic assistance offered to Egypt. Although sensitive to the potential domestic ramifications of such assistance, Kennedy repeatedly authorized the signing of sizable PL-480 agreements with Cairo. The most important of these was a three-year agreement, negotiated in the autumn of 1962, for the sale of more than $400 million in grain. Nasser's need for grain gave him concrete incentives to remain on good terms with the United States, but Ambassador John Badeau warned against overt exploitation of Egypt's dependence.[86]

Civil war in the Congo in the autumn of 1964 brought the question of reciprocity to the table. Clear evidence of Egyptian aid to the Congolese rebels emerged in early December, spurring calls to suspend *all* aid to Cairo. Komer sought a middle path between maintaining aid and cutting it off entirely, writing:

> If we flatly cut off aid to any radical African country, the reaction would be violent (a la Suez). Having nothing to lose, a Ben Bella, Nasser, or Nkrumah would shout to high heaven about our taking food from hungry mouths for punitive purposes. These nuts might even increase aid to the rebels and make it overt. As JFK said repeatedly, once you've cut off aid you've used up your leverage. And the result is to give a free ride to the Soviets and Chinese.

He argued, instead, for covert efforts to exert leverage, observing: "The trick here is to threaten credibly, privately, and if possible unofficially." In almost every case, Washington had the option of simply stalling on pending aid requests.[87]

Made days before Nasser's fiery Port Said speech, in which he told the United States to drink from the Red Sea, this was a prescient recommendation, anticipating White House strategy. Eschewing outright cutoffs, Johnson instead delayed responding to aid requests, paring them down from relatively long-term to short-term quantities. The White House attempted to steer a middle course between Congressional foes of aid and Nasser, appeasing neither party.[88]

Aid emerged as the main source of contention with Egypt in 1965. Nasser's outburst in the Port Said speech came as a direct consequence of his belief that Washington sought to use food aid as leverage. Nasser believed the threat had been made in a meeting between U.S. Ambassador Lucius Battle and Egypt's Minister of Supply Ramzi Stino.[89] The French ambassador in Cairo reported

---

[86] Telegram 2586, Cairo to Washington, May 4, 1964, NSF, CF, box 158, "UAR, Vol.1, Cables [1 of 2]" folder, LBJL.

[87] Memorandum, Komer to Bundy, December 18, 1964, NSF, RWKP, box 11, "Algeria, December 1963-March 1966 [1 of 4]" folder, LBJL.

[88] Johnson's approach to Egyptian food aid is chronicled expertly in William J. Burns, *Economic Aid and American Policy Toward Egypt, 1955–1981* (Albany: SUNY Press, 1985), 149–173.

[89] Telegram 2251, Cairo to Washington, December 30, 1964, RG-59, CFPF: 1964–1966, box 2767, "UAR-US, 12/1/64" folder, NA.

that Nasser's speech had been a direct response to U.S. coercion.[90] Assistant Secretary of State Phillips Talbot concluded that Washington's "Fabian tactics in the aid program" constituted "the root cause of Egyptian resentment of U.S. policy."[91]

Nasser, for all his rhetorical bravado, did not wish to lose the food aid promised to him for the first half of 1965, nor did he intend to relinquish the possibility of a successor agreement after the 1962 agreement expired in June. Thus Cairo visibly sought to mend relations. The UAR was not, however, desperate. Nasser assumed that Egypt's importance in the Middle East would make it difficult for the United States to cut off aid. A study commissioned by the UAR's Ministry of Foreign Affairs, which fell into the hands of a CIA source, provides a rare window into Egyptian thinking in the immediate aftermath of the Port Said speech. The report reasoned that Washington would not wish to seem to be attaching political conditions to aid, was loath to provide Moscow an opportunity to expand its influence, and understood the influence and power of Egypt in the broader Middle East.[92] The UAR clearly felt it had cause for confidence.

In the wake of Port Said, advocates of engagement sought a middle ground on discussions of aid with the UAR. A memorandum from Bundy to Johnson captured the fundamental ambivalence he felt on the question of reciprocity:

Our probable response will simply be to stop talking with him about aid for a while, but not to engage in a public row. Most of us feel that there is no gain in pushing him still further into a public frenzy. The history of Aswan and Suez is clear in everyone's minds. On the other hand, no one is particularly interested in ostentatious feeding of the hand that bites.[93]

Consequently, the administration played a delicate balancing game: maintaining existing aid to Cairo but avoiding any further commitments to Nasser. Heeding the advice of Talbot and Harriman, who warned of the regional fallout that a total breach with Egypt would cause, Rusk recommended delivering grain in the pipeline while tabling further requests for aid, including the final $37 million portion of the existing PL-480 agreement, until relations showed real improvement.[94]

As before, Congress made life difficult for the executive branch. Nasser's defiance once again sparked a Congressional assault on UAR-related aid programs.

---

[90] Telegram 13, Cairo to Paris, January 12, 1965, Amerique 1964–1970, 624, MAE.

[91] Telegram 2229, Cairo to Washington, December 28, 1964, RG-59, CFPF: 1964–1966, box 2767, "UAR-US, 12/1/64" folder, NA; Memorandum, Talbot to Rusk, December 24, 1964, ibid.

[92] Intelligence Information Special Report, April 9, 1965, NSF, CF, box 159A, "UAR, Vol. 3, Memos [1 of 2]" folder, LBJL.

[93] Memorandum, Bundy to Johnson, December 24, 1964, NSF, CF, box 159A, "UAR, Vol. 3, Memos [2 of 2]" folder, LBJL.

[94] Memcon, Rusk, Talbot, and others, December 23, 1964, in DOS, *FRUS, 1964–1968, Vol. 18: Arab-Israeli Conflict, 1964–1967* (Washington: GPO, 2000): 252–255.

After sustained effort, the White House beat back a Republican amendment that banned PL-480 sales to Egypt during 1965.[95] This represented only a momentary victory against aid's congressional foes; yet more amendments waited in the wings, necessitating further massaging of wayward legislators.

Disputes within the administration further complicated matters. In communiqués to Cairo, Rusk deemed Egyptian policy toward the Congo the "most immediate issue" with Nasser.[96] Komer heartily disagreed, thinking it a peripheral matter and a dangerous one to link to food aid. "Let's stop nattering about Nasser in the Congo or in Yemen," he wrote to Bundy.[97] Komer was chiefly concerned with the growing regional arms race. Nasser's pressure on Jordan to buy Soviet tanks had driven the Johnson administration to conclude that it would need to sell arms to Amman. This, in turn, necessitated an arms sale to Israel to reassure both the Israelis and their domestic supporters.[98] Talbot reported a common fear among the State Department's Middle East ambassadors that the Arab-Israeli conflict was moving toward an "early climactic stage," threatening U.S. interests throughout the region.[99] Such reports underscored the importance of keeping relations with Cairo on an even keel; otherwise, Nasser might act to escalate regional tensions further.

Despite these warnings, the administration continually emphasized the centrality of the Congo issue to U.S.-UAR relations. In an April 1 meeting, Rusk told the Egyptian ambassador that the Congo was the foremost issue on the minds of Egypt's Congressional critics and thus "the handiest lever by which to get the US-UAR relationship back on tracks."[100] Rusk's lever seemed a club to the UAR. One of Nasser's chief advisors, Ali Sabri, complained tearfully to Battle:

Look, I want to talk to you not officially but as a friend.... Don't you realize that the Palestine question is more important to us than Vietnam, Yemen, and [the] Congo all put together is to you? You [are] having your way in Palestine. You have pressured us to accept your selling arms to Israel.... Isn't that enough? You don't have to tell me how much we need your wheat. I know that of every two loaves of bread we eat in this country one comes from you. Now it looks as though you want to use your food to pressure us on the Congo in addition to Palestine. This simply isn't right.[101]

For its part, the White House depicted itself to Cairo as waging a difficult battle against a hostile public and Congress. Nasser believed that domestic

[95] Philip Warden, "House Votes to Ban U.S. Aid to Egypt," *Chicago Tribune*, January 27, 1965, 2.

[96] Telegram 4384, Washington to Cairo, January 28, 1965, RG-59, CFPF: 1964–1966, box 2767, "UAR-US, 1/1/65" folder, NA.

[97] Memorandum, Komer to Bundy, April 6, 1965, NSF, CF, box 159A, "UAR, Vol. 3, Memos [1 of 2]" folder, LBJL.

[98] William Glenn Gray, *Germany's Cold War: The Global Campaign to Isolate East Germany, 1949–1969* (Chapel Hill: University of North Carolina Press, 2003), 166–182.

[99] Telegram 776, Beirut to Washington, February 5, 1965, in *FRUS, 1964–1968*, 18: 298–302.

[100] Telegram 6049, Washington to Cairo, April 2, 1965, RG-59, CFPF: 1964–1966, box 2768, "POL 1 UAR-US, 1/1/65" folder, NA.

[101] Telegram 3518, Cairo to Washington, April 7, 1965, ibid.

opposition to Egypt came predominantly from Israel's supporters; the key question was whether Johnson would resist this pressure or acquiesce to it. The State Department attempted to convince Nasser that this was not at all the whole picture. As Talbot explained to Nasser: "There is [a] growing body of American opinion that feels UAR has gone beyond protection of its own interests into area of unwarranted pressure on US interests."[102] This was a delicate rhetorical balancing act. The administration strove to distinguish itself from Congress, while hinting to Cairo that some of the complaints heard on Capitol Hill were not without merit and stemmed in considerable part from something other than pro-Israel sentiment.

On April 18, Nasser accepted Washington's terms, giving notice to the visiting Talbot that he had ceased providing arms to the Congolese rebels. He also indicated grudging acceptance of U.S. arms sales to Israel and declared his disinterest in further intervention in the Cyprus dispute. Nasser's action represented, Talbot and Battle concluded, a "firm policy decision to attempt to meet conditions we have laid down for [the] completion [of] existing PL-480 agreement."[103] Komer observed, "It shows the merits of playing hard to get on aid now and then, so long as one doesn't over do it."[104] Nasser further signaled his intentions in a courteous letter to Johnson in May, stressing his interest in bettering ties. "This guy is really asking for a truce," Komer wrote.[105]

If so, the United States was slow to reciprocate. The UAR still awaited authorization of the last $37 million package of the 1962 treaty; a combination of domestic factors and uncertainty about Cairo's intentions delayed their release until some two months after Nasser's concession. What struck Washington as a prudent, tactical delay seemed unconscionably dilatory in Cairo – particularly after they had met Rusk's condition. Battle warned in May that a failure to fulfill the 1962 deal would strike Egyptians as another Aswan, posing a "potential disaster for US interests in Egypt and the Middle East." Facing the Congressional gauntlet, the administration continued to move gingerly. "Tension in US-UAR relations developing to point where you can almost cut it with a knife," Battle warned in June, observing that the embassy was literally besieged with inquires about the $37 million. Hours later, Talbot finally informed Egyptian Ambassador Mustafa Kamel of Johnson's decision to complete the purchase authorizations for the outstanding sum.[106]

---

[102] Telegram 462, Washington to Amman, February 13, 1965, RG-59, CFPF: 1964–1966, box 2767, "UAR-US, 2/1/65" folder, NA.

[103] Telegram 3652, Cairo to Washington, April 18, 1965, in *FRUS, 1964–1968*, 18: 443–444.

[104] Memorandum, Komer to Bundy, April 19, 1965, NSF, CF, box 159A, "UAR, Vol. 3, Memos [1 of 2]" folder, LBJL.

[105] Telegram 4011, Cairo to Washington, May 15, 1965, in *FRUS, 1964–1968*, 18: 456–459; Memorandum, Komer to Bundy, May 15, 1965, NSF, RWKP, box 51, "UAR December 1965-March 1966 [1 of 3]" folder, LBJL.

[106] Telegram 4214, Cairo to Washington, May 31, 1965, RG-59, CFPF: 1964–1966, box 2767, "UAR-US, 5/1/65" folder, NA; Telegram 4476, Cairo to Washington, June 21, 1965, ibid.; Memcon, Talbot and Kamel, June 21, 1965, ibid.

With the 1962 agreement due to expire, Nasser still needed to conclude another such sale. LBJ, for his part, wanted neither to offer Egypt easy carrots nor to again inflame domestic opinion by sending another bill through the rocks and shoals of the House and Senate. Kamel petitioned Rusk in July for an immediate commencement of negotiations, observing that, without more PL-480 aid, Egypt would have no choice but to turn toward the Soviets. Rusk entreated his guest to be patient, reminding him of the challenges posed by domestic opposition but also adding that the two countries needed further discussions of the nature of their common interests. Egypt's behavior had left Rusk with the impression "that non-alignment was unbalanced."[107]

Nasser had not sat by idly while awaiting the last $37 million. Other countries stood ready to supply Egypt with grain, including China and the Soviet Union. As Johnson approved the final allotment, Egypt bought 300,000 tons of wheat from the Soviet Union. This was, at best, a stopgap measure – Moscow had in fact resold grain it had purchased abroad – but it still marked a departure for Cairo.[108] "There is real danger that USSR will supplant US as major wheat supplier," Talbot wrote to Battle. The embassy in Cairo was directed to inform its hosts that the procurement of Soviet grain might "adversely affect" U.S. perceptions of Egypt, whereas the purchase of U.S.-exported wheat was "necessary to maintain neutrality."[109]

Nasser gave immediate notice that such pressure was not appreciated. On July 22, he publicly accused the United States of tying political strings to aid. As Kamel warned, Egypt had other options for its wheat purchases, and the situation struck Cairo as dangerously reminiscent of Aswan. Komer warned Bundy, "Nasser rightly convicts us of political pressure. Playing this game has its costs; for example our $37 million may have come too late, since Gamal had already burned his bridges."[110] With hostilities in Yemen again on the upswing and with renewed political unrest in Libya, Komer feared the Middle East was drifting toward another stormy period.

At the same time, the administration felt no hurry to conclude another PL-480 agreement, even after it warned Cairo against seeking further food aid from Moscow. Kamel received only vague answers when he inquired about food aid in the late summer. Battle urged the administration to act, observing that Washington's "staunchest friends" in Cairo were imploring the United States to make an offer – preferably before Nasser left for an August 27 trip to

[107] Memcon, Rusk and Kamel, July 15, 1965, RG-59, CFPF: 1964–1966, box 2767, "UAR-US, 5/1/65" folder, NA.

[108] Memorandum, Benjamin Read to Bundy, July 2, 1965, NSF, CF, box 159–2, "UAR, Vol. 4, Memos [2 of 4]" folder, LBJL. China also offered to sell 200,000 tons of corn. See Telegram 4343, Cairo to Washington, June 10, 1965, NSF, CF, box 159–1, "UAR, Vol. 3, Cables [1 of 2]" folder, LBJL.

[109] Telegram 20, Washington to Cairo, July 1, 1965, RG-59, CFPF: 1964–1966, box 2767, "UAR-US, 5/1/65" folder, NA.

[110] Memorandum, Komer to Bundy, July 23, 1965, NSF, Name File, box 6, "Robert Komer, Vol. 1" folder, LBJL.

Moscow. Failing that, it was imperative to inform the Egyptians of what would be offered by early October, when the government needed to finalize its food strategy for the coming year. Disregarding this warning, the State Department declined to offer a commitment to negotiate a new agreement either in the summer or before Battle visited Washington for consultations in September. In Moscow, Nasser proclaimed his gratitude for Soviet aid while criticizing the bombing of North Vietnam.[111]

Congress, in the meantime, passed an amendment to the FY 1966 aid bill that further limited Johnson's options. Specifically targeting PL-480 sales to the UAR, the amendment limited sales to a one-year duration and required presidential certification for Title I sales (those paid for in local currency). With the new restrictions, Congress gave indication of its continued skepticism of Food For Peace. As in the case of Indonesia, the requirement of a presidential authorization made the White House doubly hesitant to rush aid to Nasser.

Rusk ultimately recommended beginning negotiations for another PL-480 agreement, arguing that Cairo's policies had moderated visibly. The secretary warned against discontinuing aid or – ironically after his support for delaying the final increment of the prior agreement – allowing "undue delays" in responding to Nasser's request for a new agreement, predicting that the Egyptian would treat such tactics as evidence of hostility. Rusk believed in the necessity of food aid to Egypt, arguing, "Food and no strong talk is useless, but the possibility of food makes strong talk possible." A flexible approach utilizing short-term, limited agreements would allow the administration to "meter our aid on the basis of climate and UAR performance." Komer agreed, suggesting political dialogue with Nasser, and a series of six-month agreements designed to keep him "on his good behavior." Nonetheless, Johnson disapproved Rusk's request to initiate new negotiations.[112]

A month later, near the end of October, Johnson finally approved a new package for Egypt. In the intervening time, Battle had reported that even diplomats from countries unfriendly to the UAR, such as Ethiopia and Britain, urged that Washington approve food aid. The proposed deal clearly indicated Washington's willingness to drive a tough bargain, with an opening offer significantly less than what Nasser had requested.[113] Even now, however, the White House was slow to open negotiations. Battle reported in early November that the U.S. failure to begin negotiations had aroused suspicion and desperation

[111] Telegram 517, Cairo to Washington, August 18, 1965, in *FRUS, 1964–1968, 18*: 489–490; Gamal Abdel Nasser, *On the Consolidation of the Cause of World Peace* (Cairo: State Information Service, 1967), 252–261.

[112] Memorandum, Rusk to Johnson, September 23, 1965, NSF, RWKP, box 51, "UAR, 1965-March 1966 [2 of 3]" folder, LBJL; Memorandum, Komer to Johnson, September 24, 1965, in *FRUS, 1964–1968, 18*: 494–495.

[113] Telegram 980, Cairo to Washington, October 9, 1965, in *FRUS, 1964–1968, 18*: 502–503; Memorandum, Rusk to Johnson, October 11, 1965, ibid.: 503–505; Telegram 2129, Cairo to Washington, October 13, 1965, ibid.: 505–506; Memorandum, Rusk, October 27, 1965, ibid.: 509.

in Cairo, as Nasser's government frantically sought to prevent a food crisis the following year. Battle, who had generally supported administration policy, warned of dire consequences, asking, "Can't we get on with something quickly?"[114] In the subsequent negotiations, Washington obtained what Komer deemed "a pretty tough bargain." With talks concluded, Johnson certified the sale as necessary for the national interests of the United States.[115]

By all appearances, the door was open to another PL-480 agreement six months later. The first half of 1966, however, brought a dramatic worsening of U.S.-UAR relations. In the spring, the Johnson administration, yielding to pressure from Israel and the realities of the ongoing Middle Eastern arms race, decided on a sale of A-4 jets to Israel. After a lull in the autumn of 1965, the Yemeni conflict intensified again, worsening relations between the UAR and Saudi Arabia. Nasser threatened to take the war to the Yemeni rebels' bases in Saudi territory, obliging Washington to reaffirm its commitment to the kingdom's defense. Alarmed by the jet sale to Israel, U.S. support of his Saudi foes, and reports that Washington supported an "Islamic Pact" uniting the region's conservative states, Nasser abandoned the rhetorical moderation he had exercised after Port Said, likening the U.S. war in Vietnam to the Suez invasion, and charging Washington with supporting the Yemeni rebels.[116] Above all, Nasser seemed resigned to the loss of U.S. food aid. He remarked sadly to Battle that the Johnson White House had disappointed him.[117]

On June 4, 1966, the Department notified Battle that, in light of the poor state of U.S.-UAR relations, Washington was at that time unable to offer Cairo either an extension or renewal of the PL-480 agreement, set to expire within weeks. "We've tried our best to avoid a showdown," commented Harold Saunders of the NSC staff, "but Nasser seems to be forcing one." Egypt had requested a large sale of $150 million. Kamel repeatedly instructed both Rusk and Johnson on the centrality of food aid to the U.S.-UAR relationship, but to no avail. In September, as Egyptian grain stocks neared exhaustion, U.S. envoy Robert Anderson told Nasser that another agreement was impossible in light of Congressional hostility and regional tensions. "Do you want riots in the streets?" Nasser asked, vowing, "We will get wheat from somewhere."[118]

---

[114] Telegram 1171, Cairo to Washington, November 4, 1965, NSF, CF, box 159–2, "UAR, Vol. 4, Cables [1 of 2]" folder, LBJL.

[115] Memorandum, Komer to Johnson, December 28, 1965, in *FRUS, 1964–1968, 18*: 527–528, 528n. This included an Egyptian purchase of grain in dollars (Title IV) alongside a Title I sale.

[116] Hedrick Smith, "Cairo Says CIA Aids Foes in Yemen," *NYT*, June 4, 1966, 7; Smith, "Cairo Intensifies Anti-US Attacks," May 14, 1966, *NYT*, 12; Telegram 3062, Cairo to Washington, May 25, 1962, NSF, CF, "UAR, Vol. 4, Cables [1 of 2]" folder, LBJL.

[117] Telegram 2571, Cairo to Washington, April 8, 1966, in DOS, *FRUS, 1964–1968, Vol. 21: Near East Region; Arabian Peninsula* (Washington: GPO, 2000): 749–753.

[118] Telegram 6581, Washington to Cairo, June 4, 1966, NSF, CF, box 159–2, "UAR, Vol. 4, Cables [2 of 2]" folder, LBJL; Telegram 1296, Cairo to Washington, September 10, 1966, in *FRUS, 1964–1968, 18*: 636–637.

The end of 1966 witnessed the fundamental collapse of Washington's strategy to influence Egyptian policy through the dispensation of PL-480. "The Kennedy experiment is over," Saunders and Howard Wriggins of the NSC wrote.

We gambled that a three-year food deal, personal correspondence, and a certain amount of human respect for Nasser might moderate his revolutionary policies. We probably went too far too fast, but we have been frankly disappointed in results. He continued clandestine organization against the more moderate oil-rich monarchies; he ventured into the Congo rebellion; more recently, his army has become increasingly Draconian in the Yemen; Radio Cairo continues to agitate Arab 'nationalism'; his policy often parallels Moscow's.

Saunders and Wriggins advised against dropping food aid and resolving to live with a hostile UAR, advocating instead that the president consider either a series of interim food agreements or developing a new cooperative basis for the relationship.[119]

Similar conclusions had been reached in Egypt. On December 11, 1966, Nasser spoke candidly to the Canadian ambassador in Cairo, expecting that his remarks would be channeled to Battle. Nasser stated that he had ceased counting on PL-480 and no longer saw any value in raising the question with the Americans. Egypt's economic difficulties stemmed in part from having depended on such aid. Before 1959, Egypt had sustained itself without U.S. aid; afterward it had factored it into annual economic plans. Johnson's approach to food aid had proved severely disruptive to the Egyptian economy. Nasser mused that it might be best for Egypt to avoid dependence on PL-480 grain. Accordingly, he planned to secure food aid from the Soviet Union.[120]

At the beginning of 1965, the Johnson administration faced profound challenges with Egypt and in the Congress. One should not take lightly the legislative problem that confronted the administration. Still, it is inarguable that the delay in meeting Egypt's aid request, particularly the final $37 million increment of the 1962 agreement, gravely undermined relations with Cairo at a critical time and after Nasser had taken conciliatory steps on the region's foremost problem. Rusk's emphasis on the Congo – a second tier issue in comparison to growing Middle East tensions – put the cart before the horse where the UAR was concerned. Having denied Egypt aid at a time of economic crisis, the Johnson administration, moreover, sought to tell Nasser where he could and could not purchase wheat. Although the final cutoff of food aid occurred in 1966, the events of 1964 and 1965 convinced Nasser that he could not utilize U.S. food aid without compromising his sovereignty and his position in Egypt. Amazingly, the administration neglected the lessons of Aswan while dealing with the central figure of Aswan.

[119] Memorandum, Saunders and Wriggins to Johnson, December 1, 1966, in *FRUS, 1964–1968*, 18: 694–697.
[120] Telegram 1399, Cairo to Washington, December 14, 1966, NSF, CF, box 160, "UAR, Vol. 5, Cables [1 of 2]" folder, LBJL.

"THIS WILL MAKE US LOOK LIKE SCROOGE":
INDIA AND FOOD AID

Johnson experienced similar consequences in his efforts to obtain leverage from his Indian food aid program. During the critical years of 1965 and 1966, the administration confronted the dual challenges of a major Indo-Pakistani war and serious food shortages in India. Food aid long constituted a central part of U.S. outreach to India, but by 1965 Johnson and his advisors were increasingly disenchanted with the fruits of their efforts. The South Asian rivalry continued to drain the subcontinent's resources, while Indian agriculture suffered from a lack of investment and modernization. Nehru and his successor, Lal Bahadur Shastri, had emphasized developing heavy industry over improvements in crop yields, to the frustration of the United States. As Kristin Ahlberg has written, Johnson had his own designs for the foreign aid program and seized upon his frustrations with India to alter the nature and goals of food aid.[121] In 1965, renewed South Asian tensions brought Johnson's patience with New Delhi to the breaking point.[122]

The U.S. position in South Asia rested on an uneasy footing in early 1965, as Pakistan moved toward open friendship with China and India continued to procure arms from the Soviet Union. Both Pakistani President Mohammed Ayub Khan and Shastri had scheduled spring visits to the United States, but with aid legislation pending in Congress and LBJ increasingly consumed with Vietnam, the White House postponed both visits. Johnson specifically cited the unfriendly Congressional scrutiny that these visits seemed likely to draw. Another motive stood behind the deferral; as Komer put it, both states needed to "reflect on the moral that Uncle Sam should not just be regarded as a cornucopia of goodies, regardless of what they do or say."[123] Neither India nor Pakistan reacted favorably to the postponements; here, the imperative of preserving foreign aid programs had the ironic effect of damaging bilateral relationships.

This came at a critical time on the subcontinent. Border tensions between the two states festered over the Rann of Kutch, a sparsely populated section of coastal borderland along the Arabian Sea. Bowles first reported the possibility of hostilities in February; major fighting erupted in the area at the end of April.

[121] Ahlberg, *Transplanting the Great Society*, 106–114.

[122] See also Kristin L. Ahlberg, "Machiavelli with a Heart: The Johnson Administration's Food for Peace Program in India, 1965–1966," *Diplomatic History* 31 (September 2007), 665–701; James W. Bjorkman, "Public Law 480 and the Policies of Self-Help and Short-Tether: Indo-American Relations, 1965–68," in Lloyd Rudolph ed., *The Regional Imperative: The Administration of U.S. Foreign Policy Towards South Asian States Under Presidents Johnson and Nixon* (Atlantic Highlands, NJ: Humanities Press, 1980), 201–262; Robert J. McMahon, "Toward Disillusionment and Disengagement" in Cohen and Tucker eds., *Lyndon Johnson Confronts the World: American Foreign Policy, 1963–1968* (New York: Cambridge University Press, 1994), 135–172.

[123] Memorandum, Komer to Johnson, April 16, 1965, NSF, RWKP, box 22, "Shastri Visit [1 of 3]" folder, LBJL.

To the alarm of the Johnson administration, Pakistan appeared to be employing U.S.-supplied arms. Military Assistance Program (MAP) support had been furnished to both states with explicit provisions that it could be used only for the purposes of internal security, legitimate self-defense, or regional collective security.[124] Furthermore, Indian public opinion was particularly outraged by the appearance of U.S.-made arms on the Pakistani side. The clash, coupled with the postponement of Shastri's visit, aroused concern from both Americans and Indians about the future of bilateral relations.[125]

In the wake of the Kutch skirmish, the Johnson administration – as in the case of Egypt – sought to leverage its aid to India. Bowles requested that the administration move quickly on a new two-year PL-480 commitment and the sale of F-5 fighter aircraft to New Delhi. The food aid agreement held particular importance to the Shastri government, as it stood to help it build a national reserve and keep prices low. Bundy felt otherwise, writing that a two-year food aid agreement "might deprive us of major leverage" before the Johnson administration determined "what we want Indians to do in return." Moreover, continued Congressional deliberation on the FY 1966 aid bill made the submission of new aid requests unwise. "Here we must grant the President's own unparalleled sense of the rocky road the aid bill is traveling," Bundy wrote, "and his strong desire not to rock the boat till he knows what's in his pocket." Johnson's assessment of the legislative landscape came before the pleas of his ambassador in New Delhi.[126] To the amazement and frustration of Komer, Johnson also insisted on personally approving all future loans and grants, both large and small, directed to the subcontinent.[127] He also declined to sell India the F-5s.

In subsequent months, Johnson remained reluctant to authorize additional aid to India before passage of the FY 1966 bill. This dictated, in turn, a tightening of the faucet on aid to India, including on prior commitments. India awaited issuance of loans that had been incorporated into the prior year's budget. When Komer sought Johnson's authorization to dispatch them – preferably before June, the final month of FY 1965 – LBJ responded irately.[128] "I'm afraid we may have no foreign aid bill," the president wrote.[129] Johnson's concern for his aid bill stood to limit developmental assistance for India and augured his approach on the impending question of food aid.

---

[124] Telegram 1217, Washington to Karachi, April 27, 1965, in *FRUS, 1964–1968*, 25: 238–240.
[125] Telegram 3430, New Delhi to Washington, May 25, 1965, NSF, CF, box 129, "India, Vol. 4, Cables [2 of 2]" folder, LBJL.
[126] Telegram CAP 65138, White House to New Delhi, April 28, 1965, in *FRUS, 1964–1968*, 25: 240–241; Telegram 2057, New Delhi to Washington, April 27, 1965, NSF, CF, box 129, "India, Vol. 4, Cables [2 of 2]" folder, LBJL.
[127] Memorandum, Komer to Bundy, April 28, 1965, NSF, RWKP, box 22, "India Economic [1 of 4]" folder, LBJL.
[128] Memorandum, Komer to Johnson, May 20, 1965, in *FRUS, 1964–1968*, 25: 262–263.
[129] Memorandum, Komer to Johnson, April 23, 1965, NSF, RWKP, box 22, "India Economic [4 of 4]" folder, LBJL.

Food aid remained the central issue. India's existing PL-480 agreement was scheduled to end at the close of the fiscal year, on June 30, with supplies of food calculated to last until the end of August. Komer initially supported a multi-year commitment, but, taking note of Johnson's skepticism of large commitments, pared his proposal back to a one-year offer.[130] Johnson, however, was in no mood to rush an agreement, doubting that the United States should continue to send grain to India while New Delhi neglected its own agricultural sector.[131] He chafed at the lack of Indian support for his policies – particularly in Southeast Asia – and sought to communicate his displeasure by holding up the negotiation of a new PL-480 agreement and implementation of other aid programs.

He did so in spite of warnings from advisors that further delays stood to cause speculation and hoarding in India. By the estimate of Saunders, July 6 was the last date by which a new agreement could be concluded without causing any interruption in food shipments, which would finish at the end of August.[132] The day came and went. Three days later, Shastri wrote to Johnson, pleading for a new agreement.[133] The Indians were fed a stream of technical excuses for the delay in a new agreement. As Saunders worried, this duplicity stood to lay the "groundwork for destruction of good faith when the Indians find out our fellows have just been stringing them along."[134]

Johnson's aides remained uncertain about his intentions. "Could the President be determined to hold this up till trouble begins and the Indians come running to us?" Komer asked Bundy, "This will make us look like Scrooge indeed, but it might be salutary."[135] While India waited, Johnson sought to lay the groundwork for an appeal to Congress for an emergency program to address starvation in India.[136] On July 13, he explained to Ambassador Nehru that Shastri's statements on Vietnam were impeding the progress of Indian aid bills in the Senate; at the same time he asked for Nehru's help in convincing Congress that food aid was needed to avert mass starvation.[137] This message was reinforced by Johnson's Undersecretary of State for Economic

[130] Memorandum, Komer to Bundy, April 27, 1965, NSF, CF, box 129, "India, Vol. 4, Memos & Misc" folder, LBJL; Memorandum, Komer to Johnson, June 8, 1965, in *FRUS, 1964–1968*, 25: 271–273.

[131] Ahlberg, *Transplanting the Great Society*, 107–110.

[132] Memorandum, Komer to Johnson, June 17, 1965, NSF, CF, box 129, "India, Vol. 4, Memos & Misc" folder, LBJ; Memorandum, Saunders to Komer, June 22, 1965, NSF, RWKP, box 24, "Food, 1964–1965 [1 of 5]" folder, ibid.

[133] Letter, Shastri to Johnson, July 9, 1965, NSF, NSC Histories, box 24, "South Asia 1962–1966, Vol. 2, Tab B: 14–21 [2 of 2]" folder, LBJL.

[134] Memorandum, Bundy to Johnson, June 28, 1965, in *FRUS, 1964–1968*, 25: 284–285; Memorandum, Saunders to Komer, June 25, 1965, NSF, RWKP, box 24, "Food 1964–1965 [1 of 5]" folder, LBJL.

[135] Memorandum, Komer to Bundy, June 29, 1965, NSF, RWKP, box 24, "Food 1964–1965 [1 of 5]" folder, LBJL.

[136] Memcon, Johnson and Mann, July 13, 1965, in *FRUS, 1964–1968*, 25: 299–300.

[137] Memorandum for the Record, Komer, July 13, 1965, in *FRUS, 1964–1968*, 25: 300–303.

Affairs, Thomas Mann, who told Nehru that Vietnam obstructed further aid agreements.[138]

Johnson's strategy, adopted in concert with his advisors in the NSC, State Department, and Department of Agriculture, entailed shifting from long-term aid to short-term extensions of the just-expired PL-480 agreement. The first, a 60-day commitment, went into effect on July 26. This approach became known as the "short tether" strategy, and it adroitly balanced pressuring India to institute agricultural reforms with building support for food aid in Congress. The strategy also reflected Johnson's belief that foreign aid had become increasingly ineffectual, serving neither donor nor recipient. India, kept afloat by inexpensive grain, had lacked sufficient incentives to reform its faltering agricultural sector, while the United States had not received the gratitude it deserved.

A spate of border incidents in August threatened to spark a full-scale war between India and Pakistan and gave the Johnson administration further cause to rethink its South Asian aid strategy. New Delhi complained at the beginning of the month of increased Pakistani infiltration into Indian-occupied Kashmir. On the morning of September 1, the conflict escalated as a Pakistani armored column crossed the cease-fire line, triggering South Asia's first full-scale war since the partition. As during the Rann of Kutch episode, Pakistani use of MAP weaponry brought complaints from India.

Amid the conflict, the administration again received Indian requests for PL-480 grain. With the July commitment scheduled to end in the final week of October and India facing a dire shortfall, speed was needed to stave off panic and hoarding. Again Bowles requested immediate action, noting that Indian opinion was already inflamed by widespread Pakistani usage of U.S.-made weaponry. Komer wrote:

The trick is to keep on using food as leverage by only dribbling it out slowly, but to do so in time to forestall *public* reactions. Thus we keep the GOI and GOP worried ... yet don't give them or anyone else a handle to accuse us of using food as a weapon.[139]

Accordingly, Bowles was authorized to negotiate the sale of roughly one month's worth of wheat – half of what he had requested.[140] Days later, after three weeks of pitched fighting, a UN-sponsored cease-fire took effect on September 22.

The war cast the short tether strategy in a sinister light. As Bowles had warned, a number of Indian newspapers deemed Washington's refusal to conclude a long-term agreement blatant political pressure, with many fearing that

---

[138] Memcon, Mann and Nehru, July 1, 1965, NSF, CF, box 129, "India, Vol. 5, Memos [2 of 3]" folder, LBJL.

[139] Memorandum, Komer to Bundy, September 13, 1965, in *FRUS, 1964–1968*, 25: 393.

[140] Telegram 655, New Delhi to Washington, September 16, 1965, in *FRUS, 1964–1968*, 25: 399–400; Telegram 513, Washington to New Delhi, September 19, 1965, ibid.: 415n; Telegram, Bowles to Komer, September 21, 1965, ibid.: 420–421.

Johnson sought to force major concessions on Kashmir.[141] The State Department labored to dispel this impression, but the evasiveness of U.S. policymakers tended to fuel Indian fears.[142] The United States kept renewing PL-480 in one month increments, in the months following the ceasefire and preceding the Tashkent Accords, which concluded the war. The specter of coercion, thus, haunted Indian-American relations from the very debut of the short-tether strategy onward.[143]

Johnson, however, sought to craft a long-term response to the problem of Indian hunger. He envisioned using the short tether to goad India to undertake agricultural reforms. Rising worldwide demand for grain limited the available wheat for India's massive PL-480 purchases. Upon approving the one-month extension in October, he directed his aides to tell the Indians of his dissatisfaction with their agricultural performance, particularly their failure to improve crop production.[144] In November, Secretary of Agriculture Orville Freeman met Indian Food and Agriculture Minister Chidambaram Subramaniam in Rome. The two men negotiated an agreement whereby India committed to modernizing its agricultural sector through the use of fertilizers and improved wheat. Pleased by India's acceptance of his terms, Johnson authorized a three-month PL-480 agreement in December and empowered Freeman to expedite the dispatch of grain to the subcontinent.

Indian acceptance of Johnson's terms and its efforts to improve crop yields seemed to validate the president's logic. "It may be too soon to crow, but ... we seem to be achieving an agricultural revolution in India," Komer wrote to Johnson in late December.[145] Herculean efforts by Freeman facilitated the dispatch of hundreds of thousands of tons of grain to India at the end of 1965. Newly encouraged, LBJ appealed to Congress the following February for substantial revisions to the PL-480 program, including the phasing out of Title I sales and increased emphasis on promoting agricultural self-sufficiency. Johnson succeeded where Kennedy had failed: Congress threw its support behind his Indian aid program, and his strategy spurred New Delhi toward needed reforms.[146]

---

[141] Telegram 859, New Delhi to Washington, October 1, 1965, NSF, CF, box 130, "India, Vol. 6, Cables [2 of 3]" folder, LBJL; Telegram 847, New Delhi to Washington, September 30, 1965, ibid.

[142] Memorandum, Raymond Hare to Rusk, October 5, 1965, in *FRUS, 1964–1968*, 25: 443–444, 444n; Memorandum, Komer to Johnson, November 15, 1965, NSF, RWKP, box 22, "India Economic [1 of 4]" folder, LBJL; Telegram 1223, New Delhi to Washington, November 8, 1965, ibid., "India Economic [3 of 4]" folder, LBJL.

[143] See also Ahlberg, *Transplanting the Great Society*, 122–123.

[144] Memorandum for the Record, Rusk, October 27, 1965, in *FRUS, 1964–1968*, 25: 455; Telegram 800, Washington to New Delhi, October 29, 1965, NSF, RWKP, box 24, "India Food 1964–1965 [4 of 5]" folder, LBJL.

[145] Memorandum, Komer to Johnson, December 22, 1965, NSF, RWKP, box 24, "India Food 1964–1965 [1 of 5]" folder, LBJL.

[146] A contentious question in Johnson's time, the impact of his strategy remains a matter of debate. Johnson wrote glowingly of his strategy in his memoir, *The Vantage Point: Perspectives*

Despite his humanitarian intentions, Johnson had chosen a policy designed to keep India in constant anxiety, one dependent more on coercion than trust. Even in the best of circumstances, this might have engendered considerable annoyance on New Delhi's part. In the wake of the 1965 war, however, such a policy was bound to breed deep resentment in India, where Shastri's opposition charged that Washington was imposing political strings. Such conclusions were reinforced by the range of Johnson's restrictions on aid in 1965, extending well beyond PL-480. Moreover, LBJ and his advisors *had* complained about New Delhi's foreign policy, including on Vietnam *and* Kashmir. In December 1965, Johnson told Subramaniam that resolving Kashmir would strengthen Indian-American relations.[147] Political strings were apparent from the very start.

Facing high grain prices, Indian governments had little choice but to heed Johnson's diktats on agricultural modernization, but neither Shastri nor his successor, Indira Gandhi, took comfort from their dependence on U.S. beneficence. Indeed, Gandhi – although forced by circumstance to continue the policies initiated by Shastri – became particularly unhappy with this situation. As she remarked: "We want to do without aid.... It is not U.S. aid alone we want to do without, but all aid.... The giver-receiver relationship is never a happy one."[148]

FREEDOM IN POVERTY

Time and again, nonaligned states baffled Washington by seeking aid while continuing to criticize or act at cross-purposes with U.S. foreign policy. Advocates of aid to the nonaligned world had seized upon the genuine enthusiasm of postcolonial leaders for economic development. Yet they frequently misinterpreted interest in aid as reflecting a desire to favor national development over regional geopolitical agendas. After Syria's secession from the UAR, policymakers frequently opined that Nasser might now focus his energies primarily on domestic matters; one year later, he was embroiled in the Yemeni civil war. In 1962, U.S. Ambassador Howard Jones argued emphatically that Sukarno would gain economically from a peaceful resolution of the West New Guinea dispute; within months, the Indonesian leader began confronting Malaysia.[149]

---

of the Presidency, 1963–1969 (New York: Holt, Rinehart and Winston, 1971), 222–231. James Bjorkman offers a far more critical analysis in Bjorkman, "Indo-American Relations, 1965–1968," 231–240. Robert McMahon strikes a middle ground in "Disillusionment and Disengagement," 156–171. Finally, Nick Cullather provocatively examines the politics of declaring a famine in India, in *The Hungry World*, 205–231.

[147] Memorandum for Record, December 20, 1965, in *FRUS, 1964–1968*, 25: 518–520.

[148] Shashi Tharoor, *Reasons of State: Political Development and India's Foreign Policy Under Indira Gandhi, 1966–1977* (New Delhi: Vikas, 1982), 66.

[149] Memorandum, Robert F. Kennedy to Bundy, July 24, 1962, in *FRUS, 1961–1963*, 23: 608–609.

When Washington attempted to warn nonaligned recipients away from confrontational foreign policies, messages mentioning aid risked arousing ire. In October 1963, Kennedy entreated Sukarno to return to the negotiating table, noting the difficulty that he had marshaling support for economic aid to Indonesia. After reading the letter, Sukarno gathered his advisors to discuss Indonesia's options. "What now, gentlemen?" he asked the group. Sukarno's prime minister, Djuanda Kartawidjaja, reasoned:

If we have to eat stone then we will eat stone. But I don't think it will be necessary. Certainly, without American aid it is going to be rough and difficult. It means a further tightening of belts, but in this, our struggle we shall depend on our own national resources and national loyalties and ignore foreign aid. In this we shall share poverty with our people who in turn are prepared to share collectively the burden of our struggle. Our struggle would be fatal anyway if we were to get foreign aid without finding our own soul.

According to Indonesian diplomat Ganis Harsono, this remark became "the backbone" of Sukarno's verbal outburst about aid in 1964.[150]

Something similar happened that same autumn when Kennedy attempted to encourage Nasser to disengage from Yemen, reminding him of the political difficulties he faced in aiding the UAR. When warned that the conflict could imperil future aid programs, the Egyptian responded viscerally. Aid from the United States, Nasser explained to Badeau, was not essential to Egypt; if it ceased, he had alternatives in mind – especially if his Saudi enemies held such influence in Washington.[151] His 1964 Port Said speech made public what he had previously confined to private channels:

If the Americans think they are giving us a little aid to dominate us and control our policy, I would like to tell them we are sorry. We are ready to cut down in our consumption of … certain commodities. But we will maintain our independence, otherwise we will lose it completely, and the 1956 battle would have been of no use.[152]

The efforts employed by policymakers to marshal support for aid programs, moreover, carried its own psychological toll. Arguing for aid in the 1960s was a Sisyphean endeavor, requiring a high degree of conviction that the aid program was worthwhile. This, in turn, led to heightened personal investment in the policy, and exaggerated expectations of outcomes.[153] When such hopes were disappointed, the result was disillusionment on the part of those diplomats most responsible for policy. Fierce Guinean criticism of the Stanleyville operation left Americans in Conakry stunned. Ambassador James Loeb exclaimed,

---

[150] Ganis Harsono, Recollections of an Indonesian Diplomat in the Sukarno Era, ed. C. L. M. Penders (Queensland: University of Queensland Press, 1977), 248–249.

[151] Telegram 969, Cairo to Washington, October 27, 1963, in DOS, FRUS, 1961–1963, Vol. 18: Near East 1962–1963 (MS) (Washington: GPO, 1997).

[152] Text of Port Said Speech, December 23, 1964, box 159, "UAR, Vol. 2, Cables [1 of 2]" folder, LBJL.

[153] See, for example, Note, J. G. S. Beith, February 1, 1963, FO 371/172869, TNA.

"I can't understand how they can do this, considering the economic mess that they are in, and their dependence on our aid."[154]

Even in the absence of separate policy disputes, governments often clashed with Washington on both questions of strategy and American efforts to promote aid at home. U.S. economic advisors left the impression that they believed themselves obliged to tell the Guineans how to manage their economy. Of one visitor, Touré remarked, "He can have all the statistics he can find, if they are any good to him. But don't suppose he is going to alter our economic system or our Plan." Friction over aid policy goals added significant stress to U.S.-Guinean relations.[155] Similarly, the U.S. country team in Ghana faced the unenviable task of reconciling their beliefs about the country's economic prospects with Nkrumah's: while the Americans advocated investment in the agricultural sector, the president pursued a program of industrialization that struck U.S. diplomats as ill-conceived and wasteful.[156] The U.S. aid strategy for Indonesia was jeopardized in the spring of 1963 by a dispute over Jakarta's efforts to obtain a more favorable share of exports revenue from U.S.-owned oilfields.[157] Such disputes reinforced the image of the U.S. as a neocolonial power – although efforts to alter the foreign policies of recipients did far more harm overall.

Revolutionary leaders in the Third World faced immense economic difficulties stemming from both underdevelopment and their own often misguided policies. Seeking their nation's place in the sun, often in opposition to Western-allied states, they still sought – and depended upon – economic assistance from the United States. As such, they faced a paradox partly of their own making: having defined themselves as nonaligned and anticolonial states, they now faced pressure from Washington to adopt more pro-Western policies. This, in turn, risked reducing them, in the eyes of their rivals, to the status of a U.S. pawn. Aid allowed leaders like Sukarno, Nasser, Nkrumah, and Touré to wax expansively about the future of their state. It also imposed unwelcome shackles and compromised their self-images.

Most critically, aid programs failed to build lasting ties because, as measures of U.S. support, they could never come before other acts of policy. Nonaligned states sought aid but often valued assistance less than changes in policy toward colonial issues and regional conflicts. Even staunch proponents of engagement believed that aid was, by itself, insufficient to alter the policies of recipient states. Ambassador William Attwood observed that the U.S. position in Guinea depended not only on the effectiveness of aid programs, but also on developments in Angola and Algeria. He wrote, "Our failure to take anti-colonial position on these issues would largely vitiate [the] political benefits of an aid

[154] Letter, King to Le Quesne, November 26, 1964, FO 371/177194, TNA.

[155] Letter, King to LeQuesne, February 18, 1965, FO 371/177194, TNA. See Mairi Steward MacDonald, "The Challenge of Guinean Independence, 1958–1971," Ph.D. dissertation, University of Toronto, 2009, 198–208.

[156] Interview, Jack Matlock with the author, April 16, 2008.

[157] Simpson, *Economists with Guns*, 99–112.

program."[158] Tanzania's Julius Nyerere remarked in April 1963 that if he had to choose between millions of dollars in aid and a resolute U.S. position on Mozambique, he would accept the latter "without question." Nyerere believed he could still develop his country without aid, albeit more slowly; he could *not* hope to expel Portugal from his southern border without U.S. assistance.[159] U.S. policymakers were willing to concede that aid did not prevent real disagreements, but they overstated its ability to constrain states where core issues were concerned.

Worse, in the absence of policy changes, aid became a political liability to recipient governments, seeming to represent a kind of bribery. In December 1964, after Stanleyville, Nyerere delayed implementing a police training program, fearing the implications of accepting funds from a country that had been accused of trying to subvert Tanzanian sovereignty.[160] Likewise, the thaw in U.S.-UAR ties that accompanied the 1962 PL-480 accord led Nasser's Arab foes to charge that he had been bought out by the United States, giving him incentive to demonstrate his political independence of Washington – especially in the face of White House efforts to play the aid card. The angriest tirade Battle ever witnessed from Nasser pertained to the UAR's dependence on foreign grain and his resentment of U.S. press attention to that fact.[161] Successive U.S. governments did not fully grasp the political predicament that accepting aid imposed on proud national leaders, even without overt efforts at leverage.

The image of the United States as a generous benefactor, willing to aid Third World development in spite of deep policy disagreements, was always a fiction. Kennedy's aid was politically targeted and the president's eloquence on the necessity of development for its own sake masked the concrete goals behind his aid program. Under Kennedy, however, this fiction was largely sustained, and it was indisputably useful. The Congressional assault on aid did some damage to this image, but Kennedy was able – on occasion – to draw distinctions between the executive and legislative branches. Johnson's tactics erased this distinction: after 1964, both branches seemed keen to use aid coercively.

Washington's willingness to employ duplicity and stalling tactics toward nonaligned recipients worsened matters. Johnson showed little concern for the questions of planning that preoccupied nonaligned leaders. India and Egypt, among others, depended on the United States to be candid as well as generous, giving prompt notice of the quantity of grain available for sale. Johnson disregarded recommendations to provide timely word of the size and duration of PL-480 agreements, thereby forcing recipient governments to miss vital deadlines, throwing their economic planning into confusion. Nonaligned observers

[158] Airgram A-2, Conakry to Washington, July 11, 1961, NA, RG-84, Guinea, Classified General Records, box 2, "320 – Guinea-U.S. Relations" folder.
[159] Telegram 690, Dar es Salaam to Washington, April 5, 1963, DSCF, CFPF, 1963, box 4022, "POL Port-T" folder, NA.
[160] Telegram 1297, Dar es Salaam to Washington, December 16, 1964, DSCF, CFPF, box 2695, "POL 9 Tanzan-US, 12–1/64" folder, NA.
[161] Telegram 5030, Cairo to Washington, March 4, 1967, in *FRUS, 1964–1968, 18:* 768–770.

could reasonably conclude that Johnson sought to foster dependency on emergency grain shipments.

Over time, Washington's efforts to gain leverage became increasingly apparent. Nonaligned leaders took careful note of how the White House used aid; actions undertaken in one case sent broad signals to other parties of what they, too, might expect. Egypt paid close attention to Johnson's food aid policies toward India. India was alarmed by Johnson's increasingly coercive policy toward Pakistan, despite the animosity between the two countries.[162] This, in turn, served to erode the image of the United States, turning Washington's strongest card in the postcolonial world – its unparalleled financial largesse – into a source of weakness. Nonaligned leaders needed and sought aid from the great powers and usually from more than one. Such aid did not necessarily make them friends, but it quite often gave them cause to avoid being foes. Reminding them of this fact, however, spurred them to demonstrate independence from their benefactors. As Bowles sagely remarked, "We told the American people that [aid] would buy votes for us in the UN. On the contrary, as a sensitive state when you get aid from America, you're inclined to disagree with America to prove that you're sovereign."[163]

SHIFTS IN STRATEGY, SHIFTS IN IMAGE

Within the United States, the annual battle over foreign aid continued to spark efforts to reinvent the program. In January 1965, Senator J. William Fulbright, the influential chair of the Foreign Relations Committee, proposed a philosophical overhaul of the aid program. Above all he believed that bilateral aid programs, creating a creditor-debtor relationship between the United States and recipients, were no longer defensible. Fulbright was hardly an opponent of foreign aid in principle; he thought, however, that it was necessary to make aid a multilateral matter, distributed primarily through international bodies. Such reform would ease the legislative burden of the foreign aid budget, and alleviate the difficulties that aid created within bilateral relationships.[164]

The Johnson administration's experience with aid drove it in a different direction. Johnson had his own ambitions for the aid program, consonant with his Great Society program; these proposed more explicit use of aid for purposes of leverage. Johnson assembled his own committee to review the aid program, chaired by Cornell University President James A. Perkins. In January 1966 the president's committee on foreign aid presented its findings to Johnson. The committee report reaffirmed the value of foreign aid to the United States but called for a number of policy changes. It called for more emphasis on the

---

[162] Telegram 4279, Cairo to Washington, February 1, 1967, in *FRUS, 1964–1968, 18*: 754–756; Telegram 847, New Delhi to Washington, September 30, 1965, NSF, CF, box 130, "India, Vol. 6, Cables [2 of 2]" folder, LBJL.

[163] Interview, Chester Bowles, November 11, 1969, 2, OH, LBJL.

[164] Felix Belair, "Fulbright Quits as Floor Manager for Foreign Aid," *NYT*, January 28, 1965, 1.

root causes of poverty, greater use of international organizations, and renewed efforts to solicit donations from other Western states.

Critically, the Perkins committee overturned the principles espoused by Kennedy, arguing for far more explicit linkages between assistance and political goals. "Aid must be used as a carrot, and the possibility of withholding it as a stick," the report bluntly stated. It should be reserved for "countries which are not hostile to us," nor engaged in "political or military adventures."[165] Around the same time, the administration received the Korry Report, which recommended a narrowing of African aid programs, acknowledging diminished expectations on the continent.[166] Attitudes toward aid had changed dramatically. The shift away from the baksheesh model ran parallel to a mounting disillusionment with the nonaligned states and their unpredictable leaders. The era of funding the pet projects of national leaders – the age of Aswan – was at an end.

So, too, was the Kennedy promise of aid in spite of differences of opinion. Aid had become a divisive question in relations with a broad swath of nonaligned states, especially as Johnson relied on it increasingly as a means to shift the policies of recipient states. Without exception, this tactic backfired. By its own actions, the U.S. government had thrown Kennedy's pledge into disrepute throughout the nonaligned world – just as Johnson began to deploy ground troops to South Vietnam. The disaffection of nonaligned leaders on aid issues and their concurrent need to show their independence of the United States found fateful expression on this most divisive issue.

[165] Memorandum, Rusk to Johnson, January 31, 1966, in *FRUS, 1964–1968, 9*: 133–138.
[166] Terrence Lyons, "Keeping Africa Off the Agenda," in Cohen and Tucker eds., *Lyndon Johnson Confronts the World*, 260–266.

7

"A Heavy Burden for Us to Bear": The Era of Vietnam

The 1960s witnessed a dramatic deterioration in the position of the United States in the Third World. By the end of the Johnson presidency, relations between the United States and the nonaligned world stood at an unprecedented level of mutual acrimony. Diplomatic relations with the major Arab states of Egypt and Algeria had been severed for more than a year. Despite the provision of immense quantities of food aid to India, relations with New Delhi had become increasingly distrustful. African nonaligned states, embroiled in an escalating struggle against the continent's white-minority regimes, were deeply resentful over the inability of the Johnson administration to advance the cause of majority rule. A range of different causes had produced these outcomes, but one factor profoundly affected all cases: the Vietnam War.

The war brought the most profound and lasting damage to U.S.-nonaligned relations, deeply affecting every major bilateral tie. Differences among the nonaligned states ensured that its impact varied from country to country; indeed Vietnam was not the primary concern of any of them. Following the U.S. escalation of the war in 1965, however, it became the leading issue of the Cold War and a question of leading importance to each of the three major world powers. Johnson's escalation in Vietnam coincided with the deepening of two interrelated schisms: the Sino-Soviet battle for influence in the Third World and the growing doctrinal dispute within the nonaligned group. These, in turn, broadly shaped nonaligned reactions to the U.S. deployment. Although the uncommitted states each approached the conflict with their own distinct calculations of national interest and ideological perspective, a common trend transcended particular circumstances: over time they grew more critical of the war and more willing to condemn the United States. Other major events added to the acrimony: political instability in the nonaligned world, the Rhodesian crisis of 1965, and the Six Day War in June 1967.

Before examining the broad consequences of the Vietnam War, it is necessary to consider the road not taken in Southeast Asia. This story, too, reflects the U.S. experience with nonalignment, particularly the conceptual limits of Kennedy's thinking. Even though the effects of the Vietnam War were felt

almost entirely during Johnson's tenure, they might have been averted had
LBJ's predecessor been willing to extend his ideas about nonalignment further.
Both presidents must thus share responsibility for the war's impact on the pro-
ject of engagement.

NEUTRALISM IN SOUTHEAST ASIA, 1961–1963

Although the Vietnam War ultimately became a question of paramount importance between Washington and the nonaligned capitals, it represented no more
than a second-tier issue during the Kennedy years. African nonaligned leaders
worried about the Congo and the Portuguese colonies. Nasser remained preoccupied with events in the Arab world. India, although an active participant in
multilateral negotiations over Southeast Asia, had concerns far closer to home:
Goa, China, and Pakistan. Even Indonesia, just south of the former French
Indochina, remained focused on disputes of an offshore nature: first West New
Guinea and then North Borneo. India and Indonesia held a real interest in the
fate of Indochina, but this question never rose to dominate their relationship
with Washington before Kennedy's death.

Mainland Southeast Asia, however, represented a pivotal proving ground
for Kennedy's approach toward neutrality in the Cold War. His policy toward
Laos demonstrated his willingness to accept a broadly based neutral government as a substitute for an ally. Facing South Vietnam, however, Kennedy came
to a different conclusion, choosing to retain a weak ally and committing to its
defense. His decision to support Saigon opened the way, in turn, for Johnson's
escalation of the war in 1964 and 1965.

What differentiated Laos and South Vietnam? Historians of the Vietnam
War have dwelled on this question. Timing represents one key distinction. The
crisis in Laos peaked around the same time as the Bay of Pigs and the crisis
in the Congo. The Cuban disaster served to caution Kennedy against military
intervention in a remote, landlocked Asian country, where the most capable
military force by far was the communist Pathet Lao.[1] The Congo, however, provides a closer parallel. There, as in Laos, Kennedy faced a fractured country. In
the Congo, he endorsed creating a government of national unity and maintaining the territorial integrity of the Congolese state. He acted similarly in Laos,
having concluded that military options offered dim hopes at best. Neutralizing
Laos, moreover, represented a solid break with the policies of the Eisenhower
administration, affirming that his government supported the self-determination
of postcolonial states.[2] Eisenhower had backed the Laotian right against both
the neutralist faction of Souvanna Phouma and the Pathet Lao. Kennedy considered Phouma a necessary ally against the country's communist insurgency;

---

[1] On this point, see Lawrence Freedman, *Kennedy's Wars: Berlin, Cuba, Laos, and Vietnam* (New
York: Oxford University Press, 2000), 299–302.

[2] David Kaiser, *American Tragedy: Kennedy, Johnson and the Origins of the Vietnam War*
(Cambridge, MA: Belknap, 2000), 36–37

to that end, his policy succeeded in marginalizing the Pathet Lao and creating a center-right coalition.

Like the Congo, Laos represented a field of collaboration between the United States and India, which was a signatory to the 1954 Geneva Accords. Alongside Poland and Canada, India was one of the three International Control Commission (ICC) co-chairs, tasked with ensuring adherence to the provisions of Geneva. Negotiations over Laos brought a fair amount of friction between Washington and New Delhi. In the year following the agreement, U.S. observers found the Indians slow in response to reported violations. Although India praised the settlement and recommended a similar approach to South Vietnam, Washington did not share this enthusiasm.[3] Removed from the front ranks of Cold War battlegrounds, Laos lingered in a state of civil war, while serving as a communist corridor into South Vietnam. As Roger Hilsman of the State Department's Far East Bureau later noted, the amount of effort required to maintain the Laos agreement easily equaled the exertion expended to achieve it in the first place.[4]

Like other policy acts supportive of neutrality, the Geneva settlement fueled a crisis in confidence among Washington's allies in the region. Both Thailand and South Vietnam steadily criticized the agreement, questioning whether Kennedy was truly committed to their defense. South Vietnamese President Ngo Dinh Diem declared that Washington had endorsed the communization of Laos.[5] He expressed particular ire over the inability of the Laotian government to interdict communist military supplies transiting its territory. When Lyndon Johnson visited Southeast Asia, in the spring of 1961, he heard a chorus of criticism of the administration's Laos policy. As he wrote to Kennedy upon his return, "Laos has created doubt and concern about intentions of the United States throughout Southeast Asia." The ensuing reaction to Geneva had "drastically weakened the ability" of regional allies "to maintain any strongly pro-US orientation."[6] This trip clearly influenced Johnson's own later approach to the prospect of neutralizing Southeast Asia, just as the complaints of Southeast Asia Treaty Organization (SEATO) allies pressed Kennedy toward affirming his commitment to the defense of South Vietnam.[7]

In this context, it is worth reiterating that Kennedy and his advisors tolerated nonaligned foreign policies only outside the Western alliance system. Without exception, the White House frowned upon neutralism within its own camp,

[3] Telegram 1509, Karachi to Washington, March 3, 1963, in DOS, *FRUS, 1961–1963, Vol. 19: South Asia* (Washington: GPO, 1996): 219–220.
[4] Roger Hilsman, *To Move a Nation: The Politics of Foreign Policy in the Administration of John F. Kennedy* (New York: Doubleday, 1967), 155.
[5] Telegram 29, Saigon to Washington, July 11, 1962, in DOS, *FRUS, 1963–1963, Vol. 2: Vietnam 1962* (Washington: GPO, 1990): 514–515.
[6] Memorandum, Johnson to Kennedy, May 23, 1961, NSF, Papers of McGeorge Bundy, box 19, "Southeast Asia: The Vice President's Memorandum to the President" folder, LBJL.
[7] McMahon, *The Limits of Empire: The United States and Southeast Asia Since World War II* (New York: Columbia University Press, 1999), 106–112.

in cases including such allies as Iran, Turkey, Germany, and Japan. Kennedy reacted especially forcefully to independent-minded regimes in Latin America, a region the United States regarded as its own turf. The White House withdrew support from governments in Argentina and Brazil that sought dialogue with Cuba. In the case of Argentina, Kennedy accepted the overthrow of the government in Buenos Aires; in Brazil, he aided rightist anti-government factions.[8] The same concerns led Washington to dissuade its neighbors from sending representatives to nonaligned conferences. As the White House saw it, allowing an ally to turn toward neutrality opened the door to additional defections. The logic of the domino effect applied as strongly to allies slouching toward neutralism as it did to states in the throes of communist subversion. Such reasoning was only reinforced by the strident allied complaints that followed the Laos settlement.

South Vietnam could not be written off as easily. By 1963, the United States had made a sizable commitment to Saigon's defense, far exceeding what it had invested in Laos. The political situation in the Republic of Vietnam was far more polarized than that of Laos; Kennedy did not perceive an equivalent to Phouma's neutralists. More critically, however, the regional fallout from Geneva made neutralizing South Vietnam a far more difficult proposition, likely, as Rusk and McNamara advised Kennedy, to damage U.S. credibility in Southeast Asia and elsewhere. Thus, when the Diem brothers spoke increasingly of expelling the United States and talking directly with Hanoi, and when France recommended neutralizing South Vietnam, Kennedy perceived assaults on the cohesion of his alliance system. The virtual expulsion of the United States from South Vietnam would have represented an historic rejection of U.S. leadership and counterinsurgency efforts in the Third World.[9]

Consequently, Kennedy signaled his approval to a plot by South Vietnamese generals to depose the Diem brothers, hoping that the coup would bring a more reliable government to power in Saigon. His choice rested on the well-worn rationale of preserving an existing alliance and reassuring Washington's other partners in Southeast Asia. It was here that Kennedy's conceptual approach to the question of nonalignment in the Cold War fell short. He was prepared to accept it as the outlook of established nonaligned states; he could not countenance it as a policy choice for states already aligned within his camp. This was a tragic error for two reasons. First it belied Kennedy's rhetorical commitment to a diverse community of free nations.[10] Second, unbeknownst at the time, it denied him and his successor a relatively inexpensive exit from the interminable problem of propping up Saigon. Writing off South Vietnam to ˙

---

[8] See Stephen Rabe, *The Most Dangerous Area in the World: John F. Kennedy Confronts Communist Revolution in Latin America* (Chapel Hill: University of North Carolina Press, 1999), 56–71.

[9] See Fredrik Logevall, *Choosing War: The Lost Chance for Peace and the Escalation of War in Vietnam* (Berkeley: University of California Press, 1999), 1–74; Kaiser, *American Tragedy*, 258–283.

[10] See Logevall, *Choosing War*, 85–88.

neutralism – even a short-lived neutralism – would have spared Johnson the calamity of waging the Vietnam War. It also might have helped to salvage one of Kennedy's central foreign policy initiatives: engaging the nonaligned world.

"AN IMPRESSION OF DRIFT": THE DECLINE OF PRESIDENTIAL DIPLOMACY

Debate will forever rage about the differences and similarities between Kennedy and Johnson's Vietnam policies. In another area, however, a starker distinction is apparent: Johnson never established himself in the nonaligned world in the way that his predecessor did. With Kennedy's assassination, nonaligned leaders mourned someone whom they had regarded as a friend, and they naturally hoped to forge an equally strong bond with his successor. These hopes were frustrated in large part by Johnson's disinclination to engage in presidential diplomacy, which in turn constrained his ability to explain his war to the nonaligned world.

Amid the shock of Kennedy's assassination, advocates of engagement hoped for a smooth transition. Writing to Bundy on the afternoon of November 22, 1963, battling a feeling of "numb misery," Komer observed,

The Kennedy image of youth and vitality (plus the realities of his policy) has been such a priceless gain to us abroad, that every effort needs to be made to preserve them. An impression of drift at this point – instead of a quick and confident reaffirmation of what we stand for – could be of incalculable if intangible harm.[11]

The warning was prescient; it also passed unheeded. Lyndon Johnson, through a combination of deliberate action and benign neglect, created a very different image of himself throughout the nonaligned world. Nowhere did this contrast seem more evident than in the field of presidential diplomacy.

In 1961, Kennedy met Nkrumah, Nehru, Sukarno (twice), Nyerere, and Keita. Johnson met none of the nonaligned leaders before the Cairo Conference. Some meetings were politically infeasible: Nkrumah and Sukarno now seemed undeserving of the implicit approval that a visit would communicate, and Nehru's declining health made travel out of the question. Johnson was, moreover, loath to leave the country, as he lacked a vice president to serve in his absence. Yet, LBJ also seemed indifferent to the value of making the acquaintance of nonaligned leaders Kennedy had cultivated; no thought went into inviting others, such as Touré, Nyerere, or Keita. Johnson's letters to them were less frequent than Kennedy's, and they displayed less interest or personal warmth.

Johnson's approach betrayed a far more risk-averse conception of the uses of presidential prestige. Kennedy had not enjoyed easy relations with Sukarno, Nkrumah, or Keita when he met with them in 1961. These visits had served as means to an end; they were not intended to be rewards in their own right. By

[11] Memorandum, Komer to Bundy, November 22, 1963, NSF, box 322, "Robert Komer, 6/63–11/63" folder, JFKL.

1964, head of state meetings were less frequently regarded as opportunities to advance policy goals than considered as a kind of diplomatic currency, to be tendered to friends and withheld from uncooperative states. As this happened, bilateral diplomacy became a far less effective countermeasure to the radicalism of the conferences.

No immediate change in personnel lay behind this attitudinal shift. Bundy, Rusk, Rostow, Komer, and Ball all lasted well into the Johnson years; and the eclipse of the liberal triad of Bowles, UN Representative Adlai Stevenson, and Assistant Secretary of State G. Mennen Williams had occurred well before Kennedy's death. The early Kennedy years appear to have shaped the thinking of the Johnson administration: the active diplomacy of 1961 and 1962 had not forestalled serious disputes with nonaligned states in 1963. These visits were time-consuming and posed political risks to Johnson's reelection. LBJ lacked Kennedy's intellectual interest in decolonization and his advisors had lost some of their enthusiasm for presidential diplomacy.

This sentiment was not shared by most of the nonaligned leaders, who were generally keen to take the measure of Kennedy's successor. Sukarno declared that he was eager to meet Johnson, thinking him "perhaps more a man of the people than Kennedy." Johnson, frustrated with Indonesia's bellicose behavior, declined to issue an invitation.[12] Guinea's President Sekou Touré repeatedly stated his interest in visiting Washington after Johnson's reelection. The State Department, angry at Guinea's reaction to Stanleyville, demurred, citing Johnson's "heavy schedule."[13] Keita also sought to establish a personal relationship with Johnson; his requests for a visit to the White House suffered the same fate as Touré's.[14]

In 1967, the administration's seeming neglect of Africa drew criticism from its liberal opponents in Congress, most notably from Senator Robert F. Kennedy. Edward Hamilton of the NSC staff wrote, "No matter how one cuts the numbers on visits by African heads of government, the totals for the last four years aren't as impressive as those for 1961–1963." During his thirty-four months in office, Kennedy had met with twenty-eight African leaders; across a span of forty-five months, Johnson had met twenty – none of them from nonaligned states.[15] The disparity is telling.

By far the most pivotal failure to employ presidential diplomacy came in the case of LBJ's 1965 postponement of the scheduled visit of Indian Prime

---

[12] Telegram 1347, Jakarta to Washington, January 3, 1964, NSF, CF, box 246, "Indonesia, Vol. 1, Memos" folder, LBJL; Telegram 2533, Jakarta to Washington, June 9, 1964, RG-59, CFPF, 1964–1966, box 2327, "POL INDON-US" folder, NA.

[13] Telegram SecState 182, Conakry to Washington, September 11, 1964, NSF, CF, "Guinea, Cables, 1/64–1/69" folder, LBJL; Telegram 693, Washington to Conakry, January 9, 1965, ibid.; Department Telegram 734, Washington to Conakry, January 19, 1965, ibid.

[14] Telegram 493, Bamako to Washington, June 4, 1965, NSF, CF, box 94, "Mali, Vol. 1, 2/64–9/58" folder, LBJL; Telegram 279, Washington to Bamako, June 11, 1965, ibid.

[15] Memorandum, Hamilton to Johnson, August 22, 1967, NSF, CF, box 77, "Africa, Vol. V. 2 of 3" folder, LBJL.

Minister Lal Bahadur Shastri. The postponement was motivated by a number of reasons, including Johnson's concern with his aid bill and the concurrent postponement of Pakistani President Mohammed Ayub Khan's visit. Beyond its immediate circumstances, it spoke to a profound shift in the goals of presidential diplomacy, away from forming interpersonal bonds. Bundy wrote to Ambassador Chester Bowles, noting that the administration was preoccupied with Vietnam and the passage of its foreign aid bill: "Rather than have merely a polite get-together with neither party yet ready for constructive palaver, the President prefers that we both do our homework and get aid bill passed first."[16] In the Kennedy years, however, establishing a bond with the leader of the single most important nonaligned state was a goal in itself. Kennedy, interested by the challenges that postcolonial leaders faced, would have worked to make the palaver constructive – particularly as the United States became further embroiled in Southeast Asia.

Predictably, despite the wishful thinking of the White House, the postponement angered Shastri. The Indian prime minister was "hurt and very bitter," according to the later recollection of Bowles.[17] Complaining to a French diplomat, a senior staffer of the Indian Ministry of External Affairs attributed the postponement to the "growing xenophobia of Mr. Johnson, exasperated at receiving foreigners coming to solicit aid, criticize his policy in Indochina, or both."[18] Despite efforts to reschedule the trip, a confluence of circumstances kept Shastri and Johnson from meeting before the prime minister's death, in January 1966.

Johnson did, however, remain eager to meet with heads of friendly governments. Such meetings carried little if any domestic cost and served to reassure allies. Israeli Prime Minister Levi Eshkol visited the White House in June 1964. Malaysia's Tunku Abdul Rahman met with Johnson the following month, in a visit that signaled a growing U.S. commitment to the defense of the federation. Neither Sukarno nor Nasser reacted well to these meetings – made more galling by the fact that they had not been invited to Washington. Johnson's regular meetings with allies belied his claims of being overworked – Indian observers noted bitterly that other visits in 1965 seemed to be proceeding according to schedule.[19]

Changes in personnel in U.S. embassies further reduced the influence accrued during the early years of the decade. As high-profile ambassadors from the Kennedy period resigned their stations, they were invariably replaced by career diplomats. William Attwood departed Guinea in May 1963, just as the struggle in neighboring Portuguese Guinea was beginning to intensify. John Badeau departed the Cairo embassy in September 1964, after a long tenure. He and

[16] Telegram CAP 65102, White House to New Delhi, April 15, 1965, in DOS, *FRUS, 1964–1968, Vol. 25: South Asia* (Washington: GPO, 2000): 216–218.
[17] Interview, Chester Bowles, November 11, 1969, 42–44, OH, LBJL.
[18] Telegram 567–70, New Delhi to Paris, April 23, 1965, Inde 1956–1967, 228, MAE.
[19] Telegram 2175, DOS to New Delhi, April 17, 1965, NSF, RWKP, box 22, "Shastri Visit," LBJL.

Nasser had enjoyed a strong friendship, and his departure raised anxiety in the UAR, which feared an end to the policies of the Kennedy era.[20] Badeau's capable replacement, Lucius Battle, seemed to labor under his predecessor's shadow.[21] India welcomed an old friend when Chester Bowles resumed his previous post in 1963, replacing John Kenneth Galbraith, but his return could hardly be seen as triumphant after his 1961 demotion. Bowles's subsequent failure to persuade Johnson to offer New Delhi military aid undoubtedly affected Indian estimates of his efficacy – and of prevailing opinion in Washington.

These shifts attested to the changing tides of influence within the executive branch. The increasingly confrontational character of relations between Washington and the nonaligned states and the expanded influence of skeptics such as Rusk and Ball reduced the influence of advocates for engagement within Washington. Ball believed Africa unimportant to the Cold War and leaned toward the European stance on questions such as the Portuguese colonies and Rhodesia. Rusk backed his subordinate on these issues. Both men thought that the United States had overcommitted to India. Although they supported pursuing a policy of outreach to Egypt, they also backed Johnson's punitive aid policies toward Nasser in 1965. In sum, their approach to questions that pitted allies against nonaligned states meshed neatly with Johnson's.

Johnson's abandonment of presidential diplomacy came at a fateful time, as the Soviet Union, seeking to counter Chinese diplomatic efforts in the nonaligned world, was staging its own charm offensive. The overthrow of Khrushchev in October 1964 heightened the need for Moscow to engage nonaligned leaders directly. Khrushchev's successors, Aleksey Kosygin and Leonid Brezhnev, felt a clear imperative to demonstrate the continuity of Soviet outreach toward the postcolonial world by inviting a slew of nonaligned leaders to Moscow in 1965 and 1966, including Shastri, Nasser, Touré, and Keita. Their efforts were further motivated by escalating conflict within the nonaligned movement itself.

THE EVOLUTION OF NONALIGNMENT

While the administration's policies shifted, the nonaligned movement was itself riven by increasingly fractious debates about its own future. The movement remained divided between two rival organizing principles: Cold War nonalignment or Afro-Asian solidarity. India and Yugoslavia favored the former, which allowed Tito admission but kept Mao out. Indonesia, backed by China, enthusiastically advanced the latter, declaring that Africa and Asia needed to unite against the rising danger of neocolonialism.[22] At stake was the fundamental purpose of the group. A definition that accommodated China stood to render the nonaligned movement a pawn in the Sino-Soviet struggle, while

---

[20] See Memorandum, "Arab Reaction to Badeau's Resignation," William Miller to Komer, May 22, 1964, NSF, CF, box 158, "UAR, Vol. 1, Cables" folder, LBJL.

[21] Telegram 13, Cairo to Paris, January 12, 1965, Amerique 1964–1970, 624, MAE.

[22] See, for example, Telegram 723, Jakarta to Foreign Office, April 11, 1964, FO 371/178925, TNA.

jeopardizing the position of Peking's foes, particularly India and Yugoslavia. Chinese dominance stood, moreover, to alienate the United States – a concern for states dependent on U.S. aid.

These rival groups competed in early 1964, each seeking to preempt the other. In December 1963, the nonaligned states had reached a tentative agreement to stage a Belgrade-type conference; Indonesia, however leaped ahead early the following year with its own plans for "Bandung II," a second Afro-Asian conference.[23] By February it appeared that advocates of "Belgrade II" had pulled into the lead, although planning for the Afro-Asian conference proceeded.[24]

Washington seemed to watch the contest impassively. A January 1964 State Department circular observed: "This is a developing conflict over which the United States has relatively small influence, and in which any public position taken by the United States would probably be counterproductive."[25] Word of Cuban attendance at Belgrade II, however, triggered a reflexive response. The State Department sought to dissuade friendly Latin American countries from attending the conference, arguing that Cuban involvement cast "serious doubt on [the] real objectives" of the conference.[26] Washington clung to this position in spite of firm Indian suggestions that Latin American participation would serve to moderate the conference.[27]

Chester Bowles was the most prominent individual to object to the Department's policy, terming it a "tactical mistake" for the United States to try "to tell the unaligned nations what kind of meeting we think they should conduct." Such efforts would likely be "resented" and ineffectual. Moreover, the internal dynamics of the nonaligned states obligated the promoters of "Belgrade II" to make some concessions to their more radical peers. Bowles continued:

If the sponsors of the conference of unaligned nations are to hold their end up in competition with those who are pruning the second Bandung meeting, they will be forced to give their participants a little meat to chew. Otherwise Zhou En Lai, Sukarno, Nkrumah, et cetera [can] assert that they have lost their steam and no longer are representative of the peoples of Africa, Asia, etc.[28]

These points were well made – indeed, Washington had suffered in 1961 from reports that it opposed Brazilian attendance at the Belgrade Conference. Disregarding Bowles, Rusk's State Department chose to ignore recent history,

[23] Telegram 1807, Cairo to Washington, February 11, 1964, RG-59, CFPF: 1964–1966, box 1830, "POL 8, 1/1/64" folder, NA.
[24] Telegram 1301, Belgrade to Washington, February 14, 1964, RG-59, CFPF: 1964–1966, box 1830, "POL 8, 1/1/64" folder, NA.
[25] Airgram CA-6777, Washington to all diplomatic posts, January 9, 1964, ibid.
[26] Circular 1695, Washington to all diplomatic posts, March 14, 1964, RG-59, CFPF: 1964–1966, box 1830, "POL 8, 3/1/64" folder, NA.
[27] Telegram 2108, Cairo to Washington, March 16, 1964, RG-59, CFPF: 1964–1966, box 1830, "POL 8, 3/1/64" folder, NA; Telegram 1889, Washington to New Delhi, March 17, 1964, ibid.
[28] Telegram 2780, New Delhi to Washington, March 20, 1964, RG-59, CFPF: 1964–1966, box 1830, "POL 8, 3/1/64" folder, NA.

advancing a position that amounted to interference with the conference, meanwhile insisting that the United States supported the event. Well into the autumn,
it discouraged Latin American participation, particularly after Brazil, Chile,
Venezuela, Uruguay, and Bolivia signaled that they would attend.[29] In partial
deference to Washington, these friendly Latin American invitees sent observers
to Cairo, rather than full delegations. The other attendees could scarcely fail to
comprehend why the halls of Cairo bustled with observers from the Western
Hemisphere.

The White House's preoccupation with Latin American attendance came
unaccompanied by expressions of broader interest in the conference. This seeming indifference concerned several of the nonaligned powers. In a conversation
with the NSC's European specialist, a Yugoslav diplomat pointedly contrasted
Moscow's supportive attitude toward the conference with Washington's seeming "standoffishness," urging that the administration assume a more positive
stance. Tito's government continued to express concern about Washington's
seeming apathy, raising the issue again in September.[30] Although Johnson
dispatched a message to the conference, invoking the memory of Nehru and
Kennedy, the United States seemed largely disinterested in the event beyond the
peripheral question of Latin American attendance.

Once again, Washington's policy contrasted markedly with London's. Britain,
too, had cause to be wary of both conferences, but came to an altogether different decision on the question of whether to encourage friendly invitees to
attend Belgrade II. As the Foreign Office reasoned in a February telegram to its
NATO delegation:

> Although there is no positive advantage to the West in such a conference taking place we
> cannot stop it. If we opposed it or tried to dissuade our friends from attending we might
> increase the chances of the conference adopting an anti-Western posture. The conference
> will almost certainly take an anti-colonialist line. But we can hope that the more moderate
> neutrals will again be capable of standing up for themselves and resisting attempts to draw
> them into pro-Communist positions.[31]

London argued for supporting the nonaligned conference as an alternative to
Sukarno's planned "Bandung II," which stood to be exploited by the Chinese
and Indonesians.

Comparable ambivalence was felt by the Soviet Union and its allies. Fearful
of Chinese influence spreading via the "Bandung II" conference, the Kremlin

[29] Telegram 339, Washington to Rio de Janeiro, August 28, 1964, RG-59, CFPF: 1964–1966,
box 1829, "POL 8, 7/1/64" folder, NA; Telegram 184, Washington to Caracas, August 24,
1964, ibid.; Telegram 392, Washington to Rio de Janeiro, September 5, 1964, RG-59, CFPF:
1964–1966, box 1829, "POL 8, 9/1/64" folder, NA; Telegram 278, Montevideo to Washington,
September 10, 1964, ibid.; Telegram 285, La Paz to Washington, September 9, 1964, ibid.

[30] Memorandum, David Klein to Bundy, June 18, 1964, NSF, CF, box 232, "Yugoslavia, Memos
and Misc 1/64–4/66" folder, LBJL; Telegram 385, Washington to Belgrade, September 21, 1964,
RG-59, CFPF: 1964–1966, box 1829, "POL 8, 9/16/64" folder, NA.

[31] Telegram 436, Foreign Office to UK NATO Delegation, February 21, 1961, FO 371/178924,
TNA.

endorsed Belgrade II and criticized the Afro-Asian model – but not too emphatically.[32] As an East German diplomat in Indonesia observed:

For the socialist countries this problem ... is a complicated issue. On the one hand, it is hardly possible to stand against a second Afro-Asian conference; on the other hand it is presently undesirable that Chinese influence surely will be quite prominent at this conference.[33]

India and other moderate nonaligned states shared this unease. At the planning meeting for Bandung II in April, India had a novel card to play. Insisting that the Soviet Union was both an Asian and a European power, Indian delegates demanded that Moscow, too, receive an invitation for Bandung II. New Delhi also fought to seat Malaysia among the Afro-Asian invitees. These were, as a Foreign Office analysis put it, "brilliant spoiling tactics." Sukarno had neither cause nor desire to break with Moscow.[34]

The march to the parallel conferences revealed a widening schism within the nonaligned ranks. Indonesia's effort to redefine the group, its close partnership with China, and its campaign to exclude Malaysia fostered deep disquiet among its peers.[35] The Cairo meeting consequently witnessed a clash between two increasingly incompatible theses about nonalignment. Yugoslavia, India, and the UAR promoted the theme of coexistence, while declaring their support for the anticolonial struggle. Moderate delegations welcomed the relaxation of Cold War tensions and the prospect of Soviet-American détente. Indonesia and its allies rejected the notion that world tensions were ebbing; they posited that U.S. imperialism posed a dire threat to the nonaligned world. Was the Non-Aligned Movement to be a moral force between the blocs or an anticolonial alliance? A debate that had been heated at Belgrade became truly acrimonious at Cairo.[36]

Although policymakers in Washington dwelled on the lack of pro-American sentiment at Cairo, the conference laid bare the growing chasm within the movement. British and Malaysian observers savored Shastri's implied criticism of Sukarno, when he said, "We must continue to strive for peace, to resolve all differences through peaceful methods by conciliation, *as distinct from confrontation.*" India also proclaimed its opposition to any changes of

[32] Telegram 2617, Moscow to Washington, February 22, 1964, RG-59, CFPF: 1964–1966, box 1830, "POL 8, 1/1/64" folder, NA.

[33] Telegram 15/64, July 3, 1964, MfAA, A 16080, AA.

[34] Minutes, Document W7/79, April 21, 1964, FO 371/ TNA. Indeed, in 1964 even as Sukarno drew closer to China, East German diplomats reported that he also sought to broaden his ties to Moscow. See, for example, Telegram, DDR Generalkonsulat in Jakarta to MfAA, May 27, 1964, MfAA, A 16071, AA.

[35] Letter, D. K. Haskell to William Marsden, April 30, 1964, FO 371/178926, TNA; Telegram 2713, Australian Embassy to Canberra, January 10, 1964, FO 371/176471, TNA.

[36] G. H. Jansen, *Nonalignment and the Afro-Asian States* (New York: Praeger, 1966), 384–392; Telegram 1218, Cairo to Washington, October 8, 1964, RG-59, CFPF: 1964–1966, box 1829, "POL 8, 10/8/64" folder, NA.

borders "brought about by the open use of force as well as by quiet penetration of borders or subversion" – weeks after Sukarno had expanded his campaign against Malaysia to the Asian mainland. Tito issued his own veiled criticism of Sukarno when he called for the peaceful resolution of border disputes.[37]

Unmoved, Sukarno continued his campaign to redirect the nonaligned movement. One Tanzanian observer deemed him "the most impressive speaker" at the conference, communicating in "[a] language Africans could understand and which struck [a] responsive chord," even if most delegations were unswayed by his anti-Malaysian rhetoric. His adversaries had clearly lost ground, as African attendees voted against an Indian resolution opposing China's impending nuclear test. Indian delegates complained heartily afterward about newer African delegations, which had proved receptive to China's aggressive rhetoric.[38] Nevertheless, the final statement fell short of what Indonesia had sought. Although Cairo produced a coherent message against colonialism, including resolutions calling for diplomatic and economic boycotts of Portugal and South Africa, it did not resolve the growing tensions among the nonaligned nations.

The emphasis on anticolonialism and growing Chinese influence were sufficient, however, to alarm most of the NATO allies when they discussed the conference at the end of October. As one British diplomat remarked, nonalignment seemed less a matter of balancing between East and West than of balancing between China and the USSR. None of the allies disagreed with this verdict. Rusk seriously mused that it was time to call a conference of aligned states, as a counterpart to both Cairo and Bandung II (perhaps recalling Dulles's 1955 idea for a counter-Bandung conference).[39] The State Department termed Cairo a "half-step forward for Soviet foreign policy … and a challenge to [the] concept that says a bloc of non-aligned nations exists between East and West."[40] It was an ill omen for U.S.-nonaligned relations on the eve of Johnson's escalation of the Vietnam War.

THE NONALIGNED STATES AND VIETNAM

One emerging issue that had preoccupied the conference was the growing United States involvement in Southeast Asia. The Cairo Conference occurred

---

[37] Telegram 858, Cairo to Foreign Office, October 8, 1964, FO 371/176471, TNA; *Conference of Heads of State and Governments of Non-Aligned Countries* (Cairo: UAR Information Administration, 1964), 32–43, 103–109.

[38] Telegram 779, Dar es Salaam to Washington, October 15, 1964, RG-59, CFPF: 1964–1966, box 1829, "POL 8, 10/8/64" folder, NA; Ansar Harvani, an Indian delegate, complained that the "black Africans were impossible." See Airgram A-562, New Delhi to Washington, December 8, 1964, ibid., "POL 8, 12/1/64" folder, NA.

[39] TelCon, Rusk and Ball, October 18, 1964, RG-59, Records of Secretary of State Dean Rusk, Transcripts of Telephone Calls, box 51, "10/12/64–11/5/64" folder, NA.

[40] Airgram POLTO A-250, Paris to Washington, October 31, 1964, RG-59, CFPF: 1964–1966, box 1828, "POL 8, 10/21/64" folder, NA; Telegram 571, Washington to Paris, October 23, 1964, ibid.

two months after the Tonkin Gulf incident and Johnson's retaliatory bombing of North Vietnam, and the events weighed heavily on the minds of the attendees. Sukarno spoke of "outside imperialist forces" acting in Indochina, condemning the United States for establishing bases in Vietnam. His rival Tito decried "brutal foreign interference" in South Vietnam and Washington's "so-called reprisals" against North Vietnam. Others, however spoke more obliquely about the subject. Shastri merely alluded to the "long travail of Vietnam and Laos," while Nasser never mentioned the topic.[41]

Geopolitical concerns and ideological outlook primarily shaped nonaligned reactions to the Vietnam conflict. Sukarno apprehended neocolonialism at work in Vietnam, even as he mobilized against the same "Old Established Forces" in Malaysia. Yugoslavia perceived the need to affirm its credentials as a communist state by offering rhetorical support to North Vietnam, even if Hanoi remained cool toward Belgrade. Egypt, already experiencing a troubled relationship with the United States and embroiled in its own quagmire in Yemen, saw virtue in keeping a low profile on this issue. For African nonaligned states, Vietnam was a distant question; they were overwhelmingly transfixed by events in the Congo and the struggle against colonial and white minority regimes. India faced the most delicate dilemma: fearing both the possibilities of a Chinese political victory in Vietnam but also of a wider regional war pitting the United States against either or both communist powers.

The U.S. presence in Southeast Asia had long represented a potentially divisive issue but attracted little notice before the November 1963 coup in Saigon. The Egyptian press condemned the overthrow of Diem, blaming Washington. Ambassador Badeau found this a striking reversal of tone; following previously mild coverage in the Egyptian media, it seemed "a foretaste of what could happen" if relations worsened.[42] Around the same time, the Ghanaian state press began to cover Vietnam in detail, having previously paid the conflict little heed. Nkrumah spoke critically of the U.S.-backed "war against the people of Vietnam."[43] These represented rhetorical shots across the U.S. bow; they did not signify that either Ghana or Egypt yet regarded Vietnam as an issue of capital importance. When Nasser welcomed Khrushchev to Cairo in the spring of 1964, their joint communiqué addressed Cuba and Taiwan but omitted mention of Vietnam.[44]

The first major nonaligned state to devote serious attention to Washington's efforts in Southeast Asia was, unsurprisingly, Indonesia. Sukarno identified himself instinctively with Ho Chi Minh, a fellow Asian revolutionary of his generation. Angered by the effective cessation of U.S. aid and Johnson's

[41] *Cairo Conference*, 1–10, 26–30, 40, 103–110.

[42] Telegram 1089, Cairo to Washington, November 8, 1963, NSF, box 407, "Foreign Aid" folder, JFKL.

[43] Airgram A-297, Accra to Washington, December 5, 1963, RG-59, CFPF, box 3916, "Ghana-A" folder, NA.

[44] Soviet-UAR Communiqué Text, May 24, 1964, NSF, CF, box 158, "UAR, Vol. 1, Memos [1 of 2]" folder, LBJL.

support of Britain and Malaysia, and fearful of U.S. actions on the mainland, Sukarno made common cause with China and North Vietnam. In August 1964, Sukarno condemned Johnson's post-Tonkin Gulf bombing of North Vietnam, demanded a U.S. withdrawal from the region, and expressed solidarity with Hanoi. Such rhetoric suggested to LBJ that Indonesia had effectively allied with China and that its Malaysian campaign represented the southern half of a communist pincer attack on Southeast Asia.[45]

Other nonaligned states sought to mediate between the combatants and practiced greater rhetorical moderation. In April 1965, two months after the commencement of the Rolling Thunder bombing campaign against North Vietnam, a group of seventeen uncommitted states presented a plea to the combatants, their patrons, the UN, and the ICC. The signatories included Algeria, Ghana, Guinea, India, Egypt, and Yugoslavia: all the major nonaligned states, save Indonesia. Without offering condemnation, the appeal called for the cessation of violence in Vietnam and the immediate, unconditional commencement of negotiations.[46] The signatories clearly hoped that by avoiding direct criticism of the United States they might coax it toward the negotiating table.[47]

Johnson's advisors thought the proposal advantageous, not because it stood any real chance of halting hostilities in Vietnam, but rather because it reinforced their public stance that they were willing to negotiate unconditionally. Peking and Hanoi continued to require an end to U.S. bombing as a precondition to serious talks. Viewed alongside UN Secretary General U Thant's call for a temporary ceasefire, the nonaligned appeal struck Bundy as "more attractive."[48] Rusk, too, saw it as an auspicious development: if the communist nations rejected it, the United States would appear the more reasonable combatant; if they accepted it as a basis for negotiations, serious talks could commence.[49] Despite Saigon's misgivings, Rusk urged the South Vietnamese to treat it seriously.[50] Johnson reacted publicly to the seventeen-nation appeal. His major address at The Johns Hopkins University, in which he articulated his reasons for deploying troops to South Vietnam, expressed his willingness to negotiate with the North Vietnamese. At the same time, Johnson continued to approve escalatory measures for the war, including a continued heightening of the Rolling Thunder bombing campaign.[51]

[45] See Lyndon Baines Johnson, *The Vantage Point: Perspectives of the Presidency, 1963–1969* (New York: Holt, Rinehart and Winston, 1971), 606.

[46] See *DOSB*, Vol. LII, No. 1348, 611–612.

[47] See Memcon, Nicholas Andrews and Cvijeto Job, March 30, 1965, RG-59, DSCF: 1964–1966, box 1828, "POL 8, 3/1/65" folder, NA.

[48] Memorandum, Bundy, April 1, 1965, in DOS, *FRUS, 1964–1968, Vol. 2: Vietnam, January–June 1965* (Washington: GPO, 1996): 506–510.

[49] Memorandum for the Record, April 2, 1965, ibid.: 517–519.

[50] Telegram 2181, Rusk to Saigon, April 3, 1965, NSF, CF: Vietnam, box 195, "17 Nation Appeal" folder, LBJL.

[51] See NSAM 328, April 6, 1965, in *FRUS, 1964–1968*, 2: 537–539.

Among the nonaligned states, Johnson hoped for support from India, expecting that New Delhi's enmity with Peking would encourage Shastri to appreciate his efforts in Vietnam. In this, Johnson was to be personally disappointed. After the commencement of Rolling Thunder, Shastri wrote Johnson to express his concern that the raid risked the possibility of a wider war that might initially pit the United States against China and threaten to drag in the Soviet Union as well.[52] As one U.S. diplomat noted in October 1964, New Delhi was "terrified" at the prospect of Sino-Soviet rapprochement.[53] India publicly criticized U.S. bombing of North Vietnam as a violation of the Geneva Accords and as a dangerous escalation. China's entry into the nuclear club and its budding ties to Pakistan already fed feelings of insecurity in India. New Delhi had no desire to see Chinese influence in Southeast Asia expand, which might threaten its already vulnerable eastern flank.[54] Nor was Shastri eager to see the Vietnam War strengthen the Sino-Indonesian case for Afro-Asian solidarity and facilitate Pakistan's admission into the nonaligned caucus at India's expense.

By working to alleviate the conflict impartially, India sought to maintain its position among the nonaligned states and argue for the continued relevance of the Nehruvian vision of nonalignment as a mediating force between the blocs. Placing the onus on China for inflaming the conflict, moreover, would reinforce India's message that Mao's extremism was incompatible with nonalignment. At the same time, India needed to keep the United States from escalating the conflict and thereby galvanizing opinion behind the communist powers. In that endeavor, Shastri viewed the Soviet Union as a valuable ally: as with Laos, Moscow wished to avoid a Southeast Asian land war. India, moreover, depended on the Soviet Union for weaponry and support at the UN. Well before Johnson deployed ground troops to Vietnam, India seemed deeply reluctant to risk offending Moscow on this issue.[55]

Shastri hoped to foster détente on the Vietnam question with his planned spring 1965 visits to Washington and Moscow. Johnson's unilateral cancellation of the Washington visit, however, unsettled this plan, leaving Shastri baffled and frustrated.[56] As conflict with Pakistan flared over the Rann of Kutch and as he awaited approval from Washington over his request to purchase F-5 fighters, Shastri visited Moscow with a heightened dependence on Soviet

---

[52] Telegram 1633, Washington to New Delhi, February 11, 1965, NSF, CF, box 129, "India, Vol. 4, Cables [1 of 2]" folder, LBJL.

[53] Letter, Joseph Greene to Turner Cameron, October 17, 1964, RG-59, Bureau of Near East and South Asian Affairs (NE/SA), Office of the Country Director for India (OCDI), Records Relating to Indian Political Affairs: 1964–1966 (IPAR), box 6, "POL UNITED STATES" folder, NA.

[54] See Telegram 3136, New Delhi to Washington, NSF, CF, box 129, "India, Vol. 4, Cables [2 of 2]" folder, LBJL; also Mark A. Lawrence, "The Limits of Peacemaking: India and the Vietnam War, 1962–1968," in Lloyd C. Gardner and Ted Gittinger eds., *The Search for Peace in Vietnam, 1964–1968* (College Station: Texas A&M University Press, 2004), 244–246.

[55] Letter, British High Commission, New Delhi to Commonwealth Relations Office, March 26, 1964, RG-59, NE/SA, OCDI, IPAR: 1964–1966, box 6, "POL LAOS" folder, NA.

[56] Telegram 2920, New Delhi to Washington, April 15, 1965, NSF, CF, box 129, "India, Vol. 4, Cables [2 of 2]" folder, LBJL.

weaponry. Upon the visit's conclusion, Shastri and Kosygin issued a joint communiqué calling for a halt to the bombing – to the ire of the White House. Shastri had, however, argued with Kosygin about the wording of the statement, and succeeded in excising specific condemnations of the United States.[57]

At the same time, India advanced a plan for suspending hostilities in Vietnam. Authored by President Sarvepalli Radhakrishnan, the proposal called for an immediate ceasefire in Vietnam, with the interposition of an Afro-Asian peacekeeping force along the 17th parallel. Notably, it did not call for the immediate withdrawal of U.S. troops and avoided any accusations of U.S. imperialism. Johnson's advisors welcomed the proposal and instructed Bowles to convey their approval, as public praise of it would mark it for Chinese and North Vietnamese rejection.[58] Indeed, Hanoi ultimately deemed the plan unsatisfactory, since it stood to "consolidate" the division of Vietnam.[59] Nonetheless, Washington – to some discomfort in New Delhi – continued to endorse the plan long after India had abandoned it. It seemed evenhanded and likely better than other plans New Delhi could conceivably propose.[60]

Receipt of the Indian plan preceded, by a few days, a brief halt in the bombing campaign. The pause was undertaken with the dual purpose of improving the popularity of the United States among South Vietnam's Buddhist majority and as a tentative signal to Hanoi and Moscow of Washington's willingness to negotiate. Neither communist power responded favorably. With meager results in hand, Johnson felt justified in resuming the bombing a week after it had ceased.[61] His own thinking was moving reluctantly toward further escalation: the commitment of ground troops to the defense of South Vietnam. Days later he received a letter from Shastri requesting another cessation as a first step toward negotiation.[62] Johnson replied nearly two weeks later, declining Shastri's request and noting the "depressing lack of any response" to the earlier bombing pause.[63]

India had, to date, attempted to play a constructive role in the resolution of the conflict, seeking to reconcile its own fears of a regional or global conflagration with Johnson's concerns. New Delhi's language stood in sharp contrast to the increasingly pro-Hanoi stances of Indonesia and its ideological allies. Although the joint Moscow communiqué had disappointed Washington, it also reflected New Delhi's effort to claim the middle ground. The Johnson administration signaled its displeasure both verbally and in its handling of

[57] Joint Soviet-Indian Communiqué, May 19, 1965, RG-59, NE/SA, OCDI, IPAR: 1964–1966, box 11, "POL – USSR" folder, NA; Telegram 738–744, New Delhi to Paris, May 24, 1965, Inde 1956–1967, 228, MAE.

[58] Memorandum, James Thomson to Bundy, May 7, 1965, in *FRUS, 1964–1968*, 2: 620–621.

[59] Telegram 6612, Paris to Washington, May 20, 1965, in *FRUS, 1964–1968*, 2: 682–683.

[60] Letter, Leonard Unger to Joseph Greene, July 12, 1965, RG-59, NE/SA, OCDI, IPAR, box 11, "POL Vietnam, May-July 1965" folder, NA.

[61] Telegram Secto 29, Vienna to Washington, May 15, 1965, in *FRUS, 1964–1968*, 2: 664–665.

[62] Letter, Shastri to Johnson, May 23, 1965, in *FRUS, 1964–1968*, 25: 264–265.

[63] Letter, Johnson to Shastri, June 5, 1965, ibid.: 269–270.

Shastri's requests for additional food aid.[64] Such rejections left Shastri visibly upset when he entertained the French ambassador in early July.[65]

At the end of July, Shastri visited Tito in Belgrade, and the two leaders issued another communiqué calling for a bombing halt, making specific reference to the communist National Liberation Front (NLF).[66] Their lack of real rapport with North Vietnam or China posed a serious obstacle. As Shastri's advisor, L. K. Jha, explained, India's statements were conditioned by North Vietnamese obduracy.[67] Neither Belgrade nor New Delhi put much stock in their ability to reach Hanoi, believing that another nonaligned mediator with better standing in Peking might enjoy more success. Nasser and Nkrumah seemed the best available candidates.

Nkrumah was eager for the role, but his relations with the United States had been deteriorating for years. In March, he had compared Johnson's Congolese intervention to Vietnam, bringing an angry chastisement from U.S. Ambassador William Mahoney, who reported that the Ghanaian leader was irredeemably hostile to the United States. Nkrumah continued to link Vietnam and Africa's anticolonial wars; in May, he termed Johnson's intervention in the Dominican Republic "open and [undisguised] aggression by imperialism."[68] Still hoping to mediate between North Vietnam and the United States, Nkrumah announced his intention to visit Hanoi. He sought an invitation to meet LBJ, but Johnson demurred, saying he would wait to see if the visit to Hanoi bore fruit. Nkrumah never received an invitation and resented his treatment by the White House. His own rhetoric shifted further toward outright support of North Vietnam.[69]

Nasser, for his part, expressed occasional interest in playing a mediating role. After the foreign aid battles of 1964, he did not wish to anger Washington further by making common cause with North Vietnam. Nasser's understanding of the war was informed by his own embroilment in the Yemeni quagmire. He called for a halt to the bombing of North Vietnam because, as he explained to Assistant Secretary of State Phillips Talbot in April 1965, the war could not be won from the air. China, Nasser explained, was eager to discredit the Soviet thesis of peaceful coexistence and draw the United States into a ground war. Time and a bombing pause were needed to allow mediation to take hold and

---

[64] Memorandum, Komer, July 13, 1965, in *FRUS, 1964–1968*, 25: 300–303.

[65] Telegram 886, New Delhi to Paris, July 10, 1965, Inde 1956–1967, 228, MAE.

[66] Telegram 199, Belgrade to Washington, July 30, 1965, NSF, CF, box 232, "Yugoslavia, Vol. I" folder, LBJL.

[67] Telegram 201, New Delhi to Washington, August 3, 1965, NSF, CF, box 129, "India, Vol. 5, Cables [2 of 3]" folder, LBJL.

[68] Telegram 879, Accra to Washington, April 2, 1965, in *FRUS, 1964–1968*, 24: 444–446; Kwame Nkrumah, *Selected Speeches*, Vol. 4, ed. Samuel Obeng (Accra: Afram, 1997), 115–126.

[69] Memorandum, Richard Marsh, December 3, 1965, PREM 13/558, TNA; Telcon, Ball and William Bundy, August 5, 1965, LBJL, GWBP, box 4, "Ghana/Volta Project [7/31/64–4/2/66]" folder. See also W. Scott Thompson, *Ghana's Foreign Policy, 1957–1966: Diplomacy, Ideology and the New State* (Princeton: University Press, 1969), 409–412.

to strengthen Soviet influence in North Vietnam.[70] Nasser actively opposed Sino-Indonesian efforts to use the proposed Afro-Asian Conference to condemn the United States. Accordingly, in July 1965, the White House expressed its gratitude to Nasser for his moderation on this question.[71] Egypt was, therefore, not well positioned to mediate. Peking warned it away from a public mediation effort. During a visit to Cairo, Zhou Enlai roughly told Nasser to mind his own business when the Egyptian leader suggested mediation for the conflict. As Nasser later put it, "He broke my head for two and a half hours."[72] Thus chastened, Egypt kept its entreaties informal.[73]

India's position, meanwhile, was complicated by the eruption of the 1965 Indo-Pakistani war, which interrupted Shastri's mediation efforts and strained Indo-American relations. The deaths of thousands of Indian soldiers at the hands of U.S.-supplied Pakistani weaponry embittered the Indian political elite. It also focused New Delhi's attention on the conflict in Kashmir, the risk of Chinese intervention, and the subsequent peace talks with Pakistan at Tashkent. Defusing the war consumed the final months of Shastri's life and limited his ability to act with regard to Vietnam. China's threat to intervene on behalf of Pakistan aroused profound fears in India of a war on two fronts, fears that remained long after the guns fell silent.

Despite this, in the waning months of 1965, as they moved toward expanding food aid to New Delhi, Johnson and his advisors continued to expect that India would find common cause with them. "Few steps would better serve the national interest or please the President than greater Indian support on Vietnam," Komer wrote to Bowles in December 1965. "Shastri must be brought to realize that his pleas to us for help against Chicom pressure are greatly weakened by India's self-centered failure to acknowledge that we are fighting for the same purpose in Vietnam."[74] Komer sought a symbolic Indian contribution to the war effort, suggesting the deployment of an ambulance corps. He warned that India needed to show that it was "serious" about the Chinese in order to justify continued U.S. support.[75]

A new Indian approach to Vietnam did seem to be taking shape in Shastri's final months. The prospect of war with China and Pakistan made India quietly

[70] Telegram 3653, Cairo to Washington, April 18, 1965, NSF, CF, "UAR, Vol. 3, Cables [1 of 2]" folder, LBJL.

[71] Telegram 4520, Cairo to Washington, June 24, 1965, RG-59, CFPF: 1964–1966, box 2767, "UAR-US, 5/1/65" folder, NA; Telegram 200, Cairo to Washington, July 16, 1965, ibid.

[72] Intelligence Information Cable, May 12, 1966, NSF, CF, box 159–2, "UAR, Vol. 4, Cables [1 of 2]" folder, LBJL; Mohammed Heikal, *The Cairo Documents: The Inside Story of Nasser and his Relationship with World Leaders, Rebels, and Statesmen* (New York: Doubleday, 1973), 305–307.

[73] Telegram 455, Cairo to Washington, August 11, 1965, NSF, CF, box 159–2, "UAR, Vol. 4, Cables [1 of 2]" folder, LBJL.

[74] Letter, Komer to Bowles, December 16, 1965, RWKP, box 13, "Bowles 11/3/63–1965 [1 of 4]" folder, LBJL.

[75] Letter, Komer to John Lewis, January 4, 1966, NSF, RWKP, box 22, "Shastri Visit [1 of 3]" folder, LBJL.

reluctant to see Johnson withdraw from Vietnam. Bowles noted reduced Indian criticism of the war, motivated by heightened fears of China. Shastri spoke of this concern in conversation with Bowles and appeared to be considering a course friendlier to Washington. He agreed to send the requested ambulance corps, indicating that he would announce this upon meeting Johnson in Washington after his return from Tashkent.[76]

In December 1965, Johnson, heeding the entreaties of his advisors, agreed to another pause in the bombing of North Vietnam. International opinion was only one of the rationales for the halt. Johnson and his advisors sought to pressure Hanoi and Peking to accept negotiations for a permanent solution to Vietnam. With 184,000 U.S. soldiers now in South Vietnam, Johnson's advisors also felt compelled to show themselves willing to talk. The halt commenced on December 27, 1965, heralded by presidential messages to virtually every embassy in the world. Johnson's "peace offensive," as it was dubbed, was soon underway. Veteran diplomat Averell Harriman visited communist and nonaligned states, including India, Egypt, and Yugoslavia. Johnson and his advisors earnestly hoped that the suspension of bombing might facilitate negotiations, but prior experience made them pessimistic. The nonaligned states, having lobbied for a bombing pause, however, now had reason to believe their efforts had been successful and suggested making the halt permanent.[77]

To date, Vietnam had represented a divisive issue between the United States and the postcolonial world, but most nonaligned leaders had reacted with caution and moderation. Shastri and Nasser felt compelled to call for a halt to the bombing but also sought to play a constructive role in mediating the conflict. Chinese efforts to redefine the nonaligned movement fostered wariness toward Peking and also frustration with its intransigence on Vietnam. Still, no postcolonial leader could endorse the U.S. bombing campaign; as long as it continued, it represented a source of friction with Washington. The prospect of a long war in Southeast Asia caused some within the Johnson administration to fear the collapse of the U.S. position in the nonaligned world – and to ponder how this might be forestalled.

RHODESIA AND THE LIMITS OF ENGAGEMENT

The Vietnam War presented advocates of engagement with a profound dilemma. Most supported the war, viewing it as necessary for the containment of Chinese communism. Nonetheless, during 1965, policymakers working outside Southeast Asia noted the war's negative impact on U.S. prestige in the

---

[76] Telegram 1333, New Delhi to Washington, November 23, 1965, NSF, CF, box 130, "India, Vol. 6, Cables [1 of 3]" folder, LBJL; Telegram 1599, New Delhi to Washington, December 27, 1965, ibid.

[77] See, for example, Telegram 1829, Cairo to Washington, January 19, 1966, NSF, CF, box 159-2, "UAR, Vol. 4, Cables [1 of 2]" folder, LBJL.

nonaligned world. The administration's growing preoccupation with Vietnam made it less attentive to problems elsewhere. Perceiving a looming crisis in 1965, advocates of engagement sought to offset the damage of Vietnam, suffering a fateful defeat at the end of the year on the question of policy toward the question of Rhodesian independence.

Engagement's advocates reacted to the problem in different ways, dependent on their position and outlook. Bowles sought generous allotments of food aid to India, advising strenuously and unsuccessfully against linking it to foreign policy stances. Williams advocated a dramatic expansion of U.S. aid to Africa, only to have his proposal rejected by the NSC.[78] Cognizant of LBJ's reluctance to expand aid, Komer and Bundy jointly undermined Williams's plan, but Komer – stung by the rhetoric of the Cairo Conference – had his own ideas on how Vietnam's damage might be alleviated. His reaction to the growing strain of the war and the emerging Rhodesian crisis drew him closer to the liberal outlook than he had previously ventured.

Komer merits special attention here because he always was the most effective advocate of engagement in Washington, enjoying a degree of influence in 1965 that the liberals had long since lost. He had entangled himself in nearly four years' worth of policy arguments about the merits of seeking accord with the nonaligned states. Now, faced with the implications of Cairo and the sharpening rhetoric of the nonaligned states, Komer was obliged to defend his policy to an increasingly skeptical White House that was wholly preoccupied with Vietnam. He doggedly fought a war on two fronts, seeking to reverse the worsening trend in U.S.-nonaligned relations, while salvaging presidential support for engagement.

"We're in for a troubled time abroad – with few successes in the offing," Komer fretted in a July 1965 memorandum to Bundy. He stressed the need for "positive and constructive initiatives" to offset the strains placed by Vietnam and the concurrent U.S. intervention in the Dominican Republic. "Let's face the fact," he wrote,

that the things we have to do in Vietnam and elsewhere are a heavy burden for us to bear in the Afro-Asian world as well as Europe. While this heightened fear of the US course is in large measure the inevitable side-product of policies we are compelled to take (and offset by other factors), it's a real factor with which we have to deal. Clear and persuasive explanation helps, but not enough. So my sense would be to offset it by more forthcoming policies elsewhere – to compensate for, and divert attention from, and offset the impact of Vietnam and Santo Domingo by a set of measures deliberately calculated to show that we're still for peace and progress. A new gambit to rescue the UN, new disarmament initiatives, a stronger line on racism in Africa are possibilities.[79]

---

[78] Memorandum, Bundy to Johnson, June 21, 1965, NSF, MTP, box 3, "Vol. 11, 6/65" folder, LBJL; Thomas J. Noer, *"Soapy": A Biography of G. Mennen Williams* (Ann Arbor: University of Michigan Press, 2005), 287–291.

[79] Memorandum "A Rounded Foreign Policy Stance," Komer to Bundy, July 7, 1965, LBJL, NSF, Name File, box 6, "Robert W. Komer, Vol. I (2)" folder.

Komer studied African issues, seeking to replicate Kennedy's earlier successes on the continent. In June 1965, he advocated greater rhetorical support for African independence movements "even if it breaks some crockery."[80] This represented a fundamental shift in Komer's interests; during the Kennedy years he had paid little attention to sub-Saharan Africa, focusing instead on the largest nonaligned states. In his final year on the NSC, however, he shifted toward a liberal-like emphasis on symbolic issues. The travails of the Johnson years had not pushed him toward the idealism of Bowles, but they did drive him to think seriously about broader questions of prestige, about policy initiatives aimed broadly at nonaligned opinion.

The shifting bureaucratic balance within the Johnson administration now impeded advocates of engagement, however. Komer, fearful of being marginalized, complained with some regularity about LBJ failing to enunciate his views on particular issues – a problem accentuated by Johnson's disinterest in the nonaligned world. Johnson, moreover, favored Rusk and Ball. Komer and Bowles had little regard for these men; they had criticized Rusk for years. Komer angrily wrote to Bundy that "neither Rusk nor Ball ... have either particular competence or interest," in South Asian affairs. He fulminated, to Bundy's agreement, that Ball was "really quite dense on things African."[81]

Another crisis in sub-Saharan Africa loomed by the summer, as the British colony of Southern Rhodesia moved closer to declaring its independence from London. Unlike Britain's other African colonies, Rhodesia was governed by a white-minority government that refused to extend voting rights to the black majority. To no avail, Prime Minister Harold Wilson pressed the Rhodesian government, led by Ian Smith, to adopt a majority-rule system. By the autumn Rhodesia signaled that it would issue a unilateral declaration of independence (UDI). Rhodesian independence without majority rule stood to inflame African opinion in the wake of Stanleyville. Worsening matters, Rhodesia controlled the only major rail lines into neighboring Zambia; with the UDI, Zambia would be reduced to utter dependence on Smith's government. Johnson's advisors debated the relative gravity of the situation: Ball maintained that a UDI did not pose a major crisis; Komer and Williams angrily argued otherwise.[82]

Ball prevailed. Believing African issues to be of generally minor importance and suspecting that Britain sought to shift much of the Rhodesian burden onto U.S. shoulders, he argued successfully against a presidential warning to Smith.[83] Ball opposed taking strong positions where any of the white redoubts were concerned and did not wish to set a Rhodesian precedent that could be applied against South Africa or the Portuguese empire. With Rusk's approval,

[80] Memorandum, Komer to Johnson, June 19, 1965, in DOS, *FRUS, 1964–1968, Vol. 24: Africa* (Washington: GPO, 1999): 306–307.

[81] Memorandum, Komer to Bundy, October 5, 1965, NSF, Name File, box 6, "Robert Komer, Vol. 2 [3 of 3]" folder, LBJL; Memorandum, Komer to Bundy, October 13, 1965, ibid.

[82] Memorandum, Komer to Bundy, October 29, 1965, ibid.

[83] Carl P. Watts, "The United States, Britain, and the Problem of Rhodesian Independence, 1964–1965," *Diplomatic History* Vol. 30, No. 3 (June 2006), 456–459.

Ball managed the U.S. reaction to the UDI, appointing his friend William P. Rogers to head a Rhodesia interagency task force.[84]

Rhodesia declared independence on November 11, while Komer continued to lobby for a more aggressive reaction. He argued emphatically to Johnson that U.S. policy needed to address the issues of greatest importance to the Africans. "Vietnam, South Asia, or Berlin are far away," he argued, "but these African issues are seen by Africans as an intimate part of their own struggle for independence of colonialism." The inevitability of independence and majority rule throughout the continent obliged Washington to position itself preemptively "on the winning side."[85] Komer worried that sanctions would not suffice, opining to Bundy that "LBJ simply hasn't been told the likely dimensions of this mess." While recognizing the British predicament, he nevertheless feared that African anger would soon coalesce against the United States. This called for pressuring London; as Komer put it: "The harder we push the Brits, the better we'll be."[86]

The already-strained Anglo-American alliance, however, added a countervailing influence that dictated against acting forcefully on Rhodesia. Britain opposed the UDI but was unprepared to go beyond a limited course of economic sanctions. Even though London supported UN sanctions, it declined to apply full pressure to South Africa, which had opened its ports to Rhodesia-bound goods. U.S. policy remained reactive, treating Rhodesia as Britain's problem. Ball and his colleagues rejected London's requests for stringent sanctions on Rhodesia or support for British efforts to defend Zambia. While Wilson faced severe domestic criticism of his Rhodesia policy, Johnson's failure to support stronger countermeasures limited London's already narrow options. The Anglo-American response to the UDI, emerging in December 1965 and the early months of 1966, was thus limited to economic sanctions on Rhodesia. Although these restrictions lasted until the end of the Johnson administration, they proved porous. South Africa and Portugal shipped key supplies from their ports into the renegade colony. Somewhat more successful was a costly Anglo-American airlift of oil into landlocked Zambia.[87]

Sanctions on Rhodesia were not sufficient to meet African expectations. In a December letter to Johnson, Nyerere praised steps the president had

---

[84] See Thomas J. Noer, *Cold War and Black Liberation: The United States and White Rule in Africa, 1948–1968* (Columbia: University of Missouri Press, 1985), 197–202, and Anthony Lake, *The "Tar Baby" Option: American Policy Toward Southern Rhodesia* (New York: Columbia University Press, 1976), 82–85. Andrew DeRoche dissents, in Black, White, and Chrome: The United States and Zimbabwe, 1953–1998 (Trenton, NJ: Africa World Press, 2001), 120–123. At the time, however, the Rogers appointment elicited dismay from the NSC's Ulric Haynes Jr., an advocate of strong action against UDI. See Memorandum, Haynes to Komer, December 2, 1965, NSF, UHP, box 1, "Chrono file [1 of 3]" folder, LBJL.

[85] Memorandum, Komer and Bundy to Johnson, November 23, 1965, in *FRUS, 1964–1968*, 24: 313–314.

[86] Memorandum, Komer to Bundy, December 20, 1965, in *FRUS, 1964–1968*, 24: 874n.

[87] Noer, *Cold War and Black Liberation*, 202–213; Lake, *The "Tar Baby" Option*, 82–92.

taken to bolster the British position but called for the United States to support UN action against Rhodesia. Nyerere explained: "Africa simply cannot afford to wait for the slow attrition of power from Mr. Smith's government. The immediate dangers to us all – but especially to Zambia – are too great for this procedure."[88] An embassy cable from Ethiopia, one of Washington's most steadfast friends in Africa and within the nonaligned caucus, reinforced this point. Ethiopia reportedly had not "the slightest confidence in the success of economic sanctions." Britain's halfway measure would inevitably put the United States in a "ruinous position." To this, the ambassador in Ethiopia, Edward Korry, added:

> I confess that, in the light of our record of the past decade from Suez through the Congo, Dominican Republic and Vietnam, it is difficult to explain to any intelligent African why the USG is aligning itself with the British principle that the use of maximum pressures would be immoral or ineffective.[89]

To a degree, Johnson's support for British sanctions limited the damage that the UDI inflicted upon Washington's standing in Africa. At the least, the administration had adopted a stance sympathetic to the African position – and more so than its position on continuing wars in Portuguese Africa. Johnson's commitment to aiding Zambia further bolstered his credibility.

Komer, however, had seen Rhodesia and the other white redoubts not merely as vexing problems in their own right, but as opportunities for the United States to build up much needed political credit while it escalated the war in Vietnam. Johnson's reaction to Rhodesia limited the damage done by this issue, but was insufficient to achieve Komer's original goal. Additionally, it confirmed Ball's influence on African questions, precluding further action against the white redoubts. Over time the perseverance of the Smith regime underscored the inefficacy of sanctions, reinforcing the criticisms made by African leaders such as Nyerere. The problem of Rhodesia was left to fester – as advocates of engagement feared it might – with divisive consequences for the United States and Africa into the 1970s.

Although sanctions provided some cause for encouragement, Rhodesia marked a decisive defeat for advocates of engagement. Elsewhere, however, another series of events gave policymakers hope that their position in the Third World was in fact improving. Three pivotal changes of government within the nonaligned caucus fundamentally altered the tenor of that organization's politics, spelling the end of China's diplomatic advance and offering Washington fundamental reassurance of its standing in the postcolonial world – even as the Vietnam War escalated.

---

[88] Letter, Nyerere to Johnson, Undated (December 1965), NSF, Name File, box 6 "Robert Komer, Vol. 2 [2 of 2]" folder, LBJL.

[89] Telegram 792, Addis Ababa to Washington, December 21, 1965, NSF, Name File, box 6, "Robert Komer, Vol. 2 [2 of 2]" folder, LBJL. Komer passed this telegram to Johnson.

"FORTUITOUS WINDFALLS": A SEASON OF COUPS

On the morning of June 19, 1965, a military coup d'etat in Algeria overthrew Prime Minister Ahmed Ben Bella, the country's leader since independence. The coup, which brought Colonel Houari Boumedienne to power, had widespread ramifications for the nonaligned states. In the near term, Algeria's political uncertainty spelled further difficulties for Sukarno's and Mao's ill-starred Afro-Asian conference. Although planning had been underway since 1964, with Algiers set to host the event, logistical difficulties and political turmoil forced repeated delays on the organizers.[90]

The coup occurred five days before a scheduled preparatory meeting for the conference; continued unrest in Algiers convinced a number of attendees to favor another postponement, delaying the planning meeting until the autumn. Although Ben Bella's successors also supported the conference, they faced considerable suspicion among their nonaligned peers, compounding the gathering unease about the conference. Mao's government unwittingly did further damage to Bandung II by extending hasty recognition to the Boumedienne government, angering a number of African states. Ben Bella's fall, however, had another significance unknown that June. It ushered in a new period of political instability within the nonaligned movement, bringing fundamental changes to its leadership.

Indonesia was the next country to witness a violent change of government, although its ordeal far exceeded Algeria's. The bloodletting commenced on the morning of October 1, when a group of communist Indonesian air force officers attempted to assassinate a number of conservative army generals. Although six generals were killed, Major General Suharto, commander of the army's reserves, and Defense Minister Abdul Haris Nasution survived. Suharto mobilized his troops to combat the rebels. After consolidating control of Jakarta, Suharto initiated a nationwide purge of communists, implemented by the army and paramilitary organizations. The campaign effectively destroyed the PKI; it was also indiscriminate and shockingly brutal. Hundreds of thousands of Indonesians died at the vengeful hands of the army and its allies; the death toll remains unknown to this day, although estimates have reached half a million.[91]

Although the United States and Britain have been accused of directly plotting the army coup, documents from early October paint a somewhat different picture.[92] Anglo-American intelligence operations against Sukarno had been

[90] William B. Quandt, *Revolution and Political Leadership: Algeria, 1954–1968* (Cambridge, MA: MIT Press), 236–243.

[91] Adrian Vickers, *A History of Modern Indonesia* (New York: Cambridge University Press, 2005), 156–160.

[92] On this see David Easter, "'Keep the Indonesian Pot Boiling': Western Covert Intervention in Indonesia, October 1965–March 1966," *Cold War History*, Vol. 5, No. 1 (February 2005), 55–73; Bradley R. Simpson, *Economists with Guns: Authoritarian Development and U.S.-Indonesian Relations, 1960–1968* (Stanford: Stanford University Press, 2008), 171–194.

underway since 1964, but the events of the autumn caught U.S. observers by surprise. For critical days both Washington and the Jakarta embassy remained unclear about what was transpiring. Once it became apparent that Suharto meant to exterminate the PKI, the United States rushed to assist him. Washington offered material assistance to the army, including the supply of radios for secure communication and to broadcast anti-PKI messages. With London's approval, the U.S. embassy also offered Suharto the key assurance that Britain would refrain from exploiting the situation, allowing the army freedom to act. Finally, the embassy supplied the army with lists of PKI members.[93]

Sukarno remained in office, but the army's counter-coup effectively curtailed his authority. Having decimated the PKI, Suharto and Nasution began a political campaign against Sukarno's foreign minister and key ally, Subandrio. The eclipse of Sukarno's authority at home augured the end of his leadership among the nonaligned states as well. Though the balance between Sukarno and Suharto remained delicate into 1966, the PKI's destruction was celebrated by the Johnson administration, which saw little need to inquire about the bloodshed still unfolding in Indonesia. The largest country in Southeast Asia was now moving inexorably away from Chinese influence, destroying Mao's hopes of reorienting the nonaligned movement.

At the end of October, the preparatory meeting for the Algiers Conference finally cancelled the proposed Afro-Asian summit. The assembled delegations in Algiers jointly declared the present time "not congenial" for the conference, deciding instead to postpone it to an unspecified later date. In a clear victory for the supporters of the Belgrade concept, a majority of attendees – including Western-allied states such as Japan, Iran, and Turkey – supported Soviet and Malaysian participation at any future conference. India's improbable tactic had succeeded. Facing defeat on that question and losing the support of other delegations, Peking petitioned for a postponement. Contemplating a meeting riven by Sino-Soviet, Sino-Indian, and Indo-Pakistani acrimony, a majority of delegations decided to put Bandung II to sleep.[94]

The indefinite delay of the Algiers conference elicited unqualified relief in Washington. "This, of course, is the best possible outcome from our point of view," Komer wrote to Johnson:

Not only does it postpone a confab made to order for anti-US voices, but the dickering over postponement got a lot of the moderates thoroughly irritated at the Chicoms. The best tack behind-scenes is to commiserate with the moderate Afro-Asians on how the Chicoms wrecked their conference.[95]

---

[93] See, for example, Telephone Transcript, Ball and McNamara, October 1, 1965, in DOS, *FRUS, 1964–1968, Vol. 26: Indonesia; Malaysia-Singapore; Philippines* (Washington: GPO, 2001): 301–302. On CIA involvement, see Simpson, *Economists with Guns*, 140–206.

[94] Telegram 980, Algiers to Washington, November 1, 1965, NSF, CF, box 79, "Algeria, Vol. 2, Cables" folder, LBJL; Telegram 889, Algiers to Washington, October 26, 1965, ibid.; Jansen, *Nonalignment*, 393–400.

[95] Memorandum, Komer to Johnson, November 1, 1965, NSF, UHP, box 1, "Chrono., 3/1/65–6/15/66 II" folder, LBJL.

Reports throughout the Third World, meanwhile, indicated that China had overplayed its hand. Zhou Enlai had deemed Africa ripe for revolution in 1965, winning China little favor with most governments on the continent. Williams reported, at the end of an autumn trip, that African leaders were newly focused on the Chinese threat and that moderates enjoyed a strengthened position.[96] Angered by Chinese recognition of the Boumedienne government, Nyerere ceased his support of the Congolese rebels and rescinded permission granted to China to transport arms across his territory.[97] Similarly Nasser was unnerved by Zhou Enlai's disinterest in negotiations over Vietnam and lack of concern that the war could escalate. As the PRC descended into the throes of the Cultural Revolution the following year, its international influence waned further.[98]

Ghana witnessed the final coup on February 24, 1966. The Ghanaian armed forces, led by General Joseph Ankrah, overthrew Nkrumah while the president was en route to China. Of the three coups, this clearly surprised Washington the least. CIA contacts with Nkrumah's foes had been going on since 1961, and Ankrah had long been identified as a suitable replacement for Nkrumah.[99] Citing Nkrumah's ouster alongside the Indonesian coup, Komer gleefully deemed it, "another example of a fortuitous windfall," replacing a "strongly pro-Communist" government with one that "is almost pathetically pro-Western."[100] Washington rushed to aid the Ankrah regime, hurriedly offering a PL-480 agreement and hundreds of tons of emergency food. Nkrumah sought refuge in Guinea, where he spent his remaining years as a guest of Touré.[101]

After the overthrow of pro-Chinese governments in Indonesia, Algeria, and Ghana, the Johnson administration felt inclined to declare victory in the battle for influence in the nonaligned world. Against the evidence, it sought to explain the Indonesian coup – which stemmed almost entirely from local factors – as a consequence of its commitment to Vietnam.[102] To a skeptical Indira Gandhi, Rusk characterized China as having failed in "Indonesia, Africa, and at Algiers."[103] Komer diagnosed the coups in Ghana and Algeria as signaling "the beginning of the second phase of modern African history," the acts of "a dynamic educated element" of African societies "getting fed up with the ineptitude or posturing of the original leaders."[104] This current of optimism

96   Memorandum, Haynes to Johnson, November 1, 1965, NSF, UHP, box 1, ibid.
97   Telegram 145, Dar es Salaam to Washington, July 27, 1965, DSCF, CFPF, 1964–1966, box 2688, "POL 1, Gen'l Policy Background" folder, NA.
98   See Odd Arne Westad, *The Global Cold War: Third World Interventions and the Making of Our Times* (New York: Cambridge University Press, 2006), 160–165.
99   See Memorandum, John McCone, February 11, 1964, in *FRUS, 1964–1968*, 24: 412.
100 Memorandum, Komer to Johnson, March 12, 1966, in *FRUS, 1964–1968*, 26: 419.
101 On the Ghanaian coup, see David Rooney, *Kwame Nkrumah: The Political Kingdom in the Third World* (London: Tauris, 1988), 237–257.
102 See McMahon, *The Limits of Empire*, 123–124; Simpson, *Economists with Guns*, 240–242.
103 Memcon, Rusk and Gandhi, March 29, 1966, in *FRUS, 1964–1968*, 25: 598–603.
104 Memorandum, Komer to Johnson, March 10, 1966, in *FRUS, 1964–1968*, 24: 322–323.

reinforced the sense of policymakers that they had successfully met the Chinese challenge – and should continue to do so in Vietnam.

Simultaneously in Washington, fateful personnel changes further reduced the emphasis accorded to engagement. An exhausted McGeorge Bundy left the White House staff at the end of February 1966 to become president of the Ford Foundation. For a brief interregnum, Komer served as the acting national security advisor. Bundy would have preferred to hand the reins to his deputy permanently, but Johnson had other plans. He appointed Komer to serve as his special assistant, charged with managing civilian pacification programs in South Vietnam. Walt Rostow, meanwhile, assumed Bundy's former office.

Komer often referred to himself as a "pollyanna," but in this regard he held no candle to Rostow. The transition from Bundy to Rostow was interpreted in Washington as a sign that Johnson sought a special assistant more support-ive of his policies. Komer's bureaucratic instincts had long led him to bend his recommendations to suit the prevailing winds in the Johnson White House, but he also could not help but prod the president on particular issues, often to the point of exasperation. Johnson liked and trusted Komer, but remarks he made about the appointment indicated clearly that the feisty staffer was not his first choice to head Bundy's old shop.[105]

With Komer's departure from the NSC staff – occurring not long after G. Mennen Williams left the Department of State – the policy of engagement lost its most dogged, effective advocate. The disruption of the nonaligned caucus had, moreover, weakened the rationale for broadly approaching these states. After the Algiers debacle and amid the coups of 1965 and 1966, the future of the nonaligned movement seemed murky at best.

Rostow supported engagement through the Kennedy years and was the administration's most passionate advocate of development aid. By 1966, how-ever, his primary concern was the prosecution of the Vietnam War. The war increasingly limited the time and resources available for other endeavors. Rostow believed unquestioningly that Vietnam was a tough but winnable war and a necessary price to pay for progress elsewhere in the world. He was the administration's most fervent supporter of the bombing campaign. He also lacked Komer's capacity to perceive the war as a diplomatic problem for the United States.

In June 1966, Rostow posited that the world was witnessing "the decline of extremists, Communist or otherwise," specifying Castro, Nkrumah, Ben Bella, Sukarno, and Mao. On the rise were "moderates willing to damp down ancient quarrels and live with their neighbors" and a trend toward growing economic progress in Africa, Asia, and Latin America. While allowing that these were

---

[105] Johnson reportedly said of the appointment "I'm getting Walt Rostow as my intellectual. He's not your intellectual. He's not Bundy's intellectual.... He's going to be my goddamn intellec-tual and I'm going to have him by the short hairs." Komer, on the other hand, could be seen as a Bundy protege. See Kai Bird, *The Color of Truth: McGeorge Bundy and William Bundy: Brothers in Arms* (New York: Simon & Schuster, 1998), 348–349; David Milne, *America's Rasputin: Walt Rostow and the Vietnam War* (New York: Hill and Wang, 2008), 161–168.

reversible trends, and that significant problems remained, Rostow posited that the Vietnam War represented "the dam behind which a dramatic turn for the better is taking place in Asia and the world." North Vietnam, trying "in a rather old-fashioned way ... [to] pick up other folks' real estate," was running against "the grain of history."[106] Triumphalism in Vietnam was thus intermeshed with optimism toward events in the Third World, with one acting as a bulwark for the other. By confronting China in Southeast Asia, the United States was emboldening others to reject Peking – as demonstrated by the coups. The Johnson administration felt little cause to reconsider either its policies outside of Vietnam or the effect of the conflict on the U.S. image abroad.

Rostow and his peers drew false comfort from events in the nonaligned world. The coups alarmed other nonaligned leaders, seemingly validating Sukarno and Nkrumah's warnings about neo-colonialism, and KGB efforts to spread reports of CIA-sponsored coup plots.[107] The U.S.-welcomed ousters of three pro-Chinese governments cast Johnson's war in a sinister light, making it seem part of a global campaign against Third World nationalism. Nasser became increasingly fearful of CIA activity against him, and regarded the coup in Ghana as part of an "imperialist plan" against Africa.[108] Touré was angered by U.S. support of the new Ghanaian government. Far from ushering in a new era of cooperation, the season of coups and the resumed bombing of North Vietnam augured a new period of suspicion and confrontation.

TOWARD THE BREACH: VIETNAM AND THE NONALIGNED WORLD, 1966–1967

On January 31, 1966, Johnson announced the resumption of the bombing of North Vietnam. The end of the pause and of Johnson's peace offensive signaled an intensification of both the Vietnam War and the nonaligned world's reaction to it. With his focus diverted overwhelmingly to Vietnam, LBJ became increasingly resentful of nonaligned criticism – and prone to punishing it through his aid policy. The nonaligned states, made wary by the political instability in their ranks, responded angrily, setting the stage for an unprecedented level of antagonism as the war escalated.

Johnson chose to resume bombing after the apparent failure of his peace offensive. He had dispatched Harriman to Cairo, Belgrade, and New Delhi, as well as to Budapest and Warsaw. In New Delhi, Shastri approved of Johnson's

---

[106] Memorandum, Rostow to White House Staff, June 27, 1966, White House Central File, container 20, FG 11–8–1 Rostow, LBJL.

[107] See Christopher Andrew and Vasili Mitrokhin, *The World Was Going Our Way: The KGB and the Battle for the Third World* (New York: Basic Books, 2005), 314–318, 434–438. Mitrokhin and Andrew identify such efforts in the case of India, Guinea, and Ghana. One suspects there were others.

[108] Robert Stephens, *Nasser: A Political Biography* (New York: Simon & Schuster, 1971), 459–465; Kwame Nkrumah, *Kwame Nkrumah: The Conakry Years*, ed. June Milne (Atlantic Highlands, NJ: Panaf, 1990), 21.

policies but indicated that he was unable to mediate, as India lacked influence in Hanoi. Tito welcomed the pause, but urged prolonging it, so as to give Hanoi time to revise its stance.[109] Harriman's conversation in Cairo proved moderately more fruitful. Nasser recommended that the United States permanently halt the bombing, delay sending any further reinforcements to South Vietnam, and also prepare itself for a long wait while Egypt and other nonaligned countries pressed China to negotiate. Above all, Nasser stressed the need for patience.[110]

Patience, however, was something the Johnson administration had lost. Its two major bombing pauses had only elicited more invective from North Vietnam. Domestic hawks accused Johnson of waging the war half-heartedly; reports from his military advisors indicated that North Vietnam had militarily exploited the lull. When LBJ discussed resuming the bombing with his advisors on January 22, all except Ball argued strongly for a resumption. The nonaligned states and Warsaw Pact intermediaries had both pleaded for additional time to wear down the North Vietnamese. Arthur Goldberg, the U.S. representative to the UN, observed that the nonaligned states wanted "more, then more."[111] In Rusk's words, "thoroughly disillusioned" by the meager fruits of the peace offensive, Johnson felt he had no more to give to would-be mediators.[112] After January, the bombing intensified, as Johnson extended the campaign to include targets deep within North Vietnam. In June, the president authorized the bombing of petroleum storage facilities in the vicinity of Hanoi and Haiphong, bringing the war within earshot of the North's main population centers. This came as he continued to deploy U.S. soldiers to the South.[113]

The resumption signaled an escalation of the war. Predictably, it brought expressions of regret and criticism from the nonaligned states. Egypt received the news with "great regret and deep concern," terming it "a serious relapse."[114] Indian officials expressed similar dismay, prompting Vice President Hubert Humphrey to deliver a stern message to Indira Gandhi, who had come to power after Shastri's sudden death, in a subsequent meeting.[115] Tito called the decision a mistake, predicting that it would lower U.S. prestige in the world. His

[109] Telegram, Rusk to White House, January 1, 1966, NSF, Country File: Vietnam, box 148, "Pinta Vol. 2–1" folder, LBJL.

[110] Airgram 567, Cairo to Washington, January 5, 1966, NSF, RWKP, box 51, "UAR, 1965-March 1966 [1 of 3]" folder, LBJL. See also, Heikal, *The Cairo Documents*, 307–309.

[111] Notes of Meeting, January 22, 1966, in DOS, *FRUS, 1964–1968, Vol. 4: Vietnam, 1966* (Washington: GPO, 1996): 105–112.

[112] Dean Rusk, *As I Saw It* (New York: W. W. Norton, 1991), 466; Robert D. Schulzinger, *A Time for War: The United States and Vietnam, 1941–1975* (New York: Oxford University Press, 1997), 202–207.

[113] George C. Herring, *America's Longest War: The United States and Vietnam, 1950–1975* (New York: Knopf, 1979), 145–153, 165–167.

[114] Telegram 1940, Cairo to Washington, February 2, 1966, NSF, CF, box 159–2, "UAR, Vol. 4, Cables [1 of 2]" folder, LBJL.

[115] Telegram 490, Wellington to Washington, February 20, 1966, in *FRUS, 1964–1968*, 25: 575–578.

foreign minister had previously described the war as the most serious threat to peace.[116]

Embittered toward the Johnson administration, Nasser moved toward open criticism of the United States. In February 1966, the State Department reported that Egypt's UN delegation had been lobbying on behalf of the Soviet Union on a Vietnam-related Security Council vote.[117] In the spring, Nasser assented to the opening of an NLF office in Cairo.[118] While he hosted Soviet Premier Kosygin, Nasser and his guest jointly denounced the "horrifying aggression" of the United States in Vietnam.[119] As the Yemen war intensified, so, too, did Nasser's rhetoric on Vietnam. The Egyptian leader's opposition to the war was angrily regarded in Washington as evidence that he was abandoning nonalignment in favor of a pro-Soviet foreign policy. This shift played a significant role in Johnson's spring 1966 decision to deny Egypt additional PL-480 food aid. Deprived of grain and vexed by the shipment of U.S.-made weaponry to Israel, Nasser drew closer to the Soviet Union.

Like her predecessor Shastri, Indian Prime Minister Indira Gandhi was torn between maintaining her rapport with the United States and encouraging North Vietnam to accept negotiations and turn away from its Chinese ally. Unlike Shastri, Gandhi was able to meet Johnson in Washington in April 1966; the meeting, however, mostly dealt with the question of food aid.[120] Johnson hoped to explain his position on Vietnam, but made no direct requests of her. In July, however, Gandhi visited Moscow and signed a joint communiqué with her hosts calling for an end to the bombing of North Vietnam and denouncing – albeit vaguely – "imperialistic powers." As Bowles later wrote, the communiqué "demolished much of the goodwill in Washington" Gandhi had reaped by her earlier visit.[121]

The 1965 war and the failure of the United States to supply India with substantial amounts of modern weaponry turned New Delhi toward Moscow. "India has become dependent on the USSR for the bulk of its modern weapons," reported the CIA in October 1966.[122] The Indian prime minister had additional reason to take a stronger line on Vietnam. She faced a turbulent

[116] Telegram 1070, Belgrade to Washington, January 22, 1966, NSF, CF, box 232, "Yugoslavia, Vol. I, Cables" folder, LBJL; Memorandum, Bromley Smith to Johnson, February 1, 1966, NSF, CF, box 232, "Yugoslavia, Vol. I, Memos" folder, LBJL.

[117] Telegram 4280, Washington to Cairo, February 1, 1966, NSF, CF, box 159-2, "UAR, Vol. 4, Cables [2 of 2]" folder, LBJL.

[118] Telegram 2948, Cairo to Washington, May 13, 1966, NSF, CF, box 159-2, "UAR, Vol. 4, Cables [1 of 2]" folder, LBJL.

[119] Hedrick Smith, "50,000 Cheer Premier – He Joins Nasser in Denouncing U.S.," NYT, May 11, 1966, 1.

[120] Memorandum, "Final Notes on Gandhi Visit", Komer to Johnson, March 27, 1966, in FRUS, 1964–1968, 25: 593–595.

[121] Chester Bowles, *Promises to Keep: My Years in Public Life* (New York: Harper & Row, 1971), 515.

[122] Intelligence Report, "Soviet Military Aid to India," October 1966, NSF, CF, box 131, "India, Vol. 8, Memos & Misc [2 of 2]" folder, LBJL.

political environment, as the Indian left routinely accused her of mortgaging India's sovereignty to procure American food aid. Defying Washington on Vietnam offered an easy rejoinder to such challenges. At the same time, however, she also reported her willingness to help the belligerents initiate negotiations. Through the Johnson years, the Indian government sometimes acted as an informal conduit of information from North Vietnam, occasionally conveying messages from Hanoi.[123]

In public statements, however, India and its peers felt increasingly obliged to criticize the United States, particularly after Johnson expanded the bombing. An October 1966 summit between Tito, Nasser, and Gandhi in New Delhi revealed the full breadth of the gulf separating Washington from the nonaligned world. Their tripartite communiqué not only called for a bombing halt, but also recommended "the withdrawal of all foreign forces" and the participation of the NLF in any peace negotiations. Venting their frustration at the political strings tied to U.S. aid, the three leaders, while condemning "colonialism and neocolonialism in all its forms," also decried "the use of economic and financial assistance as an instrument of pressure."[124]

Washington was unimpressed. The State Department's analysis of the tripartite summit dismissed the event as a rote, unenthusiastic repetition of earlier nonaligned meetings. In his analysis of the summit, sent to Rusk, Thomas Hughes of the State Department's Bureau of Intelligence and Research observed:

The very blandness of this affair ... confirms the disarray in the non-aligned world. Widespread change in the international scene – the acquisition of independence by virtually all viable ex-colonial areas and the emergence of Communist China as a separate threat to peace – has further eroded the world role of the non-aligned grouping.[125]

Johnson's efforts to limit criticism of his policies in Vietnam compounded the damage. Alarmed at both Indian criticism and rising grain prices at home, Johnson ceased grain shipments to India in the last four months of 1966. Following Gandhi's trip to Moscow, the action was read by New Delhi as punishment for its stance on Vietnam.[126] The pressure backfired; Gandhi continued to criticize the war, but went further in May 1967, sending Ho Chi Minh a congratulatory birthday message. An enraged Rusk personally drafted a message to Bowles:

The general mood in this country does not permit us to act like an old cow which continues to give milk, however often one kicks her in the flanks.

[123] Lawrence, "*Limits of Peacemaking*," 248–254.
[124] Text of Joint Communiqué, October 24, 1966, NSF, CF, box 131, "India, Vol. 8, Memos [2 of 2]" folder, LBJL.
[125] Memorandum, "The Second Non-Aligned Non-Summit Ends with No Significant Results," Thomas Hughes to Rusk, October 24, 1966, NSF, CF, box 131, "India, Vol. 8, Memos [2 of 2]" folder, LBJL.
[126] See H. W. Brands, *India and the United States: The Cold Peace* (Boston: Twayne, 1990), 121–122; Kristin L. Ahlberg, "Machiavelli with a Heart: The Johnson Administration's Food for Peace Program in India, 1965–1966," *Diplomatic History* 31 (September 2007), 695–699.

... Perhaps my struggle here makes me a bit edgy but I really do think that those who pretend to be non-aligned should in fact be non-aligned and stay away from questions on which they are not prepared to take any serious responsibility.[127]

Dependence on U.S. food aid, fear of Chinese power, and its key position on the ICC led New Delhi to continue its awkward middle course, despite the chilly tone of relations with Washington. Indian diplomats still conveyed Soviet and North Vietnamese messages to their U.S. counterparts. Nonetheless, LBJ was frustrated by New Delhi's increasing proximity to the Soviet Union and its rhetoric on Vietnam. Mutual disaffection continued to afflict the Indian-American relationship to the very end of Johnson's presidency.[128]

Algeria experienced similar difficulties with the Johnson administration over its stance on the Vietnam War. Both the State Department and the NSC greeted Ben Bella's ouster with guarded optimism, perceiving that Boumedienne was likely to steer a more careful course. The new regime requested a new PL-480 agreement. After long deliberation and much prodding by Komer, Bundy, and Williams, Johnson approved a new agreement in February 1966 – but directed that all future Algerian aid requests be subject to his approval.[129] The very next day, however, Boumedienne published a friendly letter to Ho, who had been a longtime ally of the Algerian independence movement. In the autumn, with Algeria facing drought, Boumedienne again requested a PL-480 sale. Johnson's advisors endorsed a new agreement, reasoning that Boumedienne's opposition to the war, although irksome, was inconsequential. Harriman, after a December 1966 trip, deemed Boumedienne "worth cultivating," adding, "Nothing is to be gained by accentuating our differences."[130] Although Rusk and Rostow seconded Harriman's recommendations, Johnson waited until the late winter of 1967 before approving another sale.

Algeria reacted with much the same anger as Egypt and India. In a February conversation with the U.S. ambassador, Foreign Minister Abdelaziz Bouteflika complained with "some vehemence" about the fiscal consequences of Johnson's delay: Algeria had been forced to buy wheat at commercial rates, depriving it of funds for development programs. Bouteflika thought it apparent that Johnson was punishing Algeria for its stance on Vietnam. Algeria, Bouteflika said, would not stand indefinitely with its hand outstretched, nor would it continue to deal with the United States if Washington did not treat it as a friend.[131]

---

[127] Telegram 197663, Washington to New Delhi, May 19, 1966, in *FRUS, 1964–1968*, 25: 859–860.

[128] Dennis Kux, *Estranged Democracies: India and the United States, 1941–1991* (Thousand Oaks, CA.: Sage, 1994), 264–268.

[129] Memorandum, Komer and Bundy to Johnson, January 17, 1966, in *FRUS, 1964–1968*, 24: 51; Telegram 1579, Algiers to Washington, January 21, 1966, NSF, CF, box 79, "Algeria, Vol. 2, Memos [2 of 2]" folder, LBJL; Memorandum, Saunders to Rostow, May 25, 1966, ibid.

[130] Harriman, "Memorandum on Algeria", December 12, 1966, in *FRUS, 1964–1968*, 24: 54–56.

[131] Telegram 2575, Algiers to Washington, February 16, 1967, NSF, CF, box 79, "Algeria, Vol. 2, Cables" folder, LBJL.

Johnson's policies, however, reflected his grasp of domestic attitudes. Public opinion only reinforced the administration's insistence on solidarity. A March 1966 Gallup poll asked how the government should react if an aid recipient failed to support the United States in "a major foreign policy decision such as Vietnam." Of the respondents, 45 percent supported a total cutoff of aid; another 30 percent favored reducing aid. Only 16 percent endorsed continuing the level of aid as before.[132] Popular opinion at this point still supported the war and resented foreign criticism. Reflecting this sentiment, Congress sought to restrict aid to states that failed to show solidarity with the United States.[133]

By the spring of 1967, relations between the United States and the nonaligned world had been seriously damaged by disputes about the war. The removal of pro-Chinese governments had not improved views on Vietnam; if anything, it had fostered overconfidence in Washington and fear in the nonaligned capitals. Coercive U.S. aid policies added to the acrimony. Events in the Middle East, however, further widened the breach, while accelerating the transformation of nonalignment.

1967 AND THE AGE OF SOLIDARITY

If nonalignment faced an uncertain future after the collapse of the Algiers summit and the coups of 1965 and 1966, it gained new force after the 1967 Six Day War between Israel and its Arab neighbors. The war brought the severance of relations between the United States and Egypt; it also forged a new solidarity among the nonaligned states, as they became increasingly antagonistic toward Washington.

The tumult of June 1967 had much to do with the mutual disaffection that had unsettled U.S.-Egyptian relations since 1964. As Cairo sought aid from the Soviets in early 1967, policymakers in Washington began to rethink their earlier denial of aid to the UAR. Rostow and Harold Saunders urged Johnson to offer Egypt a new food aid agreement. Rostow reasoned, "Our experience in Indonesia is [a] strong argument for buying a little insurance against a better day."[134] That day remained distant. Nasser's deputy, Anwar al-Sadat, complained that U.S. policy toward Egypt was worse than it had been in the Dulles era, and Nasser's annual May Day speech termed the United States the

---

[132] George Gallup, *The Gallup Poll: Public Opinion, 1935–1971*, Vol. 3 (New York, Random House: 1972), 1995.

[133] An amendment by Congressman Paul Findley to the renewal of the Food for Peace program prohibited PL-480 sales to any countries found to be aiding North Vietnam. This, in turn, restricted the Johnson administration from selling PL-480 grain to Yugoslavia, which had given Hanoi medical supplies.

[134] Memorandum, Rostow to Johnson, February 14, 1967, in DOS, *FRUS, 1964–1968, Vol. 18: Arab-Israeli Dispute, 1964–1967* (Washington: GPO, 2000): 763–765; Telegram CAP 67111, Rostow to Johnson, March 6, 1967, ibid.: 771–773.

leading counterrevolutionary state in the world, accusing the CIA of plotting against him.[135]

U.S. support for Israel constituted one key factor imperiling relations with Cairo, as Arab-Israeli tensions reached new heights in 1967. In 1965, Johnson had sold tanks to Israel. A sale of advanced A-4 attack aircraft followed in 1966, intended to counter Syria's purchase of Soviet tanks. Increased conflict between Israel and Syria, fueled by cross-border raids by Syrian-supported Palestinian Fatah militants, brought Israel to strike out at both Damascus and Amman.[136] In May 1967, Syria appealed for Arab military support, after receiving false Soviet reports of a threatening Israeli military buildup.[137] Nasser responded, mobilized his army, and deployed it into the Sinai Peninsula, also ordering the departure of UN peacekeeping observers. Fatefully he also closed the Straits of Tiran and Gulf of Aqaba to Israeli shipping. From these ill-advised choices sprang the 1967 Six Day War. Nasser's choice to mobilize will be debated for decades to come, but it is noteworthy that his closure of the Straits came in spite of U.S. entreaties urging him not to risk war with Israel.[138]

Nasser's choices in this crisis undoubtedly stemmed from a complex mix of political and psychological motivations. His prestige in the Arab world, the stability of his government, and his state of mind all bear close consideration. The collapse of the U.S.-Egyptian relationship also played a critical role, however, in setting the stage for the 1967 war. Nasser's alienation from the United States arose from multiple sources. It was spurred by U.S. support for both Israel and Nasser's Saudi enemies, by a long series of disputes over regional issues, and by the effective termination of food aid. Together, these developments decisively limited U.S. influence in Cairo at a critical hour. In calmer times, Nasser had been persuaded to keep the Arab-Israeli conflict in the icebox. The decline of the relationship removed a critical reason for him to do so.[139] The strains of the Vietnam War simultaneously limited Washington's options in the crisis.

[135] Memorandum, Benjamin Read to Rostow, May 4, 1967, NSF, CF, box 160, "UAR, Vol. V, "Memos" folder, LBJL; Telegram 4793, Cairo to Washington, February 24, 1967, in *FRUS, 1964–1968, 18*: 767.

[136] See Clea Lutz Bunch, "Strike at Samu: Jordan, Israel, the United States, and the Origins of the Six-Day War," *Diplomatic History* 32 (January 2008): 55–76.

[137] See Yaacov Ro'i, "Soviet Policy Toward the Six Day War through the Prism of Moscow's Relations with Egypt and Syria," in Yaacov Ro'i and Boris Morozov eds., *The Soviet Union and the June 1967 Six Day War* (Stanford: Stanford University Press, 2008), 1–42; Boris Morozov, "The Outbreak of the June 1967 War in Light of Soviet Documentation," ibid., 43–64; Richard Parker, *The Politics of Miscalculation in the Middle East* (Bloomington: Indiana University Press, 1993), 36–98.

[138] See Memcon, Rusk, Sir Burke Trend, and others, June 2, 1967, in DOS, *FRUS, 1964–1968, Vol. 19: Arab-Israeli Crisis and War, 1967* (Washington: GPO, 2004): 237–244; Telegram 1517, Lisbon to Washington, June 2, 1967, ibid.: 233–237.

[139] On Nasser's motivations, see also Michael Oren, *Six Days of War: 1967 and the Making of the Modern Middle East* (New York: Oxford University Press, 2002), 64–75. Richard B. Parker offers a thorough examination of Egyptian decision making, in Parker, *The Politics of Miscalculation*, 36–98.

Accumulated frustration with Nasser, moreover, may have fostered some desire to see him receive his comeuppance at the hands of Israel.[140]

On June 5, a massive Israeli air strike crippled the Egyptian air force. The next day, Egypt announced its decision to sever relations with the United States. Nasser accused Washington of actively aiding the Israelis, including staging air strikes on Egyptian territory. Other Arab states followed suit, including Algeria. This represented the first suspension of relations between Washington and a major nonaligned state. Even Sukarno had not banished the U.S. embassy from Jakarta during the Confrontation. While Nasser soon sought the resumption of ties, the Israeli occupation of the Sinai and continuing regional tensions obstructed a return to even the uncertain tenor of prewar diplomacy. Although informal links existed between Cairo and Washington, formal bilateral relations did not resume until the autumn of 1973.

In place of a restored relationship with the United States, Nasser sought solidarity and support from two corners: the Soviet bloc, and his peers in the nonaligned movement. After the calamity of 1967, Soviet arms poured into Egypt, further confirming Moscow's status as Nasser's patron. Necessity made Nasser an uneasy client of the Kremlin.[141] He also, however, enjoyed the steadfast support of India, Algeria, Guinea and – in a striking break from the prewar situation – sub-Saharan African states such as Tanzania. This, too, marked a pivotal change in the nature of nonalignment.

Before 1967, African states generally held moderate stances on the Arab-Israeli conflict. Except for Guinea, the Francophone states of West Africa supported Israel at the UN. Ghana, Mali, and Tanzania each enjoyed fruitful relations with Israel, which fielded a robust technical assistance program in Africa. At the 1964 Jakarta planning meeting for "Bandung II," a Turkish attendee noted discord between Arab and African delegates on the question of Israel: the latter made the former "virtually apoplectic" by asking why the Arab states refused to negotiate.[142] At the Cairo Conference, African delegations softened the language of the final declaration pertaining to Israel. One Tanzanian delegate observed that all sub-Saharan African states supported Israel out of gratitude for its technical assistance programs.[143]

[140] See Quandt "Lyndon Johnson and the June 1967 War: What Color was the Light?" *Middle East Journal*, Vol. 46, No. 2 (Spring 1992), 198–228; Peter Hahn, "An Ominous Moment: Lyndon Johnson and the Six Day War," in Mitchell Lerner ed. *Looking Back at LBJ: White House Politics in a New Light* (Lawrence: University Press of Kansas, 2005), 78–100; Parker, *The Politics of Miscalculation*, 99–122.

[141] See Galia Golan, "The Cold War and the Soviet Attitude towards the Arab-Israeli Conflict," in Nigel Ashton ed., *The Cold War in the Middle East: Regional Conflict and the Superpowers* (New York: Routledge, 2007), 59–73.

[142] Telegram 2041, Karachi to Washington, April 23, 1964, RG-59, CFPF: 1964–1966, box 1830, "POL 8, 4/1/64" folder, NA.

[143] Telegram 779, Dar es Salaam to Washington, October 15, 1964, RG-59, CFPF: 1964–1966, box 1829, "POL 8, 10/8/64" folder, NA; Cairo Conference, 8; Note, German NATO Delegation, November 5, 1964, FO 371/178925, TNA.

Israel's retention of Arab territory, however, was something that African states could not countenance amid their own anticolonial struggles. Immediately following the war, a group of 15 nonaligned states – none of them Arab – submitted a resolution to the UN General Assembly calling for an immediate, unconditional Israeli pullback to the 1949 armistice lines. Embodying this shift, Nyerere called for the withdrawal of Israeli troops from Arab territory. Unlike the Arab states, he advocated a peace based on mutual recognition, but he and his peers no longer occupied the middle ground. While the war in Vietnam drove the nonaligned world away from the United States, the fallout from the Six Day War strengthened ties between Arab and African states. Sukarno's vision was coming true, albeit belatedly: solidarity now represented the dominant principle of the nonaligned states.

This came as U.S. prestige in the nonaligned world reached its nadir. As the Vietnam War dragged on, Nyerere, once trusted by the United States, became one of Washington's sharpest critics. In a October 1967 speech, he decried the bombing of North Vietnam, terming the war "probably the most vicious and all-enveloping war which has been known to mankind." Speaking at length on an issue to which he had devoted little attention in prior years, Nyerere called for the United States to "recover from the delirium of power and return to the principles upon which her nation was founded."[144]

Nyerere's disaffection sprung from his frustration at Johnson's refusal to act on two key issues: Rhodesia and the Portuguese colonies. Armed rebellion broke out in Rhodesia during 1967, underscoring the failure of sanctions. Portugal continued to employ U.S.-made weaponry in Africa. Frustration with the United States over this issue alienated rebels in Portuguese Africa and their sponsors in the frontline states. Touré, once a Kennedy-era success story, worried about sharing Nkrumah's fate, as he supported rebels in Portuguese Guinea. His intensifying paranoia alienated him from Washington while inflicting great suffering in Guinea.

Washington slowly drifted back toward Lisbon. Relations during the Johnson years had not been harmonious, and Portugal was slow to forget its grievances from the Kennedy era. Nonetheless, in November 1968, Rusk told Salazar's successor, Marcelo Caetano, that his country "was not leading a crusade on the African question and had no interest in the disappearance of the Portuguese presence from Africa."[145] These reassuring words were a far cry from what Rusk had personally told the Portuguese at the height of the Goa crisis in December 1961. Then he had urged them to act "promptly, even more, dramatically" – in accordance with the "historical imperatives of the day" – in offering self-determination to their colonies.[146]

---

[144] Julius Nyerere, "Tanzania Policy on Foreign Affairs," October 16, 1967, Tanganyika African National Union National Conference (Dar es Salaam: Ministry of Information and Tourism, 1967), 5–6.

[145] Memcon, Rusk and Caetano, November 19, 1968, in DOS, *FRUS, 1964–1968: Vol. 12, Western Europe* (Washington: GPO, 2001): 361.

[146] Telegram 532, Washington to Lisbon, December 9, 1961, DSCF, 753D.00/12–961, NA.

The logistical requirements of the Vietnam War further accelerated this dependence on existing allies. With a growing proportion of the United States military deployed to Southeast Asia, the Johnson administration was even more loath to risk the Azores bases. Portugal opportunistically declared itself in total solidarity with the war, linking it to Lisbon's battle against rebellion in its African colonies. The Johnson administration did not endorse this analogy but could not publicly dispute it. Lisbon, furthermore, saw advantage in supporting the bombing of North Vietnam. To Portugal, the bombing of communist rear areas provided justification for threatening its own punitive actions against African frontline states.[147]

Portugal's slow return to favor was not an isolated development. Just as Vietnam divided the United States from nonaligned states, it forced Johnson to seek greater degrees of political support from his allies. These pledges, in turn, came with strings – often in the form of reciprocal demands for Washington's support in regional crises. Vietnam also accentuated the perceived strategic value of South Africa, which offered vital port facilities for ships traveling eastward to the Pacific – particularly large vessels unable to pass through the Suez Canal. By 1967, the importance of these facilities had been amplified considerably by the rapid growth of the U.S. deployment, by the closure of the Suez Canal, and, finally, as a result of increased Soviet naval activity in the Indian Ocean and South Atlantic. With those factors in mind, the Joint Chiefs of Staff and Deputy Secretary of Defense Paul Nitze argued strongly against any policy jeopardizing access to Pretoria's harbors.[148] Policy toward the white redoubts – in which Komer had seen an opportunity to offset the damage of Vietnam – remained stuck in place, offering ineffective disapproval.

Johnson's advisors remained optimistic about the Third World. Rostow tended to single out promising reports of an improving U.S. position in the postcolonial world. Looking back in May 1968, Rostow attributed past difficulties in the Third World to "radical, ambitious revolutionaries" anxious to redraw regional boundaries in accordance with "maps in their heads." "History has not been with these men," he pronounced, "Ben Bella is gone. Nkrumah is gone. Nasser is in a weakened, difficult position ... Sukarno is gone." A new generation of pragmatic leaders had emerged in their places; Rostow wrote to Johnson in September 1968 that "the future belongs to the Houphouets and the Ankrahs."[149] Accordingly, the administration shifted its emphasis. When Vice President Humphrey embarked on an extended trip to Africa at the end of 1967, he visited friendly states such as Ghana, Ethiopia, Liberia, Congo, and

[147] Noer, *Cold War and Black Liberation*, 123–125; Letter, Commonwealth Office to Canadian High Commission, Dar es Salaam, January 25, 1968, TNA, FCO 25/293.

[148] Memcon, Senior Interdepartmental Group, December 3, 1968, in *FRUS, 1964–1968*, 24: 704–711; Noer, *Cold War and Black Liberation*, 171, 179–180; Noer, *"Soapy"*, 293.

[149] Rostow, "The United States and the Changing World," remarks at the National War College, May 8, 1968, NSF, Name File, box 6, "Rostow Memos 1" folder, LBJL; Memorandum, Rostow to Johnson, September 16, 1968, NSF, CF, box 94, "Mali, Vol. 1" folder, LBJL.

Cote d'Ivoire. Humphrey's glowing report lauded the pro-American sentiment he had encountered on every stop.[150]

Humphrey's itinerary epitomized Johnson's tendency to seek encouraging news. This represented a defining trait of an administration overwhelmed by the Vietnam War and mounting racial tensions at home. Almost as damaging as the war itself was the myopia and distraction that it fostered within the White House. Preventive diplomacy in the Middle East or Rhodesia became infeasible after Vietnam became an American war. Johnson had burdened his county with an unpopular, intractable war. Its cost to the American polity and society vexed and defeated all serious proposals to alleviate its impact elsewhere in the world.

A NEW ERA

The Johnson administration's descent into Vietnam did not cause an immediate rupture in relations with the nonaligned world. In fact, given the turbulence these ties had experienced in 1964, the reactions of a majority of the nonaligned states to Johnson's escalation were strikingly cautious. Some combination of prior experience, dependence, and prudence brought them to focus initially on encouraging negotiations. Except for Indonesia, none of the major non-aligned states saw any advantage in declaring solidarity with North Vietnam. Concern over the movement's future, particularly fears among senior members of Chinese penetration, further militated for a moderate response.

In 1966, however, a shift in the nonaligned position on Vietnam became apparent. The Johnson administration had welcomed the moderate appeals of 1965 but declined to act on them, particularly the central request for a prolonged bombing halt. The bombing evoked dismay across the postcolonial world, where elites and the public alike readily, and sometimes naturally, identified and sympathized with North Vietnam. Moreover, Johnson's willingness to link critical assistance programs – particularly food aid – to stances on Vietnam caused deep-seated alienation. Paradoxically, it made nonaligned leaders more likely to criticize the war publicly. These dissents, in turn, angered Americans of all stripes: policymakers, legislators, and ordinary citizens. They solidified a common view of nonalignment as a cynical mask, concealing hypocrisy and pro-Soviet views. In later years, the further widening of the chasm between the United States and the nonaligned group – now occupying the balance of power at the United Nations – contributed to a disastrous mutual alienation.

Vietnam had never been the primary concern of the nonaligned states. Without exception, the regional conflicts that had emerged or escalated in Kennedy's final year simmered as Washington further entangled itself in Southeast Asia.

---

[150] Report, "The Vice President's Trip to Africa," Hubert Humphrey to Johnson, January 12, 1968, in *FRUS, 1964–1968*, 24: 383–404. Humphrey also visited Zambia, Kenya, Ethiopia, and Somalia, but his itinerary omitted countries such as Guinea, Mali, and Tanzania, frequently visited by Williams.

These lingering conflicts continued to complicate U.S. relations with the major nonaligned states, driving Indonesia into the arms of China, alienating Egypt, and heightening India's perceived insecurity and dependence on Soviet arms. In Africa, the ongoing struggle against the white redoubts finally brought U.S. policymakers to turn their backs on the anticolonial promises of 1961 – despite the efforts of some to pursue engagement to its logical end.

In the immediate term, the Soviet Union profited from increased conflict in the Third World. As the Arab-Israeli conflict escalated, it became possible for the Soviets to foster dependence on their arms, although the fruits of such adventures could be short-lived. Washington's loss was not necessarily Moscow's gain. Nasser had no love of communism and retained long-standing doubts about his partnership with Moscow; after his sudden death from a heart attack in 1970, his successor, Anwar al-Sadat, was quick to abandon it. More durable was the budding Indo-Soviet bond, secured in the wake of the 1965 war.[151]

Along with Egypt, Algeria, Yugoslavia, and Tanzania, India would play a pivotal role in the nonaligned movement in the 1970s, an era characterized by polarized relations between the United States and the postcolonial world. The cancellation of the Algiers conference, the Indo-Pakistani war of 1965, coups in Ghana, Indonesia, and Algeria, and the early death of Shastri each contributed to a prolonged pause, so that the next nonaligned conference did not occur until 1970. Once again, however, predictions of the death of nonalignment proved premature. When the nonaligned states next met, in the Zambian capital of Lusaka, denunciations of the Vietnam War topped the agenda. When the NLF's designated foreign minister, Ngyuen Thi Binh, addressed the conference as an observer, she received the most thunderous applause given to any speaker.[152]

---

[151] See Vojtech Mastny, "The Soviet Union's Partnership with India," *Journal of Cold War Studies*, Vol. 12, No. 3, 50–90; Guy Laron, "Stepping Back from the Third World: Soviet Policy toward the United Arab Republic, 1965–1967," *Journal of Cold War Studies*, Vol. 12, No. 4, 99–118.

[152] Odette Jankowitsch and Karl P. Sauvant, eds., *The Third World Without Superpowers: The Collected Documents of the Non-Aligned Countries, Vol. 1* (Dobbs Ferry, NY: Oceana, 1978), 80–97; Marvine Howe, "Nonaligned Parley Ends; Liberation Groups Backed," *NYT*, September 11, 1970, 5.

Conclusion: "A Decent Respect for the Opinions of Mankind"

Amid the tumult and horror of 1968 came a fleeting reminder of the dawn of the New Frontier. In the spring of that year, Americans witnessed the winding down of the Tet Offensive, Lyndon Johnson's sudden withdrawal from the presidential campaign, the horror of Martin Luther King Jr.'s assassination, and an ensuing wave of urban riots. For a brief span, the strange prospect of a familiar pairing loomed: (Robert) Kennedy against Richard Nixon. Like the 1960 campaign, this contest have invoked discussion of the topic of nonalignment in the Cold War. Both candidates held distinct views on the matter. For Richard M. Nixon, it was time to reaffirm dividing lines. On July 29, 1967, before the exclusive, all-male Bohemian Club in a secluded woodland west of Santa Rosa, California, Nixon delivered a speech he would later term "the first milestone on my road to the presidency." Before an audience representing much of the nation's political and economic elite, Nixon elucidated his vision of foreign policy.[1]

Within a broad survey of trends in world politics, Nixon drew attention to the decline of the American image overseas, observing: "Twenty years ago, after our great World War II victory, we were respected throughout the world. Today, hardly a day goes by when our flag is not spit upon, a library burned, an embassy stoned some place in the world."[2] Part of the problem, as Nixon saw it, was an ill-conceived tolerance of nonaligned states. Discussing foreign aid policy, he observed:

The United States should use its aid programs to reward our friends and discourage our enemies. Before the recent Mid-East crisis, the fact that the U.S. had continued its aid programs to countries like the U.A.R., Algeria and Guinea when their leaders never missed a chance to condemn the United States in world forums had the effect of discouraging our friends, confusing the neutrals and bringing contempt from our enemies.

[1] Richard M. Nixon, *RN: The Memoirs of Richard Nixon* (New York: Simon & Schuster, 1978), 284.
[2] Address by Richard M. Nixon to the Bohemian Club, July 29, 1967, DOS, *FRUS, 1969–1976: Vol. 1, The Foundations of Foreign Policy, 1969–1972* (Washington: GPO, 2003): 2–10.

As counterpoints, Nixon cited four stalwart allies he believed deserving of support: Taiwan, Thailand, Iran, and Mexico. Juxtaposing volatile, anti-American nonaligned states and loyal, modernizing allies, Nixon clearly indicated where his preferences lay.[3]

Nixon made several other telling declarations. Citing the Shah of Iran, he observed that the new age was post-ideological, an age of pragmatism. "Communism, Marxism, Socialism, anti-colonialism," Nixon stated, "the great ideas which stirred men to revolution after World War II have lost their pulling power." This observation might have surprised the African movements and governments striving against the Portuguese or the white minority governments of South Africa and Rhodesia – had any of them managed to infiltrate a representative into the Bohemian Club's secluded redwood grove. Nor would Nixon's statements about Africa have particularly heartened them. "There were twelve coups in Black Africa in the last year," the former vice president observed. "No one of the thirty countries has a representative government by our standards and the prospects that any will have such a government in a generation or even a half-century are remote."[4]

With those words, Nixon voiced a resurgent resentment that Americans felt – one he had expressed while he was Eisenhower's vice president – toward the nonaligned and all their posturing. His pledge to reward the loyal and spurn the disloyal meshed neatly with the law-and-order themes of his campaign, and his description of the indignities heaped upon U.S. facilities overseas mirrored images of the riots now plaguing American cities. Nixon's statements about Africa stood as a rejection of the last vestiges of Kennedy-era promises, with their striking fusion of democratic idealism and modern social science.

Robert F. Kennedy, on the other hand, hearkened back to his brother's policy of engagement. Speaking in Portland, Oregon, in mid-April RFK decried the diminished moral authority of the United States in the world. Citing recent surveys and alluding to the Declaration of Independence, he said:

By the unilateral exercise of our overwhelming power we isolated ourselves. To many of our traditional allies and neutral friends we behaved as a superpower ignoring our own historical commitment to "a decent respect for the opinions of mankind."[5]

Like Nixon, Kennedy cited the example of Guinea. To RFK, however, Guinea was most notable for its refusal to allow Soviet flights to Cuba at the height of the Cuban Missile Crisis. Guinea had been motivated to aid the United States, Kennedy recounted, by

---

[3] Ibid.
[4] Ibid.
[5] John Herbert, "Kennedy, Calling U.S. Power-Obsessed, Appeals for a New Policy," *NYT*, April 18, 1968, 34. The phrase "a decent respect to the opinions of mankind" appears in the preamble of the Declaration of Independence.

a shared sense of what was right in relations between nations, a sense that an America which contributed its fair share to the quest for peace in the world deserved sympathy and support in a time of threat and danger to its own national security.[6]

RFK had supported his brother's policy. Though he had opposed the Volta Dam, he acted as a presidential emissary in the West New Guinea dispute and later reprised the role during the Malaysian Confrontation. Much like Chester Bowles, G. Mennen Williams, and Robert Komer in the Johnson years, the former attorney general argued vociferously for a renewed effort to aid African development, prompting one commentator to nickname him "Kennedy Africanus."[7] Engagement was one piece of his brother's legacy that Kennedy sought to salvage from the implosion of the Johnson administration – to no avail. He was struck down by an assassin's bullet on the morning of June 5, 1968. Vestiges of the policy had lingered, as a much-diminished priority through the Johnson years. One of Johnson's last acts in office, at the suggestion of National Security Advisor Walt Rostow, was to approve a sale of PL-480 grain to Guinea in the hope that its president, Sekou Touré, might yet become a "constructive force in Africa." [8] Two days later, LBJ left the White House, an exhausted man. Succeeding him, Nixon effectively abandoned what little remained of engagement.

HOW ENGAGEMENT FALTERED

The policy of engagement lived a short, stormy life. Like most unnamed policies, it died a quiet death. Emerging from the anxieties of out-of-power liberals in the 1950s, it built upon progress achieved during the late Eisenhower years. Nonetheless, engagement marked something new: Kennedy's tolerance for nonalignment was broader than Ike's and he proved willing to take greater risks for the goal of seeking concord with the uncommitted world. Kennedy's first year witnessed significant trials and disappointments; although his policies toward colonial conflicts and vigorous presidential diplomacy improved relations with the nonaligned states, the pressure of the Berlin crisis added substantial stress. The hopes he invested in the Belgrade Conference went unfulfilled, yet he was convinced by key advisors Robert Komer and Walt Rostow to forge ahead. Kennedy continued to meet with nonaligned leaders, to generally beneficial effect. He offered substantial support to their developmental ambitions. Above all, he broke with precedent, shifting policy on a number of key issues.

The sense of success felt over the course of 1962 was both deserved and illusory. Kennedy had made real headway in improving the tenor of bilateral relations with a range of nonaligned states. The New Frontiersmen, however, accorded too much significance to aid programs and too little to the gathering

[6] Ibid.

[7] C. L. Sulzberger, "Foreign Affairs: Kennedy Africanus," *NYT*, July 13, 1966, 40.

[8] Memorandum, Rostow to Johnson, January 18, 1969, NSF, CF, box 90, "Guinea, Memos and Misc, 1/64–1/69" folder, LBJL.

strength of anticolonial ideology. Deeper analysis of the nonaligned world would have buttressed the prescient warnings of ambassadors and liberals that an anticolonial reckoning lay ahead. A second wave of challenges, including growing violence in Portuguese Africa and flaring regional conflicts in the Middle East and Southeast Asia, complicated Kennedy's final year. Yet he and his advisors remained determined, regarding most setbacks as tactical. Johnson's first year, however, witnessed a series of shocks to U.S.-nonaligned relations, culminating in broad criticism at Cairo and the bitterness that followed the Stanleyville operation. Even so, the year and a half following the commencement of Rolling Thunder proved most decisive, as Johnson enmeshed himself in Vietnam, as regional and colonial conflicts deepened, and as disputes over aid grew.

Engagement's demise stemmed from four concrete failures. It ran aground on the shoals of lingering colonial disputes and then on the even more treacherous reefs of regional conflicts. Policies adopted toward the former gradually came to implicate the United States as either indifferent to the suffering of the colonized or a colonial power in its own right. Regional conflicts, however, often directly pitted the United States against nonaligned powers. Engagement also failed because U.S. policymakers disastrously overestimated the benefits of foreign aid, while underestimating the costs they would face from tying it to political goals. While aid strengthened relationships, Johnson was gravely mistaken to think that it provided leverage. Finally, the escalation in Vietnam divided the United States from other ostensible members of the community of free nations, transforming a difference of opinion into a source of division and mutual recrimination. Mired in Vietnam, the United States sought declarations of support from friends and neutrals alike. Increased regional tensions, an escalating struggle against colonialism in Africa, and a rising tide of political instability induced nonaligned leaders to put a similar emphasis on solidarity.

Of the above factors, Vietnam proved most significant. Johnson's concern with Southeast Asia limited his interest in and capacity to deal with other issues. Vietnam played on nonaligned fears of U.S. intervention, but outrage over the bombing was not the sole factor behind the widening chasm. Vietnam's effect on U.S. policy in other areas proved far more significant: the war limited Washington's ability and willingness to act in regional and colonial conflicts, while increasingly driving Johnson to link his aid policy and support of his war.

One may accept the primacy of Vietnam as a factor undermining engagement, but this answer leaves a broader question unanswered: which *types of factors* played the most pivotal role in this outcome? Were they geopolitical: the strains imposed by conflicts of various kinds coupled with Cold War imperatives and the importuning of allies? Were they political, embodied in the growing domestic opposition to engagement, which crested in the summer of 1963 and left the White House chastened and cautious in its approach to the nonaligned states? Or was this a case in which individuals mattered, wherein the changing balance of influence within the executive branch and the transition from Kennedy to Johnson played a primary role in driving events?

None of these grand factors should be discounted; any explanation that omits one of them would be incomplete. Nevertheless, one clearly stands out: the failure of engagement came as a direct consequence of the transition between Kennedy and Johnson. Systemic and domestic factors were, to a considerable degree, unavoidable. The fractious geopolitics of a world only partly decolonized and divided by regional rivalries and the nature of popular views on the Cold War made military conflict and legislative opposition inevitable. These inescapable factors, however, invested far more importance in the choices made in the White House, and these choices stemmed from individual outlooks and tendencies. Here, the key decisions occurred after November 1963. Lyndon Johnson had a preexisting disposition to bolster allies, one that was apparent by the middle of 1964. Johnson lacked Kennedy's intuitive grasp of the nonaligned world and his reservations about seeking political leverage with economic aid. Above all, as argued persuasively by a number of scholars, Johnson chose to go to war in Vietnam, ignoring an abundance of outside counsel from allies.

It is here that we may draw another distinction, for Johnson reconciled his war with his relationship with the nonaligned world in a way that Kennedy would not have done. Kennedy *might* have felt more pressure to side with allies in regional conflicts – he already had drawn back from pressing Portugal – and he *might* have sought more leverage for aid (although he clearly understood how this tactic could backfire). He was, however, someone better able to take counsel from nonaligned leaders and better able to appreciate that neutralization could serve as an inexpensive substitute for active containment. Kennedy *would not* have rejected the counsel of nonaligned leaders and allies as vehemently or as punitively as Johnson did. At the least, he would have continued to seek it in the critical year of 1964. Finally, Kennedy's particular conception of world politics, in particular his preoccupation with the position of the United States among the uncommitted states, would have served as a strong counterbalance for his concern with South Vietnam. Johnson, on the other hand, chose war in Vietnam, however reluctantly, in spite of warnings from both allies and neutrals.

In a sense, this stands as a repudiation of Kennedy. Johnson fought in Vietnam because he believed the commitment to defend the government in Saigon had already been made for him. No such verbal commitment, however, emerged with regard to engagement. Kennedy chose to keep this policy off the books. An endeavor that flourished in the informal atmosphere of his administration-wherein NSC staffers, liberal appointees, and ambassadors could circumvent the more skeptical leadership of the State Department-foundered after 1963. In part, it did so because of Johnson's reservations and because the balance of influence shifted at the outset of the new administration. The skeptical Rusk, who had lacked sway in the Kennedy White House, gained substantial influence by virtue of his formal position and bond with LBJ. Although famously marginalized on Vietnam policy, George Ball paradoxically gained influence in other areas, notably Africa. One should note, however, that Johnson followed loyally those policies and mandates made explicitly by his predecessor. Had Kennedy taken steps, publicly or privately, to state his commitment to engagement, LBJ would have hewn more closely to his predecessor's policy. In Kennedy's defense, of course, he could not have perceived the ultimate, tragic urgency of making an unstated policy public. Nor did he perceive the damage his own growing commitment in Southeast Asia would inflict on concurrent priorities.

WHAT ENGAGEMENT REPRESENTED

Engagement was a product of the intellectual climate of the late 1950s. It drew strength from the promise of modernization theory to compete with communist models of development. The policy emerged while the primary states of the nonaligned world were still governed by the leaders of their respective independence movements. It took wing at a time of real optimism in the post-colonial world, when the promises of Bandung still seemed attainable, and as newly independent states embarked upon ambitious programs of development. It preceded the economic stagnation and spate of coups that attached such dismal images to the term "Third World." Above all, however, it flowed from American fears, beliefs, and aspirations felt acutely in the late 1950s.

Nils Gilman has observed that modernization theory reflected the anxieties of its adherents, not about the problem of underdevelopment but about the future of American liberalism itself. Modernization theorists went abroad to demonstrate to themselves the intrinsic qualities of the American model.[9] The same may be said of engagement, a sibling of sorts to concurrent concerns with modernization. Its most fervent liberal advocates sought Third World affirmation of both their pursuit of the Cold War and of a specific, long-standing American role in the world as a friend to oppressed peoples. They had, as much as anyone, conceived of the Cold War as an all-encompassing global crusade. Liberal capitalist precepts informed them that the Third World mattered to the ultimate outcome; so, too, did their need to validate both non-communist models of development and a specific notion of American mission. The Manichean policies they ascribed to Dulles could, thus, be safely set aside as an aberration.

The Cold War was, in the early 1960s, still a conscious battle for world opinion. Eisenhower and Dulles had sincerely wanted neutral states to understand the U.S. position; so, too, did the New Frontiersmen. Some in the generation of policymakers taking office in 1961 had worked to establish the UN and looked upon it with paternal regard. They saw its activities, deliberations and votes as consequential – as indeed they were in cases such as the Congo. This was more than a matter of psychological reassurance; global opinion stood to influence broad questions of legitimacy. Divided or contested states – including

[9] Nils Gilman, *Mandarins of the Future: Modernization Theory in Cold War America* (Baltimore: The Johns Hopkins University Press, 2003), 12–20.

the two Germanys, the two Chinas, Israel, and Malaysia – saw the nonaligned world as possessing a critical voice, able to confer or limit international standing. At times, these concerns were exaggerated, but they were still genuine, driven by the intense, existential battles that collectively constituted the early Cold War. Each major power and numerous nations of the second tier saw the Third World as an arena in which credibility was at stake.

Engagement emerged in part from this concern with world opinion; and this, too, marks it as a product of the early Cold War. Perceived world opinion constrained U.S. foreign policy during the era of engagement: at the height of the Berlin crisis, Kennedy had thought it vital to display a willingness to negotiate; the following year, he and his brother reflected on the opprobrium that would follow a "Pearl Harbor"-like strike on Soviet missile bases in Cuba. Johnson's "peace offensive" flowed from the same concern. Implicit in these statements and actions was a belief that global opinion – a great part of which belonged to the nonaligned world – was a factor worth considering. The travails of the Vietnam era, however, conditioned Americans to disdain world opinion. The hostility of the Non-Aligned Movement (NAM) in bodies like the UN could be taken for granted – and disregarded. From this disaffection rose a greater U.S. predilection toward unilateral action on the world stage, one that substantially outlived the Cold War. The "decent respect [for] the opinions of mankind," a phrase coined by Thomas Jefferson and cited by Robert Kennedy, was in large part a casualty of the 1960s.

One may argue that the Cold War was best confined to the industrial areas of the Northern Hemisphere and that the turbulent postcolonial world was best disregarded as marginal to the struggle. Such a contention draws powerful force from our understanding of the profound human toll endured in Cold War proxy battles such as Vietnam, Angola, and Afghanistan, and from dissenters such as George Kennan and George Ball. The passage of time has strengthened this argument, but often in ways that assume facts not in evidence to our historical counterparts. We may know that the Cold War was ultimately settled in Europe, but how readily was this outcome discernible in 1961? Above all, this argument lightly discards outlooks that were common and fervently ingrained. The most comprehensive, thoughtful history of the extension of the Cold War into the Third World, Odd Arne Westad's *The Global Cold War: Third World Interventions and the Making of Our Times*, finds this escalation to have been the product of deeply rooted national mythologies, in both the United States and the Soviet Union. Belief in historical national missions and a moral (and therefore global) struggle buttressed more conventional geopolitical concerns. Arguing for the confinement of the Cold War to the industrial North is not far removed from contending that it should not have occurred at all: a laudable sentiment, but one not easily reconciled with the ideologies and uncertainties of the moment in question.

Conceding this grim fact, engagement emerges as a lost alternative to policies of intervention in the Third World. It comprehended the force of Third World nationalism, distinguishing it from communism. It recognized the development aspirations of Third World leaders, if not the best means by which they could be satisfied. Above all, taken to its logical conclusion, it could have defused potential flash points. Bowles, perhaps the most fervent supporter of engagement, perceived this. He advocated the neutralization of Vietnam, believing that Chinese power was best contained by indigenous Asian nationalism. He also counseled accepting Latin American participation in nonaligned conferences. Kennedy, by some accounts, was interested in the possibility of a neutral Cuba, still ruled by Castro but pursuing a Yugoslavia-like course.[10] Even Eisenhower had mused – perhaps remorsefully – that neutrality could be a better guarantor of a state's security than alignment with the West. Such thinking constituted a logical, though hazardous extension of engagement's core logic – and a leap into the unknown.

In considerable part, this leap did not occur because of the turbulence of the nonaligned world itself. Regional conflicts and the anticolonial struggle presented the superpowers with both opportunities and dilemmas. They weakened the ability of the nonaligned movement, as a whole, to remain aloof from the Cold War and fostered divisions within its ranks. The nonaligned states faced a bitter dilemma between Cold War neutrality and militant anticolonial solidarity. They understandably regarded this as a false choice, but a growing emphasis on the latter in the 1960s made the former more difficult. Regional conflicts heightened the potential role of the superpowers as arms suppliers. Postcolonial enmities of various forms limited the potential of nonalignment, and heightened the danger that the Cold War would further penetrate the Third World. Militant nonalignment and American disaffection with engagement acted in conjunction, each spurring the other onward.

Although coined as a Cold War strategy, engagement drew its practitioners away from the separation of the world into friendly and hostile camps. It challenged ideas of strict solidarity with allies, particularly in cases linked to empire. Most importantly, it undermined the starkly moral narrative of the Cold War, albeit unintentionally. Engagement's advocates all thought the Cold War worth fighting, but according states the right to sit it out ultimately contradicted prevailing views of the struggle. Engagement thus ran afoul of a powerful strand of popular and elite opinion, one held in large part by Lyndon Johnson. If its emergence can be attributed to Cold War anxieties, so, too, can its demise. As at other points in the conflict, Cold War ideology worked to undermine strategy, with baleful consequences.

For all the ill-founded articles of faith and mistaken reasoning held by advocates of engagement, the policy remained founded on a single essential truth: the ability of great powers to coerce uncommitted states into alignment was waning with the pluralization of world politics. Even though it was a policy designed with Cold War imperatives, it spurred its practitioners to comprehend

---

[10] Robert Dallek, *An Unfinished Life: John F. Kennedy, 1917–1963* (New York: Little, Brown, & Co., 2003), 655–665; Lawrence Freedman, *Kennedy's Wars: Berlin, Cuba, Laos, and Vietnam* (New York: Oxford University Press, 2000), 240–245.

the limits of their own power and influence. Proponents of engagement – for all their anticommunism – were the policymakers best able to step outside a Cold War framework, to perceive the localized passions that sometimes eclipsed the grand struggle. While engagement's proponents accorded undue weight to the importance of the nonaligned world in the Cold War, they grasped that relations with its leading states could be important in their own right. If neglected, the agendas of the nonaligned states could, and ultimately did, substantially affect the international standing of the United States. Engagement's advocates, in short, came closer to recognizing the postcolonial world as it was than all of their predecessors and most of their successors. Recognition, however, was not enough. The implacable logic of a global Cold War thwarted those policymakers able to perceive the complexities of a decolonizing world and the real utility of nonalignment. Sadly, engagement was fated to be a brief but genuine departure from a durable Manichean outlook that took root in the Cold War and outlived it by more than a decade.

ENGAGEMENT'S WAKE

After the New Frontier came an age of polarization. The divisions of the Johnson years were consolidated during the Nixon presidency. Nixon's continuation of the war in Vietnam only deepened nonaligned condemnations of the United States and evoked declarations of solidarity with Hanoi. A number of nonaligned states recognized the communist Provisional Revolutionary Government, which claimed to represent South Vietnam. Nixon's policies toward Rhodesia, South Africa, and the Portuguese colonies, premised on the notion that "the whites aren't going anywhere," angered black Africans of all political stripes. Nixon's embrace of Pakistan and China brought relations with India to a new level of mutual animosity after the 1971 Indo-Pakistani War.[11] Although Nixon enjoyed greater success in his approach to Egypt, particularly in the years following the 1973 October War, and in his relations with Suharto's Indonesia, the 1973 Arab-Israeli war led to a further widening of the gulf between the U.S. and the nonaligned states. In its wake came the Arab oil embargo against the United States and, as a show of iron solidarity, the severance of diplomatic relations between most of sub-Saharan Africa and Israel. Within the United States, the embargo and the incessant flow of nonaligned criticism from the floor of the UN only deepened domestic animosity toward the NAM.

Engagement was attempted again in the 1970s, as the United States strove to undo some of the damage wrought by the Vietnam War and the policies of

---

[11] See Robert J. McMahon, "The Danger of Geopolitical Fantasies: Nixon, Kissinger, and the South Asia Crisis of 1971," in Fredrik Logevall and Andrew Preston eds., *Nixon in the World: American Foreign Relations, 1969–1977* (New York: Oxford University Press, 2008), 249–268; Dennis Kux, *Estranged Democracies: India and the United States, 1941–1991* (Thousand Oaks, CA: Sage, 1994), 279–319.

Nixon. The Ford and Carter years witnessed policies more congenial to African nationalism, the signing of the Panama Canal Treaty, and Middle Eastern shuttle diplomacy. By now, the founding generation of nonalignment had largely departed, and much of Africa had turned from the hazy socialism of the immediate post-independence years to outright Marxist-Leninism. The NAM moved ever closer to the Soviet Union, debating in its 1979 conference whether to declare outright affinity with Moscow. Nehru would not have been pleased. In any event, the drastic intensification of the Cold War, at decade's end, subsumed the second wave of engagement as surely as Vietnam had the first. Discredited in American eyes by more than a decade of antagonism, weakened by crippling national debt burdens, and divided by its own unremitting debates, the NAM was relegated to the sidelines during the Cold War's terrifying final decade.

In the end, it seemed that Dulles had been right. When they overthrew their calcifying governments, the peoples of Eastern Europe and the Soviet Union dispelled forever any doubts about communism's essential repressiveness and inefficiency. The end of the Cold War, however, also came to be seen in the United States as a victory in a moral battle. Only the hard-hearted or ideologically blinded could not celebrate the sight of the Berlin Wall toppling, but ensuing waves of triumphalism obscured much about the nature of the struggle. A nation secure in its sense of moral victory, perched at the cusp of a bold new era of global leadership, was free to reinterpret the Cold War as another historical parable of American greatness, without unduly pondering the uglier aspects of U.S. policy during the conflict. Such certitude restored the idea that nonalignment in the Cold War *had* been truly immoral. U.S. preeminence in the 1990s reinforced the righteous narrative of the Cold War, while Americans wondered bemusedly why the NAM lingered on the scene.[12]

The current century has witnessed a third effort at engagement, global in scope, but mainly targeted at the Muslim world. In the wake of the September 11, 2001, attacks, the second Bush administration boosted foreign aid, launched an ambitious program to combat the AIDS epidemic in Africa, and sent public ambassadors to conduct "listening tours" of the Arab world. These endeavors, some more effective than others, were overshadowed by the Iraq War, the administration's Dulles-like rhetoric, outright efforts to coerce support from aid recipients, and the infamous use of torture.[13] For much of the decade, the administration and its most fervent advocates professed contempt for those unwilling to side with it. Grievously, unnecessarily repeating the errors of his Texan predecessor alongside those of his own, George W. Bush was no Jack Kennedy.

---

[12] See, for example, Philip Shenon, "Non-Aligned Bloc Seeks a New Reason for Being," *NYT*, September 2, 1992; Charles Krauthammer, "The Real World Order; The American Empire and the Islamic Challenge," *The Weekly Standard* 7, No. 9 (November 12, 2001), 25–30.

[13] On the question of coercion, see Mark Danner, "The Moment Has Come to Get Rid of Saddam," *The New York Review of Books*, Vol. 54, No. 17 (November 8, 2007), http://www.nybooks.com/articles/20770; Heraldo Muñoz, *A Solitary War: A Diplomat's Chronicle of the Iraq War and Its Lessons* (Golden, CO: Fulcrum, 2008), 25–77, 164–79.

His successor, however, felt differently. Barack Obama has, at times, consciously styled himself after JFK. He sought the endorsements of Kennedy family members and advisors on the campaign trail and delivered an inaugural address that echoed Kennedy's in its cadences. Alongside promises to stand firm in the global struggle against terrorism, Obama promised development assistance to impoverished nations. In successive years, traveling far more than JFK, he engaged in his own campaign of presidential diplomacy, visiting Ghana, Egypt, Indonesia, and India, among other places. The results can be judged only partially to date, and the turbulence that erupted in the Middle East in early 2011 serves as a reminder that history allows no neat analogies. The verdicts offered here are rendered modestly, with the admission that – like its 1960s antecedent – contemporary engagement is a policy often pursued quietly. There remains much that we do not know.

Still, some lessons suggest themselves. One is that rhetoric and presidential diplomacy are best used as stepping-stones; by themselves they benefited Kennedy, but they also served to increase expectations of him over time. Obama has, at times, run afoul of hopes that he, himself, raised. Another is to attach humble political expectations to foreign aid. It can win friendship but not unflinching loyalty. Admittedly, recent decades have witnessed sharp criticism of development aid on economic grounds, and these are worthy of serious consideration. Attacks predicated on the notion that aid buys obedience are not – even in these increasingly frugal times. John Foster Dulles, no Bowlesian idealist, rejected that notion in his Ames speech. A third lesson is not to underestimate the political and psychological legacy of colonialism in Africa and Asia. If Americans can still be politically galvanized by references to our own revolution and its leading figures, more than two centuries ago, it is hardly inconceivable that reminders of colonial rule in places where it still lingers in living memory evoke powerful reactions. A shared, historically founded anticolonial outlook should be one of the factors uniting the United States and the nonaligned world, not a source of antagonism.

The last lesson is the simplest. Engagement is hard work. By its very nature, in a multipolar world, it calls for a perennial balancing act between allies and others. It tests the bonds of alliance in pursuit of uncertain rewards. It opens an administration to the perennial charge of betraying a friend in order to appease an adversary; most recently, Obama's largely rhetorical outreach to the Arab world has brought hyperbolic accusations of abandoning Israel. It is easy to see why Lyndon Johnson, one of the most politically gifted presidents in U.S. history, balked at the costs this policy imposed upon him. Yet engagement is often worthwhile. For much of the Cold War, Americans believed themselves to be waging a global battle for hearts and minds. One can easily say the same about the current age, as Washington strives to combat doctrines that justify terrorism, even after the death of Osama bin Laden.

The NAM remains a large and prominent organization, representing virtually all of Asia, Africa, and Latin America. Its meetings have been widely attended, if not by U.S. observers; China is as attentive to the movement today as it was in the 1960s.[14] Afro-Asian fellowship, once largely rhetorical, is now a matter of multibillion dollar investments, as Beijing's voracious economy has led it to import massive quantities of raw materials from NAM members. The United States, too, has reason to engage the nonaligned world today. The challenges of global economic recovery, hunger, environmental degradation, and resource management must inevitably involve nonaligned states. So, too, will efforts to combat terrorism. These challenges can be approached bilaterally, or through regional or international organizations, but they also require the United States to come to terms with the meaning of nonalignment in today's world and its implications for the exercise of American power.

Nonalignment has been a frustratingly amorphous concept across its more than five decades of existence. Nonetheless, it represents the broadest, most durable notionally (if not consistently) neutral organization of states in human history. If nonalignment, then and now, can be reduced to a single concept, it represents the refusal of the world's small and medium powers – particularly those that have experienced colonialism – to be arbitrarily assigned to one or another sphere of influence. In an increasingly multipolar world, the endurance of nonalignment continues to weaken the ability of any one great power to coerce uncommitted states – if anything, it continues to encourage smaller nations to court more than one patron. Such a strategy is easier in the twenty-first century, an era in which the ideological battles of the Cold War have faded away. The phenomenal growth of non-Western economies now offers impoverished states a wide range of potential patrons and investors, making Rostow's vision of the diffusion of power a reality. As in the 1960s, nonaligned states demonstrate a continued ability to frustrate the predictions and desires of great powers, including the United States.

Perhaps that is why Americans have such a hard time with the concept. Nonalignment, at heart, implies a fundamental rejection of American claims to world leadership or an exceptional heritage and destiny. It is worth asking if our scorn toward the nonaligned states is a response to our having been demonized by the individual Sukarnos and (more recently) the Hugo Chavezes in their midst, or a response to being more generally taken off our particular pedestal and set alongside other great powers.

Nonalignment is not a phenomenon that can be wished away in a fit of hegemonic dreaming. It has transformed world politics irreversibly, and, in some ways, for the better. Its core principles of self-determination and a right to neutrality – however obscured by the day-to-day politics of the NAM – represent ideals that Americans long asserted for themselves. Kennedy was right to regard nonalignment seriously in his day, and we would be equally prudent to study it closely in ours.

---

[14] Olga Rodriguez, "China Seizes Opportunity at Cuba Summit," *The Washington Post*, September 14, 2006, http://www.washingtonpost.com/wp-dyn/content/article/2006/09/14/AR2006091400826.html

Bibliography

Archival Collections

United States

John F. Kennedy Library, Boston, MA
  National Security Files
    Countries
    Trips and Conferences
    Subjects
    Meetings and Memoranda
    William H. Brubeck
    McGeorge Bundy
    Robert W. Komer
  Oral Histories
    Averell Harriman
    Howard P. Jones
    Robert W. Komer
    Walt W. Rostow
    Phillips Talbot
    G. Mennen Williams
  Pre-Presidential Papers
  Presidential Office Files
  David E. Bell Papers
  George W. Ball Papers
  McGeorge Bundy Papers
  Harlan Cleveland Papers

Lyndon Baines Johnson Library, Austin, TX
  National Security File
    Country File
    Country File: Vietnam
    Memos to the President
    Name File
    National Security Council Histories

    Vice Presidential File
    McGeorge Bundy Papers
    Edward Hamilton Papers
    Robert W. Komer Papers
    Ulric Haynes Jr. Papers
  Oral Histories
    Lucius Battle
    Chester Bowles
    Michael V. Forrestal
    Averell Harriman
    Robert W. Komer
    Dean Rusk
    Harold Saunders
    G. Mennen Williams
  George W. Ball Papers
  White House Central Files

Dwight D. Eisenhower Library, Abilene, KS
  John Foster Dulles Papers
  Dwight D. Eisenhower, Papers as President, 1953–1961, Ann Whitman File
  White House Office
    National Security Council Staff: Papers, 1948–1961
    Office of the Special Assistant for National Security Affairs
  White House Central File

National Archives, College Park, MD
  Record Group 59
    Department of State Central Files
    Central Foreign Policy Files: 1963
    Central Foreign Policy Files: 1964–1966
    Records of the Policy Planning Staff, 1957–1961
    Bureau of African Affairs
    Bureau of European Affairs
    Bureau of Near East/South Asian Affairs
  Record Group 84
    Guinea General Records

Bentley Library, Ann Arbor, MI
  G. Mennen Williams Papers

Miller Center, Charlottesville, VA
  Presidential Recordings
    Kennedy Tapes and Dictabelts

Hoover Institution, Stanford, CA
  Howard P. Jones Papers

Yale University Library, New Haven, CT
  Chester Bowles Papers

United Kingdom

National Archives, Kew
  Cabinet Office (CAB)
  Commonwealth Office (CO)
  Defense Office (DO)
  Foreign Office Political Correspondence (FO)
  Prime Minister's Office Files (PREM)

France

Ministère des Affaires Étrangères, Quai d'Orsay, Paris
  Amérique, sub-series États-Unis, 1952–1963
  Amérique, sub-series États-Unis, 1964–1970
  Asie, sub-series Inde, 1956–1967

Germany

Politsches Archiv des Auswärtigen Amtes, Berlin
  Bestand Ministerium für Auswärtige Angelegenheiten
  B 1: Ministerbüro
  B 34: Sub-Saharan Africa
  B 36: Near and Middle East
  B 37: South, Southeast, and East Asia

Government Publications:

United States

Department of State Bulletin
Foreign Relations of the United States (Washington: Government Printing Office, for the Department of State)
1948
  6: *The Far East and Australasia* (1974)
1949
  7, Part I: *The Far East and Australasia* (1975)
1952–1954
  12: *East Asia and Pacific, Part 1* (1984)
1955–1957
  2: *China* (1986)
  8: *South Asia* (1987)
  15: *The Arab-Israeli Dispute, January 1 – July 26, 1956* (1989)
  18: *Africa* (1989)
  19: *National Security Policy* (1990)
  21: *East Asian Security; Laos; Cambodia* (1990)
  22: *Southeast Asia* (1989)
  26: *Central and Southeastern Europe* (1992)
1958–1960
  14: *Africa* (1993)
  15: *South and Southeast Asia* (1992)
  17: *Indonesia* (1994)

1961–1963
  2: *Vietnam 1962* (1990)
  5: *Soviet Union* (1998)
  8: *National Security Policy* (1996)
  13: *Western Europe and Canada* (1994)
  14: *Berlin Crisis, 1961–1962* (1993)
  16: *Eastern Europe; Cyprus; Greece; Turkey* (1994)
  17: *Near East, 1961–1962* (1994)
  18: *Near East, 1962–1963* (1995)
  19: *South Asia* (1996)
  20: *Congo Crisis* (1995)
  21: *Africa* (1995)
  23: *Southeast Asia* (1995)
  25: *Organization of Foreign Policy; Information Policy; United Nations; Scientific Matters* (2002)
1964–1968
  2: *Vietnam, January-June 1965* (1996)
  3: *Vietnam, July-December 1965* (1996)
  4: *Vietnam, 1966* (1998)
  9: *International Development and Economic Defense Policy; Commodities* (1997)
  12: *Western Europe* (2001)
  18: *Arab-Israeli Dispute, 1964–1967* (2000)
  19: *Arab-Israeli Crisis and War, 1967* (2004)
  21: *Near East Region; Arabian Peninsula* (2000)
  24: *Africa* (1999)
  25: *South Asia* (2000)
  26: *Indonesia; Malaysia-Singapore; Philippines* (2001)
Public Papers of the President: Dwight D. Eisenhower, 1956. Washington: Government Printing Office, 1957.
Public Papers of the Presidents: John F. Kennedy, 3 volumes. Washington: Government Printing Office, 1962–1964.
Public Papers of the Presidents: Lyndon B. Johnson, 5 volumes. Washington: Government Printing Office, 1965–1969.

Egypt

The Conference on the Problems of Economic Development. Cairo: Ministry of Information, 1962.
Second Conference of Non-Aligned Countries. Cairo: Ministry of Information, 1964.

France

Documents Diplomatiques Français, 1961 to 1967. Paris: Imprimerie Nationle (1961–1963)/Peter Lang (1964–1967), 2000–2008.

Yugoslavia

Conference of Heads of State or Government of Non-Aligned Countries. Belgrade: Publicisticko-Izdavacki Zavod, 1961.

United Nations

Security Council Official Records. New York: United Nations, 1961–1966.

Memoirs, Diaries, and Contemporaneous Publications:

Attwood, William. *The Reds and the Blacks: A Personal Adventure.* New York: Harper & Row, 1967.

Badeau, John A. *The Middle East Remembered.* Washington: Middle East Institute, 1983.

Ball, George W. *The Discipline of Power: Essentials of a Modern World Structure.* Boston: Little, Brown, & Co., 1968.

The Past Has Another Pattern: Memoirs. New York: W. W. Norton, 1982.

Bowles, Chester. *Promises to Keep: My Years in Public Life, 1941–1969.* New York: Harper & Row, 1971.

The Coming Political Breakthrough. New York: Harper, 1959.

Bundy, McGeorge. "Friends and Allies." *Foreign Affairs.* Vol. 41, No. 1 (October 1962), 14–23.

"The End of Either/Or." *Foreign Affairs.* Vol. 45, No. 2 (January 1967), 189–201.

Dayal, Rajeshwar. *Mission for Hammarskjold: The Congo Crisis.* Delhi: Oxford University Press, 1976.

Devlin, Larry. *Chief of Station, Congo: A Memoir of 1960–1967.* New York: PublicAffairs, 2007.

Dutt, Subimal. *With Nehru in the Foreign Office.* Calcutta: Minerva Associates, 1977.

Eisenhower, Dwight D. *The Eisenhower Diaries*, ed. Robert Ferrell. New York: W. W. Norton, 1981.

Galbraith, John K. *Ambassador's Journal: A Personal Account of the Kennedy Years.* Boston: Houghton Mifflin, 1969.

Letters to Kennedy, ed. James Goodman. Cambridge, MA: Harvard University Press, 1998.

Harsono, Ganis. *Recollections of an Indonesian Diplomat in the Sukarno Era*, ed. C. L. M Penders. Queensland: University of Queensland Press, 1977.

Heikal, Mohammed. *The Cairo Documents: The Inside Story of Nasser and his Relationship with World Leaders, Rebels, and Statesmen.* New York: Doubleday, 1973.

Hilsman, Roger. *To Move a Nation: The Politics of Foreign Policy in the Administration of John F. Kennedy.* New York: Doubleday, 1967.

Jessup, Philip C. *The Birth of Nations.* New York: Columbia University Press, 1974.

Johnson, Lyndon Baines. *The Vantage Point: Perspectives of the Presidency, 1963–1969.* New York: Holt, Rinehart and Winston, 1971.

Jones, Howard P. *Indonesia: The Possible Dream.* Stanford: Hoover Institution, 1971.

Kennedy, John F. "A Democrat Looks at Foreign Policy." *Foreign Affairs.* Vol. 36, No. 1 (October 1957), 44–59.

Guthman, Edwin, and Jeffrey Shulman ed. *Robert Kennedy In His Own Words: The Unpublished Recollections of the Kennedy Years.* New York: Bantam, 1988.

Macmillan, Harold. *Riding the Storm, 1956–1959.* London: Macmillan, 1971.

At the End of the Day. 1961–1963, New York: Harper & Row, 1973.

McNamara, Robert. *In Retrospect: The Tragedy and Lessons of Vietnam.* New York: Random House, 1995.

Morrow, John H. *First American Ambassador to Guinea.* New Brunswick, NJ: Rutgers
    University Press, 1967.
Nasser, Gamal Abdel. *On the Consolidation of the Cause of World Peace.* Cairo: State
    Information Service, 1967.
Nehru, Jawaharlal. *India's Foreign Policy: Selected Speeches, September 1946-April
    1961.* Bombay: Government of India, 1961.
    Letters to Chief Ministers, 1947–1964, Vol. 5, 1958–1964. New York: Oxford
    University Press, 1989.
    Jawaharlal Nehru's Speeches, Vol. 4: September 1957-April 1963. New Delhi:
    Ministry of Information, 1964
Nixon, Richard M. *RN: The Memoirs of Richard Nixon.* New York: Simon & Schuster,
    1978.
Nkrumah, Kwame. *Challenge of the Congo.* New York: International Publishers,
    1967.
    Kwame Nkrumah: The Conakry Years, ed. June Milne. Atlantic Highlands, NJ: Panaf,
    1990.
    Neo-Colonialism: The Last Stage of Imperialism. New York: International Publishers,
    1965.
    Selected Speeches, ed. Samuel Obeng. 5 vols. Accra: Afram, 1997.
Nyerere, Julius. *Freedom and Socialism: A Selection from Writings and Speeches, 1956–
    1967.* New York: Oxford University Press, 1968.
    "Tanzania Policy on Foreign Affairs." October 16, 1967. Tanganyika African National
    Union National Conference. Dar es Salaam: Ministry of Information and Tourism,
    1967.
Rostow, Walt W. *The Diffusion of Power: An Essay in Recent History.* New York:
    Macmillan, 1972.
    The Stages of Economic Growth: A Non-Communist Manifesto. New York:
    Cambridge University Press, 1960.
Rostow, Walt W., and Max Millikan. *A Proposal: Key to an Effective Foreign Policy.*
    New York: Harper & Bros., 1957.
Rusk, Dean. *As I Saw It.* New York: W. W. Norton, 1990.
Schlesinger, Arthur M., Jr. *A Thousand Days: John F. Kennedy in the White House.*
    Boston: Houghton Mifflin, 1965.
    Journals 1952–2000. New York: Penguin, 2007.
Sorensen, Theodore. *Counselor: A Life at the Edge of History.* New York: Harper,
    2008.
    Kennedy. New York: Harper & Row, 1965.
Williams, G. Mennen. *Africa for the Africans!* Grand Rapids, MI: Eerdmans, 1969.
Wright, Richard. *The Color Curtain: A Report on the Bandung Conference.* London:
    Dennis Dobson, 1955.

Interviews:

Thomas Cassilly
Ulric Haynes Jr.
Thomas Hughes
Jack Matlock
Elspeth Rostow
Harold Saunders
Phillips Talbot

Online Sources:

Declassified Document Reference Service

Secondary Sources:

Agyeman, Opoku. *Nkrumah's Ghana and East Africa: Pan-Africanism and African Interstate Relations*. Teaneck, NJ: Fairleigh Dickinson University Press, 1992.

Ahlberg, Kristin L. *Transplanting the Great Society: Lyndon Johnson and Food for Peace*. Columbia, University of Missouri Press, 2008.

"Machiavelli with a Heart: The Johnson Administration's Food for Peace Program in India, 1965–1966." *Diplomatic History*. Vol. 31, No. 5 (September 2007), 665–701.

Andrew, Christopher, and Vasili Mitrokhin. *The World Was Going Our Way: The KGB and the Battle for the Third World*. New York: Basic Books, 2005.

Arora, B. D. *Indian-Indonesian Relations. 1961–1980*. New Delhi: Asian Educational Services, 1981.

Ashton, Nigel. *Kennedy, Macmillan, and the Cold War: The Irony of Interdependence*. New York: Palgrave Macmillan, 2002.

ed. *The Cold War in the Middle East: Regional Conflict and the Superpowers*. New York: Routledge, 2007.

Ate, Bassey E. *Decolonization and Dependence: The Development of Nigerian-U.S. Relations, 1960–1984*. Boulder: Westview, 1987.

Bass, Warren. *Support Any Friend: Kennedy's Middle East and the Making of the U.S.-Israel Alliance*. New York: Oxford University Press, 2002.

Bill, James A. *George Ball: Behind the Scenes in U.S. Foreign Policy*. New Haven: Yale University Press, 1997.

Bird, Kai. *The Color of Truth: McGeorge Bundy and William Bundy: Brothers in Arms*. New York: Simon & Schuster, 1998.

Blackwell, Stephen. "Pursuing Nasser: The Macmillan Government and the Management of British Policy Towards the Middle East." *Cold War History*. Vol. 4, No. 3 (April 2004), 85–104.

Borstelmann, Thomas. *The Cold War and the Color Line: American Race Relations in the Global Arena*. Cambridge, MA: Harvard University Press, 2001.

Brands, H. W. *The Specter of Neutralism: The United States and the Emergence of the Third World, 1947–1960*. New York: Columbia University Press, 1989.

India and the United States: The Cold Peace. Boston: Twayne, 1990.

The Wages of Globalism: Lyndon Johnson and the Limits of American Power. New York: Oxford University Press, 1994.

Broadwater, Jeff. *Adlai Stevenson and American Politics: The Odyssey of a Cold War Liberal*. New York: Twayne, 1994.

Brogan, D. W. *America in the Modern World*. New Brunswick, NJ: Rutgers University Press, 1960.

Bunch, Clea Lutz. "Strike at Samu: Jordan, Israel, the United States, and the Origins of the Six-Day War," *Diplomatic History*. Vol. 32, No. 1 (January 2008), 55–76.

Burns, William J. *Economic Aid and American Policy Toward Egypt, 1955–1981*. Albany: SUNY Press, 1985.

Byrne, Jeffrey J. "Our Own Special Brand of Socialism: Algeria and the Contest of Modernities in the 1960s." *Diplomatic History*. Vol. 33, No. 3 (June 2009), 427–447.

Chen Jian. *Mao's China and the Cold War*. Chapel Hill: University of North Carolina Press, 2001.

Clymer, Kenton. *Troubled Relations: The United States and Cambodia Since 1870*. DeKalb: Northern Illinois University Press, 2007.

Cohen, Warren I. *Dean Rusk*. Totowa, NJ: Cooper Square, 1980.

Cohen, Warren I., and Nancy B. Tucker eds. *Lyndon Johnson Confronts the World: American Foreign Policy, 1963–1968*. New York: Cambridge University Press, 1994.

Connelly, Matthew. *A Diplomatic Revolution: Algeria's Fight for Independence and the Origins of the Post-Cold War Era*. New York: Oxford University Press, 2002.

Cullather, Nick. *The Hungry World: America's Cold War Battle Against Poverty in Asia*. Cambridge, MA: Harvard University Press, 2010.

"Hunger and Containment: How India Became 'Important' in US Cold War Strategy." *India Review*. Vol. 6, No. 2 (April 2007), 59–90.

Dallek, Robert. *An Unfinished Life: John F. Kennedy, 1917–1963*. New York: Little, Brown, & Co., 2003.

Flawed Giant: Lyndon Johnson and His Times, 1961–1973. New York: Oxford University Press, 1998.

Dann, Uriel. *King Hussein and the Challenge of Arab Radicalism: Jordan, 1955–1967*. New York: Oxford University Press, 1989.

Dauer, Richard P. *A North-South Mind in an East-West World: Chester Bowles and the Making of United States Cold War Foreign Policy, 1951–1969*. Westport, CT: Praeger, 2005.

Dell, Sidney. *Trade Blocs and Common Markets*. New York: Knopf, 1963.

DeRoche, Andrew. *Black, White, and Chrome: The United States and Zimbabwe, 1953–1998*. Trenton, NJ: Africa World Press, 2001.

Desai, Padma. *The Bokaro Steel Plant: A Study of Soviet Economic Assistance*. New York: American Elsevier, 1972.

Easter, David. "'Keep the Indonesian Pot Boiling': Western Covert Intervention in Indonesia. October 1965–March 1966." *Cold War History*. Vol. 5, No. 1 (February 2005), 55–73.

Ekbladh, David. *The Great American Mission: Modernization and the Construction of an American World Order*. Princeton: Princeton University Press, 2010.

Fain, W. Taylor. *American Ascendance and British Retreat in the Persian Gulf Region*. New York: Palgrave Macmillan, 2008.

Fairlie, Henry. *The Kennedy Promise: The Politics of Expectation*. Garden City, NY: Doubleday, 1973.

Freedman, Lawrence. *Kennedy's Wars: Berlin, Cuba, Laos, and Vietnam*. New York: Oxford University Press, 2000.

Fursenko, Aleksandr, and Timothy Naftali. *"One Hell of a Gamble": Khrushev, Castro, and Kennedy, 1958–1964*. New York: W. W. Norton, 1997.

Khrushchev's Cold War: The Inside Story of an American Adversary. New York: W. W. Norton, 2006.

Gaddis, John L. *Strategies of Containment: A Critical Appraisal of Postwar National Security Policy*. New York: Oxford University Press, 1982.

Gaitonde, P. D. *The Liberation of Goa: A Participant's View of History*. New York: St. Martin's Press, 1987.

Gallagher, Tom. *Portugal: A Twentieth Century Interpretation*. Dover: Manchester University Press, 1983.

Gardner, Lloyd C., and Ted Gittinger eds. *The Search for Peace in Vietnam, 1964–1968.* College Station: Texas A&M University Press, 2004.

Gavin, Francis J. *Gold, Dollars, and Power: The Politics of International Monetary Relations, 1958–1971.* Chapel Hill: University of North Carolina Press, 2004.

Giglio, James N. *The Presidency of John F. Kennedy.* Lawrence: University Press of Kansas, 1991.

Gilman, Nils, *Mandarins of the Future: Modernization Theory in Cold War America.* Baltimore: The Johns Hopkins University Press, 2003.

Gopal, Sarvepalli. *Jawaharlal Nehru: A Biography, Vol. 3, 1956–1964.* Cambridge, MA: Harvard University Press, 1984.

Gould, Lewis L. *The Most Exclusive Club: A History of the Modern United States Senate.* New York: Basic Books, 2005.

Gray, William Glenn. *Germany's Cold War: The Global Campaign to Isolate East Germany, 1949–1969.* Chapel Hill: University of North Carolina Press, 2003.

Gleijeses, Piero. *Conflicting Missions: Havana, Washington, and Africa 1959–1976.* Chapel Hill: University of North Carolina Press, 2002.

Hahn, Peter L. *The United States, Great Britain, and Egypt, 1945–1956: Strategy and Diplomacy in the Early Cold War.* Chapel Hill: University of North Carolina Press, 1991.

   Caught in the Middle East: U.S. Policy toward the Arab-Israeli Conflict, 1945–1961. Chapel Hill: University of North Carolina Press, 2004.

Hahnimäki, Jussi M. *Containing Coexistence: America, Russia, and the "Finnish Solution." 1945–1956.* Kent, OH: Kent State University Press, 1997.

Halberstam, David. *The Best and the Brightest.* New York: Random House, 1972.

Herring, George C. *America's Longest War: The United States and Vietnam, 1950–1975.* New York: Knopf, 1979.

Hershberg, James G. "'High Spirited Confusion': Brazil, the 1961 Belgrade Non-Aligned Conference, and the Limits of an 'Independent' Foreign Policy during the High Cold War." *Cold War History.* Vol. 7 (August 2007), 373–388.

Hoffman, Elizabeth Cobbs. *All You Need Is Love: The Peace Corps and the Spirit of the 1960s.* Cambridge, MA: Harvard University Press, 1998.

Hoopes, Townsend. *The Devil and John Foster Dulles.* Boston: Little, Brown, & Co., 1973.

Horne, Gerald. *From the Barrel of a Gun: The United States and the War Against Zimbabwe, 1965–1980.* Chapel Hill: University of North Carolina Press, 2001.

Immerman, Richard. *John Foster Dulles: Piety, Pragmatism, and Power in U.S. Foreign Policy.* Wilmington, DE: Scholarly Resources, 1999.

   ed. *John Foster Dulles and the Diplomacy of the Cold War.* Princeton: Princeton University Press, 1990.

Irwin, Ryan M. "A Wind of Change? White Redoubt and the Postcolonial Moment, 1960–1963," *Diplomatic History.* Vol. 33, No. 5 (November 2009), 897–925.

Jacobs, Matthew F. *Imagining the Middle East: The Building of an American Foreign Policy, 1918–1967.* Chapel Hill: University of North Carolina Press, 2011.

Jansen, G. H. *Nonalignment and the Afro-Asian States.* New York: Praeger, 1966.

Johnson, Robert David. *Congress and the Cold War.* New York: Cambridge University Press, 2006.

Jones, Howard. *Death of a Generation: How the Assassinations of Diem and JFK Prolonged the Vietnam War.* New York: Oxford University Press, 2002.

Jones, Matthew. *Conflict and Confrontation in South East Asia, 1961–1965: Britain, the United States and the Creation of Malaysia*. Cambridge: Cambridge University Press, 2002.

"A 'Segregated' Asia?: Race, the Bandung Conference, and Pan-Asianist Fears in American Thought and Policy, 1954–1955." *Diplomatic History*. Vol. 29, No. 5 (November 2005), 841–868.

Kahin, George McT. *The Asian-African Conference, Bandung, Indonesia, April 1955*. Ithaca: Cornell University Press, 1956.

Kahin, George McT and Audrey Kahin. *Subversion as Foreign Policy: The Secret Eisenhower and Dulles Debacle in Indonesia*. New York: W. W. Norton, 1995.

Kaiser, David. *American Tragedy: Kennedy, Johnson, and the Origins of the Vietnam War*. Cambridge, MA: Harvard University Press, 2000.

Kalb, Madeleine G. *The Congo Cables: The Cold War in Africa – From Eisenhower to Kennedy*. New York: Macmillan, 1982.

Karabell, Zachary. *Architects of Intervention: The United States, the Third World, and the Cold War, 1946–1962*. Baton Rouge: Louisiana State University Press, 1999.

Kaufman, Burton I. *Trade and Aid: Eisenhower's Foreign Economic Policy, 1953–1961*. Baltimore: The Johns Hopkins University Press, 1982.

Kent, John. *America, the UN and Decolonisation: Cold War Conflict in the Congo*. New York: Routledge, 2010.

Kerr, Malcolm. *The Arab Cold War: Gamal 'Abd al-Nasir and His Rivals, 1958–1970*. New York: Oxford University Press, 1971.

Khrushchev, Sergei. *Nikita Khrushchev and the Creation of a Superpower*. University Park: Pennsylvania State University Press, 2000.

Kolko, Gabriel. *Confronting the Third World: United States Foreign Policy, 1945–1980*. New York: Pantheon, 1988.

Kux, Dennis. *Estranged Democracies: India and the United States, 1941–1991*. Thousand Oaks, CA: Sage, 1994.

The United States and Pakistan, 1947–2000: Disenchanted Allies. Baltimore: The Johns Hopkins University Press, 2001.

Lake, Anthony. *The "Tar Baby" Option: American Policy Toward Southern Rhodesia*. New York: Columbia University Press, 1976.

Larson, David L. *United States Foreign Policy toward Yugoslavia, 1943–1963*. Washington: University Press of America, 1979.

Lederer, William J., and Eugene Burdick. *The Ugly American*. New York: W. W. Norton, 1958.

Lees, Lorraine. *Keeping Tito Afloat: The United States, Yugoslavia, and the Cold War*. University Park: Pennsylvania State University Press, 1997.

Leffler, Melvyn P. *For the Soul of Mankind: The United States, the Soviet Union, and the Cold War*. New York: Hill and Wang, 2007.

Lerner, Mitchell, ed. *Looking Back at LBJ: White House Politics in a New Light*. Lawrence: University Press of Kansas, 2005.

"'A Big Tree of Peace and Justice': The Vice Presidential Travels of Lyndon Johnson." *Diplomatic History*. Vol. 34, No. 2 (April 2010), 357–393.

Lijphart, Arend. *The Trauma of Decolonization: The Dutch and West New Guinea*. New Haven: Yale University Press, 1966.

Little, Douglas. *American Orientalism: The United States and the Middle East Since 1945*. Chapel Hill: University of North Carolina Press, 2004.

Logevall, Fredrik. *Choosing War: The Lost Chance for Peace and the Escalation of War in Vietnam*. Berkeley: University of California Press, 1999.

Logevall, Fredrik and Andrew Preston eds. *Nixon in the World: American Foreign Relations, 1969–1977*. New York: Oxford University Press, 2008.

Louis, William R., ed. *Ends of British Imperialism: The Scramble for Empire. Suez. and Decolonization*. New York: Palgrave Macmillan, 2006.

Louis, William R. and Hedley Bull eds. *The 'Special Relationship': Anglo-American Relations Since 1945*. Oxford: Clarendon, 1986.

Lüthi, Lorenz M. *The Sino-Soviet Split: Cold War in the Communist World*. Princeton: Princeton University Press, 2008.

Mackie, J. A. C. *Konfrontasi: The Indonesia-Malaysia Dispute, 1963–1966*. New York: Oxford University Press, 1974.

MacDonald, Mairi Stewart. "The Challenge of Guinean Independence, 1958–1971". Ph.D. dissertation, University of Toronto, 2009.

Maga, Timothy P. *John F. Kennedy and the New Pacific Community, 1961–63*. Houndmills: Macmillan, 1990.

Mahoney, Richard. *JFK: Ordeal in Africa*. New York: Oxford University Press, 1983.

Martin, John Bartlow. *Adlai Stevenson of Illinois: The Life of Adlai E. Stevenson*. New York: Doubleday, 1976.

Mazov, Sergey. *A Distant Front in the Cold War: The USSR in West Africa and the Congo*. Stanford: Stanford University Press, 2010.

McFarland, Linda. *Cold War Strategist: Stuart Symington and the Search for National Security*. Westport, CT: Praeger, 2001.

McKeever, Porter. *Adlai Stevenson: His Life and Legacy*. New York: Morrow, 1989.

McMahon, Robert J. *The Cold War on the Periphery: The United States, India, and Pakistan*. New York: Columbia University Press, 1994.

　Colonialism and Cold War: The United States and the Struggle for Indonesian Independence, 1945–1949. Ithaca: Cornell University Press, 1981.

　The Limits of Empire: The United States and Southeast Asia Since World War II. New York: Columbia University Press, 1999.

McNamara, Robert. *Britain, Nasser and the Balance of Power in the Middle East*. Portland, OR: Frank Cass, 2003.

Merrill, Dennis. *Bread and the Ballot: The United States and India's Development, 1947–1963*. Chapel Hill: University of North Carolina Press, 1990.

Milne, David. *America's Rasputin: Walt Rostow and the Vietnam War*. New York: Hill and Wang, 2008.

Newsom, David. *The Imperial Mantle: The United States, Decolonization, and the Third World*. Bloomington: University of Indiana Press, 2001.

Noer, Thomas J. *Cold War and Black Liberation: The United States and White Rule in Africa, 1948–1968*. Columbia: University of Missouri Press, 1985.

　"Soapy": A Biography of G. Mennen Williams. Ann Arbor: University of Michigan Press, 2005.

　"The New Frontier and African Neutralism: Kennedy, Nkrumah, and the Volta River Project," *Diplomatic History*. Vol. 8, No. 1 (January 1984), 61–80.

Nutting, Anthony. *Nasser*. London: Constable & Co., 1972.

Nwaubani, Ebere. *The United States and Decolonization in West Africa, 1950–1960* (Rochester Studies in African History and the Diaspora, number 9). Rochester, NY: University of Rochester Press, 2001.

Oren, Michael. *Six Days of War: 1967 and the Making of the Modern Middle East*. New York: Oxford University Press, 2002.

Pach, Chester J., and Elmo Richardson. *The Presidency of Dwight D. Eisenhower*. Lawrence: University Press of Kansas, 1991.

Paterson, Thomas, ed. *Kennedy's Quest for Victory: American Foreign Policy, 1961–1963.* New York: Oxford University Press, 1989.

Pearson, M. N. *The Portuguese in India.* New York: Cambridge University Press, 2006.

Penders, C. L. M. *The West New Guinea Debacle: Dutch Decolonization and Indonesia, 1945–1962.* Honolulu: University of Hawaii Press, 2002.

Prados, John. *Keepers of the Keys: A History of the National Security Council from Truman to Bush.* New York: Morrow, 1991.

Prashad, Vijay. *The Darker Nations: A People's History of the Third World.* New York: Free Press, 2007.

Preston, Andrew. *The War Council: McGeorge Bundy, the NSC, and Vietnam.* Cambridge, MA: Harvard University Press, 2006.

Quandt, William B. *Revolution and Political Leadership: Algeria, 1954–1968.* Cambridge, MA: MIT Press, 1969.

"Lyndon Johnson and the June 1967 War: What Color was the Light?" *Middle East Journal.* Vol. 46, No. 2 (Spring 1992), 198–228.

Rabe, Stephen G. *The Most Dangerous Area in the World: John F. Kennedy Confronts Revolution in Latin America.* Chapel Hill: University of North Carolina Press, 1999.

John F. Kennedy: World Leader. Washington: Potomac Books, 2010.

Rao, R. P. *Portuguese Rule in Goa.* New York: Asia Publishing House, 1963.

Roadnight, Andrew. *United States Policy towards Indonesia in the Truman and Eisenhower Years.* Palgrave: Hampshire, 2002.

Ro'i, Yaacov, and Boris Morozov eds. *The Soviet Union and the June 1967 Six Day War.* Stanford: Stanford University Press, 2008.

Rooney, David. *Kwame Nkrumah: The Political Kingdom in the Third World.* London: Tauris, 1988.

Rotter, Andrew J. *Comrades at Odds: The United States and India, 1947–1964.* Ithaca: Cornell University Press, 2000.

Rudolph, Lloyd, ed. *The Regional Imperative: The Administration of U.S. Foreign Policy Towards South Asian States Under Presidents Johnson and Nixon.* Atlantic Highlands, NJ: Humanities Press, 1980.

Schaffer, Howard. *Chester Bowles: New Dealer in the Cold War.* Cambridge, MA: Harvard University Press, 1993.

Ellsworth Bunker: Global Troubleshooter, Vietnam Hawk. Chapel Hill: University of North Carolina Press, 2003.

Schmidt, Elizabeth. *Cold War and Decolonization in Guinea, 1946–1958.* Athens: Ohio University Press, 2007.

Schoenbaum, Thomas J. *Waging Peace and War: Dean Rusk in the Truman, Kennedy, and Johnson Years.* New York: Simon & Schuster, 1988.

Schulzinger, Robert D. *A Time for War: The United States and Vietnam, 1941–1975.* New York: Oxford University Press, 1997.

Schwartz, Thomas. *Lyndon Johnson and Europe: In the Shadow of Vietnam.* Cambridge, MA: Harvard University Press, 2003.

Selverstone, Marc J. *Constructing the Monolith: The United States, Great Britain, and International Communism, 1945–1950.* Cambridge, MA: Harvard University Press, 2009.

Sheehan, Neil. *A Bright Shining Lie: John Paul Vann and America in Vietnam.* New York: Random House, 1988.

Shepard, Robert B. *Nigeria, Africa, and the United States: From Kennedy to Reagan.* Bloomington: Indiana University Press, 1991.

Simpson, Bradley R. *Economists with Guns: Authoritarian Development and U.S.-Indonesian Relations, 1960–1968.* Stanford: Stanford University Press, 2008.

Sorley, Lewis. *A Better War: The Unexamined Victories and Final Tragedy of America's Last Years in Vietnam.* New York: Harcourt & Brace, 1999.

Statler, Kathryn C., and Andrew L. Johns eds. *The Eisenhower Administration, the Third World, and the Globalization of the Cold War.* New York: Rowman & Littlefield, 2006.

Stephens, Robert. *Nasser: A Political Biography.* New York: Simon & Schuster, 1971.

Taubman, William. *Khrushchev: The Man and His Era.* New York: W. W. Norton, 2003.

Tharoor, Shashi. *Reasons of State: Political Development and India's Foreign Policy Under Indira Gandhi, 1966–1977.* New Delhi: Vikas, 1982.

Thompson, W. Scott. *Ghana's Foreign Policy, 1957–1966: Diplomacy, Ideology and the New State.* Princeton: Princeton University Press, 1969.

Toma, Peter A. *The Politics of Food for Peace: Executive-Legislative Interaction.* Tucson: University of Arizona Press, 1967.

Vickers, Adrian. *A History of Modern Indonesia.* New York: Cambridge University Press, 2005.

Wallerstein Mitchel B. *Food for War – Food for Peace: United States Food Aid in a Global Context.* Cambridge, MA: MIT Press, 1980.

Watts, Carl P. "G. Mennen Williams and Rhodesian Independence: A Case Study in Bureaucratic Politics." *Michigan Academician.* Vol. 36 (2004), 225–246.

"The United States, Britain, and the Problem of Rhodesian Independence, 1964–1965." *Diplomatic History.* Vol. 30, No. 3 (June 2006), 439–470.

Webster, David. "Regimes in Motion: The Kennedy Administration and Indonesia's New Frontier, 1960–1962." *Diplomatic History.* Vol. 33, No. 1 (January 2009), 95–123.

Weissman, Stephen. *American Foreign Policy in the Congo: 1960–1964.* Ithaca: Cornell University Press, 1974.

Westad, Odd Arne. *The Global Cold War: Third World Interventions and the Making of Our Times.* New York: Cambridge University Press, 2006.

ed. *Brothers in Arms: The Rise and Fall of the Sino-Soviet Alliance, 1945–1963.* Stanford: Stanford University Press, 1998.

White, George H., Jr. *Holding the Line: Race, Racism and American Foreign Policy toward Africa, 1953–1961.* New York: Rowman & Littlefield, 2005.

White, Mark, ed. *Kennedy: The New Frontier Revisited.* Houndmills: Macmillan, 1998.

Wolfers, Arnold, ed. *Alliance Policy in the Cold War.* Baltimore: The Johns Hopkins Press, 1959.

Yaqub, Salim. *Containing Arab Nationalism: The Eisenhower Doctrine and the Middle East.* Chapel Hill: University of North Carolina Press, 2004.

Zeiler, Thomas W. *Dean Rusk: Defending the American Mission Abroad.* Wilmington, DE: Scholarly Resources, 2000.

Zubok, Vladislav, and Constantine Pleshakov. *Inside the Kremlin's Cold War: From Stalin to Khrushchev.* Cambridge, MA: Harvard University Press, 1996.

Index